GERTRUDE WEIL

LEONARD ROGOFF

{ GERTRUDE WEIL }

Jewish Progressive in the New South

THE UNIVERSITY OF NORTH CAROLINA PRESS

Chapel Hill

*This book was
published with generous support provided
by the Southern Jewish Historical Society and
with the assistance of the Z. Smith Reynolds Fund
of the University of North Carolina Press.*

Manufactured in the United States of America
Designed by Richard Hendel
Set in Miller and Didot types
by Tseng Information Systems, Inc.

The University of North Carolina Press
has been a member of the Green Press Initiative since 2003.

Cover illustrations: Front, courtesy of the State Archives
of North Carolina; back, courtesy of David Weil

Library of Congress Cataloging-in-Publication Data
Names: Rogoff, Leonard, author.
Title: Gertrude Weil : Jewish progressive in the New South / Leonard Rogoff.
Description: Chapel Hill : The University of North Carolina Press, [2017] |
Includes bibliographical references and index.
Identifiers: LCCN 2016032976| ISBN 9781469630793
(cloth : alk. paper) | ISBN 9781469630809 (ebook)
Subjects: LCSH: Weil, Gertrude, 1879–1971. | Women social reformers—
North Carolina—Biography. | Women civil rights workers—North Carolina—
Biography. | Suffragists—North Carolina—Biography. | Jewish women—
North Carolina—Biography.
Classification: LCC HQ1413.W4 R64 2017 | DDC 303.48/4092 [B] —dc23
LC record available at https://lccn.loc.gov/2016032976

CONTENTS

ILLUSTRATIONS

PREFACE

Gertrude Weil had a "lovely time" as she led her African American neighbors into a segregated hotel. Her invitation to the political reception had asked her to bring her friends. Now in her eighties, she had enjoyed a long career defying convention. As always, Miss Gertrude was perfectly poised even as her clear blue eyes glimmered with mischief. A southern lady, she was raised to be modest and courteous. A New Woman, she thought progressively and acted courageously. A cosmopolitan Jew, daughter of an immigrant, she had learned to fit into a society that was Christian and traditional. Negotiating complexities within herself, Gertrude would change the world.

Although rooted to her native Goldsboro, North Carolina, Gertrude represented a generation of educated women who advocated for women's rights, social welfare, and world peace. Among them, too, were Jewish women newly risen to the middle class and politically emancipated. Broadly read and deeply thinking, Gertrude felt she was acting according to her own standard of justice. The first North Carolinian to graduate from Smith College, she returned to Goldsboro, where as "Federation Gertie" she joined a Women's Club movement that transformed communities, pulling women from the hearth into the civic marketplace. After leading the state's woman suffrage campaign, she founded its League of Women Voters. Intent on reform, she fought relentlessly for labor rights, economic justice, and social welfare. When civil rights for African Americans could no longer be denied, she committed to the cause with an energy that belied her years. Beyond her borders, she campaigned tirelessly for world peace. She saved her German family from the Holocaust and, an ardent Zionist, worked to establish a Jewish state in Palestine.

Though her life was momentous, Gertrude Weil would not have wanted this book written. She would have dismissed her biographer as a "damn fool." The eminent women's historian Anne Firor Scott, who knew her well, felt differently: "Gertrude Weil deserves a full-scale biography, and when one is accomplished perhaps many complexities and mysteries of her life will be illuminated."[1] Scott was charmed by her character and awed by her achievements. That she still found mysteries to be unraveled is revealing since in books like *The Southern Lady: From Pedestal to Politics, 1830–1930* Scott has done more than anyone to cast light on women of Gertrude's time and place.

The challenge of writing Gertrude Weil's biography is to tell many stories at once, personal and epochal, thematic and chronological. As Scott notes, when Gertrude died in 1971 at the age of ninety-one, she had lived nearly half the nation's history under the Constitution.[2] Born in the wake of Reconstruction, she saw ex-slaves and Confederate veterans hobble down the street. Nearly a century later she watched African Americans march for civil rights. Gertrude's life spanned the agrarian Old South, the urban New South, and the suburban Sunbelt South. She was raised middle class in a mill and market town amid cotton and tobacco fields. Her family was typical of the new townspeople who changed the South. They built the stores, banks, factories, and warehouses that turned country crossroads into thriving commercial cities. Immigrant Jews, beyond their material contributions, fostered new ideas, new ways of connecting to the world.

Gertrude Weil's political evolution from belle to belligerent needs elucidation. Her life documents a constant expanding of interests and a growing willingness to transgress social custom and political norms. In her last years, she quipped that she was becoming ever more radical, laughing that she would die a communist.[3]

Gertrude missed little. As Frank Porter Graham observed, "She feels that she never knows enough, joins enough, sees enough, or travels enough." Historians have cited her as "the mainstay" of the state's social welfare movement, as "the most prominent leader among the state's organized women" who brought progress to North Carolina. Her colleagues were mostly Christian women inspired by the Social Gospel. Women's Clubs launched them into civic careers that transformed political culture and social relations. Their stories need telling, too, if the narrative of state—indeed, of national—history is to be told.[4]

Gertrude, like her colleagues, was both southern lady and New Woman. Drawing on imagery dating to antebellum slave times, the southern lady represented a pure and pious ideal of a wife and mother who was the paragon of domesticity. Gentility was expected of Victorian women of means generally, whether in Britain or America, but in the American South this feminine paradigm was central to the region's understanding of itself. Southern white men of the upper class idealized women, wanting them in their domestic place, wanting to maintain the social order that gave them privilege. As Goldsboro physician G. B. Morris wrote Gertrude in the 1920s, our "fathers bled for the defence and honor of that most sacred thing on earth, Southern Womanhood." Race was a distinctive factor in the South. Southern white men imagined themselves gallant guardians of defenseless women against the threat of allegedly rapacious blacks. Civil War and

Reconstruction only weakened the stereotype without destroying it. Conflating race and gender, southern white men resisted granting women autonomy or extending the franchise to them. Gertrude, like other southern suffragists, appealed to the chivalry of southern gentlemen in asking for women's vote and legal protections.[5]

As a Jew and a town dweller, a social reformer educated in the north, Gertrude seemed to defy the stereotype. Newspapers saluted Gertrude as a model of southern womanhood even as she advocated as a New Woman, who was independent, reform minded, and active in public spheres. Middle- and upper-class women, held to their maternalism, intervening in society to benefit women and children on such domestic issues as education and sanitation. Social welfare, Gertrude often said, was the motivating force of her life. Scott observes the paradox of accomplished, progressive southern women like Gertrude who remained "lady-like" and "modest about their achievements." Although Gertrude urged women to step down from their pedestals, she eschewed militancy and, in her suffrage campaign, conceded the racial status quo.[6]

Gertrude as a Jew had an oblique relationship with southern society, not assuming what others took for granted. From a national perspective, she belonged among the reform-minded, Jewish women activists in her commitment to suffrage, birth control, and antiwar movements, but she advocated in a conservative society where her views were often unpopular, sometimes violently so. As she represented Jewish viewpoints at secular agencies, so too she brought her social welfare agenda to Jewish organizations. Gertrude's primary interest was southern farmers and millworkers, especially children and women, rather than the immigrant urban poor who became the focus of northern Jewish women. Her involvement with race issues also had a regional dimension, given the South's peculiar history.[7]

At a gathering of Jewish women, Gertrude urged them to raise "the torch of idealism." That image evokes the uplift, leadership, and dedication to principle that lit her way. These values she imbibed in an immigrant household imbued with the ethics of prophetic Judaism and the German spirit of *Bildung*, or self-improvement. Classically educated, she measured herself by absolutes of truth, beauty, and goodness. "I am one of the idealists," Gertrude wrote, "who believe that we shall eventually develop a pattern of actual living that will put into operation these ideals." That ethic, to live one's ideals, was constant, and she rooted it in Judaism. German idealism lay at the heart of a modern Classical Reform Judaism that valorized moral conduct over revelation. The endearing modesty that led Gertrude to forever disparage her achievements was in measure the self-judgment of a woman who felt a religious duty to do ever more. Jews, she believed, were to be the light onto the nations.[8]

Southern lady, New Woman, Reform Jew, Gertrude Weil embodied complexities and paradoxes. Unmarried, she formed intimate relationships with other women but remained in the "bosom of family."[9] Educated in the North, she viewed her native region as both insider and outsider. She died in the house in which she was born, but she traveled so often that friends joked about finding her home. She invited African American women to her parlor to organize for civil rights but rang a bell to summon her manservant. A faithful Sabbath worshiper, she speculated freely on spiritual experience. She was a harbinger of what historians now call the Global South, yet neighbors recall her as flower show judge or library board member. Those who knew Gertrude well described her character as seamless, integrated.

In his pioneering book on southern Jews, Eli Evans labels them the "provincials."[10] That may be true from a New York perspective—often taken as the Jewish one—but Gertrude Weil was a cosmopolitan, the daughter of a German immigrant educated at the North's finest schools. She discoursed on Kant, heard Nellie Melba sing, and summered at Villa I Tatti in Italy. Populating her "crowd" were leading lights of twentieth-century culture and history, from Senda Berenson, mother of women's basketball, to Henrietta Szold, seminal figure of Zionism. Literally and figuratively, Gertrude was all over the map, on the road for conferences and conventions, touring gardens and museums, or visiting family and friends. In her eighties, she circumnavigated the globe.

Gertrude Weil offers a counternarrative to the stereotype of a South that is provincial, patriarchal, traditional, and Protestant. That North Carolina has been exceptional among southern states as a contending ground of progressive versus conservative forces has given it a certain cachet: in the 1890s in the Democratic South, North Carolina voted in a black-supported Populist-Republican Fusion government; it least resisted racial integration but remained the most segregated; it repeatedly elected liberals and reactionaries. Observers frame this debate as a conflict between urban and rural, modernity and traditionalism. Scholars speak of the state's divide, paradox, and contradiction. Often in the crossfire, Gertrude negotiated these differences, acting locally but thinking globally. She was a citizen of the world as much as of Goldsboro, a cosmopolitan with roots.[11]

One simple reason for Gertrude's achievement was that she was a Weil. As *The State* magazine editorialized in 1953, "Thousands of North Carolinians who know nothing else about Goldsboro know it is home of the Weils … and in North Carolina few names can match it for solid and enlightened citizenship."[12] Weil men were distinguished as entrepreneurs, philanthropists, and civic leaders. Gertrude's models and mentors were her mother, Mina, and her aunt Sarah, extraordinary for their communal and Jewish enterprise. Widely admired, Weil men and women became intimates of the state's elites as they served on boards and committees. Beyond the parks, hospitals, campus buildings, scholarship funds, welfare programs, and lecture series that the Weils endowed were the black ministers whose churches were helped, farmers who received loans rather than foreclosures, rural students lent money for school, barefoot kids outfitted with shoes ... Gertrude Weil needed no introduction.

Gertrude, a zealous guardian of her privacy, would not enjoy being the subject of a biography, much less being crowned with a halo of hagiography. Her rapier wit would have punctured any puffery just as she dismissed as fools those who did not see things her way. She recognized that she had inherited racial prejudices common to white southerners of her generation. In the fractious politics of women's suffrage, labor advocacy, and welfare reform she compromised her ideals to reconcile disparate factions and achieve incremental results. Deploring injustice and inequity, she nonetheless defended her native city, state, and region. One cause, eugenics, was the progressive position of her day but has been thoroughly discredited for its class, racial, and gender biases. Yet, taking her life as a whole, an honest biography of Gertrude Weil will be an immodestly admiring one. Like her dear friend Frank Graham, she was beloved as well as respected.

A final reason for a Gertrude Weil biography, then, is that she has much to teach us on how to live a meaningful life. Those most inspired by her often say it was her very being, rather than anything that she pointedly said, that was life changing. "She made me want to be the best that I can be," observed Amy Meyers Krumbein, a former Sunday school student.[13] Gertrude's clear blue eyes twinkled with fun. Perennially youthful, she laughed quickly and often. She took her causes seriously but never herself. Honors embarrassed her, and her interest was others. Friends were for life, she believed. Spirited and spiritual, she gloried in roadside lilies and a line from Shakespeare. Always she was committed to do the right thing, to address the need of the day as she said of her mother, as an organic element of her being, not as an adornment of her character. On her deathbed she was full of humor, curiosity, and ambitions for a better world. The biography of Gertrude Weil will tell of a life well lived.

GERTRUDE WEIL

{ I }

MY DEAR ONES
German, Jewish, and Southern

Gertrude, Gettler, Gettla, or Sister—as a child, Gertrude Weil answered to many names. To the African American help she was *Miss* Gertrude. Sister befitted her, too, as family defined her. Currents of the German, Jewish, and American past flowed through her. As a Jew, she was the offspring of a great European migration to America that transformed the Jewish people. As a German, *Kultur* suffused her household with art, music, and literature. As a southerner, she was raised in a North Carolina redeeming itself after a cataclysmic war. On her dinner table were barbecue and goose cracklings. While classmates played after school, she was off to the temple for Hebrew and German lessons. A cosmopolitan in the provinces, Gertrude resided in several worlds at home.

As Gertrude threw herself into national and even global causes—women's suffrage, economic justice, labor rights, racial equality, Zionism, the antiwar movement—she remained a faithful daughter of her family and a loyal citizen of Goldsboro. However expansive her perspective, however much of the world she traveled, she was rooted in her German-Jewish heritage and small-town southern community. Gertrude Weil cannot be understood without visiting them.

Auf Deutschland

Gertrude's father and grandparents—Weils, Rosenthals, and Oettingers—immigrated to America in the 1840s and 1850s among some 140,000 Jews from German-speaking lands. They were village Jews residing in the Black Forest countryside on the border of Württemberg and Bavaria. Restricted in livelihoods and taxed into penury, Jews had worked in widely despised trades as cattle dealers, money lenders, and most typically peddlers. With their peculiar religion and Judeo-German language, these alleged killers of Christ remained a people apart. Periodically, riots left Jews beaten and murdered. Jews suffered further as the industrial revolution dispossessed artisans and small tradesmen from a distressed rural economy.

The trends transforming nineteenth-century German Jewry shaped Gertrude's family and the milieu in which she was raised. As village Jews, her forebears adhered to a folkloric, rabbinic Judaism that governed their lives with daily rituals, dietary laws, and communal obligations. The Haskalah, the Jewish Enlightenment, rationalized Judaism, reconciling it to science and philosophy, to citizenship in a civil society. States sought to hasten the Jews' German acculturation and, ideally, their assimilation into Christianity by granting them conditional rights.[1]

In 1848, liberal revolutions aspired to overthrow monarchial regimes across Europe and establish civil states that promised, among other liberties, to emancipate Jews. A year later Prussian troops crushed these democratic hopes. Bavarian Jews accelerated their American exodus. Neighboring Württemberg followed as a reactionary regime rescinded Jewish civil rights. Taxation, forced military service, and scant harvests aggravated their plight. From 1848 to 1862 Jews left for America at rates doubling those of the general population. Immigrants wrote letters and reports urging kin to come. Württemberg Jewish author Berthold Auerbach wrote of an "addiction to America." Not only the poor but also increasingly the wealthy left, among them Gertrude's father, aunts, uncles, and grandparents.[2]

Jews like the Weils entered modern society through their German acculturation. They embraced *Bildung*—moral education and self-improvement—which harmonized with Jewish laws and traditions that commanded study and ethical practice as pathways to God. *Bildung* was an aspiration for "higher things," a Platonic ideal where truth, beauty, and goodness were one. Education in classical languages and literature and cultivation of an aesthetic sensibility were portals into bourgeois society. Jews flocked to concert halls and art museums as if they were houses of worship. Respectability—honesty in business, pride of family—entitled Jews to citizenship. Many German Jews, especially among elites, converted to Christianity either from conviction or from self-interest, but Weils, Rosenthals, and Oettingers remained loyal Jews as they adopted German culture. In his native Oberdorf young Heinrich Weil, Gertrude's father, received a secular education in French, English, geometry, and geography but wrote his name in Hebrew on his schoolbook cover.[3]

Gertrude's family emigrated culturally as well as geographically. One side, Weils and Oettingers, originated in neighboring villages on the Bavarian-Württemberg border while another line, the Rosenthals, came from north-

The extended family were Gertrude's "dear ones." Jacob and Yetta Weil are at the center, first row. Second row, from the left, are Henry, Mina, Herman, Fanny, Solomon, and Sarah. Courtesy of David Weil.

ern Bavaria. Her grandparents, Jacob and Yetta Weil, had been antique dealers, and family folklore was that the "Weils came here with money."[4] The grandparents owned beautiful things, and their children and grandchildren, Gertrude included, were art lovers, bibliophiles, and collectors. Weil men and women alike studied Latin, and Henry shared the German devotion to Shakespeare, which he trained his manservant to spout. Gertrude would be classically educated and avidly attend theater, museums, and opera houses.

The Weils fit the pattern of family chain migration, as one drew another until the clan transplanted to America. First were teenage sisters Jeanette and Bertha Weil, the eldest of five children. Then came, in 1858 their brother Herman, sixteen. In 1860 Henry, Gertrude's father, then fourteen, departed Hamburg for Baltimore in steerage. His younger brother Solomon followed, and then their parents, Jacob and Yetta, arrived and opened a dry goods store. In America the clan of cousins, aunts, and uncles, settled mostly in Baltimore, some in New York, while others traveled rivers and railroads to places like Scranton and Toledo, as well as rural eastern North Carolina. As they had in southern Germany, the family clustered in nearby towns: Kinston, Wilson, Raleigh, and Goldsboro.[5]

Through constant visiting and letter writing the family network remained tight. When Gertrude's father became engaged to her mother, he "spread the intelligence broadcast all over the land, both in the New & old World." Letters were addressed to "my dear ones," and extended family spoke of "our crowd" or our "whole Jewish crowd." They vacationed together in Atlantic City and gathered in Baltimore, where they dined and danced at the Concordia, a German-Jewish club. They sailed to Europe to see cousins, aunts, and uncles. News of births and deaths, weddings and graduations were received with full hearts. For Gertrude no family member was ever distant.[6]

Baltimore served commercially and religiously if not politically as the capital of Jewish North Carolina, and Goldsboro became its colony. Economic distribution routes along sea lanes and rail lines were also channels of cultural communication. Not only cotton, capital, and commerce traversed railroad tracks, but also matzah and mothers-in-law, rabbis and religion, kuchen and corned beef. With the German migration Baltimore's Jewish population swelled from 120 in 1820 to 15,000 in 1874. A young immigrant—hardy, ambitious, and poor—could obtain goods on credit from a kinsman or landsman in the city, take a train or coastal steamer south, throw a pack on his back, and head into the countryside to peddle notions, fabric, or house wares.[7]

The Weils illustrate historian Jacob Rader Marcus's quip that no Jew was ever the first to arrive in a community. He was always preceded by his uncle, or in this case by an aunt. Jeanette Weil was engaged to Henry Oettinger, a Baltimore peddler who, since about 1850, had traveled eastern North Carolina with a horse and wagon. He had worked his way to a store on Goldsborough's Center Street. When he needed a clerk, he sent to Baltimore for his brother-in-law Herman.[8]

The arrival of Weils, Rosenthals, and Oettingers in North Carolina owed much to self-selection. Württembergers had been the most rural of German Jews, and North Carolina resembled the place they had left. As they had in Europe, Jewish peddlers and storekeepers brought commerce to the countryside. They assumed the classic Jewish role as retail middlemen between city and country, wholesaler and customer. Family members clerked in one another's stores, loaned one another money, and partnered in enterprises. Familial intramarriages were common, and Weils, Einsteins, Oettingers, and Rosenthals were so knotted that a sister-in-law was also a niece and first cousins were husband and wife. For Gertrude the household constantly filled with relatives, some from next door and others from Ohio, Maryland, New York, or Pennsylvania.[9]

As Jews, they were a clannish minority, whose acceptance depended on the tolerance of Christians. The Weils needed to cultivate goodwill if they were to succeed in business and raise their children without prejudice. Happily missing were the legal restrictions and public discrimination that had daily affronted their dignity and challenged their livelihoods in Germany.

Golden Land of Goldsborough

What did they find when they arrived in Goldsborough? The Carolina coastal plain was flat and fertile, a patchwork of field and forest, swamp and stream. English planters had settled along the muddy, meandering Neuse River, but more typical were yeomen, subsistence farmers who were poor, independent, and in contrast to the cultured gentry, stubbornly uneducated. Slave gangs worked plantations even as local Quakers sought to manumit them. Antebellum North Carolina was the Rip Van Winkle state, its economy stagnant, its people abandoning farms and towns for richer opportunities out west.

In 1840 the Wilmington & Weldon Railroad arrived, at 161 miles the world's longest. A hotel arose where tracks crossed the coastal road to New Bern. It was named Goldsborough Junction to honor an engineer. In 1847—after the town well was allegedly spiked with moonshine—citizens voted to incorporate Goldsborough as the Wayne County seat. In 1856 Goldsborough became the eastern terminus of the North Carolina Railroad that crossed the state to Charlotte. With north-south, east-west lines, Goldsborough became an economic hub.

Goldsborough was typical of mill and market towns sprouting along tracks, places where farmers brought cotton, peanuts, or tobacco to sell or warehouse, sites for textile mills and tobacco factories with access to northern markets. On Fridays millworkers and managers had paychecks to buy shoes and ready-made clothing. On Saturdays farmers arrived to market produce and buy supplies. Newcomers were wanted for their capital, commerce, and civic enterprise.[10]

When brothers Herman and Henry Weil arrived in North Carolina, "Jew peddlers" were familiar, and their careers followed a typical progression. Backpack peddlers worked up to a horse and wagon and then to a store, which might grow into a wholesale "peddler's headquarters" where new immigrants resupplied.[11] Across the South Jews created an ethnic economy in dry goods. Many failed and moved on, but successful storekeepers purchased farm land, built warehouses, speculated in cotton, and invested

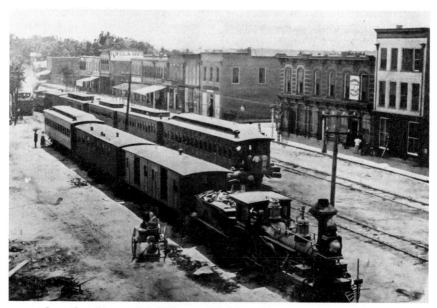

The railroad created Goldsborough. The Weil store is in the background.
Courtesy of the Wayne County Public Library.

in mills and banks. Jewish-owned department stores anchored southern cities.

Local society was fluid, and as newcomers the Weils felt welcomed. At their boarding house the brothers joined a table with merchants, ministers, and railroad agents. Hardscrabble North Carolina lacked the social hierarchies of the plantation states to its north and south. Distrust of outsiders was evident — nativist Know-Nothings made respectable electoral showings in the 1850s — but not severe enough locally to prevent the immigrants' swift integration. The foreign-born were too few to be threatening, and southerners were also hospitable to strangers. Along with the prevalent Baptists and Methodists were Quakers, themselves religious dissenters. The Weils, arriving two years after the North Carolina Railroad, were part of a small immigrant flow. In the late 1860s an immigration society, meeting in Goldsboro, sent recruiters to Germany. European settlers were wanted to preserve white dominance.[12]

Stepping from the Goldsborough train, the Weil brothers saw opportunity in stores lining the tracks. Nearly a thousand people lived in the budding town. At least three German Jews owned stores. The Weils settled shortly after Goldsborough's founding and became a chapter in the town's creation narrative, a situation that historically enhances the acceptance of Jews in a community. (The Weil homestead was the site of the town's legendary spiked well.) They became close friends with the town's first families.[13]

The Weils experienced little of the hostility that often greeted Jews heading south. Southerners resented northern economic exploitation even as they sought its trade and finance. Creating their own credit and distribution networks outside conventional channels, Jews were suspect. The bankers, merchants, and attorneys who wrote credit reports for R. G. Dun & Co. often described "Israelites" or "German Jews" in derogatory terms. Local anti-Semitism was evident in 1857 when "nearly every Jew left town" after a courtroom fracas between Falk Odenheimer and Dr. John Davis that left the "Jew merchant" with a cracked skull and the doctor with a bullet wound. T. T. Hollowell, a local Quaker, thwarted an anti-Semitic lynch mob. Jews soon returned, and the episode did not dissuade Herman and Henry Weil from settling there. The Dun & Co. reporters invariably described Weils, Oettingers, and Rosenthals as men of "strict integrity" who "stand high," "hardworking," and "very energetic & enterprising." Uncle Isaac Oettinger "stands remarkably well for a Jew."[14]

When Civil War erupted, Weil men, like other Jewish immigrants, demonstrated loyalty to their new southern homeland. Although the family had not been slaveholding, they were swept with war fever. A month after Fort Sumter, Gertrude's uncle Herman Weil, just three years in America, volunteered for the Confederate army. Another uncle, Leopold Oettinger, enlisted in the infantry only to be killed at Seven Pines. Her grandfather Emil Rosenthal served in the Home Guard and purchased cotton as a Confederate agent. If she wanted, Gertrude could join the United Daughters of the Confederacy.

With its railroad serving as "the lifeline of the Confederacy," Goldsborough Junction was a target of General Sherman's 1865 march through the Carolinas. At nearby Bentonville some eighty thousand Union and Confederate forces battled in March, leaving more than four thousand casualties. A month later the war was over. Although "bummers" ravaged the countryside, Goldsborough survived unscathed, and rail service soon resumed. War bankrupted the state. Repudiation of the Confederate debt exhausted its banks. Planters were reduced to poverty. A Freedman's Bureau challenged the racial balance of power. And yet business was to be done. Three Union armies had converged on Goldsborough, and some one hundred thousand Union soldiers, including black troops, were stationed nearby.[15]

With the plantation economy crumbled, and African Americans holding political rights, southern society unraveled. Conservative Democrats contended with blacks and Republicans. From 1867 to 1869 Ku Klux Klan violence wracked the state. The Klan was especially strong in eastern North Carolina. Despite unrest, across the South immigrant Jews saw opportunity in a devastated economy rebuilding itself. White southerners looked on disapprovingly. A credit agent disdained one local Jew as a "carpet bag," a "low Jew" who does a "mongrel trade with negroes." Weils, Rosenthals, and Oettingers as former Confederates did not bear such a stain. In 1867 Reconstructionist authorities appointed Emil Rosenthal to the Wilson town council despite a state constitutional religious test limiting public office to Christians. Lauded by a credit agent as a "Southern Jew," Rosenthal was elected in 1870 to the first of several council terms. His personal politics are not known, but his future son-in-law, Henry Weil, like many southern Jews, was an ardent Democrat contemptuous of black voters and Radical Republicans.[16]

Henry Weil, after clerking for Emil Rosenthal in Wilson, had replaced his soldier brother Herman in the Goldsborough store. At war's end, the brothers purchased a small wooden building along the tracks for $1,050. The store prospered—1865 was a good crop year, and the federal garrison provided plentiful customers. A year later younger brother Solomon, seventeen, joined them: "H. Weil & Bros." read the sign. The enterprising brothers sold toys and baby carriages, brick and lumber, crockery and jewelry, shoes and suits. In 1866 they purchased a town lot and a year later won a public auction for more lots. The next year they bought a 155-acre farm. In 1869—as the budding city renamed itself Goldsboro—the brothers acquired the property next door and then replaced the wooden store with a two-story brick building with an iron front. The store's brick came from a yard they purchased on the Neuse River. Sales rose from $30,000 in their first year to $100,000 in 1875 to $400,000 in 1890. In 1882 they erected an armory and office building, at three stories the town's tallest. Over two decades, Weils were partners or incorporators of nearly every major enterprise in the city. They were merchants, bankers, cotton speculators, manufacturers, and warehousemen. Weil enterprises produced tea and ice, brick and cotton, fertilizer and rice flakes.[17] The brothers exemplified to a high degree the Jewish entrepreneurship that helped build an urban, commercial New South. Business success led to civic leadership.

Reconstruction lasted until 1877, the token federal military occupation ending but two years before Gertrude's birth. The past was never dead. She heard tales of Confederate bravery and Yankee perfidy. Walking the streets, she recalled, were "characters" who were "faithful leaders of unending loyalty to the Confederacy." In 1895 a teenage Gertrude was decked in the red and white sash of the Hampton Guards to escort an aged Confederate general to the dedication of the Bentonville monument. "Alas," she remembered, "the heavens poured forth such volumes of rain" that she missed the ceremony.[18] Her community basked in Lost Cause nostalgia. In 1905 local Baptist minister Thomas Dixon Jr. exploited the alleged outrages of Reconstruction in Wayne County in his novel *The Clansman: An Historical Romance of the Ku Klux Klan*.

More influentially, Gertrude Weil was raised in the enterprising spirit of the New South. The Weils' success in Goldsboro owed to a confluence of historical factors. The postwar South welcomed the economic energies, the new sources of trade and capital, that Jews brought to a region that saw its salvation in commercial and industrial development. The New South, as Atlanta journalist Henry Grady proclaimed in 1886, would remake southern society, creating racial harmony and bringing newcomers to its emerging cities. Immigrants enjoyed an advantage through family networks. War did not break the commercial ties linking southern and northern Jews. Weils turned to their Einstein kin in Boston to supply their Goldsboro store with shoes, and Henry financed his Baltimore nephew, Elias Ries, a pioneering electronics inventor.[19]

The store integrated the Weils into town society. They employed neighbors as managers and bookkeepers and partnered with leading businessmen in banking and industrial enterprises. As Jewish entrepreneurs in the New South, the Weils were hardly alone. The Cone brothers in Greensboro, sons of a Bavarian immigrant, began as drummers for their father's Baltimore wholesale house and, investing in mills, created a textile industrial empire. Employing country pickers, the Wallace brothers of Statesville built the world's largest herbarium. The local *Daily Argus* hailed the Weils: "People like these, people of high character and strict personal integrity, are wanted in every community, for upon such men ... depends the safety, stability and the advancement of the city that possess them, the state and even the nation."[20] The family's multiple identities—emancipated Jews, cultured Germans, and progressive New Southerners—were more consonant than dissonant. Gertrude did not feel conflicted.

Family Life

Having secured their fortunes, the Weil brothers established families. Henry and Solomon, seemingly joined at the hip, married six weeks apart in 1875. Henry's bride was Mina Rosenthal of nearby Wilson, while Solomon wed a Bostonian, Sarah Einstein, whose uncle Moses owned a Goldsboro store. As was typical, marriages tightened the family knot. When Henry

Weil married Mina, his sister Jeanette was married to her uncle Henry Oettinger. His sister thus became his aunt. Gertrude's maternal grandparents Emil and Eva Oettinger Rosenthal were Bavarians who had arrived by 1859 in Raleigh and settled four years later in Wilson. As Emil's former clerk, Henry Weil had observed his future bride, he recalled, since she had crawled on the rug.[21]

The economic rise and social integration of these Jewish families were local examples of a global trend: the ascent of Jews into the middle class. In a society where illiteracy was widespread, German traditions of *Kultur* and *Bildung* identified Jews with the educated classes. Through literary culture they entered polite society as southern ladies and gentlemen. Mina attended the Wilson Collegiate Seminary for Young Ladies, under the churchman Dr. John DeBerniere Hooper, a professor at Chapel Hill. At eleven she was awarded a "Certificate of Praiseworthy Diligence and Success" in Greek and Roman history, geography, and mathematics. Hooper's wife, Mary, remained Mina's friend and affectionate correspondent.[22]

Mina's influence on Gertrude was formative—"if any good shall come from my life, it will be due to you," Gertrude once wrote her—and the daughter cannot be understood without an appreciation of the mother. Excepting her high school and college years, for her entire life Gertrude shared a house with Mamma, with the daughter caring for her widowed mother twenty-seven years. Mina had been raised in a Jewishly observant home. In their parlor her father, Emil, prayed morning and evening, often with Mina at his side. A local editor recalled him as "a man of deeply religious sentiments, unostentatious piety." Rosenthal opened his business ledger with an emphatic "Mit Gott!"[23]

Gertrude recalled grandmother Eva Oettinger Rosenthal as a "devoted wife and mother, wrapped up in her family." Judaism's traditional patriarchy blended with Victorian family values. Jewish women did not have liturgical responsibilities in the synagogue, but by custom and commandment they oversaw household rituals, dispensing charity, reading Bible and psalm books daily, and gathering family on Friday nights for Sabbath dinners. "All depends & comes from a higher Being & to Him we will trust," Eva wrote her "dear children." When Mina married, Eva advised, "Nothing is nicer for a wife than to make home pleasant for her husband."[24]

Emil Rosenthal said that he preferred giving charity to being wealthy, and he gave quietly and generously, including to a country Methodist minister whom he befriended. Along with Kate Connor and Mary Daniels, Eva formed a Jewish, Catholic, and Methodist trinity known in Wilson as the "Three Graces" for their benevolence. Daniels's son Josephus—who would become publisher, secretary of the navy, and ambassador to Mexico—remembered the Rosenthals warmly in speeches and memoirs. He recalled a day townspeople stood on the post office steps sympathizing with a farmer whose house had burned: "'I am sorry,' spoke up a well-to-do citizen. 'How sorry are you?' asked Mr. Emil Rosenthal, a prosperous Jewish merchant. 'I am sorry twenty dollars' worth,' he said." Others then gave. Daniels commented, "That was characteristic of the Rosenthals," whom he stereotyped as "rich Jews."[25]

Small-town neighborliness, childhood friendships, multigenerational familiarity all led to intimate social conviviality between the immigrant Jewish families and their native Christian neighbors. "Our friendship began in the old days when your grandmother and my mother 'went about doing good' in Wilson," *Raleigh News and Observer* publisher Jonathan Daniels wrote Gertrude in 1943, "so I feel there is a lasting bond of affection in our families." Another neighbor, Collier Cobb, later an influential professor at the University of North Carolina at Chapel Hill, recalled how as a child, bedridden after a horse trampling, he was brought daily treats by the Rosenthals. His aunt described these Jews "as the best Christians in this town."[26] In a South wary of outsiders, Gertrude was warmly greeted as one of its own.

Small-town Jews fit in. In 1873 Mina Rosenthal "could think of nothing but Christmas." Weils and Rosenthals exchanged "goodies" and enjoyed eggnog as children hung stockings. The state's most venerated politician, Civil War governor and U.S. senator Zebulon Vance, in his philo-Semitic speech "The Scattered Nation" honored Jews as his "wondrous kinsmen."[27]

Founding a Family

Henry Weil and Mina Rosenthal became engaged in 1873 when she was but fourteen and he was twenty-seven. Such a courtship was not unique among rural Jews given the dearth of potential spouses. Her parents were concerned for the propriety of the relationship, and Henry acknowledged that "public gossip" kept him from Wilson. At a time when female school teachers were expected to be chaste and unmarried, an engaged school girl raised concern. Mina wrote Henry that the mayor, Colonel Kenan, "called to see me last night. He said he always calls on young ladies when they stop school."[28]

The Rosenthals, while approving of Henry, vetted the couple's correspondence and restricted visits to weekends. She was his "little Kally," a Yiddish diminutive for bride, and he tutored her in Hebrew and German. The wedding was postponed until Mina finished school. When Henry expressed

loneliness, his "Pineywoods girl" counseled "patience." Separation intensified their ardor. Henry promised kisses by the hundreds, if not the thousands. By December, he was "at last permitted open & above board to express freely my deep feeling of love which has burned in my heart bosom."[29]

Gertrude remembered a mother mature beyond her years. At sixteen
Mina had ended her childhood and formal schooling. Atypical for Jewish
parents, Mina and Henry rarely pressed Gertrude to marry or raise a family.
Gertrude enjoyed a liberty that Mina never experienced. Mina received a
modern education, and Gertrude would attend the country's finest schools
for women. Henry confessed that he was "jealous" of Mina's love for "Calcu-
lus, Chemistry, and Trigonometry," subjects beyond the curriculum female
seminaries offered to groom southern ladies. Henry assured Mina that after
marriage she could realize her ambition to study medicine, if she so chose,
and he supported his daughters' education even more generously than his
sons'. Nearing a quarter century of marriage, Henry joked, "After various &
sundry experiments I found the best method to train a wife ... is to let her
have her own way."[30]

On 24 March 1875, Mina Rosenthal and Henry Weil wed at the Hanover Street Temple in Baltimore with Rabbi Benjamin Szold officiating.
This congregation, Oheb Shalom (Lover of Peace), was founded by German Jews who negotiated a conservative compromise between Orthodoxy
and Reform.[31] Mina became friends with the rabbi's daughter Henrietta, a
pioneering figure in American Jewry who founded Hadassah, the women's
Zionist society, in 1912. Mina's ardent Zionism, atypical of German Jews
in the South, was passed to her daughter. More typically, German Jews
asserted their Americanism, and their Reform Judaism dismissed Zionist longings as parochial and impractical, no longer claiming Judaism as a
nationality.

Weeks after Henry and Mina's marriage, Solomon Weil married Sarah
Einstein at Hanover Street Temple. Anticipating families, the brothers built
adjoining, nearly identical, eight-room houses on Chestnut Street in Goldsboro, a short walk to the store. These Italianate houses proclaimed the success and sophistication of the immigrant brothers. Neighborly porches welcomed passersby for chats, and parlors hosted town society for formal social
calls. Weils were noted for elegant dinners. The newspaper described the
houses, set in a magnolia grove with a fountain between them, as "pala-
tial."[32] On a buying trip to New York Henry furnished both houses from the
city's finest purveyors. When Mina and Henry wanted portraits, they went
to high-society photographers at Bachrach Studios in Baltimore.

Despite the grandeur of the Weil dwellings, Goldsboro's streets were un-

Gertrude's lifetime home: 200 Chestnut Street, Goldsboro, North Carolina.
Courtesy of the State Archives of North Carolina.

paved, rutty, and muddy. Water came from a household well, and an out-house served as privy until a backyard tank brought running tap water. Not until the 1890s did the city connect water and sewage. Innovations—bath tub, furnace, refrigerator, gas lighting, and telephone—followed. One nightly entertainment for Gertrude was to watch the lamplighter with his long torch make his rounds.

Gertrude was raised in material comfort, but even more formative was the embrace of a large and loving clan. Uncle Herman, the steady oldest brother, died in 1878, and his widow, Fannie, and children departed for Baltimore, but Henry and Solomon established a multifamily enclave on Chestnut Street. The brothers, busy with enterprises, deferred to their strong-willed wives. At the dinner table Mina sat at the head, with Henry to her right. Gertrude never lacked cousins and siblings for companionship or aunts, uncles, and grandparents for security and guidance. Across the street lived Grandma and Grandpa Rosenthal, and around the corner were Uncle Joe, Mina's brother, and more cousins, the Spiers and Josephs. Einstein in-laws joined the family circle, and Oettingers were always nearby.

Mina and Sarah's relationship was both complementary and competitive. Where Mina was a native North Carolinian versed in its mores, Sarah remained a Bostonian ambitious to bring New England civilization to the benighted South. The "Yankee girl" teased her younger sister-in-law about being so credulous and trusting. If Mina gave charity personally and quietly, Sarah led campaigns to create a public library and, with a Presbyterian minister, a city hospital. Mother and aunt set demanding standards for their children.[33]

In 1876, after a year of marriage, Henry and Mina had the first of four children to grow into adulthood, a son, Leslie. Gertrude followed on 11 December 1879, and then Herman in 1882 and Janet in 1892. An infant daughter, Madlin, died in 1885, despite Henry and Mina's efforts to find a healthier clime in Virginia. The siblings stayed close throughout their lives, with all but Janet remaining in Goldsboro, and she only as far as nearby Wilmington. Birth order fixed family roles. Leslie was big "Brother," who set a model of academic achievement, civic engagement, and social deportment. As middle child, Gertrude enjoyed a measure of freedom. Short and slight, fair skinned and blue eyed, Gertrude even in childhood appeared younger than her years. Herman was Gertrude's fun-loving playmate, like her a sports devotee. Gruff, at least on the outside, he aroused her stubborn, competitive streak.[34] For Janet, Gertrude was proverbial big "Sister," and given the thirteen years between them and their mother's ill health, Gertrude tended to her with near-maternal solicitude.

Next door at Aunt Sarah and Uncle Sol's house were cousins Edna, Lionel, and Helene, also bright, accomplished children. At times residing there were Oettinger and Altmeyer cousins, clerks in the Weil store, and Sarah's much younger sister Hilda and their widowed mother Sophie Einstein. Children of the two households were raised communally, and doors opened for dinners, sleepovers, and nightly card playing. Each morning at 8:30 a two-horse double phaeton drove Gertrude, Leslie, Herman, and cousins Lionel, Edna, and Hilda to school, returning at 2:30 for dinner. Gertrude remained close to her cousins. Little Leslie and Hilda were so tight that Henry once told his two-year-old son as they sat on the porch to call Sophie Einstein his "Sweiger Mutter," or mother-in-law. Leslie and Hilda indeed married twenty years later.[35]

Despite the security of wealth and relations, the family was not without suffering. Having lost an infant when Gertrude was five, Mina was an anxious parent. Gertrude had been a colicky baby who kept her parents up. Nearing her second birthday she fell ill, eliciting "fervent prayer" for the "little darling." In 1887 Mina's sister Mattie was fatally injured when a coach driven by cousin Adolph Oettinger was struck by a train in Wilson. Then, in 1892, two months after Janet's birth, Mina's beloved father, Emil, died suddenly. Gertrude recalled her mother as "feeble," an image contrary to her reputation as an inexhaustible host and clubwoman. Mina had a sickly youth and after marriage strained a muscle that made walking difficult. She suffered spells that were diagnosed as "nervousness," a syndrome commonly affixed to women. When Gertrude was six Mina suffered a prolonged bout, and she consulted doctors and visited spas for therapy; sometimes Gertrude accompanied her. In the 1890s eye problems prevented her from reading. Gertrude, too, suffered headaches and eye troubles. Mina's anxiety typifies stereotypes of the Jewish mother. As a twelve-year-old traveling with Uncle Joe in Virginia, Gertrude wrote her mother, "Aren't you lonely, without anybody to worry you?" Gertrude later became her mother's caregiver.[36]

Born in the antebellum Old South when women were bred to be dependent on fathers or husbands, Mina had been raised during the Civil War and Reconstruction when women were often left to be self-reliant. She became wife and mother in a New South when women were asserting independence. Though Mina never wrote a check while her husband lived, she participated in the economy as consumer and household manager. Mina was indifferent to material goods—Henry furnished the house—and she chided Gertrude on the vanity of fashion. Yet much mother-daughter correspondence was expended on dresses and millinery, and fabric swaths were mailed in style consultations on shirtwaists and bicycle skirts.[37] Holiday visits to New York included expeditions to Arnold Constable or Altman's, with charges made to "H. Weil."

As befit the Weils' wealth, domestic staff served the homes. Mina held high standards, and Henry compared her household leadership to Lincoln firing his generals. Cooks came and went. Black domestic help were addressed customarily by first names. Butlers Judge and Prince provoked humor about the "high character" of their names. As was common among white southerners, Gertrude was raised in a household where race privilege was assumed. Distrusting the help, Mina and Sarah kept pantries locked, and Mina carried house keys in a small basket.[38]

While African Americans cooked, gardened, and cleaned house, childcare was entrusted to an uneducated, white country woman known affectionately as Norny. She had raised Mina and her siblings in Wilson, and for twenty years she raised a second generation in the Weil home. Gertrude held warm memories of her sitting in a rocker singing Methodist hymns. When Norny retired to a farm, the family brought money and clothes from the store. Gertrude always had domestic help. She advocated positions contrary to her class interests while enjoying the entitlements of wealth.

The Weils' African American butler's photograph was labeled "Le Prince Noir."
Courtesy of the State Archives of North Carolina.

If commerce had brought Weils to Goldsboro, home acculturated them to the South. Contrary to the stereotype of the Jew as one who "sojourns" but does not "dwell," as Zebulon Vance observed, Weils planted roots in local soil. Gertrude inherited from her mother a love of flowers and with cousin Etta Spier planted her own garden. Between the houses was a grape arbor. The backyard provided play space for neighborhood children, and behind that were vegetable gardens and pens for ducks and geese.[39]

Gertrude enjoyed a southern childhood. On the corner were the Galloways, where the children relished breakfasts of ham and biscuits while Mrs. Galloway read her beloved Dickens. The Galloways often joined the Weil dinner table. In contrast to their urban cousins, who lived in largely Jewish enclaves, small-town Jews integrated into local society. On Sundays Weil children walked the railroad tracks to the Howells' home, where they played in the sand yard and flew skyward from a huge swing. Or Gertrude was off

Addie Ritter, affectionately called Norny, raised two generations of Rosenthal and Weil children. Courtesy of the State Archives of North Carolina.

to friends to play or to work on school projects. The Spiers' house around the corner served as a hangout. With five children, the Spiers hosted their Weil cousins for dinners and sleepovers. Their yard sported a tennis court where the children played summer nights, ending with Aunt Amelia's fresh biscuits.[40]

Foodways illustrated the family's "braided" cultures. Like many German-American Jews, Weils abandoned kosher laws, which Reform Judaism eschewed as "foreign" to a modern people. Mina's signature dish was fried oysters in butter sauce. African American cooks brought their cuisine into the household. Bacon and battercakes, pickled oysters and kuchen were breakfast fare, and all enjoyed barbecue. Mammy Lucy, Sarah's cook, packed sardine biscuits for school lunches. Desiring German delicacies, Henry would award Ma Rosenthal's *ganz Grieben* (goose cracklings) a gold medal at the state fair and devoured her *Apfelkrapfen* (apple crepe).[41]

Gertrude was raised in a multicultural and multigenerational household. On her thirteenth birthday Leslie congratulated her on becoming a "Barmitzvah Madchen." Uncle Sol's library held *The Book of Thoughts*, which recorded the family's inner worlds. Grandpa Emil's inspirational poets were biblical David and Solomon, while father Henry preferred German master poet Schiller and American satirist John Godfrey Saxe, and mother Mina chose Tennyson and Longfellow. Grandpa's favorite music was the "Blast of the Shofar" on Yom Kippur, while his son in law liked Mozart and musical theater stars Harrigan & Hart. Their tastes demonstrated a generational American acculturation.[42]

Correspondence reveals people conversant with a wide world. Letters among parents and children recommended articles in *Harper's*, *Century*, *Atlantic Monthly*, or *Cosmopolitan* and the latest novels of Stevenson or stories of O. Henry, as well as now forgotten Victorian novelists. Siblings argued Walt Whitman's poetry, George Eliot's religious views and relationships, and Israel Zangwill's assimilationist novels. Henry and Leslie collected first editions. Trips to Baltimore and New York were not just to purchase store stock and to visit family but also to see plays and concerts. Gertrude attended theater so avidly that after a matinee of *The Mikado* she quipped, "Of course I have to go to keep up my reputation."[43]

Parents kept Gertrude and her siblings in the ethnic and religious fold. On Saturdays she attended Sabbath School from eight to nine. After public school were German School on Tuesdays and Hebrew School on Thursdays.[44] Gertrude interrupted games and bike riding for piano lessons. She enjoyed dance class, which was thought necessary for proper society. Gertrude eagerly anticipated Goldsboro's balls and Germans as well as Jewish high society at the Baltimore club Concordia.

Gertrude held warm memories of home life. After supper Mina called the children to the living room and read from the Bible or Longfellow, *Evangeline* being a favorite. An avid reader, Mina shared poems from *The Century* and *Atlantic Monthly*. A proficient pianist, although incapable of singing on key, Mina assembled the children for parlor musicales. Other times they sat around "nice, sweet" Papa who read light verse, "Singing through the Forests" or "How Goes the Money?" from favorite poet Saxe.[45]

Visiting centered southern social life. Weils joined neighbors for teas and luncheons. Trips to Wilson, Kinston, and Baltimore bonded Gertrude to her Weil, Rosenthal, and Oettinger relatives as the parents passed their Jewish world on to their children. After the thirteen-year-old visited Kinston,

Gertrude wrote home, "It seems to me if we, Cousin Hennie's & Bertha's children, and I get together, there is a crowd," employing her parents' term to define her social circle. With her cousins, she enjoyed horseback riding and carriage rides to a farm or to the Seven Springs resort for picnics. One highlight was a trip with her father and Herman to their Joseph cousins in Chicago for the 1893 World's Fair. Joined by ten relatives, Gertrude walked until her feet hurt. Although all enjoyed Buffalo Bill's Wild West show, Papa refereed a fight when Herman lingered at the bicycle exhibit while Gertrude pulled them to the French dolls.[46]

Jewish and American cultures harmonized on basic family and community values. Children were set on a course of sobriety, industriousness, and self-improvement. Gertrude felt that she differed from neighborhood children only in the directions they headed for church on Sunday mornings. Family photos show children posed with bicycles and large dogs. Gertrude's diary, kept when she was twelve, recorded daily social rounds with neighborhood kids. Like her parents, she maintained parallel Jewish and Christian crowds. With Leslie and Herman, Edna, and Lionel she played tiddledywinks; her Spier cousins were good for paper dolls, and the Cohen and Rosenthal girls knew German games. In 1891, at a bar mitzvah party, Mrs. Ike Fuchtler organized the Young Folks Literary Society with Leslie as president and Gertrude chief contributor of poems and stories. They published the *Literary News*. It lasted but two years, when Leslie headed to college and the rambunctious ten-year-olds had interests other than literature.[47]

However different their religion and ethnicity, the children shared an upbringing that embraced the free spirit of American youth. Gertrude fitted comfortably into an emerging, late-nineteenth-century "American girl culture." As gender roles evolved, girls went beyond traditional "morality and domesticity" to embrace new models of "blooming health, independence of spirit, and cultivated taste." Bodies as well as minds were exercised, and schools added physical education for girls. According to Progressive Era gender codes, boys tested their manliness while girls showed womanly vigor. From her youth Gertrude kept physically fit. While her mother struggled to climb stairs, Gertrude hiked and biked, swam and rowed. Always fond of the outdoors, she spent evenings walking the woods with cousin Etta and their friend Susie Fulghum.[48]

Weil children as both fans and athletes were struck with the sports mania sweeping America. In 1893 "bike fever" hit Goldsboro, and Gertrude, given a two-wheeler, reveled in the freedom. "Sister rides splendidly and all over town," Mina wrote Leslie at the University of North Carolina at Chapel

Gertrude as a child. Note the six-pointed star on her hat.
Courtesy of the State Archives of North Carolina.

Hill. With Leslie she avidly followed UNC football, and with Herman she attended Goldsboro baseball games. Evening card playing pitted Grandpa and Sister against Grandma and Brother. Gertrude obsessed over the latest card craze, particularly bridge. She did not like to lose. One story retold in later years recalled how Gertrude bopped Herman on the head with a croquet mallet. Her mother demanded an apology, but Gertrude refused. From an early age, as Herman himself warmly recounted, Gertrude had a stubborn sense of justice, unwilling to submit to authority or defer to a male.[49]

Mina's and Henry's gender roles were both properly Victorian and traditionally German Jewish. Henry was the provider. "Anyone engaged in a Business is but a slave to it," he observed, and he spent long hours tending to his enterprises. Stocking a department store, brokering cotton, and financing mills meant frequent travels to Raleigh and Wilmington, as well as buying trips to Boston, New York, and Baltimore. Yet Henry was "dear Papa," quick to write his daughter a check whether she asked or not. A bright-eyed, perpetually humorous dreamer, Henry was legendarily absentminded. Though indulgent and affectionate, he was distant, in contrast to her mother's intimacy. At family gatherings, Gertrude recalled, her father and uncle "would go over in a corner of the room and discuss business, oblivious to what went on around them." Writing Gertrude when she was nineteen, he confessed that "Mamma gave me such a good lecture ... that I was negligent to not appearing to take much interest in my children & so on." He continued, "Well, you know I never can & have always been a poor hand to attend to anything appertaining domestic affairs." Mina's household efficiency "spoiled" him.[50]

Of the factors inspiring Gertrude's civic career, the family's example was most influential. As a child, Gertrude observed her father as a school board member, university trustee, civic benefactor, synagogue officer, merchant, and industrialist. This self-made immigrant moved easily among native-born men who were legislators, governors, and university presidents. Gertrude had also the example of Uncle Sol, who served intermittently as town alderman from 1881 until 1905, when his son Lionel succeeded him. The Weil civic presence was visible in downtown Goldsboro in 1890 when Henry and Sol donated Herman Park in memory of their brother. Its dedication was marked with an elaborate parade led by the Goldsboro Rifles, the fire department, and a military band. Local dignitaries speechified. Later the brothers added a pavilion.[51] The Weil name became widely known for philanthropy and civic betterment, opening doors for Gertrude and shielding her when she took unpopular positions. In towns across the nation successful Jewish merchants rose swiftly into leadership.

A path was laid for daughters as well as for sons. Gertrude's mother and grandmother were among the Jewish women joining their Christian sisters as community builders. Mina was a formidable woman tirelessly civic and generous. "I always thought my mother had no sense of beauty," Gertrude reflected, "except of holiness." Mina was a traditional wife and mother, mistress of the household, yet she also joined the vanguard of women entering the civil sphere. "The public life of nearly every Southern woman leader for forty years," writes Anne Firor Scott, "began in a church society." Though the Social Gospel inspired the women's movement, Weil women drew from Jewish culture—albeit one imbued with an American progressive spirit shaped by the Protestant environment. In Jewish community development, the benevolence society traditionally preceded organizing a congregation, honoring commandments to welcome guests, succor the poor, visit the sick, and bury the dead. In the 1880s Mina and Sarah had led Hebrew Benevolence and Ladies Aid Societies. As social gatherings, the Jewish societies paralleled the home and missionary societies of Protestant churches but without evangelical intent or outreach.[52]

Mina, following her mother's example in Wilson, helped organize an interfaith Ladies Benevolent Society in Goldsboro. In March 1885 eighty women chose Sarah as president, a post she held for nearly thirty years, while Mina chaired its relief committee. The women directed their efforts to the sick and poor in the Goldsboro working-class neighborhoods of Webbtown and Edmundsontown. "In the scorching days of summer, in the frigid days of winter they were on hand to offer help," recalled Mina's daughter-in-law Hilda. Mornings found Mina in her buggy taking medicine, wood, and coal to the "poor folks." When a parent-teacher chairman counted schoolchildren who needed shoes, Mina responded, "I don't care how many it is, just send them to H. Weil & Bros."[53]

"From my earliest childhood I have seen poor people at my mother's door," Gertrude recalled in tribute. Plainspoken, Mina was no soft touch to those who knocked asking for school tuition or money for a doctor. One recipient recalled, "She'll fuss at you, but she will give you something." Mothers were instructed to clean their children, and no-goods were lectured on being better husbands and fathers. As a seven-year-old in 1886, Gertrude was enlisted in her first charitable campaign, a bazaar to benefit victims of the Charleston earthquake. Her mother sent her to fetch sheets as backdrops for their homemade wares.[54] The parental examples inculcated in Gertrude a duty to the poor and the responsibilities of citizenship.

Social Ambivalence

As Jews, the Weils still felt their position as outsiders more than their neighbors perceived. Jews were too few to enter into public consciousness, and Mrs. Hooper meant well when she customarily ended her letters to the Weils with blessings in her savior's name. In 1893 when the Methodist Church held a Goldsboro revival, attended by Norny, the Weils looked out their window as missionaries knocked on doors of Jewish homes, "going to Spier's, Einstein's, and Schwab's."[55] If not overt religious prejudice, such behavior suggested Christians were oblivious to Jewish feelings.

In the 1870s anti-Semitism was evolving from a religious to a racial prejudice, intensifying as the East European Jewish immigration brought millions of allegedly swarthy aliens regarded as incapable of assimilation. Social discrimination was institutionalized. In 1907 Jewish philanthropist Bertha Rayner Frank was turned away in Atlantic City, a favorite Weil vacation spot. Mina was a devotee of spas and resorts, where she took note of Jewish guests even as she enjoyed the society of Christian friends. Weils traveled frequently, staying often at the best hotels. As acculturated southern German Jews, they did not much resemble the unwanted northern Jewish parvenus or Russian immigrants.

Mina did recall one slight pointing to underlying social discrimination. At a Recreation Club reception in 1900 for some one hundred guests to honor Sallie Southall Cotten, the state's "Mother of Clubs," Mina noted that everyone was invited afterward to Sue Collins's house for refreshments except Jews, who all went home. Mina thought it "funny." Exceptional Jews, like the Weils, often found access where other coreligionists were unwelcome. Appreciation of a Jewish neighbor coexisted happily with a general anti-Semitism. Yet Weils were intimate with elite families like the Grahams, Graves, and Cottens, and their social calendar listed invitations to balls and weddings. The New South lacked the first family hierarchy of the Old, and small towns were less exclusionary.[56]

Whether feeling excluded or wanting to be among their own, Weils, like Jews everywhere, maintained separate Jewish social circles and institutions. The principal way that the Weils expressed their Judaism was through association with "our Jewish crowd." The Weil men took leadership roles in organizing and financing the congregation, while the women formed a Ladies Benevolent Society and Auxiliary Society of the Atlanta Hebrew Orphans' Home. When a Chautauqua organized in 1892, its half-dozen members were all Jews, with Mina and Sarah leading. They studied the *Nieblungenlied* and *Nathan the Wise*, railroads and Shakespeare. Later, a few prominent Christians joined.[57] Growing up, Gertrude lived in a circumscribed Jewish social world, but she freely entered other spheres and did not feel anti-Semitism personally. Her parents, conscious of themselves as Jews, did not express anxiety as to their own racial status or any need to demonstrate their whiteness.

The Jewish Church

When Gertrude was born, some 250,000 Jews lived in America. After the Civil War, Jews from Prussia and western Poland arrived in growing numbers. Goldsboro Jewry grew to 147 in 1878. As immigrant peddlers and storekeepers came and went, Weils persisted as community leaders. Prior to organizing, local Jews had hosted home services but, diverse in ethnic and religious origins, had yet to unite into a congregation. Henry Weil distinguished "our crowd" from the "Polakim," Polish Jews.[58]

The late 1860s and 1870s were birthright years of institutional Judaism in America. A Union of American Hebrew Congregations (UAHC) and a Hebrew Union College were founded in Cincinnati. New congregations and synagogues arose in the hundreds. In 1875, following Jewish custom, Goldsboro Jews took their first communal step by purchasing a burial ground in Willow Dale Cemetery. That year, the women organized a Ladies Hebrew Assistance Society. Across the state, new cemeteries, congregations, and burial and benevolence societies sprouted, including a first synagogue in Wilmington in 1876.

A synagogue was the Jewish church, a place for Jews to worship and gather as a people but also to stake civic space in the faith community. To be respectable in the South meant joining a church. The movement for a synagogue occurred as Goldsboro was growing into a city. A building boom brought new factories, schools, and stores. With population growth Roman Catholics erected a sanctuary. Church building, synagogues included, was a civic duty, and peoples of all faiths contributed. As a child, Gertrude went with her mother to the Methodist fair. So many Jews attended the Catholic bazaar, noted a church historian, "that one would think plans were being made for a synagogue."[59]

In Jewish communities too small to factionalize by ethnicity or religious orientation, congregations accommodated diversity. Even within the Weil family, Gertrude's parents shared a Jewish culture but had different religious upbringings. In Württemberg Henry received a traditional religious education. He sprinkled Hebrew in his courtship letters to Mina, comparing his periodic visits to ritual counting of the *omer* (grain) between "Pesach &

Shevuoth." Excepting her Baltimore sojourns, Mina was raised without a synagogue or resourceful Jewish community. Home was her Jewish setting. When expressing religious views, she spoke a feminine language that borrowed from Protestant rhetoric in its stress on feeling and personal spirituality. "I don't think religion lies in forms, but that in our daily life must we live the religion of our hearts," Mina instructed Gertrude. "Our consciences are our only guides, but we must see that these remain pure and unselfish." But Mina also confessed to Gertrude: "I feel my shortcomings towards you mostly from a religious point of view, and I almost wish my own good father could have lived long enough to instill more of his religious spirit into his grandchildren."[60]

The family's observance was marked by inconsistencies as they negotiated between tradition and modernity. Small-town Jews, distant from metropolitan centers and rabbinic authorities, accommodated Judaism to their own situation. If the household did not keep kosher, they lived the Jewish calendar. Pesach—Mina always used the Hebrew for Passover—meant ritual housecleaning and gathering the family for "sedah." Excluded from synagogue rituals, women engaged in daily Bible reading, a custom common among Christians. Henry learned the practice from Mina, reading testaments New and Old. Nightly, Leslie read his Bible and "tphilla" (prayers), and likely Gertrude was so instructed. What persisted was folkloric Judaism. Purim was observed German style with a glass of "gut old Winkler-Hasensprung." Gertrude's grandparents taught her to associate blooming lilacs with the approach of Pesach. New Year meant ritual letter writing to relatives. Honoring a commandment, neither Mina nor Sarah wrote on the Sabbath.[61]

Immigrant Jews who came to North Carolina were searching for economic opportunity, not Jewish community, which was abundantly more available in Baltimore or New York. Starting in the early 1880s, some two million East European Jews flowed into eastern port cities, with a trickle heading into heartland America. When Goldsboro Jews reached the critical mass and material prosperity to build a synagogue, they turned to Baltimore. There, Weils had gone to be married, to observe holidays, and to bury brother Herman. Baltimore was a cauldron of Judaisms, offering the gamut from traditionalists committed to Hebrew worship and strict Sabbath observance to conservatives streamlining ritual and historicizing theology to radicals inventing an American Judaism consonant with Ethical Culture or Unitarianism. When visiting Baltimore and New York, Weils attended synagogue but sometimes slept late or shopped. Frequently, Saturday morning worship was followed by a theater matinee or dancing school.[62]

Building the Temple

On 15 February 1883, thirty-three people "who called themselves Israelites" met at Goldsboro's Odd Fellows Hall, "united for the purpose of building a synagogue." Sol Weil introduced Rev. Dr. Alois Kaiser, eminent cantor of Oheb Shalom in Baltimore. Kaiser had composed a hymnal that was distinctly American yet still traditional with prayers in English, German, and transliterated Hebrew. Four days later they voted to adopt Oheb Shalom's name, constitution, ritual, and prayer book. Ladies, as was traditional, were entrusted to raise funds, furnish the synagogue, and provide social welfare through their benevolence society. In January 1884 a "neat sum" was raised when Jewish statesman Simon Wolf, a Weil family friend, delivered an ecumenical lecture at the opera house, "Have We Not All One Father?" H. Weil & Bros. lent space in their armory for services. A lot for a synagogue was purchased on James Street, around the corner from the Weil homes.[63]

The 1886 synagogue dedication was front-page news. Temple Oheb Sholom replicated the neo-Romanesque architecture of the Baltimore mother synagogue while fitting in with neighboring churches. The ornamental, white-and-gold Goldsboro ark resembled its parent. Stained glass adorned the windows. As the Jewish church, the synagogue testified to prosperity and permanence. It had the grandeur of a city cathedral scaled for a provincial town. At the temple's dedication, "a large audience" of Jews and Christians gathered for a ceremony both civic and religious. Doors opened to an organ fanfare. Leading a procession of girls, presumably including Gertrude, her ten-year-old cousin Edna presented keys to congregational president Adolph Lehman. In a prepared speech, Edna spoke to shared values: "While our beautiful city, Goldsboro, increases in wealth and refinement and makes religion and education the object of her culture, may this edifice stand among its sister churches, which point their spires to heaven, as an evidence of the devotion of the Hebrew community of Goldsboro to the truth of their faith, and of their regard for the reputation of their city for moral and intellectual elevation."[64] The chorus sang Hallelujah. The Torah was placed in the ark. Rev. Dr. Max Moses prayed to "the Father of all mankind." The temple, he continued "shall teach you that Israel's mission is universal." Some two hundred enjoyed a "grand banquet." The *Daily Argus* editorialized that "the Jews are among the chief promoters of the development of humanity and civilization."[65] Attending synagogue, Gertrude was sensitive to aesthetics. At Oheb Sholom she found truth, beauty, and goodness.

From childhood an unshakable Jewish value was implanted in Gertrude: each Jew was responsible for the other. Jews commonly employ the metaphor of family in describing the bond that unites them as a people, and Gertrude felt it. She lived Judaism through family. That sentiment kept her within the bounds of Judaism and Jewish community even as her spiritual outlook, intellectual interests, and social commitments expanded. "She was Jewish to the core," a Goldsboro resident observed.[66]

Jewish observance in the Weil home was idiosyncratic, and Gertrude felt free to create her own way. She always insisted that her religious views were personal, however consonant they were with larger Jewish trends. If Weils could not cite Talmudic verse to justify their behaviors, they absorbed values and practices from the Jewish folk culture that owed to traditional Judaism. They preferred giving charity anonymously in a way that empowered recipients rather than supported dependency. They regarded study a necessary prelude to practice. They honored their parents, and they valued their good name in the community. Gertrude's family lived the Jewish calendar, and that became her lifelong habit. Siblings, cousins, aunts, and uncles filled the house on holidays. They ate matzah during Pesach and fasted on Yom Kippur.

In a small congregation every Jew was needed, and at temple Gertrude learned lessons of community, to be inclusive and to conciliate differences. Oheb Sholom negotiated a conservative compromise bridging the ethnic and ideological differences dividing American Jews. In Gertrude's family, her grandfather Emil was a traditionalist while her uncle Sol wanted reform. In 1885 the UAHC conference, meeting in Pittsburgh, issued a platform defining a distinctly American Classical Reform Judaism that rationalized belief and anglicized worship, complementing liberal Protestantism. Certainly, Goldsboro Jews followed national debates as they mediated between Jewish tradition and American democracy. According to the Oheb Sholom bylaws, worship would be governed by "Biblical injunction rather than by expediency," and in Hebrew rather than in English. Men were required to cover their heads, although Uncle Sol prayed defiantly hatless. As in a church, women sat with men in family pews while an organ played and choir sang.[67]

Gertrude was raised in a traditional Jewish milieu trending toward Classical Reform, and her views and practices reflected a modernizing ethos. In 1890 the congregation joined the UAHC, which became the Reform governing body, but did not adopt its Union Prayer Book until 1913. After several rabbis came and went—Grandpa Rosenthal led services—the congregation in 1890 brought from Statesville Rabbi Julius Mayerberg, who remained thirty-four years. He and his family became Weil intimates. Born in Lithuania of Orthodox background, he had been educated in historical Judaism at a German university and supplemented his income as a lawyer.[68]

In ideology if not in always practice, Reform Judaism granted equality to women. Jewish tradition had confined women religiously to the home, segregating them in a synagogue gallery, but the Reform temple seated them equally. Mixed-gender choirs gave voice to women in prayer. The temple acculturated women as Americans while affirming their Jewish identity. In the late nineteenth century, the synagogue no less than the church was undergoing a feminization. Men still led Oheb Sholom's worship and governance, but women increasingly occupied the pews, a reflection of Christian trends. Weil women did not yet insist on voting rights or full membership privileges, which many Reform congregations had already granted.[69] Gertrude's mother, lacking formal Jewish education, still held to the domestic pieties.

Gertrude saw her parents take leadership roles within prevailing gender roles. Her father and uncle as synagogue officers sat on the bimah (prayer platform) flanking the ark. Mina's primary duty was to organize the annual Purim ball and *spiel* (play) held at the opera house. The ostensible purpose was to raise funds for the Atlanta Hebrew Orphans' Home, and Christians were welcomed. As a six-year-old Gertrude played Queen Vashti to Leslie's King Ahasuerus in a Purim play and then was a Spirit in a Chanukah revel. Gertrude's lifelong love of theatricals had its start in the congregation's holiday pageants. In 1886 Weil men founded a fraternal lodge of B'nai B'rith, linking them to a global network of Jewish charity and civil liberties defense.

By 1895 Goldsboro's "Russian contingent" conducted separate Orthodox holiday services, with the rabbi leading them after Reform worship. East Europeans joined community societies and sent their children to the temple's religious school. The conflict was not only religious—the Reform of the former and the Orthodoxy of the latter—but also one of class and Americanization. Accommodating traditionalists retarded Oheb Sholom's progress toward Reform. Small-town Jews were highly mobile—the local Jewish population declined to 125 in 1905. As German Jews left, East Europeans arrived. Jews drew social and ethnic lines among themselves. Gertrude's mother warned Janet about dating a Jewish student at Trinity College (later Duke University) since he was from Durham, where Jews were "ordinary," that is, East European. (This boy, Louis Isaac Jaffe, later earned a Pulitzer Prize.) Gertrude inherited this bias but overcame it.[70]

Concern for the Jewish future of American children was a prime motive in organizing. Borrowing from public education, the male trustees appointed a school board with the rabbi as superintendent. The Jewish schooling was democratically American, not just for promising boys as in the old country. In May 1883, fifteen boys and girls alike enrolled in Sabbath School. Hebrew primers from the 1880s and 1890s bear Gertrude's signature. She learned to take pleasure in ritual and observance, Although she complained about the stern rabbi's reprimands, she felt affection for the temple, the place where she enjoyed dancing lessons. Most important was the children's Jewish bonding. Gertrude had a crush on the rabbi's son Isie, dreaming of a wedding announcement in 1912: "Mr. and Mrs. Weil request your presence at the marriage of Miss Gertrude Weil to Mr. Isie Mayerberg. Mr. Mayerberg was *interested* & well he might be."[71]

Politics of Progress

Gertrude was raised in a progressive household, yet that did not imply liberality on issues of either race or gender. "We grew up with prejudices," she later acknowledged. Weil business ledgers listed customers by color. During Reconstruction Goldsboro fell under Republican rule, with a Union Army veteran as mayor and blacks on the town council. Henry drew cartoonish stereotypes in deploring "a crowd of dark-skinned radicals and dark-hearted white-skin radicals." He claimed to have assisted "Negroes" who battled in the streets against the "few darkeys who would have voted," the differing terms for African Americans suggesting his racial distaste for black political aspirations. White businessmen, bent on redemption, cloaked their racism in the rhetoric of reform. In 1894 black voters helped elect a Fusion state government of Populists and Republicans, and Democratic white supremacists launched a bitterly racist campaign to overthrow them.[72]

In the 1898 election, the national spotlight focused on North Carolina as racial tensions exploded in Wilmington, where a black and Republican coalition governed. Mina wrote Gertrude not to believe the "sensational reports," because Papa had just taken a business trip there and found it "quiet politically." Henry's Goldsboro friend Charles B. Aycock, a progressive Democrat, delivered race-baiting speeches to night-riding Red Shirts while Josephus Daniels fanned racial flames in his *Raleigh News and Observer*. After the Wilmington race riot, Mina informed Gertrude that nine blacks had died. Mina expressed unusual empathy, blaming the riot on white "rowdy ringleaders." She continued, "The worst of such an affair is the race feeling it engenders. How the negroes can be expected to have any feeling but enmity after such a day, is not easy to comprehend." White leaders justified the violence as necessary to restore clean government. Two years later Weil men traveled to Raleigh to celebrate Aycock's inauguration as governor, elected on a progressive Democratic platform of educational reform, economic development, and black disfranchisement.[73]

In Gertrude's childhood, racism was engrained. Minstrelsy drew laughs. One Goldsboro Jewish Ladies Society baby show was performed in blackface. At a temple benefit Aunt Hattie Spier tutored costumed children to perform cakewalks and sing "coon songs." Yet racial attitudes were not polar but a spectrum. A white supremacist like Aycock advocated black uplift of the Booker T. Washington kind, economically but not socially or politically. When Henry Weil served on the school board, it took responsibility for black grade schools, and newspapers reported whites attending commencements. Weils sponsored Goldsboro's "colored German club," which elicited ironic comment. Personal relations, however paternalistic, might temper the harshness of segregation. Grandma Rosenthal visited the black sick as well as the white, and Mina's charity included blacks. Grandpa's business ledger did not note the color of his customers. When considering a boarding school for Gertrude, her parents chose racially integrated Horace Mann School in New York.[74]

Women's issues were the subject of Weil table talk. As early as 1874, during their courtship, Henry had asked "dearest little Mimmi"—without irony—"Are you a women rights man?" In the laggard South a few scattered outspoken women advocated women's suffrage, but, linked historically to abolitionism, it lacked the groundswell for a movement. Gertrude's cousin Etta Spier's "pet topics" were women's rights, Democratic reform, and women's ambition. When Leslie raised the subject at dinner, Etta "wouldn't talk about them as she said we were not capable of arguing about them." Not until the 1890s, with prominent men speaking out, did southern women organize. Weil women had a cosmopolitan perspective. Although a traditional wife and homemaker, Mina recommended to her daughter the "superior woman," who blended beauty of form and intellect. One such woman was her cousin in Toledo, Rosa Kaufman, whose letters were erudite and learned. In 1894 Kaufman wrote, "It seems as if woman's suffrage were going to be the next thing." She was ambivalent as an unmarried, German-born woman not yet naturalized. She had "never been able to see it in a favorable light chiefly from the physiological stand point, but you may be assured that if we do get the chance I will not neglect my opportunity." Gertrude came into maturity as women's rights, if not yet a movement, became household conversation.[75]

Whatever differences Gertrude felt as the daughter of an immigrant or a Jew in the South, she was a happy child, secure in her family and community. Surrounded by rural and industrial poverty, she enjoyed the comforts of wealth. She smiled a lot, and her complexities coexisted in happy harmony. That confidence never left her. The bicycle-riding child who had the liberty of her small town pursued freedom but within limits. A nervous mother kept her close, and she was both dutiful and independent. That habit of mind was engrained in her. She would be loyal to Judaism but define it in her own way. Enjoying privilege, she was taught social responsibility. On race and gender, she inherited prejudices but learned to question them. Before her was the example of her parents. In disposition, she inherited from her mother a generous and benevolent heart, sympathetic to the poor and loyal to friends and family, and from her father a buoyant, humorous spirit, intellectually curious, civic minded, sometimes oblivious to social convention. The household *Bildung* implanted within her an aspiration for higher ideals. To further her education, she would need to look beyond Goldsboro.

{ 2 }

HIP! HIP! HOORAY!!!
The Education of a New Woman

Gertrude Weil pursued the finest educational opportunities available to women, but in 1895 that meant leaving North Carolina. Her father seemed content with her choices, but her mother conveyed mixed messages. Having dashed her own educational ambitions for marriage, Mina encouraged her daughter to seek the best, but she also wanted to keep her in the bosom of family. Sixteen-year-old Gertrude faced the adolescent dilemma of declaring her independence while assuring her family of her love and loyalty. Prep school and college would take her beyond the domesticity of the southern lady into the freer, public domains of the New Woman. Home or career? Goldsboro or New York?

Gertrude's education began in the public schools. For a family that prized learning, the Weils lived in a state whose school system ranked among the country's poorest. In the 1880s progressives promoted school reform, based on Prussian models, as the foundation on which to build the New South. "Graded school fever" swept the state. Cities competed to gain an economic edge. Gertrude attended school during "flush times." In 1885 Goldsboro was among a dozen North Carolina cities to have a graded school open 180 days, triple the average. Children were imbued with the spirit of enterprise and individualism. Free thinking replaced rote recitation and religious indoctrination. Universities began sponsoring teacher institutes for women. In 1891 the State Normal and Industrial School for white women opened in Greensboro. Over the next thirty years the percentage of female teachers rose from 40 percent to nearly 90 percent. The movement, too, invited parental involvement. When Goldsboro schools lacked funds in 1887—Gertrude was then in elementary school—a public meeting was held to raise money. This appeal failed, so Sol Weil volunteered to pay expenses to keep the schools open.[1]

Importantly for Goldsboro—and Gertrude's career—local school reformers became state and regional leaders. In 1889, with Henry Weil on the school board, its chair was Charles B. Aycock, later North Carolina's "Education Governor," and the superintendent was E. A. Alderman, later president of Tulane, the University of North Carolina, and the University of Virginia. Like Henry Weil, they were largely self-made, middle-class men of the New South. Henry Weil served over twenty years. Young Gertrude saw him roving school halls, inspecting steam boilers, or visiting a crowded sixth grade that needed a classroom. At commencement a boy and girl each received a $20 gold Weil Prize. In 1897 Republican governor Daniel Russell appointed Henry Weil a trustee of the University of North Carolina, a remarkable achievement for an immigrant who was a Democrat and not an alumnus.[2]

As a student, Gertrude showed curiosity, diligence, and high intelligence. She did well academically, but not at the expense of her social or sporting life. Always she had friends waiting and games to play. "Gertrude does not seem to be worried with her lessons," Mina wrote Leslie, "nor does she give me the impression that she is studying hard, but she studies most of the time she is out of school." Gertrude enjoyed algebra and physiology, less so history. Leslie, at Chapel Hill, advised the seventh-grader to get her Latin verbs "downpat." Classical languages and literature, according to modern pedagogy, were not merely taught by drilling or recitation but studied in historical context for moral, social, and political lessons. Gertrude's classical education reinforced her idealism.[3]

Public school wove Gertrude into the fabric of her community. Classmates like Susie Fulghum and Sallie Kirby became lifelong friends. Teachers were recalled as both "capable instructors" and "loyal southern ladies." When Miss Anna taught state history, she made excuses for Confederate losses. Gertrude recalled Miss Humphrey, a northerner, as a mentor and continued to write and see her beyond school years. Gertrude joined the Sigma Phi Literary Club, a group of twenty-one girls and fifteen boys.[4]

Public school acculturated Gertrude into the Protestant ethos that was America's civil religion. Each day began with Christian Bible readings, and hymns were sung at assemblies. A Goldsboro school guide noted that "Onward Christian Soldiers" and "In the Cross of Christ I Glory" were "patriotic songs" fit for "public worship." The report continued, "We endeavor to inculcate Christian principles" but then added—oblivious to irony—"Of course, nothing denominational is permitted in these teachings."[5] Her father, the rabbi, and the B'nai B'rith protested to little effect, but Gertrude rarely objected to public displays of Christianity.

The civic ethos of the school reinforced lessons of home. Graded school inculcated values that Gertrude always prized: independence and citizenship. Students collected food and clothing for the poor. Teachers sorted them, and the Ladies Benevolent Society distributed them on Thanksgiving Day. Mina, as relief society leader, doubtlessly was involved. Superintendent Alderman declared, "Civilization is largely a question of personal improvement," a principle reinforcing the Weil household *Bildung*. At commencement in 1895 Gertrude read aloud her paper "Philosophy of Wordsworth." The superintendent announced that the Weil Prize would be awarded not to a boy and a girl but to two girls since the "girls had so far out-distanced the boys." Three girls—Gertrude and her friends Louise Hicks and Susie Fulghum—ranked best, although Gertrude's grades were highest by a "fraction." To "unbounded applause," Gertrude declined the prize awarded by her father. The newspaper headlined, "Miss Gertrude Weil's Generous Act of Self Denial."[6] Even as a youth she demonstrated the modesty and empathy, as well as accomplishment, that endeared her to her townspeople. Lifelong she shunned honors.

Gertrude's schooling was exceptional but not unique. American Jewish girls in diaries and memoirs often expressed their desire to excel, to go beyond domestic roles, at a time when less than 3 percent of women attended college. Next door, both Hilda Einstein and Edna Weil were sent to Chicago for high school before matriculating at Cornell. Etta Spier could only afford the state woman's college in North Carolina, but she continued to Columbia for her master's degree and returned to Greensboro as professor of rural education. Cousin Ruth Heyn of Ohio, a student of ancient languages, graduated Phi Beta Kappa from Vassar. She married cousin Lionel and settled in Goldsboro. Within her family circle, Gertrude joined a peer group of superbly educated women.[7]

Such achievement reflected class as much as ethnicity. In 1893 Gertrude and Julia Howell published in *The Round Table*, the school newspaper, a list of 125 Goldsboro Graded School alumni who had pursued higher education. They included school superintendents, professors, numerous teachers, and Dr. Clara Jones, the state's first woman physician. Five girls attended Mount Holyoke. Gertrude became the first North Carolinian to graduate from Smith College, but the third to enroll.[8]

Continuing Education

German-Jewish parents did not universally accept that girls needed post-secondary education, and Mina expressed her doubts. Marriage and a career were still considered incompatible. In 1893 a national study reported that "insignificant" percentages of boys went to college, and for Jewish girls the percentages were even smaller. In 1895 another survey revealed that half of women's college graduates had not married, and those who did averaged fewer than two children. Family advocates were alarmed. Concerns were expressed for the mother-daughter relationship. Behind these objections were older prejudices that women lacked the rational or physical capacity for the rigors of college. Questions were raised whether women could climb stairs or move between campus buildings. Gertrude had a running argument with Mina on the "necessity" of college and her separation from family. Over time, Jewish girls followed rising national trends as parents overcame their ambivalence.[9]

Gertrude's family situation may have pushed her from home. Mina was suffering from "another & protracted spell of nervousness." She had charge of both toddler Janet and widowed mother Eva. Leslie was at Chapel Hill, and Herman soon followed. Uncle Albert Rosenthal, an engineering graduate of Columbia residing in New York, insisted on "getting" Gertrude to attend Horace Mann laboratory school established at Columbia's Teacher's College in 1887. Based on developmental principles, the curriculum compared with the finest college preparatory schools. Although a "Christian institution" with daily chapel, it was "non-sectarian in spirit." The 1890s marked increasing discrimination against Jews, but religion was not an issue at liberal Horace Mann. Gertrude was not as exceptional as African American students, among them the children of Charles Chesnutt, a writer from North Carolina.[10]

As a rite of passage, going away to school meant a break from home and family. Mina and Gertrude traveled to New York to visit the Horace Mann School. Gertrude's move was hardly a rupture. Mina took her to synagogue. In New York were Uncle Albert and later his wife Aunt Kala and "the Oettinger crowd," all of whom acted very much in loco parentis. Living nearby and constantly visiting were an endless procession of aunts, uncles, and cousins. Buying trips brought Goldsboro visitors, and some hometown friends now lived in the city.

Not unexpectedly, Gertrude was at first unhappy. "Oh! I'm homesick," she scribbled on a school program, wishing she could baby talk with her sister, Janet, wanting to help Herman with his Latin, and needing advice from Norny. Always appreciated were gifts of violets, roses, and jonquils sent fresh from the garden. She assured her anxious Papa that "I remember that I am in N. York & am very careful & watchful." But the most fervid correspondence passed between Gertrude and school friend Susie Fulghum. "I wish we were together to kiss & hug and room together," Susie wrote passionately, and a month later, "I would love to shake & squeeze you all night-dear sweetheart." She anticipated next winter when "we'll be together in the same bed" and described herself as "your true friend (more than friend)." To a modern sensibility the intensity expresses a homoeroticism beyond "the enthusiasms of adolescent girls," yet in the Victorian era female friendships often succumbed to a "romantic rhetoric" that was "both sensual and platonic." Other Weil letters were full of similar feminine effusions clearly in ways that had no sexual implication. When Uncle Albert became engaged, his fiancée, Kala Strauss, wrote Mina that she would smother her in kisses, throw her arms around her neck, and love her with her "whole heart."[11]

By October, Gertrude assured her family that she was "not in the least homesick." In a class of twenty students, Gertrude formed friendships for life, most notably with Helen Chamberlain and Beulah Evans. Despite its progressive curriculum, Horace Mann still functioned as a finishing school, and Gertrude was groomed in the social art of balls and dances. She lamented the dearth of dancing boys, observing a "clicky ... in it" crowd, but she "knew nearly all the girls and danced to my heart's content." For German conversation she enjoyed teas with her professor Miss Kase and attended a recital at the elegant parlor of Mrs. Untermeyer on Fifth Avenue. (Yes, she assured Mina, Mr. Untermeyer was Jewish, but not his wife.)[12]

Gertrude was instructed to send three letters home weekly, and mother reminded daughter constantly of her "obligation" to write this aunt or visit that cousin. Gertrude formed her strongest attachment to Uncle Albert and Aunt Kala. Weekends found her at their apartment in Yorkville, the city's German quarter, and later at 97th Street, closer to Columbia. The family tie was maintained in her adherence to Judaism, but here too she was seeking her own way. She went synagogue shopping, dutifully informing her parents of her attendance at Sabbath and holiday services. She found "too much Hebrew" at the 65th Street temple but enjoyed the grand Temple Emanuel, where services "were much like ours at home." Uncle Albert or cousin Mattie accompanied her to the 43rd Street temple, but she preferred the "fine" music at the 74th Street temple. Sometimes she went alone. She disliked that "D'utch talk," the German sermon, but enjoyed hearing Dr. Kaufmann Kohler, advocate of Radical Reform, speak "in the American tongue." Though she missed "Pesach" in Goldsboro, she was well stocked with matzah. Was homemade jelly "kosha?" Taken by three friends to an Episcopal church, she enjoyed the music. Later she took Beulah Evans to Temple Emanuel, whose architecture inspired her. Completing the Sabbath aesthetic, Saturday afternoons might be spent at theater matinees or the art museum.[13]

New York City provided an education in itself, and Gertrude became a devotee of high culture. She responded with girlish glee when celebrity

Leslie noted Sister's fashionable fur tails.
Courtesy of the State Archives of North Carolina.

spotting after theater at Delmonico's. When she heard the pianist Ignacy Jan Paderewski at Carnegie Hall, she enthused, "I never saw such wonderful hands." She became an opera buff, too tired to sit through a campus lecture but willing to suffer standing room at the Metropolitan Opera. She enjoyed *Faust* and *Carmen*, found Italian opera as funny as minstrel shows, but felt passionate about *Siegfried* and *Lohengrin*. As befitted her heritage, she reflected, "Maybe I was built for Wagnerian operas." Her cousins took her shopping at Altman's and Bloomingdale's. Leslie, returning from a postcollege European tour, was surprised to find Sister in a "very pretty" fur piece to which she added "four new tails, a great number of which are very desirable this winter."[14]

Over time, Gertrude tested her freedom. By her second year, it "occurred" to Mina that Gertrude had "been at Temple very little." Once, Gertrude decided to go for a "change." Traveling the city alone, she felt irritated that cousin Mattie worried about her. Visiting Goldsboro friend Lizzie MacDonald downtown, she wrote her mother, "I felt so proud of myself going down all alone in the Broadway car." Gertrude learned to express her desires against her mother's drumbeat of family obligation. In 1896, after a surprise visit from Aunt Kala the night before exams, Gertrude pled, "It is very nice to have a whole lot of kin folk here to make you feel at home, but there can be too much even of a good thing." Months later, when Mattie promised to bring more cousins, Gertrude bristled, "Of course, I'd like very much to see them," but not now.[15]

Gertrude inherited a charitable disposition, and at Horace Mann she learned to give it ideological and institutional foundations, a step in her political education from benevolence to social reform. Her physical education teacher was Margaret Stanton Lawrence, daughter of women's rights and social justice advocate Elizabeth Cady Stanton. Hearing Lawrence speak on war, Gertrude wrote, "Oh! You'll see me come home a thorough reformer." After Maud Booth's lecture on prisons, she "felt like joining the Volunteers [of America] first thing," overlooking its Christian evangelical mission. Although Gertrude paid extra tuition since she did not enroll in the teachers' program, by her second year she took interest in the kindergarten movement. Saturday afternoons Gertrude volunteered for a free kindergarten held at a gymnasium on 127th Street. In 1897 "nine of us girls" formed a club working with Irish immigrant children. Though some were "pretty tough . . . and dirty," she found them "sweet" and "bright." She loved the work. The girls held a fundraising party, and Mina so "enjoyed" hearing about it that she pledged a donation.[16]

If Gertrude developed a passion at Horace Mann, it was—prescient for a North Carolinian—basketball. The 1890s were the game's birthing years, and when Horace Mann played an interscholastic game in 1897, the stands were packed with noisy, "half crazy" fans. "My blood begins to run faster every time I think of it," Gertrude wrote Mina. "Study is almost impossible with the excitement of the approaching game." Gertrude was enthused to be a sub and played in a co-ed scrimmage. A faculty row erupted when newspapers printed "horrid" illustrations of a game that, to Gertrude's distress, depicted the female athlete as if she were a "new woman in the comic weeklies." For a rematch, the faculty banned spectators.[17]

Although physically active, Gertrude was diagnosed with curvature of the lower spine and sent to a specialist, Dr. Caroline Cabot. She put exercise rings in her rooms and embarked on a vigorous treatment program. Gertrude took avidly to gymnastics as taught by Margaret Stanton Lawrence and joined her on a rigorous ten-mile bike ride. Throughout her life, Gertrude's erect posture elicited comment as a reflection of her upright character. She never let illness or a diagnosis handicap her.

College

Horace Mann graduation renewed Gertrude's ongoing negotiation with her mother on education. On a draft of an application letter, Gertrude had scribbled "Smith," "Vassar," and "Wellesley." Aunt Sarah endorsed Smith, but Mina, wanting her home, was reluctant. She continued to assert the family claim: "Just think of all the years it means we must do without you, and then may be when you get through you'll wish to do something that will again take you from us." Mother was not Gertrude's sole concern. Unsure of herself, she feared the Smith entrance exams, holding "little hope that I won't flunk everything." Her Horace Mann grades, she felt, "weren't very pleasant," especially in Latin and German. She hired a Vassar graduate to tutor her. Unlike Vassar or Wellesley, Smith did not offer compensatory college preparatory courses and was reputedly the most rigorous of women's colleges. Mina again gave Gertrude a mixed message: "I do not wish you to study too hard because to overwork yourself just might harm you more than the Smith course could ever benefit you." But then she added, "Going to Smith College means a great deal to us." Most Horace Mann girls remained in New York to study at Barnard or Columbia, but Gertrude sought Smith alumni for advice.[18]

Smith was a good fit for Gertrude. Rural, small-town Northampton, Massachusetts, felt familiar. Gertrude assured Papa that Northampton is "a pretty place" and Mamma that it was a "good winter resort." For a Jew, Smith was Christian but the least evangelical of women's colleges. For a woman of aesthetic sensibility who loved to draw, Smith maintained a curriculum in art and music, even though other women's colleges had dropped them as more appropriate for finishing schools. Moreover, Smith appealed to Gertrude's independent streak. Unlike its sister colleges, where students were confined to one building for both residence and classes, Smith was built on a "cottage system," which allowed girls to live in either boarding houses or home-like dormitories. Smith had the largest women's enrollment of any college in the world, numbering over a thousand when Gertrude arrived in 1897.[19] On 21 June, accompanied by her father, Gertrude left for Northampton to take entrance exams. Returning in September, she still felt inadequate, fearing that she would be sent home.

"Hip! Hip! Hooray!!! The joyful news be spread! Gertrude Weil is a member of the class of 1901!" she wrote her dear ones. She had been accepted with conditions in rhetoric, algebra, and history, but these she quickly resolved. Smith's curriculum reflected the evolving social and political status of women. Debates had focused on women's intellectual capacities, their ability to withstand college rigors, and the moral consequences for their domestic roles as wives, mothers, and housekeepers. Smith and its sister colleges modeled themselves on the finest men's prep schools and colleges, with emphasis on a classical curriculum. Gertrude's entrance exams required her to list the dates of Roman territorial expansion prior to 133 B.C. and define the historical infinitive in Latin.[20]

On her first day at Smith Gertrude confronted the choice whether to remain the dutiful daughter of a southern Jewish lady or become the rebellious New Woman. College opened on the Jewish New Year, but Gertrude chose classes, not synagogue. After a month on campus, she insisted on having a bicycle sent from home despite her mother's concern about hilly roads. Proudly assembling it herself, she was soon riding with friends, enjoying the New England countryside even as her cautious mother warned her not "to meander at your own sweet will." When she took a sleigh ride from Northampton to Amherst with her classmates, she was offended to learn that she had violated college regulations: "Those little silly rules make me sick—as if it could be any harm for four girls to go without a *chaperone* to an old village that happens to contain a small man's college." She complained that it was "pretty ridiculous" to need a chaperone to attend a play. By her sophomore year, she exulted, "O, the bliss of not having to have a chaperone!" She reacted defiantly to house rules. Smith's intent was to create a domestic family setting for women, but Gertrude, like other students breaking from home, demanded "masculine prerogatives."[21]

Enjoying her autonomy, Gertrude was learning to rebel against authority.

She bristled at her mother's letter-writing regimen. Not having heard from Gertrude for a week, Mina accused her of causing them "worry," adding with unintended irony, "even if we are not of the worrying kind." Gertrude replied tartly with a mea culpa: "Meek and contrite do I feel—fit to be scourged to the stake or burned at the rack—humble and penitent. Would twenty, fifty, or a hundred candles suffice as expiation?" Each Jewish holiday elicited a motherly "don't forget" with the admonition that "there are times when religious observances rise above our personal comfort." Such rebukes became necessary.[22]

Mina questioned Gertrude whether Smith compelled students to attend "Church services if your Parents prefer otherwise?" To exempt herself, Gertrude screwed up "a terrible amount of courage" and entered the "awe-inspiring chamber" of eminent college president L. Clark Seelye. "Of course," the liberal-minded Seelye told her, she need not go to chapel, although he felt that weekly worship was a good thing. Gertrude assured Mina that she attended chapel but once since then. Yet she enjoyed vespers and went the next three years faithfully both for the music and inspiring sermon, often by Seelye himself.[23]

For her first Yom Kippur, Gertrude was directed by Mary Cable, her landlady, to the downtown store of Mr. Cohen. On the street she stumbled into his family, who brought her to an Orthodox service in a small, second-floor room. The strangeness alienated her: a rough box holding the Torah, the men draped in a "wide 'tallas' (is that right?)," and the praying a disagreeable "noise." Joining the Rosenthals in New York for High Holidays, she reflected, "I don't know about my going to Temple this year." She found Aunt Kala's Judaism at an 1898 Passover "a queer kind of religion." Kala was learned in Hebrew rote prayer but thoughtless as to the religion's content. Moreover, Gertrude objected to the patriarchy of traditional Judaism where women need not do anything if the "men go to schule and pray." By her sophomore year her mother was resigned: "I know you did not think of Schule last night or to-day." If Gertrude did not attend synagogue but enjoyed vespers, she still fasted on Yom Kippur and ate matzah during Passover. Seeing Israel Zangwill's *The Children of the Ghetto*, she contrasted the play's dysfunctional family with her own memories of the "sweetness and peace of the Jewish home." An exploring college student, she was seeking her Jewish way outside tradition.[24]

A generation gap opened between Gertrude, a thoroughly American youth, and her parents. "It is rather difficult to be a Jew at Smith isn't it?" mother wrote her daughter. But Gertrude did not find it so. Mina had directed her to seek out Jewish students, including a Selma Weil from Boston, no relation but from a family known to Aunt Sarah. Gertrude had little interest in a Jewish crowd, if one were to be had at Smith. She retained, however, her Jewish self-consciousness as she embraced women's college culture. She internalized the prejudice that took Anglo-Saxon standards as measures of beauty and fashion. She found one campus "Jewess—a *very* pretty, decidedly non-Jewish looking girl," in contrast to Miss Cohen, who was "no startling oriental beauty—and no New England one either."[25]

Colleges responded to the challenge of women's changing expectations by moving away from the traditional canon and offering electives. In her first years Gertrude took the time-honored curriculum. Though she had her fill of Marlowe and Milton, she loved Ruskin and Rossetti. Her junior year, attending a student production of a play by Plautus, she observed, "It was very good, but I think something modern better suited to the genius of college girls." In 1899 Smith introduced courses in ethics and economics, which Gertrude enjoyed. Smith advanced Gertrude's political education, expanding her awareness of the need for systemic social reform. In 1900 she took classes on Political Economy and Problems of Poverty, with a course outline that included "Poverty is Preventable," "Reform in Women's Wages," and "doing away with war."[26] These issues became Gertrude's own political causes.

Courses were taught from a historical-critical perspective. Lectures focused on the destructive effects of industrialization on family structure and class and gender inequalities in the wage system. The theories of Smith, Marx, and Engels were applied. The lecturer emphasized women's role in confronting social injustice through trade unionism and their political and economic emancipation and empowerment. Gertrude also read such modern social reformers as Jane Addams, Felix Adler, and Jacob Riis. In her senior year, Gertrude observed, "The whole system of courses is in a state of transition between the old and the new regulations." Her senior year was her "finest." She still delighted in the pre-Raphaelites—Ruskin's books, she hinted, would make a nice birthday present—but she also took a course in social science focusing on "the problems of poverty, the unemployed— employment of women and children."[27] The seeds of her radical sympathies were planted.

Gertrude's notebooks also reveal her inquiry into spiritual and philosophical principles. She always sought religious ground for her social and political views. A psychology course explored ego and spirituality. One notebook contained the insight: "Object of educat.=to develop those powers wh. are in us & make us most effective as members of a social body." A senior paper on Kant, written days before graduation, included: "The law of the mind is not outside itself.... The moral life is ruled by reason." A rationalist, she saw the unity of the moral and aesthetic. In notes on *Macbeth*, she underlined six times: *"Evil is ugly."* Her passion for Ruskin likely owed to his view of art as a moral and social craft and his critique of industrial capitalism.[28]

If Gertrude had not yet declared herself a suffragist, she was excited about a campus mock presidential election that saw McKinley defeat Bryan by nearly ten to one. Yet even Gertrude grew "everlastingly tired of hearing girls talk politics." When the Spanish-American War erupted, she was swept by the romance of "inspiring music and jolly camp fires." She trumpeted "Hurrah for U.S.!! Hurrah for George Dewey! And for Manila!" Her Papa justified America's right to intervene in Cuba, although other family elders recalled Civil War horrors and demurred. Enthused to hear Harvard's Charles Eliot Norton speak on campus, her "affection" for him was shaken when he denounced the war and declared his intention to keep students from enlisting.[29]

Gertrude's education in racial equality progressed tentatively. At a reception, she wrote her family that she just "happened to talk to two negresses" from Hampton, studying at Harvard, who seemed "very nice and intelligent." After North Carolina disfranchised blacks, she found "very interesting" a campus debate her senior year on "Shall the Federal Government give aid to the negro in keeping his right to vote." She "heard" that "the negative side" had the "greater advantages," but "the affirmations made their points tell stronger." Days later she expressed pride in the inauguration of Aycock as her native state's governor, who advocated both black uplift and disfranchisement. And days after that, she felt amused—likely because of her southern accent—to be cast as the black mammy in the historical drama *White Aprons*. Smith had admitted a black student in 1898 but, with its Banjo Club playing "coon songs," was hardly free from the racism that pervaded popular culture.[30] Still, college experiences challenged her racial assumptions.

Off-campus relationships expanded her worldview. Her freshman year she boarded at the home of Mary Louise Cable, whose brother George Washington Cable was the noted southern progressive and national littérateur. Mrs. Cable was "motherly to the girls," but a visit by the great man inspired five exclamation points in a letter home. Cable came for dinners and stayed to recite stories. When he traveled, Mary read aloud his letters portraying J. M. Barrie, George Meredith, and Rudyard Kipling. More lastingly for Gertrude, Cable described how he had conceived Home Culture Clubs. Like settlement houses, these reading clubs embraced Progres-

In this photo, likely taken at Mrs. Cable's Northampton boardinghouse,
Gertrude is in the second row, center, in a white blouse.
Courtesy of the State Archives of North Carolina.

sive Era uplift. People across lines of age, sex, class, ethnicity—and race—
gathered in "fireside groups" to discuss literature and topical issues. Since
Cable founded them in Northampton in the 1880s, they spread internation-
ally, numbering ninety-four by 1900.[31]

Another welcoming Northampton family was the Berensons. Rachel
was a Smith student, and her sister, Senda, was Gertrude's physical education instructor, who achieved sports immortality as the Mother of Women's
Basketball. Absent was brother Bernard, who, the Weils learned, was an
"art critic" in Florence; in fact, he was the great connoisseur of his age. Although Mrs. Berenson was a Russian Jew with an accent, Gertrude found
her "nice and homelike and motherly," and the family "among the brightest
people I ever met." Senda was a New Woman conscious of the liberating
effects of women's sports. By a curious coincidence, the Berensons were related to the Goldsboro rabbi, Julius Mayerberg. Their friendship with the
Weils was sealed when mother and daughter Berenson vacationed three

months in Goldsboro. The Berensons had not been "congenial" with German Jews, but Mina received them warmly, finding them "highly cultured people." Mina was surprised that Mrs. Berenson was now a Christian Scientist and expressed shock that her "son marries outside the faith of his fathers" as would her daughters, but they remained friends.[32]

College took Gertrude beyond home truths. At the Berensons, Gertrude met Anglo-Jewish author Israel Zangwill. She was "very anxious" to hear his lecture on "The Ghetto," but she found him the "ugliest Jew—or otherwise that I ever looked at." It was a Weil assumption, consistent with *Bildung*, that truth and beauty were one. Mina responded that he has "brains in inverse ratio to his good looks." At the Philosophical Club her junior year she heard Stanley Hall, founder of the American Psychological Association who pioneered the study of child development, speak on "The New Psychology," which she found "very interesting." When physician-novelist S. Weir Mitchell lectured on the virtues of the domestic arts and the superiority of marriage over careers, Gertrude dubbed him an "old fogy."[33] College experiences, in and out of the classroom, were breaching lines of race, class, and ethnicity that had ordered her Goldsboro childhood.

Gertrude's college friends consisted of a circle of Protestant girls from the Northeast and Midwest. These classmates formed her crowd, and alumna attachments were enduring. Over school breaks, roommates wrote her ardently wishing to see her again and planning adventures. Gertrude showed little predilection toward leadership, excepting one occasion when a "committee" anointed Gertrude "chairman" to confront their tyrannical housemother. Most often she preferred to blend in with the crowd. If Gertrude had an ethnic identity, it was not as a Jew but as a southerner. According to a senior-class poem, "when people said 'Hurry!' Ne'ever did she worry— This deliberate young southerner named Weil."[34]

Another identity was her "athletic self," as a friend addressed her. Gertrude maintained a rigorous sports regimen. The junior physical listed her a trim five feet, two and a quarter inches, 104 pounds. With Senda Berenson as friend and teacher, she still gushed over basketball but also played tennis, swam in the pool, a large tank, and joined a golf club (no longer keeping score after once shooting 105 over seven holes). Game for adventure, Gertrude organized riverbank walks, mountain hikes, and rowing trips on the Paradise and Connecticut Rivers.[35]

Over her college years Gertrude expressed growing autonomy. In her junior year she was excited when Leslie, Aunt Sarah, Uncle Joe, and cousins Edna and Lionel visited. Gertrude wrote her mother, "Not a bit homesick," adding that she "would like to be with you" but then qualifying it with "once in a while." The incessant reminders from her mother to write Grandmamma, meet Aunt Bertha, or visit Baltimore cousins elicited resistance. Touring Ohio in 1900, she received a sympathetic missive from Leslie: "Gertrude, have you started your numerous duty calls yet? Poor child I pity you."[36]

Unresolved was her leaving home for Smith. "Of course I know what your argument is—what it always is—about college not being a necessity—but ... it makes me feel better," Gertrude wrote her mother, "although I am without any absolute necessity, staying away from you for a little while. Goodness knows I hope it will do some body some good some time and that I'll be of more use and a pleasure to you than I am now." She reassured Mina that her desire for independence was not a rejection of her love. The holiness that Gertrude saw in her mother was felt as burden and judgment as well as obligation. "O Mamma it's a blessing to be allowed to know anybody like you—much more to have her for a mother," Gertrude wrote, "and if we seem to be going to the bad sometimes, just know it's for desperation of ever being as good as you." Another time she wrote, "If I could ever be one-half what you are."[37]

Gertrude suffered spells of "blueness" of "varying degrees of severity." Living far from home aroused guilt. She blushed with "shame, as I sit here alone, to think how careless, lazy, negligent, ungrateful, and every other bad thing I have been." She always felt modest about her achievements, inadequate and undeserving, especially measured against her mother's selfless devotion to family and community. One spring day in 1900, lying in a hammock in a campus orchard, refreshed by bracing air and distant church music, Gertrude meditated on William James, convincing herself to "believe that I am a very pious person depriving myself of so much for the sake of other people." With typical self-deprecating humor, she invited her mother to "hurry up and send me another sermon" so that she won't get "too stuck on myself."[38]

In invoking God's blessings for Gertrude's eighteenth birthday, Mina reminded her of the "highest duties of a true woman. ... I want you still to feel that you must live for others, too." She observed approvingly that Smith had "a tendency to teach kindness and thoughtfulness for others." Gertrude always asserted that home, not college, first inspired her commitment to social justice. Smith was less a crucible of feminism than an incubator of womanliness. Even as it encouraged the autonomy and professional abilities of the New Woman, the college did not challenge separate gender spheres, nor did it foment suffragism. Yet at Smith women's opinions were valued, and the campus bonded a sisterhood. Gertrude was taught to see social injustice through the lens of gender. She learned that "social problems of the time ... slums, disease, illiteracy, prostitution and crime" could not be "solved until women had full rights."[39]

Movement at Home

Even as Gertrude was wanted home, Mina fomented a women's revolution in Goldsboro. In May 1898 the Ladies Benevolent Society brought to town a superior woman of international repute, Charlotte Perkins Stetson (later Gilman), a utopian socialist and feminist whose recently published *Women and Economics* advocated independence from sexual and economic subjugation. Gilman had argued for making housework and childcare professional to free women for public lives. Her lecture series to benefit the graded school library focused on the New Woman. Mina was disappointed that only twenty-five attended the first talk at the opera house. Subsequent talks moved to the courthouse and Baptist church, drawing larger crowds. A relationship formed, and the southern housewife and visionary reformer stayed in touch. Mina herself led efforts to create a childcare center for working women in a nearby mill town. Gilman's calls for labor reform and new gender relations were radical to southerners but acceptable discourse in Gertrude's home.[40]

Like her mother, Gertrude was drawn to a "superior woman" as a mentor, a role she later assumed. At Horace Mann she had fallen under the influence of Margaret Stanton Lawrence and admitted to a "crush" on Dr. Cabot, the doctor who treated her spine. In Northampton she became infatuated with Adeline Moffatt, general secretary of the Home Culture Club. Miss Moffatt "can have me any day," Gertrude wrote. "She is very tall & graceful & dignified ... with a beautiful face & voice.... But most winning of all is her manner—such cordiality and such sincerity." Like Gertrude, Moffatt was an artist and native southerner. Socially prominent, she reciprocated Gertrude's affection by inviting her and her friends to teas. Gertrude volunteered for the club, doing double duty as Moffatt's assistant and teacher of writing, reading, and arithmetic to immigrants. Gertrude speculated on establishing a Home Culture Club in Goldsboro.[41]

Days after Gertrude wrote of Miss Moffatt, Mina had a fortuitous encounter. Mina was stopped in the street by Clara Royall, who "discoursed" for twenty minutes about creating a woman's club in Goldsboro. Plans were vague, but Mina recalled talk of jails, hygiene, and reading rooms in working-class community of Webbtown. Church groups would serve as charitable agencies. Mina wrote Gertrude, "How does this accord with Miss Moffat?" Could Gertrude send her Home Culture Club literature? Mina

Gertrude, Janet, and Mina. Courtesy of the State Archives of North Carolina.

hesitated to act until a purpose for a woman's club was defined. Echoing a common critique, she could not see the point of just hearing "women talk about doing so much" with nothing to show other than a meeting. She suggested focusing on "just one rather easy thing" for town betterment. She and Sarah made calls.[42]

At a March 1899 meeting at the opera house, with Charlotte Perkins Stetson (later Gilman) and Sallie Southall Cotten, founder of the state's women's club movement, as speakers, Mina was asked to serve as chair. Not knowing how to preside—or so she claimed—she descended from the stage carrying a paper and asked each woman to sign as a charter member. The club provoked nervous, defensive humor from men and women alike. Mina recalled "little knots of men gathered on the street corners discussing" the new club: "What was it for? What would it do? Would it try to get votes for women?" Would "radical change" disturb the "quiet, peaceful life of Goldsboro?" Henry wrote Gertrude that a gavel was an appropriate gift for her mother as an "insignia of authority," but until then her lungs and tongue were sufficient. A year later Mina reported efforts to create a free kindergarten, and still later, with Aunt Sarah as chair, establish traveling libraries. A mental club organized, and the women attended health talks. Gertrude joked about her mother "sitting up into the small hours of the night over heated discussion in the ultimate perfection of the human mind" and expressed mock concern for "poor little Janet—growing up in that fearfully intellectual atmosphere of clubs."[43]

Mina had her own mentor in Sallie Southall Cotten, "Mother of Women's Clubs." Cotten was another superior woman, a stately Southern Lady, a leader in literary and educational circles as well as the United Daughters of the Confederacy. Mina and Sarah scored a social coup when they hosted Cotten at their homes. Mina found her a "comfortable guest," a well-informed conversationalist with men as well as women. At an April 1900 reception, Goldsboro's finest arrived in "gala dresses" to meet Cotten at an elegant reception at Sarah's flower-bedecked house. Cotten spoke of Weil women as her dear friends.[44]

A Mother's Blessing

For the Jewish New Year 1900, Mina sent Gertrude an ethical letter. Such letters were a Jewish genre dating to the middle ages in which a parent left a moral rather than a material legacy to a child. Letter writing at the New Year was a Weil family ritual. Typically, like the Christian Christmas letter, it updated friends and relatives on family news, but Mina confessed that this letter was different. Expressing "Papa's wish," Mamma assured Gertrude that "since that illness of your babyhood you have caused us no pang except those of the parents' maternal solicitude and which was unconscious in your heart." She confided that "my big daughter is just all I could have her" and that any "lack may be due quite as much to my training as to her actions." Mina again addressed their separation: "May be I expect you to be more thoughtful and considerate and helpful than your many years from home warranted me to expect from you to be, but so many people's comfort always depends largely on a woman's forethought, and I lay much weight upon this." She then reiterated the family covenant: "My greatest desire is to feel that my children have been so raised that the world will be the better for their having lived—not great things but good is what I wish them to do." She sealed the covenant with a benediction to "our Heavenly Father to always be with you, and to so guide you that your every deed may be good in his sight." Her blessing validated her daughter's decision to choose her path away from home: "With every breath draw in the best influences the Massachusetts air can give you."[45]

Gertrude's responded at once to the "blessed Mother and Father of mine" with exclamation: "How can I tell you how I feel! You are so good.... When I look at my poor self—well if it weren't for being loved by you, I should be utterly nothing." Any good in her owed to her mother's "inspiring love." She knew that she had "many" and "serious" shortcomings but thanked her mother for setting ideals to attain.[46]

Gertrude soon tested her blessing. As graduation approached, Gertrude attended a talk by Mary Kingsbury Simkhovitch, a social reformer working at the Friendly Aid Settlement House in New York. Smith was a leader of the college settlement movement, and Gertrude accepted an invitation to visit Lower Manhattan for a tour of the Italian, Chinese, and Jewish quarters. She did not make it to the Jewish neighborhood, although the tour stopped by Lillian Wald's Henry Street Settlement. The college girls walked single file through crowded streets with "filthy" Italian and Chinese immigrants pressing against them. "The funniest remarks were made at us on all sides as we passed by," Gertrude observed. "I don't wonder that we were as big a show to them as they to us." The playgrounds and Nurses' Settlement on Henry Street impressed her. The following days found her in "another country," shopping for hats, attending theater, joining the Rosenthals for Passover, and visiting her college friend Lillian See in suburban Mount Vernon. Choices were starkly before her.[47]

Mina—not Henry—raised the question to Gertrude of "work as a necessity at the close of College." She asked, "What would you do?" That question was expressed in the title of a popular 1896 manual "for girls," *After*

College, What? Women, if they did not marry, the manual asserted, needed "something to do." Finishing schools prepared women for marriage and normal schools educated teachers, but women's colleges offered intellectual fulfillment, not vocational training. When Gertrude entered Smith it followed a classical liberal arts curriculum and then added electives on contemporary social issues. "I don't know that I am especially fitted for teaching," Gertrude wrote Mina, "or for anything else for that matter." She described herself as "unskilled labor." Behind the questions were larger issues of women's autonomy, conflicts between their duties as wives and mothers and new opportunities in the professions.[48]

Mina chided Gertrude that she did not "relish having you away from us any longer—six years is almost enough to alienate home ties." Gertrude responded, "Your question, Mamma, about earning a living for myself comes right in line with my thoughts lately." Given her pleasure at drawing, but doubting her talent, she considered book design. She tested her mother's tolerance of a further separation: "If I were going to be away from home I should try to teach in one of the slum schools of New York." A reform movement in New York public schools was replacing "miserable teachers, many of them ignorant brutes," with college girls. The salary was good, and a Smith alumna had "pull" with "Mr. Somebody."[49]

Mina gave Gertrude's letter some "thought," confessing that she was "selfish enough" to want her home. Mina asserted maternal authority even as she encouraged her daughter's independence. If Goldsboro lacked mountain hikes, Mina was sure that Gertrude could run errands for her "whenever I wish you to" by walking the mile to Leslie's house. Rather than teach in New York, Mina made a counteroffer: "We have no manual training of any sort in our graded school so it seems to me if you can arrange to teach some drawing and sewing perhaps to the lower grades the school would be the better for it." Book design might be worth an inquiry, Mina conceded, but Gertrude needed "systematically to know Woman's work, making clothes and working, for as a rule these are the necessary qualifications for a good home-maker." She added, "I have a horror of a helpless girl—a dependent one."[50]

Whatever the influence of Charlotte Perkins Gilman, Mina expressed a southern lady's ideal of "woman's work": charity and domesticity. Her concern that Gertrude become self-supporting perhaps owed to memories of war and Reconstruction when southern women, bereft of men, had to depend on themselves. Economic panics in 1893 and 1896 rendered even the wealthy insecure. Women's advocates saw education as the means to economic independence.[51] Other German-Jewish families employed sisters and daughters as buyers or clerks in their stores, but Gertrude did not take such work, although she enjoyed the fruits of family wealth.

Gertrude's career plans were likely not even convincing to herself, and she offered feeble resistance. "I agree with you about some regular occupation after I get home," she replied. She had considered a sewing class, but only if the children were very young as her own needlework needed improvement. "No doubt there will be plenty to keep busy at it if I try hard," she demurred. Gertrude pushed the conversation beyond charity work. She had just heard Florence Kelley lecture on the newly founded National Consumers League, the antisweatshop movement, and asked Mina about getting its label on "things at home." Advocacy of labor rights was wholly alien to the anti-union bias of the New South, Gertrude would have well known.[52] As plans were made for Gertrude's graduation, Mina fell ill with erysipelas but recovered sufficiently to attend the ceremony with Janet.

The full press of family fell on Gertrude. Aunt Sarah recognized Gertrude's "conflicting emotions" but urged her to "give a thought to your absent ones who are thinking of you." She expressed happiness that "your college education is finished and . . . you will enter the Home life again." Sarah pled, "We need you among us—with your fresh ideas, your wholesome optimism. Your enlarged sympathies to say nothing of your personal service; in some of my own schemes—too?" The consensus of those who knew Gertrude, Uncle Joe advised, was that "she is imbued with the idea that a young woman who can have luxuries should have the more willing to aid in benefitting mankind less fortunate. She will do something *real*."[53]

Gertrude's situation exemplified the dilemma that reformer Jane Addams had recognized in herself and college-educated women of her generation: the competing claims of society and family. As Addams wrote, graduates felt a "social claim," a responsibility to serve society, but were confronted with a "family claim," an obligation to their parents. The social claim was "vague and unformulated," and Gertrude could not articulate a career path beyond musing about book design or a teaching job through "Mr. Somebody." Her self-doubt contrasted with her mother's self-assurance. As Addams noted, daughters had been raised to be "self-sacrificing, to consider the good of the whole before that of the ego." In letters Gertrude and her schoolmates constantly apologized for seeming "egotistical." Though it had yet to acquire its Freudian resonance, the term was current in popular psychology. In one class Gertrude was asked to contrast the ego with the "spiritual self." For Addams frustration was inevitable: "Modern education recognizes women quite apart from family or society claims" and offers them "training" for the independence that had been men's prerogative. Yet back home, the graduate was left alienated, an "unhappy woman" as expectations went unfulfilled.[54]

Many women college graduates, at some point, did hold paid jobs, mostly in teaching. The number of female physicians increased, and doors to graduate study begrudgingly opened. Though most students were, like Gertrude, middle class, Smith was exceptional in enrolling students unable to afford tuition. Gertrude felt it unfair that graduates like herself have "peace and plenty" while scholarship students "should have to scramble around so desperately" finding jobs.[55]

Gertrude's quandary was shared by college friends as they returned to the parental fold. In their correspondence they talked of Jacob Riis's documentation of immigrant life in city slums, Jane Addams's work at settlement houses, and the National Congress of Mothers. Her friend Louise Hicks returned to her mother in Columbus, Ohio; Lillian See went back to her parents in New York; and Beulah Evans was home in Marion, Indiana, all wondering what was next. Other classmates married or toured Europe. Those with lesser means took teaching jobs, for which they often expressed ambivalence. Compared with duties owed God and family, new ideologies could not yet marshal sufficient forces to grant Gertrude the liberty to which she aspired.

The Weil family claim was especially intense. Jane Addams had argued that the claim on sons was "urged much less strenuously." Although women's opportunities were circumscribed, Weil brothers also felt the family's gravitational pull. Mina reminded her "dear son" Leslie that he had "many inherited obligations." After Chapel Hill Leslie and Herman, too, returned to Goldsboro for a lifetime in the home, business, and synagogue. Mina and Aunt Sarah were not wholly insensitive to Gertrude's aspirations. Addams simplified in posing social and family claims as contraries. Sarah, wanting Gertrude's "fresh ideas," seemed keenly aware that social welfare needed to move beyond charity to reform. Indeed, Gertrude graduated at a historical moment when the older generation of benevolent volunteers was being superseded by trained professionals, and religious societies were yielding to public agencies. College-educated women, conversant in the new psychology and sociology, took a scientific approach beyond the Social Gospel. Gertrude's youth and experience would be welcome.[56] She weighed her choices.

"I think just now we are selfish enough to want you at home for a while," Mina wrote Gertrude in May 1901. "(I can see the disadvantage of the little town)," the mother conceded, but then added, "I think if you look for it you can find something to do that will benefit a very needy class here."[57]

Six years had passed since Gertrude had left Goldsboro, first for Horace Mann School at Columbia University and then for Smith. Smart and fun loving, the young woman had taken to New York with the enthusiasm of a country girl dazzled by the big city. There was theater with the divine Sarah Bernhardt, Nellie Melba singing at the Met, golf in Van Cortlandt Park, and a stroll down belle époque Fifth Avenue on Easter Sunday. Relatives provided home comforts for the Sabbath and Jewish holidays. Family wealth gave Gertrude license to choose her pleasures, to travel at leisure. If she wished to marry, in New York she could meet Jewish men of education and refinement.

Gertrude had been a devoted daughter, and however much she enjoyed shopping for millinery at John Wanamaker or indulging in lobster Newburg at the Waldorf, she took seriously the motherly admonition to pursue a life of moral purpose, to benefit the needy. The obligation to be socially useful was a family covenant. In Massachusetts and New York she had been excited by the New Women who were reforming schools and organizing settlement houses. As an urban German Jew, she might, like Lillian Wald, apply herself to the relief of the immigrant Jewish poor. Settlement houses employed single women.

Pulling Gertrude southward was the family chain. Although she had shaken herself from its pull, she was devoted to her large, extended family. Whatever her frustrations, she loved her mother dearly. She was still fond of the home folk, Norny, her neighbors. Grade school friends were now, like her, educated sophisticates. She craved town gossip and relished clippings from the *Argus*. Gardening remained her passion. At home were needy of another kind, farm and factory laborers, children and women toiling in field and mill.

On that May day, as she considered her choices, the *New York Times* would have enticed her with a review of a drama by Irish playwright W. B. Yeats and faculty news from the education departments at Barnard and Columbia. By contrast, the *Goldsboro Argus* reported on cotton prospects, gossip from Mt. Olive, and the Woman's Club Traveling Library Committee chaired by Aunt Sarah.[58]

Home is where Gertrude Weil headed.

{ 3 }

WHEN I CAME HOME

Federation Gertie as Citizen Activist

"A lady of leisure" was how Gertrude Weil described herself after returning to Goldsboro. Her Smith friends speculated whether she might be writing "personals for the 'weekly whistle,'" studying music, climbing mountains, or "perhaps abroad enjoying herself to the fullest." In fact, Gertrude's life resembled that of other Smith alumnae sufficiently wealthy to live free from the workplace. Like their mothers, they managed households, taught Sunday school, worked for charities, and joined women's clubs. "So you are rushing about doing whist clubs, teas, country club larks etc etc," her friend Anna Collins wrote her. "I don't see how you get time to sleep at all!"[1] Gertrude enjoyed Goldsboro, the dances, card parties, amateur theatricals, temple affairs, and baseball games. Returning to family and friends, she was a southern lady.

Yet Gertrude lived in other worlds, too, and her look of contentment masked deeper tensions. For one thing, Gertrude and her friends, homesick for Northampton, never truly let go of Smith. Letters wistfully recalled golden days, updating gossip, lamenting loneliness, and begging for visits. Some spoke of European tours, new beaux, or settlement houses. They continued their intellectual life, recommending books and reviewing plays. As a New Woman in a New South, Gertrude was seeking her place in a changing society where women's roles outside the home were being reconsidered. In the progressive spirit of the age, new women's organizations arose to address inequities caused by urban and industrial growth. Gertrude's situation was typical of woman college graduates, daughters of the new urban middle class. Educated to realize their individuality, alumnae found at home "only traditional models of young womanhood available," historian Joyce Antler observes. "Uncertain" as to how to apply college skills and talents, these women felt "alienated from their families and communities."

Jane Addams described daughters and parents who "cannot comprehend each other."[2]

As she dutifully returned home, Gertrude was still negotiating her autonomy. "I'll not put the question After College What?" Aunt Sarah wrote Gertrude, "remembering the College girl is only human." But then she instructed, "Say to your mother & father that I'm happy with them, that your college education is finished and especially at the thought that you will enter the Home life again." She wished "God's blessing." In a 1902 letter Mina infantilized her twenty-two-year-old daughter: "Be a real good little girl, and mind your Auntie, unless her orders should run counter to mine, which are most likely to do since I have you so far." Gertrude answered deferentially but ironically: "I am trying to follow out all your numerous injunctions, dear Mamma, as well as Tante's, which are about as numerous."[3]

Domestic tranquility came at psychic cost. Family claims, Jane Addams observed, left the college girl anxious, even depressed, her "life is full of contradictions." In a 1903 letter to her Smith friend Mary Brinson in Chicago, Gertrude vented. Waxing nostalgic for "old Hamp!" the "little North Carolinian" made a rare cri de coeur:

> As for myself, I found it was high time I got back home when I did. Not that anybody had been missing me much or suffering from my absence, but from the feeling of "strangeness" that I had, I fear a prolonged absence would have made me a stranger sure enough. It did take me so long to settle down and get used to things after three months of gadding about and good timing. I must say—on the sly—that Goldsborough seemed stupider and duller than ever, and I missed the girls immeasurably more than I ever did before. I have entirely got over the "strange" feeling and am convinced beyond a doubt that I am home to *stay*, and yet I still feel a longing for something that I have not.[4]

Gertrude busied herself with domestic duties. Her friends were amused that Gertrude, a notoriously bad cook, was "keeping house." Betty asked the "domestic angel," "Can you make good apple-dough, and the thousand and one delicacies a college trained maiden ought naturally to turn off easily and gracefully?" Gertrude by no means rebelled. Her father felt "well satisfied" that "housekeeping is no task for Gertrude." Though never fond of the house's gingerbread ornament, she had an artist's eye and oversaw the décor and remodeling. Now that Leslie and Hilda were parents, she delighted in nieces and nephews whether at Chestnut Street or her brother's new estate a mile away. With her mother's debilities and spa retreats, she parented Janet, helping pack her off first to Sweet Briar and then Women's

College in Greensboro before she followed Sister to Smith. "It feels so good to be living home again even if I do have to keep house," Gertrude wrote Janet in 1909. A year later Gertrude described a daily routine of decorating, visiting, parties, literary readings, and club meetings that "I hardly have a minute for the leisureliness of social correspondence." Like other older sons and daughters, Gertrude was enlisted to teach Sunday school, which she enjoyed even with "Edwin, Isaac & Hyman to control." By 1918 she was its principal. She led, taught, or supervised there for fifty years.[5]

Social and family claims were not simply polar, nor did they necessarily impede a woman's progress. The family might also serve as the "mediating" agency between "educated women and society at large," making "possible a continuing process of growth." Through the family network, Gertrude met the political and intellectual luminaries of progressive North Carolina, and the family's civic engagement drew her into causes of her own. In describing her plans, Gertrude echoed Sarah's words luring her back to Goldsboro: "I have all sorts of schemes for the fall and winter—all of course, in embryonic force—and let us hope that is easier for a girl during her second year out of college after she has somewhat found herself to carry out her plans and live out her ideals than during that first year of indecisive readjustment."[6]

"Goldsborough"—as Gertrude ironically spelled it—may have seemed old-fashioned compared with New York, but in truth Gertrude enjoyed a lively local crowd. Through clubs and societies she worked with highly educated women who shared her literary and social justice passions. Part of her, too, was still the down-home girl who delighted in gardening and horseback riding. She made country visits to Norny, her childhood nanny. She busied herself at milliners and dressmakers or shopping for "pink slippers … to match my evening gown." Mina drew limits—reminding Gertrude that "being a woman, she is not at liberty to go anywhere she chooses alone." Perhaps recognizing the price Gertrude paid returning home, her parents indulged her travel and summer studies.[7]

From her porch Gertrude could see her country town rapidly urbanizing. As industrial growth pulled farm folk to the mills, Goldsboro's population doubled from 5,877 in 1900 to 11,296 in 1920. Among the new immigrants were Syrians and East European Jews, who peddled or opened stores. A building boom brought a new city hall and courthouse, all in monumental style, as well as rows of stores, banks, hotels, and office buildings, including a six-story skyscraper. Streets were paved. A trolley car linked downtown to new suburbs. The Weil armory became the Paramount Theater where Gertrude enjoyed movies and vaudeville. From the new Union Station she could take trains to Raleigh, Norfolk, Baltimore, or New York.

Gertrude as a lady of fashion. Courtesy of the State Archives of North Carolina.

Love and/or Marriage

Behind the family claim lay the assumption that Gertrude would one day marry and manage a household. Yet among German Jews an unmarried son or daughter at home was a "social tradition." According to one story, Gertrude's father was so jealous of any potential beau that "he had a fit." Mina regarded Gertrude's domestic work as a marital apprenticeship even as she wanted her as her caregiver. Perhaps lessening pressures on Gertrude, Leslie provided five grandchildren. Mina was also kept busy vetting gentlemen callers at Janet's door. For women, family and career were still regarded as incompatible—female school teachers were expected to be single—and marriage and birth rates were falling. College-educated women wed later, and more than half of full-time professionals never married. Yet, as her Smith friend Jess wrote Gertrude in 1909, "Marriage among our college friends is such an everyday occurrence." She asked whether Gertrude felt "sad" over her lack of a husband. Henry and Mina seemed not to have pushed marriage upon their independent, strong-willed daughter. When Leslie raised the issue, Gertrude thanked him for his "kind wishes for my future married welfare." Mina, she knew, would tolerate only a Jewish spouse, and choices were few in North Carolina. When uncle Joe Rosenthal married Elizabeth MacDonald, a former Weil employee, Mina suffered "conflicting feelings" at her brother's intermarriage with a Christian. The family bitterly divided, though Aunt Lizzie became a beloved family member.[8]

Gertrude gave notice that she prized her autonomy. Attending her first Jewish ball in Baltimore in 1902—an obvious marriage market—filled her with dread: "I like to have a good time, but I can think of lots of things that are more fun than balls." Of the debutantes, several of whom were cousins, she wrote, "I have made observations of Society—some of them tickle *my sense* of humor almost to the laughing point. How a girl can do nothing but this and look forward to nothing but this is beyond my understanding." Once, at the Concordia, she committed the faux pas of mistaking "one of the swellest society swells" for the head waiter. Fond of dancing, she enjoyed balls in Goldsboro, which drew Jew and Gentile alike, but accompanied by her brother Herman, a cousin, or other women.[9]

Gertrude's disdain for the "dissipations" of the "sporty life" did not mean that she was not sociable. Men found her charming, but her wit, erudition, intelligence, and sharp tongue made her formidable. In later years, when asked why she had never married, Gertrude quipped, "Who asked me?" In truth, suitors were aplenty. In New York a Mr. Frank accompanied her one night to a magician and the next day to temple and a walk in Central Park, and a certain Henry in Massachusetts begged the "pleasure" of a letter. Alexander Blumberg of Baltimore pressed his case: "Few girls talk so sensibly as you, and it is a pleasure as well as a treat to be in the company of one so bright." A Baltimore cousin, Isaac Heller, appealed to the "red blood in her veins, a throbbing heart, keen animation, burning interest, active desire, determined hopes, wishes, aspirations, and ambitions," but Gertrude rebuked him for his "consummate skill at saying unpleasant things," noting they shared nothing but "blueness of eye." She was friendly with Greensboro Jews, enjoying a country car ride with mill executive Julius Cone and discussing books and debating law with attorney David Stern, recipient of a Weil fellowship to Chapel Hill. Other than Jews, she corresponded for two years with George Thompson, an Englishman who had once lived in the Weil home as a graphic designer for Weil products. Abandoning business for art, he expressed his desire to see her, but her letters focused more on painting than on romance, which was apparently his interest.[10]

The ardent suitor who most inspired Gertrude was Victor Jelenko, a lawyer in Baltimore, with whom she corresponded for four years, starting in 1907. His family were members of the Jewish crowd. Their letters were witty, intense, and literary, so much so that he jokingly suggested saving them for publication. They shared gossip, bared their souls, and indulged in silliness. Not knowing how to address each other, they agreed to forgo salutations. Their mutual sympathy owed much to their similar situations, with Jelenko caring for a mother and sister afflicted with "nervousness." Gertrude wrote her own "wail of too-much-family." As she told her "dolorous tale of inactive Goldsboro," he regaled her with his opera, concert, and theater going in Baltimore. Jelenko sought to dispel "Gertrude's modest self-abasement." When she apologized for her "lightness," he asked to be "enlightened."[11]

Gertrude had met her match intellectually. Victor "devour[ed]" books, and she sought his views on socialism, suffragism, the Anglican Oxford movement, and settlement houses, as well as informed comment on writers ancient and modern from Virgil through Maeterlinck. He sent her a subscription to *The Bibelot*, a literary magazine. She sent him articles by the University of North Carolina's polymath professor Archibald Henderson. When she enthused over O. Henry, he praised that writer's grasp of the "comic and pathetic." Gertrude had attempted fiction, which he requested to see. Nearly all his letters ended, "Aren't you coming to town soon?"[12]

Gertrude, who kept intimate female friends at safe emotional distance, opened her soul to Jelenko. The Gertrude Weil gadding about Goldsboro card parties and Baltimore balls was privately engaged in deep reading and thinking. Always a religious seeker, Gertrude lived in an age of spiritualism, and within her circle were friends and relatives who had explored Unitarianism, Christian Science, and Ethical Culture. Though Jelenko confessed that he had "not troubled myself overmuch in outward professions" on the "Jewish topic," he agreed to discuss Gertrude's "live issue of Jewishness or non-Jewishness." In the way of religion, he recommended, "Do justice, love mercy," admitting that it was a "very broad creed" that may lack the "comfortable warmth of more elaborate systems." This prophetic ethic seemed a "good working start for a busy man."[13]

Jelenko tested Gertrude with the journals of Henri-Frédéric Amiel, a mystical Swiss poet-philosopher whose *Journal Intime* expressed a "gripping soul philosophy" in a "beautiful dressing of moral principles." She feared that Amiel's "minute introspection" and "soul searching" led to "isolation." To avoid becoming the "recluse," she pointed to Felix Adler, whose Ethical Culture "has a creed of morals to preach." Two years later they were still arguing Amiel. He advised, "Open one's ear to the sweetness and beauty of his conceptions of life and love and spirituality." Amiel's impracticality, his "renunciation of the world" that so troubled Gertrude, Jelenko argued, was a "soothing influence," a "salutary check" on the materialism of the age. Gertrude was seeking spiritual foundations for her social and political activism, and Jelenko challenged her to translate creed into program: "Of course, all of us are theoretically, socialists, just as we are theoretic suffragists or theoretic angels, but when it comes to applying the yard rule of common sense and practice to our 'isms,' we are stumped."[14]

Gertrude told Jelenko that her attendance at a leap-year ball in 1908 had been the "last chance many of you will have." He dismissed her threat of withdrawal from the social—that is, the marital—marketplace as "a gratuitous and superfluous self-derogation," arguing "you know very well you didn't mean it." He, too, despised the "old system of choosing mates." Three years later, Jelenko delicately broached personal feelings. He admitted that men profess to be "wary of entanglements and brag about the pleasures and privileges of bachelordom," but that is only a "habit to sidestep discussion of vital subjects.... That gets us nowhere and leaves most of us in the dark as to the real sentiments." Would she "loosen up" with a visit? The correspondence soon ended. Feeling a threat to her emotional privacy—perhaps even a marriage proposal—Gertrude retreated. In March 1912, Mina mentioned to Janet that Victor Jelenko was engaged to Minna Rosenheim, a nurse.[15]

In Baltimore's Jewish circles, cousin Bessie Blum wrote, Gertrude was becoming "more and more eligible." After a performance of *Die Walküre,*

Bessie reported that Monroe Block asked for her and that Ben Katzenberg was still interested. At a cotillion in December, Gertrude's dance program listed "the most eligible members of Baltimore society." She added immodestly, "I did look lovely. My dress made quite a hit." By now she noted "my mature age." Gossip "went around" about Gertrude and Frank Graham, who was seven years younger, but "she did not want to marry a non-Jew." In 1914 Janet, a social butterfly, jokingly addressed Gertrude as her "dear old maid sister." She was in her mid-thirties, had embarked on a public career, and apparently committed to an unmarried life.[16]

Bonds of Sisterhood

Gertrude's deepest and longest relationships were with women, yet even here she maintained a reserve that, as Jelenko had put it, precluded "real sentiments." Rosa Kaufman, fascinated by Gertrude, wrote Mina, "For that little bit I saw of her was just a tantalizing prelude and I want the whole book." But she wisely discerned, "I believe, however, that the owner permits few to read it deeply." A pattern emerged in her correspondence: women declared their love but insisted on more intimacy than Gertrude was willing to give. Frances Towers, a former Goldsboro school teacher, wrote Gertrude insistently, much of it literary talk, some political, but most confessional. In 1909 she pled, "I want to see you and I do love you very much. Whether you care or not it is so." She continued, "You hate personal talk but I feel that it is sometimes necessary." And, ever more desperately, "I wish you would write and tell me you love me—whether you do or not." Towers, abrasive at times, was depressed after several family crises, and Gertrude helped her with loans. In 1914 Towers married. Gertrude's Smith friend and travel companion Anna Collins also married. Her relationship was similar with childhood friend Sallie Kirby, who declared, "I'd love to have you more than anybody I know" even as she eyed available men at her school. She offered to share her "single bed" if Gertrude would join her in the mountains. "I can't think of any words that might convey to you the great love that I have for you," Sallie wrote Gertrude. Sallie also suffered the "blues," and in 1911 Gertrude nursed her through a "nervous breakdown." Sallie, too, married.[17]

A chance meeting in the North Carolina mountains introduced Gertrude to the woman who became her most enduring companion. In 1912 Gertrude traveled to Boone to join Sallie Kirby, then teaching for the summer at the Appalachian Training School for Teachers (forerunner of Appalachian State University). To reach the mountaintop campus required an arduous surrey ride. Among the passengers was Harriet Payne, Vassar, '03, on her way to visit Bertha Lindau Cone, widow of textile magnate Moses Cone. Benefac-

Harriet Payne. Courtesy of the State Archives of North Carolina.

tor of the Training School, Cone resided in a twenty-three room mansion set in a thirty-five-hundred-acre game park on a scenic ridge outside Blowing Rock, North Carolina. After settling in a Boone hotel, Gertrude hiked to Cone's, losing her way in the woods until rescued by a voice, "Miss Weil! Miss Weil!" It was Harriet Payne. She pulled Gertrude to the top. At the mansion Gertrude found a somber scene. Bertha Cone, garbed in black, had never stopped mourning Moses, dead now four years. Her "saturnine sister" Clem Lindau sat dourly and silently beside her. Gertrude, bright and sprightly, was the proverbial "change of air," and Cone grew fond of her, insisting that she stay for weeks. More meaningful to Gertrude, she and Harriet were kindred souls. "She is very good company," Gertrude wrote Mina, "always full of good cheer and in lively spirits." Conversant in "all the languages afloat," Harriet was a cosmopolitan who had taught abroad. Like Gertrude, she was an energetic mountain hiker. Politically, she was a suffragette (leading Cone to shake her fist). In turn, Harriet described Gertrude as "most lovable, charming and intelligent."[18]

In later years Gertrude jested that the only person whom she ever could have married was her brother Leslie. Sometimes she added Frank Graham. Sometimes she added Harriet Payne. When they met, Gertrude was disappointed to learn that Harriet had a partner, Jane, with whom she owned a tea room in Connecticut. Gertrude visited there, and Harriet in her trips to Goldsboro became so close to the Weils that she brought matzah during Passover. Harriet was bookish, opinionated, and "side splittingly funny." She sent Gertrude Jung's *Psychology of the Unconscious* and Frederic W. H. Myer's *Human Personality and Its Survival of Bodily Death*, which failed to relieve her doubts that "this world is not the end." A suffragist, she shared Gertrude's passion for social reform. By 1914 Harriet dissolved her partnership both emotionally and financially and relocated to Upstate New York, where she taught French. Like Gertrude, she was limited by duties to a dependent mother. She also lacked resources, and Gertrude loaned her money. Mina ripped up the ious. Harriet prized her autonomy, advising Gertrude, "Perhaps yours will be the next matrimonial venture. I certainly never shall." And, on another occasion to Gertrude: "My heart is tout a toi." The women sought opportunities to be together. "How I wish our house & interests were in Goldsboro!" she wrote in 1917. Each admired the other's ability to rise above the limitations of family and their provincial hometowns. "Although you live in the conservative South, you are far more active than we are here in every way," Harriet wrote Gertrude in 1915.[19]

Such "bonds of sisterhood" as Gertrude enjoyed were typical of middle- and upper-class women, especially among graduates of same-sex colleges. Living in a separate sphere of domesticity, women found sustenance and intimacy among themselves. For married women, these relations were socially acceptable. Through literary culture they shared a language of feeling, and club work tightened social bonds. Entering public spaces, women drew together in solidarity. The expressions of love that passed among Gertrude and her friends, most notably Harriet Payne, were common, and historians note that "many middle-class women shared a physical and emotional closeness that was erotic as well as spiritual," moving easily between them. However much Gertrude may have held such feelings, she shielded her private life. Though they visited and traveled, Gertrude and Harriet never established a domicile together, but such prominent women as Jane Addams and Lillian Wald did have lifelong domestic relationships with women. Gertrude remarked to a great-niece that she could have lived with a woman, presumably Harriet, but did not think Goldsboro was ready.[20]

A New Woman

After college, what? remained unanswered. Gertrude's description of herself as a lady of leisure was both candid and ironic. As usual with her, the struggle was to balance contrary demands, to be loyal to her family and community but to preserve her independence, to enjoy herself but to live with moral purpose. Mediating conflict within herself, Gertrude became adept as a conciliator among factions in her various organizations. Her task was to find her place as a progressive woman in conservative Goldsboro.

A lady of leisure meant not that Gertrude had nothing to do but that she was free to control her time. In so labeling herself Gertrude was archly referencing Thorstein Veblen's *The Theory of the Leisure Class*, a popular book published in 1899 that described a caste of wealthy women who consumed conspicuously, entertained lavishly, paid social calls, and complained about the help. Gertrude's predicament was typical of college women who, if not pursuing professional careers, were searching for a place beyond "unproductive leisure." She had little interest in business, as her financial needs were amply provided. As she aged, she became less the consumer, and her adolescent fervor for fashion faded. Her one excursion into enterprise came in the early 1900s when she and her mother enthused over the Carolina Rice Flakes produced at a Weil mill. The box reprinted Mina's recipes. They sent samples near and far, but for Mina and Gertrude marketing cereal was more about entertainment than entrepreneurship.[21]

Gertrude enjoyed life. As a Weil, she was welcomed into elite Goldsboro society. Mina and Henry were noted for the elegance of their dinner parties—a 1903 bill from a Baltimore grocer listed imported cheese and herring, Nova Scotia salmon, and smoked meat. As a southern lady, Gertrude busied herself penning thank-you notes and sending small gifts—gloves, handkerchiefs, local yams, holly wreaths—to friends and relatives for this holiday or that birthday. Visiting Goldsboro from New York in 1902, Aunt Kala Rosenthal wrote Gertrude: "Without realizing it, my dear, you do a lot of people a lot of good." She added, "Each one's world lies so close to himself, and it is good to see anyone who can become broad within a narrow circle and find, as you do, that there is good in everything."[22]

Sports offered one arena for Gertrude to exercise her freedom. She maintained her vigorous college regimen, playing golf and tennis and rowing the river. She was still the baseball fan. Like society at large, she was afflicted with bridge madness, sometimes crowding in two games a day. Modest Gertrude was unabashed about her card skills. In 1908 she purchased her own horse, naming it Waffles for her favorite meal at Seven Springs, a country resort noted for its restorative waters. In 1910 she fell from the horse. What she resented most about her mishaps, like her illnesses, was being the "invalid lady," fussed over by doctors and a mothering Mina.[23]

The Weils' integration into the upper echelons of small-town society was noteworthy in an era when anti-Semitic social discrimination was commonplace in urban America. Ethel Borden "must have taken a fancy to the tribe," Mina noted of a prominent Christian woman with many Jewish friends. Visiting Atlantic City in 1911, Mina confessed, "I'll take a Southern or even non-Jewish crowd anywhere for sociability." Yet the Christianity pervasive in civic culture discomfited. Weil women sat at social service conferences as resolutions passed urging Christianity as a cure for public ills. One 1916 session featured "The Teachings of Jesus as They Bear upon the Solution of Modern Social Problems." The state Federation of Women's Clubs resolved to "use its influence in having the Bible read daily in the graded and public schools." When the Goldsboro school board endorsed religious instruction, Mina wrote a dissenting report. Henry and Lionel Weil successfully lobbied the legislature against a constitutional amendment to require school Bible reading, and their B'nai B'rith lodge opposed religious instruction in the schools.[24] If Gertrude, a third-generation American, felt excluded, she did not then raise her voice. Living in the churchly, evangelical South, Jews grew accustomed to accommodating.

According to gender divisions of the time, Weil women engaged in moral campaigns for social welfare while Weil men held posts in commerce and government. For Sol and Henry, and Leslie and Lionel, public service was one aspect of larger, lucrative careers. Mina and Gertrude ran a nursery school while Weil men served on school boards, a right denied women. Although women were more likely to fill the pews of Oheb Sholom, men sat before the ark as officers. Lionel, as an alderman from 1904 to 1922, led a reform movement to end patronage and adopt a city-manager government, the first in the state to do so. He wrote a manual on the subject and served on the Council of the National Municipal League. He expanded Weil enterprises into scientific agriculture, published research in technical journals, and patented a machine to transplant longleaf pines.[25]

As Weils acculturated to the South, they identified with its cosmopolitan elements. Concerned about her nervousness prior to a European tour, Mina consulted Dr. George Kirby, a Goldsboro friend who directed New York's Wards Island asylum. He wrote his Swiss colleague Dr. Jung in Zurich— "his specialty is psycho-analysis"—about a consultation. If Jung were unavailable, Kirby recommended Viennese physician Dr. Freud. Weils were sociable with Trinity College historian John Spencer Bassett, who ignited a national furor in 1903 when he dared to compare Booker T. Washington to Robert E. Lee in his *South Atlantic Quarterly* article "Stirring Up the Fires of Racial Antipathy." During the so-called Bassett Affair, the professor was vilified—the *Argus* was "aghast" that such a "vicious, deadly reptile" hailed from Goldsboro—and calls arose for his dismissal for breaching the color line. Weils continued their friendship, as well as their *Quarterly* subscription, after Bassett joined the Smith faculty in 1906.[26]

The young, progressive Chapel Hill professors invited to lecture in Goldsboro were guests in the Weil home, and relationships grew. University of North Carolina president Edwin Alderman, former Goldsboro school superintendent, advised Mina on women's club issues. The brilliant Archibald Henderson, explicator of Albert Einstein, biographer of George Bernard Shaw, and friend of both, was another houseguest. His wife, Barbara, a poet, shared Gertrude's interest in women's suffrage. Edward Kidder Graham, who became university president at thirty-four, was another guest, and his wife Susan Moses, a professor of literature, was Gertrude's friend. Through them, the family came to know his cousin Frank Graham, then a young history professor at Chapel Hill.

Gertrude's closest Goldsboro friends were teachers. Conflicts with principals, a new superintendent, or hirings and firings pulled Mina and Gertrude into school politics. In 1909 her friend Frances Towers wrote Gertrude in outrage after a superintendent passed two students who had been failed for cheating. When a rumored pregnancy led a district nurse to resign and leave Goldsboro abruptly, she wrote Gertrude a heartfelt letter as a confidante who never listened to "busy bodies."[27]

Gertrude enjoyed book talk and sought the company of avid readers. A home library inventory listed 1,435 volumes. In one 1912 book order Gertrude purchased the complete works of Henrik Ibsen and four volumes of Oscar Wilde, while Mina requested *A Montessori Mother* and *What Is Judaism*. Gertrude read the popular novels of H. G. Wells, George Meredith, and George Eliot, and correspondents recommended progressive writers like Upton Sinclair. The Weils subscribed to Charlotte Perkins Gilman's feminist magazine *The Forerunner*. Henry George's *Progress and Poverty* advocated an innovative single tax on land to redress the inequities of the industrial economy. Gertrude wrote familiarly of *Doll House* and *Hedda Gabler*, which dramatized independent women contesting social norms. Liz Kohn in Brooklyn, part of her Jewish crowd, was raising her son on the "advanced mode of living" of Gilman and Ellen Key, a Swedish feminist who promoted free love and nontraditional family models. Gertrude sent Key's novel *Rahel* to cousin Rosa Kaufman in Ohio.[28] The utopian visions and radical solutions of these writers reinforced Gertrude's idealism and offered measures to assess her own activism. With new technologies, notably a proliferating popular media, living in a remote southern mill town did not preclude Gertrude's engagement with the international intelligentsia.

Wandering Jews

Gertrude Weil lived successfully in Goldsboro because she could escape it. As befitted their immigrant heritage, Weils had wanderlust, and Gertrude traveled incessantly. Travel allowed her to exercise her independence while retaining her fealty to home and family. Her return from Smith with her parents included a leisurely detour to Buffalo for the Pan-American world's fair, as well as to Montreal. Besides frequent trips to Greensboro, Kinston, Raleigh, Wilson, or Chapel Hill to visit her crowd or attend meetings, Gertrude was well known in Baltimore and New York Jewish circles. One spring trip in 1902 to Baltimore, New York, Scranton, Ithaca, and her beloved Northampton lasted nearly two months. She reprised this itinerary in 1904. Starting in 1907, she spent summers in the North Carolina mountains, whose beauty she found rhapsodic. Vacations renewed her. Gertrude accompanied her mother to spas, hospitals, and resorts in Chase City, Atlantic City, Pinehurst, or Lithonia Springs, West Virginia. In 1913 she spent two weeks in Richmond while Mamma underwent a "rest cure" and "anti-toxin treatment." In 1915 she was away three months to California and the Pacific Northwest.[29]

European excursions were de rigueur for people of the Weils' class. In 1903 and 1906 Gertrude embarked on grand tours and planned a third. Beyond the obligatory cultural capitals, these trips were also sentimental journeys to the *Heimat* to renew family ties. Visiting cousins in Württemberg, Uncle Sol cried. Henry's bad memory of steerage kept him home until 1903 when he and Mina took Gertrude and Janet to Europe. Three years later Gertrude embarked by steamer, chaperoned by Mary Jobe, "a very pretty and stylish" school teacher, and her Smith friend Anna Collins. Always the enthusiast, Gertrude looked at Europe with wide eyes: "Just think of it— Shakespeare's real Avon." London, she judged, "doesn't hold a candle to Paris." She pitied overworked streetcar horses but thrilled to tea with a "real M.P." at the House of Lords.[30]

In Europe Gertrude reveled in museums, opera houses, and concert halls. On her 1903 tour Gertrude felt sympathy for the "poor artist class" who "all look half starved." A devotee of Ruskin, she sought art's social and moral dimension. She was drawn to the pre-Raphaelites, whose paintings were naturalistic but spiritual. She admired Belgian lace but was repelled at the exploitation of female needle workers. She noted admiringly that Belgium had abolished capital punishment and opened reformatories.[31]

If Gertrude was a cosmopolitan among provincials in Goldsboro, in Paris, Koln, or London she was a hometown girl. On a London street she met by

Gertrude with her parents. Courtesy of the State Archives of North Carolina.

chance Sallie Kirby's brother George, and in Germany she rendezvoused with honeymooning uncle Joe Rosenthal and his bride, Lizzie. Her European relatives had joined the Jewish migration from the countryside to the cities and, like their American kin, had acculturated into the middle class. In Strasbourg she met Oncle Emanuel, Tante Babette, and cousin Ernst, a university student who serenaded her with his violin. "I felt so at home there" with her "jolly" family, Gertrude wrote, wishing Grandma Rosenthal could be with them. In Paris cousin Emil Oettinger dazzled her with a romantic dinner, sunset carriage ride, and "too much champaign [*sic*] for little Gertrude." Dutiful, she attended Sabbath services at the Rue Victoire synagogue, whose ritual reminded her of "Roman Catholic forms." In London cousin Max Oettinger, charmed by the young American women, exhausted them with museums and theater.[32]

Her European grand tour accorded with the social expectations for a well-to-do college graduate. So did collegiate summer study. In June 1904 Gertrude joined her cousin Helen Weil at Cornell, where she audited courses in civil government and European history and enjoyed a performance of *Hedda Gabler*, a "masterpiece." She began a habit of daily newspaper reading. There, too, she deepened her friendship with Susan Moses, a North Carolinian pursuing a master's degree in literature. Mina was "afraid" that Gertrude would "be wanting to go back" to Cornell, and a year later Gertrude returned for summer school, this time with her friend Sallie Kirby, to study Shakespeare and "Evolution and Revolution in Politics." In 1909 she was at Vassar with Ohio cousin Ruth Heyn and five years later back at Cornell. Northern trips were timed so that she could return to Smith for commencements. "Oh—it is glorious to be here again," she wrote from Northampton in 1904.[33]

The adolescent who had resented maternal marching orders found herself as a young adult enjoying family visits. After a stay with Oettingers and Rosenthals in Washington and Toledo in 1904, Gertrude wrote, "They are truly delightful to know and be with. From the very first meeting, I felt that I had known them always." When Gertrude extended an Ohio stay into a fourth week, Mina worried that she was abusing the hospitality: "The best time to go home is when everybody is asking you to stay." During a 1908 Toledo visit Gertrude enjoyed "long talks" with cousin Rosa Kaufman, a "citizen of the world" and a "progressive wonder of learning." Gertrude could not name a book Rosa had not read. She grew close to younger cousins Ruth and Margaret Heyn. Two years later cousin Nat Kaufman, a wit, took Gertrude boating to a Lake Erie resort where he proffered a comic menu that included "Young Pig stuffed with Matzos, a la Wayne County." The Kaufman home was a "hotbed of agnosticism," and Gertrude heard "fine" lectures at the Unitarian and Christian Science churches. Gertrude assured Mina that she also attended "schule" for Purim and should not fear for her Jewish soul. As much as she enjoyed the Ohio family's uproarious iconoclasm, she expressed discomfort with the "wholesale way old-time traditions are swept away."[34]

The Jewish crowd reinforced Gertrude's progressivism. Rosa Kaufman remained a confidante of the Weil women, corresponding often and exchanging visits. She was their sounding board on political issues. Rosa derived many of her views from her Toledo friend Pauline Steinem, prominent in women's and Jewish affairs (and grandmother of feminist Gloria). Visiting Baltimore in 1902, Gertrude made a courtesy call to the Szolds, another family noted for intellectuality and social activism. By chance, that very day Henrietta Szold had received a letter from Mina. "They are a lovely family altogether including their wonderful dog Creole," Gertrude observed. "We were speaking of how intelligent the creature is when someone very aptly asked, 'Well, what kind of a dog would you expect to find at Szolds?'" Also on Mina's visiting list was the Fels family in Philadelphia. Lazarus Fels, apparently a distant Weil relation, had been an antebellum merchant in Yanceyville, North Carolina. His son Joseph made a fortune manufacturing Fels-Naptha Soap, and with his wife, Mary, endowed Henry George's single-tax land movement, as well as Zionist and suffragist causes. Gertrude had visited the Henry George Jr. Republic in Upstate New York. Although not catching Fels at home, Gertrude took interest in the George colonies.[35]

As she traveled, Gertrude explored Judaism beyond her home truths. During one New York visit, given the choice of lectures by a rabbi at Temple Emanuel or Felix Adler at Carnegie Hall, she chose Ethical Culture. After partying Friday night with Smith friends in New York in May 1902, Gertrude rose early for temple but abandoned prayer for a springtime walk in the park. "The lecture may have been fine, but I doubt whether its religious influence was any stronger than the sermons in the rocks, boat pond, and the spring foliage," she wrote, referencing Shakespeare. Indeed, her synagogue going was exceptional at a time of religious disaffiliation, with an estimated 80 percent of American Jews "unchurched." One New York Sabbath in 1905, she confessed that she had not attended services for a "long time," but she so enjoyed Temple Emanuel's "beautiful" choir and organ that she wondered why more were not present. She explored the uptown synagogues, hearing sermons from America's rabbinic luminaries. One Saturday she arose early to attend Orthodox services. The lifelong reader of William James was interested in spiritual experience and comparative religion. Gertrude retained her outward conformity to Judaism and Jewish community, but as in other aspects of her life, her conventionality masked a robust, questioning inner life. Her rationalism, universalism, and nature worship created tensions with organized religion. Yet she came from the small-town South where churchgoing was expected and from an affiliated synagogue family. Gertrude honored her mother and father.[36]

One Weil grand tour that Gertrude did *not* take resonated. In 1909 Mina, Henry, and Flora Oettinger cruised the Mediterranean, detouring to Jaffa and Jerusalem. Henry was astonished to find Württembergers in Jerusalem, including an Oberdorfer whose father had purchased the Weil home. Henry appreciated receiving synagogue honors in the Holy Land. Reporting to the *Argus*, he confessed, "My heart beats a little faster" approaching Jerusalem. But he dismissed Zionism as "criminal ... since it has for its purpose the settling of poor Jews ... on barren soil" where they will depend on charity or starve. Mina, "devoted to learn about things Jewish here," drew contrary lessons. She met Miss Faber, a former Baltimore neighbor of Bertha Weil, who taught at Jerusalem's Rothschild School for Girls. Mina counted some forty organizations, all needing money, all jealous of one another. She toured institutions resembling American settlement houses. In 1913 Jane Addams would visit. Thanking Mina for a donation, Annie Landau, the English-born principal of the Rothschild School, described her work with deserted wives and abandoned children and her efforts to teach lace making as a "home industry," programs not unlike Mina's in Goldsboro.[37]

Gertrude's Zionism, like so many of her commitments, was a maternal inheritance that inspired local community organizing in service to a global mission. The Weil women broke from Classical Reform Judaism in their Zionism. In 1885 Reform Jews in Pittsburgh had famously proclaimed, "We consider ourselves no longer a nation, but a religious community." They did not anticipate the restoration of the Jews to Palestine. Southern Reform Jews are often stereotyped as the least Zionist of American Jews, but that owes more to a few prominent anti-Zionists in national Jewish organizations than to popular sentiment. Prominent Classical Reform rabbis like David Marx of Atlanta, Edward Calisch of Richmond, and Moses Jacobson of Asheville fulminated against Zionism from pulpits, yet their communities all supported active Zionist societies. Non-Zionists, in contrast to anti-Zionists, might oppose a political Jewish state in Palestine but still philanthropically support the needy there. Gertrude conceded that Zionism may suggest a "dual loyalty," but she felt "safe in declaring the undivided loyalty of our people to our country and my deep appreciation of the blessing of the Constitution."[38]

The Holy Land tour reinforced the women's Zionism, their feeling that Jews everywhere belonged to an extended family with a shared destiny. Mina's friendship with Henrietta Szold gave their Zionism a personal dimension. Szold's work in Jerusalem with the poor and children, inspired by American progressive movements, fit the Weil women's social ethic. Gertrude thought her father's indifference to Zionism "lacked foresight." On Gertrude's bookshelf was George Eliot's romantic, proto-Zionist novel, *Daniel Deronda*. When Szold founded Daughters of Zion in 1912, Weil women joined. Two years later it was renamed Hadassah: The Women's Zionist Organization of America.[39]

Municipal Housekeeping

Gertrude always said that her social activism was learned at home. Grand-mother Eva and mother Mina had led interfaith charitable societies in Wilson and Goldsboro. Increasingly, women saw the social issues confronting them as systemic, beyond religious benevolence. They would move from charity to reform, from personalism to politics, from local activism to national organization. Whatever alienation Gertrude had felt from her mother yielded to their shared commitment to social welfare.

Gertrude possessed traits common to clubwomen. She was wealthy, college educated, and without responsibility for children. She had the means and time to dedicate herself to civic activism. Grandmother Eva observed in 1905, "Gertrude is always kept at something." Herman recalled a day when "Gertrude is trying to phone everybody in town and … has only gotten to 35." "Municipal housekeeping"—a term Gertrude employed—describes metaphorically how women extended their domestic responsibilities from home to city. Women's maternal duty was "protection" of the family with laws that safeguarded women and children. Among the women's clubs' first acts were academic scholarships and public health campaigns. Weils participated enthusiastically in the "educational awakening" launched in the early 1900s by Governor Charles B. Aycock, the former Goldsboro school superintendent.[40]

Mina enlisted Gertrude in her program in Edmundstown, a working-class neighborhood. Mina had established a daycare nursery for "factory children," likely inspired by Charlotte Perkins Gilman, who had advocated the communal raising of children, and by the settlement house movement. According to the racial and gender division of labor prevailing at the time, nearly all the 30,000 workers in North Carolina's mills were white and mostly women. While Mina entertained the children with surrey rides, summer watermelon, and winter Christmas parties, Gertrude organized a Monday afternoon sewing class for twenty-five children. Gertrude, fresh from college, wanted to expand the nursery into a kindergarten. During a 1902 trip to New York she inquired at Columbia's Teacher's College about securing an educator who could both teach and train the locals. "It was mission work" with low pay, Gertrude apologized. She collected reports from the College Settlement Association and visited programs in New York and Chicago, including Hull House. At a 1908 ceremony that Gertrude hosted, mothers were invited to see their children's hand-sewn bags and hear them perform poems and songs. The children "do think 'Miss Gertrude' is *the thing*."[41]

In later years Gertrude scoffed at her Edmundstown efforts, citing an uncle who counseled her that "it would be much more to the point 'if you would go to the board of directors of the mill and tell them to pay these people a decent wage.'" She reflected, "Our old-timey 'charity' had been a superficial amelioration," which left unaddressed deeper social and economic abuses. "It was worth a great deal to know how the poor lived," she recalled.[42] Edmundstown had been a volunteer, charitable endeavor. In the coming decade Gertrude affiliated with new, progressive social service organizations that approached welfare scientifically and were committed to political lobbying and legislative relief.

Jewish Social Gospel

Prohibition was the moral cause that inspired progressive women to organize for social reform. Protestant ladies, including close Weil friends, flocked to the Woman's Christian Temperance Union (WCTU) branch that formed in North Carolina in 1883, ten years after its founding. Weils, like other Jews, remained outsiders. Under the Social Gospel banner, the WCTU, joined by the Young Women's Christian Association, sought to "bring the masses to Christ." Their crusade included causes dear to Weil women: prison reform, child labor laws, and minimum wages. Gertrude would have endorsed the WCTU's suffragist advocacy, but it was adopted not as a feminist initiative but as a "Home Protection Ballot" to secure Prohibition. The WCTU's culture of abstinence and moralism was alien to Jews like the Weils, who drank wine ritually and enjoyed schnapps yet avoided alcoholism. Hymn-singing women smashing saloons appalled Jews, especially since respectable Jews were involved in the alcohol industry. The first president of Goldsboro's Oheb Sholom, Adolph Lehman, owned a liquor store. Prohibitionists targeted Jews. An anti-Semitic sermon by a "great & eminent Divine" blamed Goldsboro's Jews for the city "voting wet." "A Jew"—likely Henry Weil—rebutted the "Reverend Gentleman" whose sermon did "lower & degrade" Jews by "classifying them with Negros & Beerkeeping." He admonished "religious fanatics." Gertrude thought Prohibition hypocritical when everyone knew where to buy bootleg.[43]

Weil women followed a typically Jewish national pathway to civic engagement. In 1893 the Chicago World's Fair hosted both a Congress of Representative Women and a World Parliament of Religions. Sallie Southall Cotten represented North Carolina on a planning Board of Lady Managers and was inspired to create a North Carolina Federation of Women's Clubs. Jewish women organized a National Council of Jewish Women.[44] Both efforts drew the Weil household.

Gertrude was fourteen when she attended the Chicago fair and went for fun, not feminism, but Weil women followed the proceedings. One parliament speaker was Henrietta Szold, who lectured on "What Judaism Has Done for Women." Cousin Rosa Kaufman did "peep into the hall" of the Jewish Women's Congress. Like many of her background, she had "left everything of Jewish ceremony and observance" but retained "the fibre of memory." Rosa's indifference was more typical of Jewish women than Mina, Sarah, and Gertrude's affiliation. Modeled on the WCTU and General Federation of Women's Clubs and inspired by the ethical precepts of Reform Judaism, the Council took as its mission to educate an assimilating generation of Jewish women on Judaism. Where Christians were inspired by the Social Gospel, wanting to bring the masses to Christ, Jews cited "prophetic calls for justice." Like other women's groups, the Council saw woman's role as a mother in the home. Theirs was a social or domestic feminism, promoting women's interests in health, education, and the workplace.[45]

Unlike her parents' generation, Gertrude did not have an acute sense of Jewish difference, an issue the women's movement debated. Elizabeth Cady Stanton argued in *The Woman's Bible* that Christianity had imbibed from Judaism the "insidious poison" of women's inferiority, leading to tensions between Jews and feminists. At Horace Mann Gertrude was mentored by Stanton's daughter Margaret Lawrence. Gertrude in later years said that she was unfamiliar with Stanton's *Bible*, but she likely heard arguments blaming Judaism for patriarchy. In the 1890s American suffragist leaders like Anna Howard Shaw and Carrie Chapman Catt, who became Gertrude's personal heroes, spoke a nativist rhetoric that labeled Jewish immigrants as undesirables.[46]

To the contrary, the National Council of Jewish Women rooted progressivism in Jewish values. Council members were welcomed into women's clubs, which were religiously inclusive. Nationally, the Council was often the portal through which Jewish women entered secular organizations. Gertrude's Judaism was always a liberal religion committed to social justice. Mina and Gertrude followed Council debates and traveled to conferences. In April 1902, Gertrude joined Council women in Baltimore to hear "brilliant" Rabbi Emil Hirsch advocate workers' and women's rights. In 1912 Mina wrote Janet, "Sister is reading aloud the report of all the rumpus that has lately been raised with the National Jewish *Council*." With Reform Jews leading, women argued over religious diversity and whether the Council should emphasize its founding religious mission to combat assimilation or commit to social welfare. Personal conflicts inflamed meetings. As New Yorkers assumed leadership, resentment grew over the Council's focus on providing relief to urban East European Jewish immigrants.[47]

Goldsboro received but a trickle of East European Jews. Escaping urban sweatshops, they tended to be self-employed, upwardly mobile peddlers and storekeepers. As small-town Jews, the Weils did not have a ghetto nearby, but they joined national German-Jewish philanthropists who contributed to relief and Americanization programs. Politically, they opposed immigration restrictions. Weil men joined boards of the Hebrew Orphans' Home in Atlanta and the National Farm School in Pennsylvania. Mina sent her Ohio cousins *The Promised Land*, Mary Antin's autobiography of her Russian immigrant experience.[48]

Gertrude and Mina showed interest in the Council in the early 1900s but did not sustain their commitment. Goldsboro never organized a Council section—although four North Carolina communities did so. Gertrude disdained partisanship and was likely cool to an organization beset by personal and political squabbles. Weil women directed their energies toward secular, progressive organizations in their city and state, committing local Jewish groups to their social welfare agenda. Mina and Gertrude's focus remained the rural and industrial poor. They joined the middle- and upper-class activist women who sought to forge alliances with working-class women through groups like the National Consumers League and Women's Trade Union League.

Clubwomen

The North Carolina Federation of Women's Clubs became the platform of Gertrude's early activism, and her public career followed its trajectory. The club movement began in 1868 in New York, and by 1895 dilatory North Carolina had its first club, in Wilmington. In 1899 Sallie Southall Cotten, a poet and teacher, sent letters to prominent women urging them to form local clubs. With Cotten and Charlotte Perkins Stetson [Gilman] at her side, Mina Weil had presided over the first Goldsboro Woman's Club meeting in 1899. Nationally, Jewish women flocked to the movement. However, Jews were few in North Carolina, and clubs maintained a Christian ethos. At a 1902 Goldsboro meeting, Mina noted that the chairman took her cues from

"Methodist conferences," and at one state meeting the Federation president called upon women to display "Christian tactfulness." But rabbis also adjourned conventions with benedictions. Despite its background in church societies, the women's club movement spoke in spiritual rather than sectarian terms. "Unity in diversity" was the General Federation motto. "The Women's Club has done more to eliminate denominational lines and enlist the women of Goldsboro in a common effort for the public good than any organization," the *Daily Argus* exulted.[49]

In writing her *History of the North Carolina Federation of Women's Clubs*, Sallie Southall Cotten did not just draw from the Bible but boldly evoked Darwin and Freud. She did so at a time when the state was embroiled in the evolution debate. "A psychic Call from the Infinite stirred the soul of womanhood and unconsciously woman responded," she wrote. The women were fulfilling "God's law of evolution which forever calls for higher types." They would emancipate themselves from the "'inferiority complex,' which was simply the habit of sex-submission." Cotten spoke of the club as a "university." Gertrude would have identified with that progressive, modern ethos.[50]

When the North Carolina Federation of Women's Clubs first met in Winston-Salem in 1902, Sarah and Mina attended and signed onto the Library Extension and Education Committees, respectively. That year, the Goldsboro club counted sixty-eight members. Cotten often cited Goldsboro as a model and echoed Sallie Kirby's nickname for Miss Weil, "Federation Gertie." Alone among the seven founding state clubs, Goldsboro called itself a Woman's Club, the others focusing on art, embroidery, or, most often, literature. Goldsboro was notable for its progressive "high ideals, broadminded principles, and a wide scope of earnest work," while other clubs were dedicated to a more ladylike "self-improvement and social enjoyment." Mina was president in 1903, and Gertrude served three terms: 1908, 1916, and 1932. In 1905 and 1915 the state Federation held its annual conference in Goldsboro. When Mina was elected, Gertrude—with the defensive humor women often employed as they stepped outside the home—penned a satirical letter that expressed pride but deflated lofty ambitions: "Methinks I see before me a noble and puissant city under the regime of Mrs. Henry Weil," or at least "a grand boom to the day-nursery enterprise." She warned her mother, "Don't take the responsibility so seriously."[51] That unwillingness to take herself seriously underlay Gertrude's equanimity. She was always conscious, often humorously so, of the gulf between ideals and achievement, between the reality of the problem and the ameliorative action. Hence, she was perpetually modest, belittling her own contribution.

Under Cotten's guidance, Gertrude climbed the organizational ladder. In 1906 she delivered welcoming remarks to the fourth convention in Charlotte and a year later was elected General Federation state secretary. In 1908 when Gertrude was asked to revise the Federation's constitution, Cotten taught her to consider the larger politics and bureaucratic "perplexities." Elders who had written the charter needed to be co-opted into the process. She advised her to use the newspapers, which were widely distributed and unburdened by postal regulations. As local club reporter and chair of the Federation's Publications Committee, Gertrude became adept at utilizing public media.[52]

The challenges facing the Goldsboro Woman's Club were typical of the New South as agrarian market towns rapidly turned urban and industrial. From 1899 to 1919 the number of industrial laborers in North Carolina more than doubled, and the urban population grew from 10 percent to 20 percent. The club's municipal housekeeping was both traditional and progressive. The focus remained domesticity. Classes were held in social hygiene. Household finance and management were taught as the new science of home economics. Sarah, chair of the library department, stated the "ultimate object ... is to create within the people a desire for better homes, cleaner homes, a demand for common school education" as well as "thirst for knowledge." Sarah was "a missionary" intent on saving boys from delinquency and girls from "all kinds of indiscretions." The club sponsored get-togethers with teachers and mothers that led to formal parent-teacher associations. Inspired by the White City of the 1893 World's Fair, the City Beautiful movement sought not just to enhance urban aesthetics through gardens and tree planting but also to introduce higher standards of sanitation in places where livestock wandered the streets.[53]

In 1903, with Mina as president, the club reported triumphantly in the *Weekly Argus*, "Three years ago when our woman's Club was suggested ... it was caricatured, criticized and misrepresented." Women "suddenly found themselves the subject of sneering comments or vulgar would-be wit on the part of men." Now, however, the club had brought "a new gospel of learning," inspiring "in every sense the moral awakening to the full glory and meaning of life."[54] That the club proved unthreatening also suggests that the women minded their southern manners.

North Carolina clubs retained an Old South ethos. At Federation luncheons women stood to sing *Dixie*. In 1900 the General Federation acceded to the wishes of southerners in denying representation to a black club from Boston. The 1916 convention in High Point featured an "appetizing luncheon" hosted by the United Daughters of the Confederacy, who gifted each member a rebel flag. Touring a local mill, each woman went home with a souvenir of raw silk tied daintily in baby blue ribbon. This genteel hospitality occurred as Gertrude and other clubwomen were agitating on behalf of exploited child and female millworkers. The irony was not lost on Anna Hardwicke Pennybacker, General Federation president, who attended the meeting. She declared that "reports on health, literary work, social service, and civic cleanliness would produce more happiness than club flowers and club colors—once so prominent."[55]

Gertrude and Sallie Southall Cotten exemplified the women's club's multigenerational culture. "Our club women have the virtues and accomplishments of the 'old-fashioned' woman with the mental equipment of the Woman of To-Day," read a 1908 statement. The Daughters of the American Revolution affiliated. The clubs continued their earlier incarnations as literary societies, social gatherings, and venues for self-improvement. In 1906 the Goldsboro women studied Shakespeare's plays as well as Emilie Poulsson's *Love and Law in Child Training*. These progressive women also adopted a club flower and exchanged recipes. In 1912 Gertrude, a theater buff, acted in "My Marriage," a play written by Ruth Weil from a sketch in *Ladies Home Journal*. The annual book reception might feature Etta Spier lecturing on drama or Sallie Kirby singing. Originally meeting in rooms above a Chinese laundry, the women in 1912 began a collection to build a Goldsboro clubhouse.[56]

Generational wheels were turning in club politics. At Wilmington in 1907 Gertrude was elected state General Federation secretary, which positioned her to advance progressive policies as the liaison to the national Federation. A youth rebellion was afoot. A year later in Greensboro, Federation president Margaret Lovell Gibson engaged Gertrude in political stratagems. Gertrude had revised the state bylaws to conform to the national ones. Gibson wanted to sidestep an old-guard conservative from Goldsboro who had helped frame the original document. So as not to show "discourtesy to an older person" Gibson had Miss Weil introduce the resolution and chair the committee. Charming and likable, amenable to southern ladies and New Women, Gertrude negotiated troublesome issues without offending. Yet her frustration was sometimes palpable. When she attempted to create a free kindergarten in Goldsboro, other members preferred to spend the funds on a fountain at the public school, a City Beautiful project. "Now it seems the Club cannot see its way clear to establish the kindergarten," the newspaper reported. In her own household, Gertrude and her mother shared progressive views on juvenile justice and child labor reform, but a generational divide persisted on women's suffrage.[57]

At its best, women's club work reconciled Gertrude's multiple identities. Her trip to the General Federation of Women's Clubs' Biennial in May 1910 demonstrated club work's holism. She accompanied Aunt Sarah to Cincinnati. There, with family friend Belle Lowenstein, she took country rides and visited the Jewish Kitchen Garden Association and Trade School for Girls, where she observed "dress-making, embroidery, millinery, cooking, and house-work." She lunched with Smith alumnae and enjoyed a recital at a National Council of Jewish Women reception. She attended temple, where she heard a sermon on child labor. At a club meeting with Esther Straus, she joined "very interesting women both Jews and non."[58]

The women's club became Gertrude's friendship circle, reconciling family and social claims. Federation Gertie led, spoke, wrote, edited, chaired, performed, and organized. In 1909 she headed the Federation's Publications Committee, while her mother served on Industrial and Child Labor Committee and Sarah on the Legislative Committee. Sarah's passion was the library extension department, while Mina worked on education. Cousin Edna, chairing the Village Improvement Committee, organized the town's garden club. In 1906, when Sallie Kirby was club president, Mina served as vice president and Gertrude as recording secretary. Gertrude was the North Carolina reporter to the *Keynote*, a regional club newsletter published by noted Charleston activist Louisa Poppenheim, a Vassar graduate and pioneering new southern woman. Reviving the moribund North Carolina column, Gertrude established a statewide network that would prove useful in her suffrage and social welfare campaigns. Gertrude often took the role of writer. If only the public were educated, she believed, citizens would recognize the rightness of the cause. Joe Robinson, editor of Goldsboro's *Weekly Argus*, gave the local woman's club a column, which was signed "Club Woman" or "Gertrude Weil."[59]

A Social Justice Agenda

Gertrude's cause was to commit the Women's Club movement to social welfare and economic justice. At the state Federation's convention in Goldsboro in 1905, Dr. A. J. McKelway, a Presbyterian minister and crusading editor of the *Charlotte News*, rallied the women to child labor reform. Introduced by Charles B. Aycock, McKelway described factories where he witnessed "little children spending all their days that should be filled with sunshine and laughter in the mills." He urged women to take up the cause and help enact legislation. As McKelway sat down, Mina rose to describe the Goldsboro club's program for millworkers' children.[60] Labor advocacy, Gertrude knew, was radical in the industrial New South. By lobbying, women intruded into male political precincts.

At Edmundstown, Gertrude had been educated firsthand in the conditions of the laboring poor. Her interest deepened in workers' rights. In 1903 the North Carolina General Assembly passed a law, without enforcement provisions, forbidding employment of those under twelve and limiting the work week for those under eighteen to sixty-six hours. In 1904 the National Child Labor Committee was formed, and supported by the likes of Charles B. Aycock and Josephus Daniels, a campaign gained momentum to raise the working age and require schooling of children. With Mina serving on its Industrial and Child Labor Committee, the Federation in 1908 lobbied for a compulsory education law to keep children out of the factories.

In 1909, when Greensboro textile industrialist Julius Cone invited Gertrude horseback riding, she responded by describing her mill town sewing class and "spoke out" for workers' "welfare." He asked her not to "overlook the fact there are two sides to this question" and sent her literature explaining the manufacturers' viewpoint. He had been "made to feel the ingratitude of our laborers." A year later Gertrude sent inquires to Greensboro attorney David Stern concerning taxes on labor agents. Her advocacy would be built on "fact finding."[61]

Gertrude's challenge was to overcome the elitism inherit in the ladies' bountiful calls for labor reform. Class differences challenged solidarity with their working-class sisters. At a Monthly Mothers Meeting in Edmundstown, clubwomen attempted "through pleasant talks and intercourse with these women to enrich their lives & lead them to higher ideals." Through traveling libraries the women selected literature that they believed uplifting. The women's movement expressed social Darwinist rhetoric about "higher types."[62]

Birth control and eugenics, advanced by national advocate Margaret Sanger, engaged the Weil women. Then regarded as progressive policies, they were popularly disdained as radical and socialist. Among the supporters was Jane Addams. In 1913 Mina had attended eugenics lectures and read literature that warned against the "inbreeding of the feeble-minded." Two years later the Federation convention featured Dr. C. Banks McNairy of the North Carolina School for the Feeble Minded at Kinston, who declared that the "only way to wipe out this menace to the population is by segregation, education, and sterilization." He wanted North Carolina to take the lead. Gertrude's friend Susan Moses Graham sent her literature from

Sanger on birth control. In 1916 Sanger had opened a clinic, which led to her arrest for disseminating obscene material. Sanger believed that women's vote would lead states to enact birth control legislation. Though it was politically contentious, Gertrude joined the campaign.[63]

If Gertrude could not prevent the birth of delinquent youth, she worked to rehabilitate them. Prison reform had interested her since Horace Mann. Nationally, women's organizations, including Jewish ones like the Council, were dedicated to juvenile justice and prison reform. Since 1906 Gertrude had served as a probation officer for the Goldsboro Juvenile Court. She joined Federation campaigns to separate youthful offenders from hardened criminals, advocating reform schools for boys and then girls, first for whites and then for blacks. In 1909 the state responded with the Stonewall Jackson Manual Training and Industrial School, followed nine years later by Samarcand Manor, the State Home and Industrial School for Girls. In 1915 the legislature passed a Probation Courts Act with a separate judicial track for juveniles. In 1919 Kate Burr Johnson, state director of child welfare, wrote Gertrude, "Your juvenile court here in North Carolina is splendid and gives us the machinery to do most progressive work."[64]

Not Yet Race

Gertrude's prison advocacy led to the more obdurate issue of race. The deplorable condition of African American prisoners in the Wayne County jail offended a committee from the Goldsboro Woman's Club. In March 1902, the Village Improvement Committee published in the *Weekly Argus* a scathing report on the jail signed anonymously "Club Woman"—the byline belonged to Gertrude, and one can hear her voice. The article described as unfit for dogs the "degrading" and "demoralizing" treatment of presumably innocent prisoners awaiting trial: "You say they are negroes.... Are they not the nurses for our children? Are they not the cooks in our kitchen and the laborers in our fields? And yet in a city of churches, a civilized land, they are imprisoned in a hostel infested with lice, without ventilation, given no exercise ... [they] march up and down their cells like the wild animals we see in circuses." The ladies' committee protested to the chairman of the Board of County Commissioners. When a Mr. Briggs disputed the facts, the club reporter attacked him as a "worthless, weak character about town" who "presumes to ask the citizens of Wayne county to believe his testimony" and not that "by six of Goldsboro's women whose evidence would be taken in any court in the United States." Such rhetoric from a white woman was intemperate, coming soon after black disfranchisement. Political campaigns commonly depicted blacks as criminals and rapacious beasts. Beyond race, the reporter refuted any challenge to women's legal status as witnesses. The county responded by investigating and then agreeing to enlarge and improve the jail.[65]

Gertrude did not yet identify publicly as a racial liberal. Nine years later, writing to attorney David Stern of Greensboro, she was not so solicitous of civil liberties. In 1910 Stern had defended a "bad, bad Negro" convicted of his fourth crime who had been sentenced longer than the law prescribed. Gertrude saw a conflict of "right & justice" versus "carrying out the law." She could "somewhat forgive" Stern for taking the case but accused him of "confusing the means with the end."[66] This exchange took place when lynching challenged the rule of law. Some clubwomen were involved in interracial work, which was permissible within the racial code if it concerned economic uplift and involved what was deemed the better class of educated African Americans. No record suggests Gertrude yet participating.

Civic Education

The women's club was Gertrude's postgraduate school. She had lamented matriculating at Smith unskilled, but under the professorship of Sallie Southall Cotten she was learning public relations, organizational management, government affairs, and political gamesmanship. Like Adeline Moffatt in Northampton, Massachusetts, Cotten proved a savvy mentor. In contrast to Mina, whose demands Gertrude could rarely satisfy, Cotten did not tolerate Gertrude's self-abasement. After Gertrude as recording secretary apologized to President Cotten for her editing of the Federation yearbook, Cotten in a jocular letter threatened to "punish" her for slandering herself. Gertrude was a friend of her daughter Agnes and visited Cottendale plantation frequently—on occasion Mother Cotten addressed Gertrude as "Child." Sallie observed in her diary how much she enjoyed Gertrude's visits, how the two busied themselves all day reading minutes and editing the yearbook. They traveled together organizing clubs. When Wilson women gathered in May 1915, Cotten spoke on the need to be progressive and to cooperate with men, while Gertrude explained the club's function and structure. A 1917 diary records the two visiting small towns across eastern North Carolina—Mt. Olive, Washington, Seven Springs, Rosewood, Fremont—seeding clubs. Cotten was grooming Gertrude for leadership, and her blessing gave her protégé cachet. At the 1910 General Federation Biennial in Cincinnati, Gertrude was appointed an "inspector of tellers" for ballot boxes and learned the mechanics of running a fair election. In 1916 Gertrude was again elected state secretary.[67]

Francis Squire Potter of the General Federation invited Gertrude—

after admonishing her as "entirely too modest"—to serve on its national Literature and Library Extension Committee. Gertrude, experienced in "study clubs of small towns," complained of a "tendency" to "cover much ground superficially." Clubs needed to "extend their aim from Self-culture to community culture" through public lectures. Gertrude apologized that her own tastes were literary and offered to make study outlines of Browning or perhaps Ibsen, Maeterlinck, Shaw, or Wilde. The growth from self-improvement to civic action, from literary societies to public campaigns, lay at the heart of an evolving women's movement.[68]

Club work for Gertrude, as for her circle of women, served as a springboard to civic and professional careers. Gertrude worked closely with Laura Weill Cone, Annie Land O'Berry, and Kate Burr Johnson. Like Gertrude, all were northern educated. In 1919 Johnson, studying at the New York School of Social Work, wrote that "that there is no one from 'down home' that we would love so much to have with us in New York . . . as Gertrude Weil."[69] Each would break precedents in working for social reform, racial justice, or public service.

Women's clubs followed a process of civic engagement: the club identified a problem, initiated a program, lobbied government to take responsibility, and then after reforms were enacted took on a new challenge. Women's club causes—education, social welfare, labor rights—all required political action and passage of new laws. In 1902 Sarah led drives to create traveling county libraries, which inspired the city to open its first public library. The Federation lobbied for a state library commission, and when the legislature created one in 1909, Sarah was appointed vice chair.[70]

Gertrude's public health advocacy followed a similar path. Through the Goldsboro Woman's Club, Mina and Gertrude paid personally for a county public health nurse. North Carolina clubs lobbied for each county to establish health departments and pressed the legislature to adopt such a law. The Goldsboro Club's first effort was to keep pigs and chickens off the streets and to have food stores install screens. The women pressed for clean water and milk. With Goldsboro's Club leading, women, inspired by federal legislation, pushed the state legislature to create a model pure food bill. In 1909 the state instituted a public health director, and counties were entrusted to create health departments. Clubwomen were appointed welfare directors. Public health nursing was introduced statewide. In 1914 the Goldsboro Club reported that "one of their long and dearly cherished dreams has been realized," the appointment of a veterinary surgeon as sanitary inspector to examine the milk supply, meat slaughter, and sale of food stuffs. The

Ladies Benevolent Society became the Charity Organization Society, with Gertrude as caseworker.[71]

If women were to achieve their civic goals, Gertrude well knew, they needed to secure the vote. The "development from religious societies to self-improvement clubs, to civic improvement, to suffrage" was not an orderly process.[72] Although men and women organized the state's first suffrage group in Asheville in 1894, it soon disbanded. A women's suffragist bill introduced in the North Carolina General Assembly was referred to the committee on insane asylums. National suffragists visited North Carolina only to find the state preoccupied with black disfranchisement. Sallie Southall Cotten herself was "leaving the suffrage question to the younger women." At home Gertrude and grandmother Eva were "fighting," and neither Mina nor Sarah shared Gertrude's suffragist sympathies. Leaders of the National Council of Jewish Women—including its founder, Hannah Solomon—joined the campaign, but the membership failed to pass a suffragist resolution. In 1907, when a Federation officer requested that the "charming Miss Weil" attend a lecture in Wilmington by Dr. Elizabeth Delia Dixon-Carroll on "Women in Civics and the Home," Aunt Sarah responded that the "family are very much opposed" to her going. Gertrude's friends Sallie Kirby and Susie Fulghum pulled her in the other direction, and she defiantly went.[73]

Gertrude recognized the utility and good work of the women's club, but she was reconsidering her priorities. Gertrude served as first vice president of the state Federation in 1914, and a year later her nomination for president was greeted with such "a spontaneous ovation" that "several minutes elapsed before Miss Weil could be heard, declining the honor." The members rejected her refusal, insisting that she had served ably and broadly. Colleagues noted in Gertrude, as a club historian wrote, a character that was "keen in mind . . . fearless and courageous" but also "modest and retiring." On boards she took working positions like secretary or, if petitioners persisted, she agreed to "acting" chair or president. She was adamant in declining the Federation presidency, perhaps eyeing the suffrage campaign ahead.[74]

Gertrude, as she became more political, maintained the demeanor of the southern lady. In 1909 when clubwomen, meeting in Raleigh, visited the governor's mansion, Gertrude, dressed in "pink suisine with old lace and pearls," stood in the receiving line with the governor. The magazine *Everything*, profiling Gertrude in 1913, admired her "trained intellect," "fidelity," and "tact." It continued, "Although still young she possesses a poise which comes only from experience, and which is stimulated but never overpowered by her enthusiasm.... Positions of honor come to her because she has proved her ability to fill them." It concluded, "Progressive yet sane, cultured yet unassuming, she possesses always that sweet graciousness of manner" which is the mark of "southern womanhood." She was "beloved."[75]

Gertrude learned to negotiate complexities. She made peace with her mother. Through the Woman's Club, she could fight for unpopular causes while preserving decorum. Women recognized that, as Annie Nathan Meyer, a National Council of Jewish Women member and founder of Barnard College, suggested, "to put any radical scheme across, it must be done in the most conservative manner possible." Even radical Charlotte Perkins Gilman argued for incremental progress. Relative to British feminist militants who resorted to violence, American activist women were well behaved. In the conservative, tradition-bound South, propriety was both a custom and a strategy.[76]

Educated at Smith in the new ideologies of social and political reform, Gertrude was moving beyond the North Carolina consensus in her growing involvement in women's suffrage and labor rights and her tentative forays into racial justice. Her political outlook was that of a college-educated New Woman eager to apply the modern practices of social science to systemic economic problems. She envisioned expanded roles for government. Feeling frustrated at the pace of change, she sought new agencies beyond the Women's Club to realize her ideals. In 1910 she wrote Janet, "I shall be 31 years old to-morrow. What do you think of that! It sure does sound astounding. I only hope that when you reach that mature age you can be prouder of your accomplishments than I."[77] The problems of the South required political action beyond benevolence and club work. However sweet and well mannered, Gertrude was harboring radical thoughts. The contradictions of her character gave balance to her life as she tempered her idealism with pragmatism. She was progressive but sane, *Everything* reported.[78] Sanity and progress would be put to the test as Gertrude Weil fought new battles to bring the vote to women, and the world prepared for war.

{ 4 }

HOLDING HER BREATH
Conflicts Personal and Global

Now in her thirties, at home in Goldsboro, Gertrude Weil was living her ideals. Behind her was the college student asserting her autonomy and the lady of leisure bereft of purpose. On Chestnut Street she became her mother's guardian, a stalwart of her temple, and a leading citizen activist. She would not marry, guarding her independence, but would retain her fealty to family, faith, and community. Even as she upended established gender and political hierarchies, she alluded to her "provincial bringing up" and the "good of social conventions." She wanted change, but orderly change that befitted her modest character and conservative society. She became a woman at ease with herself, so likable with her kindly manner, ready laugh, and youthful enthusiasms, so admirable with her high intelligence and selfless dedication to her causes. Circumstances, personal and global, soon tested her resilience.

Prior to the Great War, Gertrude's primary platform for activism remained the Goldsboro Woman's Club, but she was pulling it in more political, confrontational directions. In its early years, Gertrude reflected, the club "occupied almost all our attention—it was an end in itself." As women grew "more accustomed to its machinery," she continued, women "realized that it was a mere tool to use for something more real and vital" for "good ends," such as public health, child welfare, and labor justice. Although Women's Clubs effected changes in "laws and conditions," they had done so through "indirect influence," Gertrude observed. Increasingly, she recognized, "We have felt a lack of power to make *effective* our ideas."[1]

By 1911 the state Federation began addressing legal and political disabilities that discriminated against women. Their initiatives—protections for children's and women's labor, minimum wages, and maximum hours—could be achieved only if women secured the ballot. In 1911 Sallie Southall

Cotten interviewed North Carolina attorney general Thomas W. Bickett, who convinced her that women had no legal standing under state law and were not entitled to hold appointive public office, not even on school boards. Cotten left wondering, "Must we all become suffragists?"[2]

Gertrude struggled to rouse other women, including her aunt and mother. She had returned from Smith a convinced suffragist. "When I came home I wondered why people made speeches in favor as something so obviously right," she recalled. In 1908 she wrote a Trinity College professor correcting him for overlooking the fact that women had "citizenship" even without the "privilege" of suffrage.[3] The Women's Club practiced democracy, with women voting for officers on "an official ballot" in a public election. Yet, even among her Smith classmates, suffrage was not popular. A poll at her tenth alumna reunion revealed that forty were "violent antis" and only eleven "do want" the ballot; another twenty admitted that they "ought to want to," while another nineteen were either "on the fence" or made "no reply." After hearing suffragist Maud Wood Park, Gertrude's former classmate Louise Kilton wrote from Ohio that she would have affiliated, "but so far I have had sufficient strength of mind and regard for dear Pres. Seelye's ideals of womanliness to stay in my peaceful, happy home instead of in public life."[4]

At home Gertrude's task was generational. In 1913 Sarah Weil invited state supreme court justice Walter Clark, a nationally known advocate of women's suffrage, to speak at the Federation's annual meeting in New Bern on "The Legal Status of Women in North Carolina." Prior to his lecture Clark sent the text to Sallie Southall Cotten, who suggested that he "omit some of it." Cotten expressed a southern lady's sensitivity to accusations of feminist militancy, advising Clark to follow "the lesson of the automobile": "To progress slowly—at the expense of possible speed is better than a wreck caused by too much speed." Clark traced women's legal status in marriage and property rights from English common law to the present day, which he disdained as "unjust." He mocked man's "idea of his superiority to woman" as something that ought to have been "spanked out of them by their mothers when they were little." He climaxed his speech with a call for women's full suffrage. Sarah Weil was so "enthusiastic" that she foresaw a new day for women: "Now they are awake!" The lecture was distributed as a pamphlet.[5] By 1911 Gertrude had joined the National American Woman Suffrage Association, and she was affiliated with the Equal Suffrage League of North Carolina chartered two years later. Women's vote was heatedly debated among the four candidates in the 1912 presidential election, which Woodrow Wilson won as a suffrage advocate. Yet, to Gertrude's dismay, neither Cotten nor her mother or aunt was yet willing to commit to the suffragist campaign. The state legislature repeatedly failed to pass laws grant-ing women voting rights in primaries or municipal elections.

If North Carolinians were reluctant to join women's march to the ballot, progress was made on other legal fronts: property rights, divorce, and equal pay, for teachers especially. Each was a struggle. In 1915, after a legislative fight, a woman won appointment as a notary public. The North Carolina General Assembly conferred upon married women the right to enter into contracts, supposedly granted by the 1868 constitution. One legislator cau-tioned, "This bill was only an entering wedge for woman suffrage in the State." He warned that the camel's nose was in the tent but behind it was the hump.[6]

Prior to suffrage, school board membership had been women's primary political goal, supported even by conservatives. That was the focus of the first state suffrage meeting in Asheville in 1894. By law women were eligible to hold "positions," but without the vote they could not hold "offices." The legal question was, what constitutes an office? Sarah learned a bitter lesson when the state library commission removed her as vice chairman after Fed-eration sponsorship ended. In 1913 the General Assembly twice killed a bill drawn by Justice Clark to permit women to hold appointive posts like the school board. Clubwomen "bombarded" legislators with letters and tele-grams. Cotten told a legislator, "We do want it." It passed a third reading when the Speaker broke a tie. The answer to Cotten's question was, yes, we must all become suffragists.[7]

A North Carolina Conference for Social Service

Frustrated with the pace of progress, Gertrude considered the larger poli-tics. In 1912 a meeting was held in Raleigh to organize the North Carolina Conference for Social Service. Such state conferences had spread across the South, starting in Virginia in 1900. "North Carolina Forward—for Human Betterment and a Richer Civilization" drew 311 attendees, with Sallie Southall Cotten speaking for the Women's Clubs. Within months over two hundred more joined, including Mina, Sarah, and Gertrude. The confer-ence inventoried causes needing legislative remedy: child labor, school at-tendance, public health, illiteracy, alcohol abuse, prostitution, and coopera-tion between church and social service agencies. It called for a state board of public welfare. A 1913 talk—reflecting the racist paternalism that under-lay progressivism—was titled "We Must Lift Up the Negro or He Will Drag Us Down."[8]

From the first the conference brought together lay leaders and university professionals. It met each spring, debated a cause, and organized a campaign of lectures, forums, and publications to arouse public awareness. Not merely content just to educate or change hearts, the conference worked to reform public policy and enact laws. The members drafted resolutions and lobbied the General Assembly. Returning from the 1914 conference meeting in Raleigh Mina agreed to chair the local club's Betterment Committee. In 1917 Gertrude lectured the conference on "The Need of a State-wide Survey of the Social and Economic Conditions of Women and Girls," and a year later she titled her talk emotionally "The Cry of the Children." Drawing from her Goldsboro casework, she described a "weakling" father and "immoral" mother with four daughters, the eldest of whom had succumbed to prostitution and illegitimate births, while the youngest was rescued from a "future of pain and vice and crime." The cry was "an appeal to our heart and intellect in equal force." She called for an "organized social service" to conduct a scientific survey, a "comparatively new" field that had yet to fix its principles. Resolutions supported state training schools for delinquent boys and girls, both black and white, as well as compulsory school attendance and child labor laws. Another perennial subject was prison reform, with calls to end flogging, dark cells, and capital punishment. Addressing the meetings was the sitting governor or headliners like Josephus Daniels or William Jennings Bryan. As Gertrude rose in the leadership, she worked intimately with Chapel Hill progressives like Howard Odum and Frank Graham, who were agents of regional change. At the conference's instigation in 1917, the State Board of Charities added "Public Welfare" to its title, and Kate Burr Johnson, Federation president, was appointed state director of child welfare.[9] Women's political future advanced in step with the progressive political agenda.

Family Catastrophes

While Gertrude busied herself in Federation and conference work, calamity twice struck her family in 1914. In August, Henry and Mina were vacationing in Atlantic City when Henry took ill. Hospitalized at Johns Hopkins in Baltimore, he died unexpectedly at sixty-eight. Seven weeks later, Solomon fell ill while traveling in New Hampshire, and he, too, died suddenly. In death as in life, Solomon followed Henry in lockstep. Tributes flowed to the homes, and newspapers eulogized. Cousins Leslie and Lionel, close as brothers, assumed patriarchal duties. Like their fathers, they lived in neighboring homes, managed family enterprises, led the synagogue, and took board positions with the city, university, and philanthropies. In their fathers' memories, Leslie and Lionel endowed at the University of North Carolina at Chapel Hill the Weil Lectures in American Citizenship, with

William Howard Taft delivering the inaugural speech in 1915. The will left Gertrude well provided. Gertrude and Mina remained in the Chestnut Street manse. In January 1915 Gertrude traveled with her mother to Hot Springs in the North Carolina mountains for a prolonged stay. Later that year Mina, Gertrude, and Janet, joined at times by Herman, took a long, re-storative cross-country journey as far west as Vancouver. Gertrude became caretaker for her dependent mother. The two women bonded in their public welfare work, and Gertrude pulled Mina toward politics. In 1915 Mina took her late husband's seat on the Goldsboro school board. The newspaper ex-claimed, "The election of Mrs. [Mina] Weil to the Board of Trustees of the graded schools of Goldsboro marks the beginning of a new era in the edu-cation life of the progressive city, and a new era in the status of women in municipal government."[10]

World at War

After her father's death, Gertrude continued serving on Club committees, although she declined the Federation presidency. By 1916 she was again president of the Goldsboro Woman's Club. Increasingly her priority be-came organizing for suffragism. The outbreak of war in April 1917 diverted her attentions. The Weils joined women engaged in volunteer work with the Red Cross. Gertrude was appointed an instructor of surgical dressings and membership chair, traveling as a recruiter. Mina chaired the Civilian Relief Committee and set up an office in her living room, where she as-sisted families of servicemen and collected old clothes for Belgian relief. The family donated fifteen hundred dollars for an ambulance in memory of Henry and Sol.[11]

In 1917 Gertrude's Women's Club colleague Laura Holmes Reilley, state director of the Council of National Defense, appointed her state chair of the Department for the Maintenance of Existing Social Service Agencies. Its purpose was to ensure that social services did not collapse with the on-set of war as had happened in Britain. Her bailiwick covered "associated charities, the orphans home, the hospitals and all philanthropic institutions in the state." The central committee in Washington sent her circulars list-ing policies to adopt locally. Despite objections, Reilley boldly maintained a racially integrated program. By December 1917 Gertrude reported that the committee had covered thirty-four counties. Rather than create new associations, she would "secure the support and cooperation" of existing ones. The task was unrelenting. North Carolina, Gertrude noted, was "a state of rural communities and small towns and cities," and local agencies were "in no case highly organized." Women, she found, lacked "initiative," so she made her proposals as "definite as possible." The department's primary work was publicity to ensure that financing charities was regarded a need rather than a "luxury."[12]

In 1918 Gertrude served as county chair of the World Relief Committee under the U.S. Food Administration. Gertrude delivered patriotic speeches calling upon public sacrifice. Women were encouraged to plant year-round gardens to increase food production. Responding to widespread starvation in Europe, which continued beyond war's end, she organized schoolhouse meetings to instruct "dear friend and patriot" on food conservation. "The people of our country have an opportunity to render the world and humanity a service that will not be forgotten as long as history is read," she told one crowd.[13]

As president of the Goldsboro Woman's Club, Gertrude held study sessions on the social and political implications of the war. She led semimonthly book reviews while also lecturing on garden fertilizers. Gertrude threw herself into the war bond campaign of the Woman's Liberty Loan Committee. The drive gave women practical experience in fundraising and in building a national grassroots organization. The campaign had a domestic theme: "A Bond in Every Home." Gertrude advised her neighborhood canvassers to "go over your assigned territory EXHAUSTIVELY" and "report to district chairman." Her notes recorded who was "hopeless" and who had a "rich husband," and she reminded them to "always stay cheerful." In 1918 the state chairman congratulated Gertrude for having raised $106,400 in Wayne County, which included $6,000 from Mina, $6,000 from the Rosenthals, and $5,000 from Aunt Sarah.[14]

The Weils' German heritage—family still lived there—did not temper their patriotism. The unity fostered by the war effort marked these native-born children of Jewish Germans as normative Americans. When German artillery approached Paris, Gertrude "pictured the Louvre in flames and the Arc de Triumph shattered." She was holding her "breath—since weeping would be useless." Gertrude worried about her friend Harriet Payne, who, after undergoing a tonsillectomy and hysterectomy, sailed to France with the Red Cross in June 1918 to work in a children's home and soldiers' canteen. From Paris she wrote Gertrude that she was lonely and homesick. The two women agreed that "bloodshed … is too depressing." Payne added, "Weltschmerz! It's almost incurable."[15]

The war left the Weils grieving. Arthur Bluethenthal, Herman's friend and brother of Janet's husband, Herbert, had joined the French Flying Corps after graduating from Princeton, where he had been a football All-American. In 1918 he was shot down and killed, the first North Carolina fatality. Days before his death he had written Mina thanking her for a box of candy. Mina sent roses and then rushed to the Bluethenthal home in Wilmington. "Poor Arthur," Mina wrote Gertrude, "went down in a flame of glory in the fields of France." Wilmington observed citywide mourning and named its airfield for him. Gertrude sent candy to another soldier, Edward Blum, a Baltimore cousin. His father forwarded a newspaper report from him describing battlefields strewn with decomposed bodies and stacked corpses. Jumping into a foxhole, he landed on a severed arm and leg.[16] For Gertrude, antiwar feeling was visceral.

In her Red Cross work Gertrude was dedicated to the soldiers' welfare. With her mother she hosted picnics at camps, wrapped bandages, and sent Christmas packets. She compiled lists of Wayne County soldiers, tracking down addresses to send them "Smileage Books," which contained coupons for admission to wholesome theatricals. "Sure appreciated it to the highest of pleasure," soldier George Franklin wrote her. At war's end Gertrude wrote "home folks" asking them to donate letters from their boys at the front for a Wayne County memorial. The letters, some written from hospital wards, described the "hell" of bombardment, frozen limbs, and gas in the lungs, always expressing wishes to return to a mother or father. Some were all the more eloquent for being semiliterate. In years following Gertrude committed herself to antiwar work through suffragist and women's organizations. On the first Armistice Day, she reflected on the "war to end wars:" "Shall we be realists in our ideals? Or shall we discard our ideals as impracticable?"[17]

The war had a specifically Jewish dimension for the Weils. East European Jews were trapped between the lines, accused by Germans and Russians alike of disloyalty. Hundreds of thousands were starved, expelled, or massacred. Prominent New York philanthropists, Jewish and Christian, created a Jewish War Sufferers campaign. North Carolina's goal was set at $100,000, with Lionel Weil as state committee chair. Governor Thomas W. Bickett proclaimed Jewish Relief Day, and one Sunday churches held a "union service" followed by an "intensive campaign." Well over three hundred communities contributed almost $150,000, and Lionel's North Carolina Plan of a statewide appeal to Christians as well as Jews became a national model. Goldsboro was the state's most generous community, raising over $13,000. Coming when nativism was rising nationally, and only three years after the Leo Frank lynching in Atlanta, the campaign demonstrated goodwill toward Jews. In an appeal, the Raleigh News and Observer declared the Jew "proves in this country a useful and valued citizen."[18] Politicians who became targets of Gertrude's suffragist lobbying—Bickett and

O. Max Gardner current and future governors, among them—prominently lent their names.

Scarcely had the war ended when North Carolina was struck by the influenza epidemic, which killed 50 million worldwide. Janet wrote of people walking the streets covered with face masks. Gertrude abandoned her "refined surroundings" and with Mina tended the poor. Once Mina pulled up in her buggy at a home to inquire how the family was coping. A man on the porch told her, "fine," that a Red Cross nurse was inside. When Mina discovered that worker was Gertrude, she laughed, knowing how little her daughter knew about nursing. "You are indeed a heroine to go into the homes of the poor to nurse," a friend wrote. "It takes courage of a high order to face dirt, germs, and degeneracy." Early in 1919 Gertrude became "one of the many victims of the Influenza." With her mother "watching ... like a hawk," Gertrude dismissed it as a "light case."[19] Gertrude was doubtlessly mindful of her dear friends Susan Moses Graham, who had died in 1916, and her husband Edward, president of the University of North Carolina, who had succumbed months earlier. By the end of January Gertrude recovered, and she was soon traveling.

"Influenza has certainly crippled our work," Julia Dameron, a Warrenton teacher and woman's rights advocate, wrote Gertrude on behalf of the North Carolina Educational Association in 1918. Dameron's group had suggested forming an umbrella council consisting of representatives from a coalition of women's organizations as a legislative lobby on education. "You can have some idea of how we feel about you," Dameron wrote Gertrude in asking her to lead, "from the fact that you and you only were suggested at our first meeting as chairman."[20] Such a legislative council did not form until 1921.

With peace abroad, the nation turned to domestic needs. In 1919 the *Raleigh News and Observer* saluted Goldsboro's urban and industrial growth, but Gertrude, signing herself "A Citizen of Goldsboro," wrote the editor that more significant than "material progress" was the city's reform with a managerial system of government, including a superintendent of public welfare. The public library held forty-five hundred volumes. The Charity Organization Society supported a public health nurse, and War Camp Community Service work was transitioning to peace time. The writer failed to mention that a Weil led, financed, or helped implement every reform.[21]

Death, war, and epidemic, all tested a still relatively young woman idealistically committed to reforming her community and the world. Her twenties had been years of questioning her place as a Weil, Jew, and citizen. Personal trauma and global events consumed her attention without diverting her from her vision of a just society. That meant the civic betterment of Goldsboro and North Carolina. To end war, it also meant supporting Woodrow Wilson's crusade for a World Court and a League of Nations. These ambitions, she knew, could be realized only if women achieved their rights. Gertrude said that she would not compartmentalize her life. In coming home, Gertrude also grounded herself spiritually, and if she held to her ideals in troubled times, it owed to the durability of her religious foundation.

{ 5 }

GREATER HEIGHTS OF
SPIRITUAL ACHIEVEMENTS
A Jewish Light unto the Nations

Addressing the Fifth Annual Conference of the North Carolina Association of Jewish Women in Durham in 1926, President Gertrude Weil told
the members that rather than bore them with a report she would "suggest
a standard by which to measure our progress": "Our one big purpose, it
seems to me, is to hold the torch of idealism before our people, and so to
the rest of the world, to remind our Jewish people not only of their noble
past and their leadership in by-gone days, but to prod them to still greater
heights of spiritual achievements—to stimulate our consciousness of the
great, the good, the beautiful in the unseen world of mind and a consequent
ennobling of our daily lives."[1]

If Gertrude Weil's mysteries need illumination, as historian Anne Firor
Scott suggests,[2] they can be elucidated through her Judaism. It was her
spiritual core, a constant in her variegated career as social welfare activist
and peace advocate. Gertrude's Judaism was anything but the fossil religion
of its detractors. In Judaism she rooted her aspiration to realize the ideal.
Conceptually, this transcendental trinity of "the great, the good, the beautiful in the unseen world of mind" may seem more Platonic than Mosaic, but
her views reflected an American Judaism undergoing profound historic reforms during the near century that she lived. Her theology was consonant
with reason and science; her practice, with social justice and progressive
politics. Hers was a Judaism acculturated to the times, affirming its commonalities with other faiths and universalizing its message to other peoples.

The image of the uplifted torch suggests an Israel that was to be, in the
words of the prophet Isaiah, a "light unto the nations." If Gertrude wanted
Israel's beacon to shine on the nations, so too did she want the nations to

enlighten Israel. The imagery evokes the Statue of Liberty, which, though a classical icon, became for Jews a specifically Jewish-American symbol with the welcoming words of poet Emma Lazarus engraved on its pedestal.

The torch-bearing feminine icon also highlighted woman's role as the transmitter of Judaism. As Reform Jews of German origin, Gertrude, Mina, and Sarah were typical of the progressive Jewish women flocking to social justice organizations. Embracing the ethics of Classical Reform Judaism, Jewish women shared the commitment to national moral reform that Christian women found in the Social Gospel. Jewish women, too, could cite biblical verse or prophetic example to justify their civic activism as a religious mission.

In her own speculations on religion Gertrude spoke generally of Judaism but rarely referenced Reform platforms or theology. In 1909 she considered her continuing adherence to Judaism a "live issue." Lifelong she explored the spiritual foundations of social justice. She was conversant with the ideological debates coursing through American Jewry, and in her travels she sought the deep thinkers of the American rabbinate: conservative Alexander Kohut in New York and radical reformers William Rosenau and Emil Hirsch in Baltimore. Attending a lecture series by the "brilliant" Rev. Dr. Hirsch, she endorsed his "great big ideas" rather than his "small discrepancies." Hirsch was an ethical monotheist committed to social justice who battled Felix Adler's Ethical Culture, a movement that attracted Gertrude. At Cincinnati's Plum Street temple, she suffered through a "dull uninteresting sermon" on nineteenth-century German Reform theologian Abraham Geiger, but she appreciated a recently ordained, "up to date" rabbi who preached on child labor. She always described her beliefs as "personal," but like many contemporary Jewish women, her religious views largely if not entirely fit the precepts of Classical Reform Judaism.[3]

Believing ethics to be the essence of Judaism, Gertrude expected all Jews to work for social justice. Few Jewish women led national secular, progressive organizations, but they were well represented in local and state leadership positions, including in the South. Southern women like Sophie Weil Browne of Columbus, Georgia, paralleled the Weil women's trajectory from Jewish benevolence societies to Women's Clubs to civic activism. Writing of North Carolina, Goldsboro's Emma Edwards reported, "The Jewish woman gives of herself to Jewish and non-Jewish organizations alike." On the national stage Gertrude certainly knew of Lillian Wald, who founded New York's Henry Street Settlement, and Rose Schneiderman, who presided over the Women's Trade Union League for thirty years. Through her New

York visits and attendance at national conferences, she was likely familiar with Maud Nathan, who was a grande dame of social, labor, and suffragist movements, including the National Consumers League.[4]

Sisters

In 1913 Reform congregational women's auxiliaries coalesced into the National Federation of Temple Sisterhoods. Aunt Sarah served on its national board. Intended to unite local auxiliaries, Sisterhood adopted a national peace and social justice agenda, and it rivaled the National Council of Jewish Women, which was beset by factionalism and personal disputes, for Jewish woman's loyalty. In 1912 Gertrude referred to the "erstwhile Council," and her involvement faded. Weil women were charter members of the Oheb Sholom Sisterhood. Sisterhood emphasized home ceremonials, temple attendance, and Bible study. Mina, Sarah, and Gertrude had always been notable in their religious observance.[5]

Jews in small towns often enjoyed richer, more committed religious lives than those in larger metropolitan communities, where being Jewish could be taken for granted. However much Gertrude's personal beliefs challenged traditional Judaism, throughout her life she considered a duty to family, congregation, and the Jewish people a home truth. Every Jew was needed to sustain congregational life in Goldsboro, and small numbers made them more conscious of their difference. The community had declined to 125 in 1905 as German Jews died or departed. By World War I newly arriving, religiously Orthodox Polish, Latvian, and Lithuanian immigrants outnumbered established German Jews. Rabbi Julius Mayerberg, Lithuanian born, helped the immigrants, working in their stores and conducting Orthodox services after finishing Reform worship. Admitted to the bar, Mayerberg assisted Jewish lawbreakers until temple elders, jealous of the community's good name, asked him to stop. The Weil family underwrote the rabbi's salary and congregational finances, adding a temple annex in 1915 in Sol's memory.

Crossing ethnic, class, and ideological lines, Weil women welcomed the immigrants. Mina visited the new families to enlist their membership in Oheb Sholom, and they enrolled their children in Gertrude's Sunday school. The congregation wavered in its movement toward Reform Judaism as it sought to accommodate immigrant traditionalists, who held separate services in a rented hall. Oheb Sholom had joined the Union of American Hebrew Congregations in 1890, but it rejected its Union Prayer Book until 1913, when it was adopted for Friday nights only. Otherwise, the conservative Szold prayer book prevailed. Within her congregation Gertrude encountered varieties of religious experience. Oheb Sholom minutes record conflicts between liberals and traditionalists. Gertrude expressed democratic and egalitarian religious views, which likely put her in conflict with the rabbi, who shared the immigrants' religious background. Not until 1924, when Rabbi Mayerberg retired, did the congregation wholly commit to Union worship, with more English brought into the ritual. When American-born, Reform Rabbi Abe Shinedling arrived, women were granted full membership.

Social and religious distinctions lessened over time as East European Jewish peddlers and storekeepers climbed into the middle class, sent their children to college, and acculturated as Americans. Amy Meyers Krumbein, daughter of Latvian immigrants, recalled that Gertrude, her Sunday school teacher in the 1920s, "couldn't have cared less" about Jewish ethnic divides. Reflecting on Goldsboro, Gertrude felt that the German Jews' airs of superiority were "ludicrous," and differences with East Europeans were "superficial," a matter of having immigrated a "few years earlier."[6] From her congregational experience, Gertrude learned to accommodate, and she spoke inclusively of "Judaism" and the "Jewish people," eschewing divisive ethnic or movement labels.

As immigrant Jews moved into the American heartland, Goldsboro remained an outpost on the Jewish map. The town received a stream of itinerant schnorrers, Jewish beggars needing money for a meal or a bus ticket to Miami or New York, and meshulachim, rabbinic emissaries collecting funds for a yeshiva in Brooklyn or an orphanage in Jerusalem. Sometimes they were hard to tell apart. They came to the Meyerses' second-hand furniture store, Amy Meyers Krumbein recalled, and her father brought them to the Weils: "It didn't matter how busy Leslie and Lionel were in the store, they would stop what they were doing and take care of him and give him money." Gertrude was also an easy mark. Her check registrar includes small sums for an orphan's kitchen, a Talmud Torah school, and the Shaare Zedek Hospital in Jerusalem.[7] That each Jew was responsible for the other was inscribed in the family covenant, nor did they want Jewish beggars to embarrass the community.

The family's Zionism embraced a Jewish nationalism contrary to the universalism of Classical Reform Judaism. What gave the Weils' Zionism special resonance was Mina's continuing friendship with Henrietta Szold, founder of Hadassah, which grew into America's largest Zionist organization. Modest and learned, the self-sacrificing Szold was a revered, even saintly figure. Her presence in Palestine validated American Zionists who had no intention of moving there. A socialist with pacifist leanings, Szold was both idealistic and pragmatic. Szold had begun her social justice career educating the Jewish immigrant poor in Baltimore. "The neighborhood idea is not well developed here," Szold wrote Mina from Jerusalem in 1921, "nor is public spiritedness or the power of public opinion.... So several of us Americans set to work at organizing the women of Jerusalem by neighborhoods." Among her early efforts were infant welfare stations and school hygiene and nurses' training. In 1921 Mina sent Szold six hundred dollars, half for the Rothschild School, and the other half, Szold wrote, was for something that "could always be referred to as 'Mrs. Weil's.'" Szold purchased tents for the Jewish scouts. She visited their first encampment on Mount Scopus, observing that it was land on which Hebrew University would arise. Szold appreciated Mina's trust when American donors often dictated to their Palestinian partners.[8]

Jewish Teacher

Upon returning from college Gertrude was recruited to teach the religious school children and did so for more than a half century. Congregations enlisted secularly educated college students not only to impart Jewish learning but also to acculturate immigrant children as American Jews. German lessons ended. Gertrude recognized that Jewish children confronted new opportunities of assimilation in an open society. Small-town Jews lacked critical mass, and they lived in communities that were pervasively Christian and churchgoing. By 1918 Gertrude was religious school principal.[9]

Gertrude took religious school seriously, but she felt disaffection among her thirty-two students. In her 1920 report as principal Gertrude noted that attendance was "not altogether satisfactory, a good many absences for insufficient reason." Three years later she observed that parents seemed "indifferent" if their children were tardy or absent and returned report cards unsigned. In 1924 she reflected, "In the days of the Ghetto there was no press of other opinions on the Jewish child, but today at every turn the child meets different ideas." The 1920s were times of growing materialism and secularism. Where Jews were once dedicated to Americanizing immigrant children, they now grew concerned about losing their Jewish identity. Women assumed school leadership, taking responsibility for the "transmission of Judaism." Gertrude's commitment to Jewish children and their education expressed a domestic feminism. Sisterhoods supported Jewish education for adults as well. Gertrude's first step was to have parents clarify their own beliefs so they could pass something to their children.[10]

Traditional Jewish education had largely focused on the rote drilling of boys for the bar mitzvah. To the contrary, Gertrude held that "the object of our religious school is to develop ideals of character and conduct as men and women and as Jews." In undated notes, Gertrude cautioned that "it is not enough that our children learn facts or acquire knowledge—our responsibility to quicken the soul life of the Jewish child, to aid in the development of his divine spirit." Children were to be educated as "messengers of truth and righteousness and a light to the nations," echoing the precepts of Classical Reform. In her 1923 report, Gertrude reiterated what she had learned in her own family: "The home is, after all, where we must look for the most decisive influence in the child's life." She ended by quoting a favorite verse, Deuteronomy 30:11–14, ending "The word is very nigh unto thee, in thy mouth and in thy heart, that thou mayest do it." That was a Gertrude truism consistent with *Bildung*, that by educating the self the ideal could be made actual.[11]

For Reform Jews decorum had become a synagogue value, in contrast to the Hebrew and Yiddish cacophony that often typified Orthodox worship. The graybeard rabbinic disciplinarians, the strange tongues and antique rites yielded to a decorous, distinctly American Reform Judaism. The opening exercises came from the Moses hymnal, a popular collection intended as a Jewish response to Christian worship. "Come Forth and Bring Your Garlands," the children sang at the springtime flower service. Hymns were followed by Bible readings and speeches. Rather than the bar mitzvah for boys, the coming-of-age ceremony was now Confirmation for boys and girls alike. Children marched in solemn procession—boys in suits, girls in white dresses clutching bouquets—while the choir sang "Father, See Thy Suppliant Children." They recited their catechism "I am a Jew" and "Confession of Faith." The rabbi blessed them, after which Gertrude presented Bibles and Leslie handed certificates. The school borrowed from the public schools in issuing grades and report cards. At year's end the children enjoyed a picnic. As school principal, Gertrude became a theatrical impresario for a new generation reprising her childhood roles in "Purim Play in Five Acts" or a "Chanukah Jumble." Casts included great-nieces and nephews.[12]

Decorum also involved acculturating immigrant children as Americans, in Gertrude's case as southern ladies and gentlemen. Amy Meyers Krumbein, from a poor immigrant family, recalled how in the 1920s "Miss Gertrude" brought Sunday school students to her home for dinner, where they ate on fine china. "She welcomed you as an equal," Krumbein observed, "regardless of your station in life." At one such dinner a student mistook the finger-dip bowl for soup. "Miss Gertrude was an idol to me," Krumbein recalled. "We all wanted to be educated because she was educated."[13]

Gertrude instilled feelings of responsibility for global Jewry as an extended family. Children brought coins, the money donated to charities like the Hebrew Orphans' Home in Atlanta or the War Orphans Bureau. In 1923 Goldsboro's children adopted five-year-old Alan Mindel in the shtetl of Danilowitz, Russia, sending him one hundred dollars a year as well as a cap, sweater, and stockings.[14]

North Carolina Association of Jewish Women

Gertrude's principal Jewish organizational commitment was to the North Carolina Association of Jewish Women (NCAJW), founded in 1921 when Aunt Sarah convened a statewide meeting at Oheb Sholom. Gertrude and Mina were among the fifty-seven charter members. Gertrude recalled, "The purpose, I fancy was somewhat vague in the mind of Mrs. Sol Weil." Her intent was to "get the women acquainted … develop solidarity" and "know their Judaism, why they are Jews."[15] Gertrude was a lifetime board member. In 1924 she served the first of her three terms as president.

The NCAJW was unique nationally as a state Jewish women's organization, and it reflected the specific character of North Carolina. Sarah recognized the difficulty of unifying North Carolina Jewry. Coastal Wilmington was far culturally as well as geographically from Appalachian Asheville. Jews, who needed community for sustenance, were scattered in small towns across a distant landscape. North Carolina did not have a Baltimore or New York City to serve as an in-state Jewish capital. Goldsboro could support a congregation and Sunday school, but not Mount Olive or Swannanoa. A 1929 survey revealed forty-eight towns with one to five Jewish families. The NCAJW would "extend a sisterly hand" to the "families living in isolated sections" and "let them know that though far away from Jewish contact, they were not forgotten by their more fortunate sisters."[16]

Typically, Jewish women were united through local chapters of national organizations like Hadassah, Sisterhood, or the National Council of Jewish Women. Excepting Hadassah, which as a Zionist society appealed especially to women of East European origin, these groups tended to be led by Reform Jews of German descent. They reflected the fractures in American Jewry. National Jewish women's associations, including the National Council of Jewish Women, wanted the NCAJW to affiliate under its banner, but the North Carolina women decreed "no entangling alliances." Their ambition was to bring women together regardless of ethnic background, movement affiliation, or Zionist orientation. They wanted to avoid the political factionalism and personal conflicts that tore at national groups, including resentments over New York's growing dominance. After a year the NCAJW

Jewish Synagogue. GOLDSBORO, N. C.

Oheb Sholom (1886) replicated the Romanesque architecture of its Baltimore parent synagogue. Courtesy of the State Archives of North Carolina.

claimed 556 members in forty-six towns. By 1927 it counted 781 women in sixty-six towns.[17]

"It makes no difference to me if such leaders be orthodox or reform, are members of Hadassah, Council, or Sisterhood," Gertrude reported as chair of an NCAJW advisory committee. "Whatever their little differences of background or custom (which are of no importance), they should be broad minded, generous and capable of working for the common good." She noted that in the NCAJW, "again and again this uniting of Jewish women has been emphasized."[18] Her frequent calls for unity suggest that community divisions persisted.

Gertrude traveled to small towns where scattered Jewish families gathered for holidays and social occasions, especially to bond with their children. Gertrude's datebooks report her visiting places like Plymouth, Hamlet, and Enfield. When she spoke at a home in Weldon, Harry Kittner recalled, men gathered on the front porch while women held a district meeting in the parlor. Gertrude was "always held in awe," he observed. She built relationships with Jewish activist women who formed not just an organizational network but also a friendship circle. Her immersion in the NCAJW was total: among her many efforts, she revised its constitution, chaired its Student Activity Committee, helped found its Youth Association, and headed its Program Committee. At one conference the women honored her as "the Jack of All Trades" and serenaded her, "Let us tell you, Gertrude, we're in love with you."[19]

That the NCAJW formed a year after the enactment of women's suffrage was no coincidence. As models the NCAJW followed the examples of Women's Clubs and the League of Women Voters, and its leaders came from those ranks. Traveling the state, Gertrude often did double duty, meeting with Jewish women for lunch and then speaking at a League meeting after dinner. Following the Club and League plan, Gertrude divided the state NCAJW by districts. Among its first acts was a cause dear to Sarah Weil from her club days, a traveling library of Jewish books. Sarah also created in her mother's memory the Sophia Einstein Loan Fund to support college students, again modeled on a club program. Although it resisted national affiliations, the NCAJW supported the national agenda of progressive organizations, both Jewish and secular, like the National Council of Jewish Women or League.

Importantly, these women transformed the American synagogue. National Jewish leaders like Rebekah Kohut rooted political suffrage in Jewish traditions and pressed for religious reform. After winning the vote and organizing the NCAJW, women demanded equal congregational membership. Gertrude's suffragist colleagues Etta Spier and Miriam Lindau won such rights at Temple Emanuel in Greensboro in 1923, and a year later Goldsboro's Oheb Sholom granted women "full privileges of membership ... with voting rights."[20]

As chair of the NCAJW Religious Education Committee, Gertrude organized statewide teacher institutes, starting with a one-day affair attended by thirty-five in 1924. Six years later it met at Camp Osceola near Hendersonville for ten days. At statewide gatherings, Gertrude met the leading lights of American Judaism. At one Jewish Leadership Conference, held at the ecumenical Wildacres Retreat in the North Carolina mountains, she heard Reform Judaism's pioneering director of education Emanuel Gamoran, who bridged traditional Jewish learning with modern pedagogy. He urged women to learn Hebrew. As NCAJW president in 1927, Gertrude introduced the keynote speaker, Dr. Julian Morgenstern, president of Hebrew Union College, the reform seminary in Cincinnati.[21]

If Gertrude's campaigns for women's rights and social justice frustrated her, she could take satisfaction in her efforts to organize Jewish community. The NCAJW women had boasted in 1923 that "North Carolina is the Palestine of America." Jews commonly extolled their community as a New

Jerusalem when expressing local pride. A Reform rabbi touring the Southeast in 1929 reported that the "religious situation is not as acute" in North Carolina as in other states "due in large measure to the active work that has been undertaken by the NCAJW." Although he found small communities "heterogeneous" and outside the Jewish mainstream, his North Carolina journey was "most stimulating and encouraging." He discovered active Sunday schools, congregations forming, and bonds between cities and towns. Invited by Gertrude to speak before the NCAJW, Rabbi Stephen Wise of New York's Free Synagogue declined, writing her that North Carolina was "so finely loyal from the Jewish point of view that it is much less in need of help and stimulus from outside."[22]

Not simply an American of Jewish persuasion, Gertrude synthesized her Judaism and Americanism, rooting democracy and social justice in the canon of Israel. She felt no conflicting loyalties as an American Zionist. Jewish history was not autonomous, and women's progress in institutional Judaism proceeded apace with their American acculturation and entitlements in civil society. A coeducational religious school, an empowered Sisterhood, and women's synagogue membership attested to a democratic Judaism. For Gertrude, to be a light onto the nations meant securing the vote for women.[23]

{ 6 }

BREATHING THE SAME AIR
The Battle for Women's Suffrage

Having just elected officers, the 1919 Convention of the North Carolina Federation of Women's Clubs prepared to adjourn when the ladies were interrupted. Sallie Southall Cotten immortalized that moment in Hendersonville in her club history:

> Just before the close of the meeting Miss Gertrude Weil, President of the North Carolina Suffrage League, entered the Convention Hall, and the President, who seemed to understand, said "Miss Weil to the Platform, please." She obeyed, face smiling, and too full of joy to rescue her handsome evening wrap which was dragging the floor in her excitement. She held in her hand a yellow paper which often means joy or sorrow to some one, and which all recognized as a telegram. She read the message aloud "The Suffrage Bill passed Congress, two votes to the good." She was too full of joy to respond to the call for a speech, except to say "Victory will not be ours until North Carolina has ratified." But she held fast to the yellow paper, declaring she wished it for a souvenir. Much applause greeted her announcement.

Thirty-six states needed to ratify the Nineteenth Amendment for women to secure the ballot. Victory in North Carolina became Gertrude Weil's passion. She could not have known then how consequential her effort would become—in the end, after thirty-five had done so, it came to two, either Tennessee or North Carolina. "The eyes of the country are turned to North Carolina," Gertrude would write suffragists across the state.[1]

North Carolina was not a cauldron of suffrage militancy. In such a conservative society women were more resistant than in northern states. Gertrude observed, "Goldsboro was very un-suffrage minded. The women just weren't interested in the right to vote." Indeed, when the local Women's Club first met in 1898, men gathered outside and warned, "They'll be wanting the vote next and that will be too dreadful." Gertrude was typical of suffragist leaders, with roots in the urban mercantile class, college education, and progressive politics, but Goldsboro was still situated in eastern North Carolina, the state's Black Belt, dominated by a plantation economy and culture. Male opponents of women's vote included veterans of black disfranchisement who argued that any expansion of suffrage threatened white supremacy. Opposition to suffrage was greater where black population was larger. Racial fears had gender consequences.[2]

Southern ladies of the upper classes remained committed to traditional gender roles. Nor did working women—exhausted by long hours in the mills, with hungry mouths to feed—see the vote as a priority. African Americans, though supportive, were cautious, given recent white supremacist campaigns. Lynching and discrimination were more pressing concerns. Suffrage lines were thus drawn not simply by sex but also by class and race. Like many suffragists, Gertrude, though not working class, knew the situation of laboring women through her voluntarism.[3] Among the virulent opponents of voting women were manufacturers who wanted a free hand with labor and liquor interests that feared Prohibition.

Gertrude's status as an educated, middle-class progressive New Woman was typical of suffragists, but her religion was not. Unlike in Britain, where a separate Jewish League for Woman Suffrage formed, American Jewish suffragists did not feel excluded or a need to unify. However much they traced their civic spirit to Judaism, they acted through secular affiliations. In Tennessee Sophie Friedman fought for ratification and later became a prominent lawyer. Attorney Felice Cohn wrote Nevada's suffrage bill.[4] Jewish women in Asheville, Charlotte, Wilmington, and Greensboro joined Gertrude in the suffrage campaign. Fitting in, they did not fear courting political controversy.

"Social welfare—that's the chief interest I have ever had," Gertrude often said in later years.[5] Like activists Jane Addams or Florence Kelley, who were also ardent suffragists, Gertrude saw women's vote not as a feminist ends but as a means to create a more just, humane society, even bring world peace. Women's vote became another battlefield in North Carolina's perennial war between progressives and conservatives over such issues as Prohibition, labor rights, road funding, and the teaching of evolution.

North Carolinians lagged on women's suffrage. In 1913 a bill to grant women municipal suffrage was introduced into the General Assembly, but it sparked little interest and was tabled. Women reassured men that suffrage posed no threat to domesticity or to the hierarchy of gender. Concluding a North Carolina Federation of Women's Clubs conference in Chapel

Hill in 1914, president Clara Lingle, an ardent suffragist, pleaded with "her sister club members to honor the American man ... to whom we owe it all—and let our sister suffragettes be careful what they say about them." In 1914 the national General Federation of Women's Clubs adopted suffragism, but the North Carolina Federation failed to act. Annually, the state convention debated a resolution on suffrage, but to Gertrude's chagrin votes were tabled "in respect to many who believed in it but thought the time for action had not come."[6]

North Carolina awoke slowly. Since 1890 a united National American Woman Suffrage Association (NAWSA) had focused on a federal amendment rather than state-by-state legislation. Southern suffragists, dilatory in organizing, at first favored the states' rights approach before subscribing to the national agenda. After some initial electoral successes, the movement fell into the "doldrums" until 1910 when Washington State passed a suffrage referendum, invigorating a second wave. Gertrude joined NAWSA in 1911. The four-way 1912 presidential election proved a watershed. Theodore Roosevelt's Progressive Party, with Jane Addams and Maud Nathan helping to write its platform, endorsed suffrage. In response, Democrat Woodrow Wilson, who supported state amendments, proposed a New Freedom that promised progressive reform on tariffs, banking, and business trusts. With women voting in suffrage states, some women suspected that Wilson's commitment was more expedient than principled.

NAWSA's policy was to be nonpartisan, to the chagrin of many suffragists. In 1912 Alice Paul and Lucy Burns, two young American veterans of British suffragette "guerilla warfare," with arrest records for civil disobedience, took leadership of NAWSA's Congressional Committee.[7] They revived the campaign for a federal amendment. Inspired by Britain's Pankhurst women—Paul had thrown a shoe at the prime minister, breaking a window—they attracted radicals ready to fight. At Woodrow Wilson's inauguration, Paul organized a parade down Pennsylvania Avenue that drew eight thousand marchers and half a million spectators. Hostile bystanders rioted, and cavalry quelled the violence. Unlike the nonaligned NAWSA, Paul and Burns held Democrats culpable for the failure of suffrage and pledged to defeat not just Wilson but all party candidates—including suffragists. NAWSA expelled Paul and Burns, and in 1914 they organized the Congressional Union (CU), which two years later became the National Woman's Party. Headquartered in Washington, the party sent workers to the states, including North Carolina.

Gertrude, who subscribed to the *Women's Journal and Suffrage News*, would have been conversant with the international movement, particu-

Gertrude (far left) as suffragist. Courtesy of the State Archives of North Carolina.

larly British suffragette militancy, with its mass arrests, hunger strikes, and forced feedings. Her correspondents kept her up-to-date. Harriet Payne mailed her literature and wrote of canvassing in New York, while Frances Towers paraded in Washington. In North Carolina the state suffrage league was largely moribund, but local clubs began forming.[8]

In November 1913, women from a half dozen towns gathered in Charlotte to organize the Equal Suffrage Association of North Carolina (ESANC) and elected Barbara Henderson of Chapel Hill as president and Gertrude second vice president.[9] It affiliated with NAWSA. Henderson invited some fifty women to hear Lavinia Engle, an NAWSA spokesperson from Maryland. Engle, twenty-one, was described by the newspaper as a "tall, graceful, pretty and smart ... Southern woman" who dispelled stereotypes of the unwomanly suffragist. She spoke in eight North Carolina towns organizing clubs. On 17 April 1914 she addressed a crowd of men and women at the Kennon Hotel in Goldsboro. Engle argued that the government regulated education, sanitation, and working conditions, which all fell in women's domestic realm. Women thus deserved representation. Twenty-one women gathered to organize the Goldsboro Equal Suffrage League and elected as president Gertrude Weil. Her only relative to join was Elizabeth Rosenthal, uncle Joe's wife. Although Mina was not yet convinced, Gertrude opened their home two weeks after the founding for a local league meeting to discuss "The Individual Responsibility of College Women." In March the Goldsboro league sponsored Madeline Breckenridge, a Kentucky suffragist. Like Engle, Breckenridge was a southern lady whose elegance and pedigree refuted prejudices.[10]

North Carolina belatedly enlisted in the movement. In 1914 women in Charlotte held the state's first suffragist parade. In October Gertrude attended a statewide suffrage meeting hosted by Barbara Henderson where her professorial husband Archibald and North Carolina chief justice Walter Clark spoke. Clark saw no reason to deny women the vote: "Why should the mothers, the daughters, the wives, and sisters of the white voters of North Carolina be thus grouped with idiots, lunatics, convicts, and the negroes?" In December Clark spoke before the Goldsboro league at the courthouse. Men—Josephus Daniels, Henderson, and most notably Clark—sometimes pushed faster and farther than women felt comfortable going. That was especially true of Clark, who mapped political strategy and laid legal groundwork for women's vote, donating one hundred dollars to finance the campaign. Gertrude gave as much, but no one gave more. In 1913, when Clark encouraged the Woman's Club of Raleigh to support suffrage in municipal elections, the women thanked him and then "voted unanimously not to take it up."[11]

In May 1914 Mina opened a letter for Gertrude from Miss Carrie, "the President"—Carrie Chapman Catt of NAWSA—full of newspaper clippings. Gertrude could not but have contrasted the dawdling local scene with the national momentum. She kept a suffrage scrapbook of newspaper articles, meticulously documenting NAWSA but saving nothing on the National Woman's Party, or its predecessor, the CU, although its demonstrations and civil disobedience drew headlines. The CU had but a minimal presence in the state and, concerned with a federal amendment, ignored state legislators but lobbied congressmen. In 1915 Lilian Exum Clement, a criminal lawyer, organized a CU branch in Asheville. The National Woman's Party's executive secretary was a North Carolinian, Virginia Arnold, who would be jailed for picketing the White House. Gertrude's friend Frances Towers marched in the fateful Washington suffragist parade, and Harriet Payne asked her, "Have you joined the woman's organization to defeat Wilson?"[12]

Gertrude was born and bred in the Democracy, as the party was known, but had shown little partisan zeal. She knew well that in conservative North Carolina militancy alienated the public. When the Democratic National Convention was held in Baltimore in 1912, Josephus Daniels offered tickets to Henry Weil, who invited his daughter to join him. Gertrude emphatically told her father that she "positively will *not* go."[13] Gertrude, along with other

North Carolina women, sympathized with the CU's goals, but its disruptive tactics were beyond the boundaries of southern ladies. As ESANC met in Charlotte in 1915, militant English suffragette Christabel Pankhurst demanded "immediate action" at the Southern States Woman Suffrage Conference in Chattanooga. ESANC, however, affirmed allegiance to NAWSA. "The Congressional Union is a strong organization," Barbara Henderson declared, "but its methods would not suit the conditions of the Southern States."[14] Gertrude agreed. In truth, NAWSA and CU complemented each other. Women's suffrage would be achieved through both state advocacy and federal action, by agitation in the streets and by lobbying in Washington.

Gertrude struggled to build a suffrage network. Like the Women's Clubs, ESANC appealed to women socially as well as politically. For a fundraiser in February 1915, the Goldsboro women, led by Gertrude, held a barbecue, divvying duties to make slaw and cornbread. The Goldsboro women were hardly repudiating their domesticity. Gertrude pressed them to recruit more women. One meeting drew but fifteen, and election of officers had to be postponed for lack of a quorum. Yet ESANC reported "marked increase in the interest ... from every age and class." President Henderson noted, "The question is constantly being debated in the schools." The number of state clubs grew to fifteen.[15]

In January 1915, the U.S. House of Representatives considered a federal suffrage amendment, but it was defeated 204 to 174. Weeks thereafter, the North Carolina General Assembly considered state legislation, "An Act to Amend the Constitution so to give Women an Equal Right to Vote with Men." To win its passage, ESANC opened headquarters in the Yarborough Hotel in Raleigh as a lobbying post and propaganda distribution center. Dominating the office was a map depicting suffragist progress across the forty-eight states. Gertrude likely did not play a direct role in this campaign as she was now ensconced for a "prolonged" stay in Hot Springs with her still mourning mother suffering from various ailments.[16]

The national suffrage leadership came to Raleigh to press for the state amendment. William Jennings Bryan, former presidential candidate and now secretary of state, spoke stirringly to the legislature, arguing for suffrage's inevitability. On 2 February women from a coalition of suffragist groups testified before a joint legislative committee, but the day belonged to Dr. Anna Howard Shaw, president of NAWSA. The English-born Shaw, a Massachusetts resident, was an imposing speaker, witty and engaging, a Methodist minister as well as a physician. Gertrude was enamored of her. God's choir has a soprano as well as a bass, Shaw told the legislators. Americans ridiculed the divine right claimed by the German emperor, but it was no "more ridiculous than our American divine right of sex." The newspaper was impressed with the "dignified body of women." That night, Shaw delivered a public lecture where she argued that women's vote would better conditions for working women and children. Gertrude saved the program, copies of Shaw's speech, and newspaper reports. Folded in her papers was Shaw's portrait.[17]

The state house of representatives voted to postpone consideration of the state suffrage amendment by a vote of sixty-seven to thirty-eight, while the senate tabled the measure. Objections were raised that suffrage would "unsex" women, displace them from the home, violate biblical precepts, soil women's purity, topple them from their pedestals, and equate negro women with white women. These allegations were commonplace, and Shaw had rebutted them all, but the accumulated social and cultural prejudices that had deified and dehumanized the white southern lady could not be overcome in one lecture. "The defeat was a foregone conclusion," ESANC reported at its 1915 meeting, but "as a method of arousing public interest in the question ... the Equal Suffrage Bill was triumphantly successful."[18]

Gertrude was hardly disheartened. Meeting in Asheville in 1915, with Gertrude as the Goldsboro delegate, ESANC decided not to submit a full suffrage bill to the legislature but rather to focus on municipal suffrage and presidential electors. A "modest, ... prominent Goldsboro suffragist," undoubtedly Gertrude, wrote a newspaper that "gentle, unobtrusive 'entering wedge'" strategies were "half measures to palliate our disabilities" and "have not proven effectual." The one legislative victory that women had won proved transitory as the North Carolina Supreme Court, with Walter Clark dissenting, overthrew the law allowing women notaries. Nothing less than a change in the constitution would put women on "an equal political footing with men," Gertrude wrote.[19]

Winning Plan

At NAWSA change was afoot. Although personally admired, Anna Howard Shaw was an ineffective organizer. Splinter movements challenged her leadership, not only the CU but also the Southern States Woman Suffrage Conference, which in 1914 revived the campaign for state amendments. In 1915 Shaw was replaced by her predecessor, Carrie Chapman Catt. Although not an orator in Shaw's class, Catt was a talented and energetic "field commander." She reorganized the NAWSA office with an elite staff and in 1916 launched a "Winning Plan" for a federal amendment. Rather than confront Wilson, she sought his counsel, and a year later the president abandoned his states' rights approach and called upon Congress to enact the federal amendment. For ratification, Catt would focus on one or two states at a time, working through a designated leader in each.[20] In North Carolina she appointed Gertrude Weil as that commander.

In February 1917, NAWSA sent three directors to Raleigh to conduct a four-day school in public speaking, fundraising, organization, and parliamentary law. They rallied women at a mass meeting. The legislature considered a first bill to allow a municipal referendum on women's suffrage when 10 percent of voters, all *male*, so requested. After a familiar debate, the house rejected it. Days later a second bill was introduced to enfranchise women by amendment to the state constitution with women voting on the proposal in a primary. It was tabled. Next, a bill was presented to grant women presidential suffrage. After warnings of a "black peril," this bill was rejected. Bills to allow municipal suffrage in several western towns where sentiment was strong succeeded in the senate but died in the house.[21]

As progress stalled, complaints arose at the 1917 ESANC convention about its leadership. ESANC had lobbied politicians, written letters, and distributed literature. Occasionally, women hosted out-of-state suffragettes on lecture tours. Despite growing numbers of clubs, by 1917 ESANC reported but 175 members. The previous year it had failed to hold a convention. The women were divided on whether to proceed with state or federal amendments. One lecturer warned that woman's apathy was more of an obstacle than man's opposition.[22]

When the militant CU—now the National Woman's Party—sent an organizer from New York to Charlotte in spring 1917, sixty-two women joined, some of whom were ESANC members. Gertrude, ESANC third vice president and chair of the Committee on Organization, asserted herself. Following Catt's "Winning Plan," Gertrude appointed district chairs who in turn selected county chairs. A "conference" replaced the "convention." Writing to her friend Laura Cone from Blowing Rock, Gertrude outlined the strategy: "It is my immediate aim to get the whole state so well organized by then that we may have a representative from every county at that meeting."[23]

The 1917 conference, held in Goldsboro, consisted of sixteen delegates from nine cities. Membership had dramatically risen to more than a thousand. The following year Anna Howard Shaw and Jeanette Rankin of Montana, the first congresswoman, lectured in Greensboro. Efforts were expended to create suffrage clubs at women's colleges, despite resistance from trustees and administrators. The women directed letters and telegrams to the state's congressional delegation urging support of the federal—or, as it was popularly known, the Susan B. Anthony—amendment.

The war stalled suffrage momentum. Do not act, Gertrude cautioned

Laura Cone, "pending war measures are disposed of." NAWSA leaders, most notably Catt, had been active in international peace movements—Congresswoman Rankin cast a lone dissenting antiwar vote—but, reluctantly, suffragists yielded to the national patriotic mood. When the North Carolina Federation of Women's Clubs met in Raleigh in 1918, "everybody was doing World War Work." General Federation president Ione Cowles praised the women for selling Liberty Bonds and war savings stamps and "unceasing Red Cross work." She cautioned suffragists "to allow no criticism of the President nor of the United States Government." Suffragists recognized that it would be impolitic and unpatriotic to challenge or disparage government when sons and brothers were dying overseas. As women answered the call to meet manpower shortages, suffragists saw an opportunity to demonstrate their citizenship. In 1918 ESANC contributed $350 to the Overseas Hospital Fund.[24]

With war and influenza ending, attention returned to unmet demands on the domestic front. "Women in war service have opened the eyes of the men of North Carolina to the fitness of women of all kinds of service," said Mrs. John Cunningham, ESANC president, "and surely suffrage has won more converts." Their just reward was the ballot. As Woodrow Wilson proclaimed in his war declaration, America was fighting for a world "made safe for democracy." How could it deny its own citizens rights granted by tyrannies it opposed? Not only democratic Canada granted women the vote, suffragists argued, but even Bolshevist Russia.[25]

Gertrude tried again to enlist women's clubs in suffrage. At the 1918 North Carolina Federation of Women's Clubs conference in Raleigh the "long delayed storm burst." Suffrage was the last and thirteenth resolution put forward. Even then, the resolution justified "enfranchisement of women" not on grounds of gender equality or natural rights but for their "valuable service" to the "teaching profession." Wartime shortages had opened more classrooms to women teachers, and they needed the ballot to qualify as school superintendents. Gertrude spoke in favor. The resolution "passed amidst great applause" with but two dissenting votes. The Federation sent telegrams to U.S. senators Lee Overman and Furnifold Simmons endorsing a suffrage amendment to the Constitution.[26]

A Federal Amendment

In January 1918, the Susan B. Anthony Amendment revived in the U.S. House of Representatives. President Wilson delivered an impassioned appeal on the eve of the vote, hailing women's service in wartime. The House responded by passing it, one vote over the necessary two-thirds, and sending it to the Senate. From Washington NAWSA president Catt sent Gertrude marching orders. As state congressional chairman of ESANC, Gertrude directed "*all our efforts*" to lobby Senators Simmons and Overman. Her campaign called for "*many* and *influential* men and women" to write letters, compile petitions, and send last-minute telegrams.[27]

The nominally nonpartisan suffrage movement was drawn unavoidably into politics. When Republicans and Democrats held state conventions in 1918, suffragists played the political game. Gertrude asked the Washington NAWSA office to enlist Marion Butler, a former North Carolina senator and national Populist Party leader, but he was unavailable. Carrie Chapman Catt was convinced that North Carolina Democrats would not adopt a suffragist plank, but if the Republican Party were to do so, it might "influence" Democratic senators Simmons and Overman. "Of course the suffragists are largely, if not entirely Democratic," Catt wrote Gertrude, although she was "very much amazed … to learn that there is large Republican white vote" in the state. She asked Gertrude to interview the "moving spirits" of the Republican Party to get pledges of support. She was not to do so, however, unless she was "sure" that she had the votes.[28]

Gertrude tested Catt's strategy on Walter Clark, who advised her to proceed regardless of consequences. He did not doubt that Republicans would pass it. He warned her that Democratic "'machine' men are very much alarmed," but they feared opposing the president, Congress, and Democratic National Committee, all now suffragist. The machine politicians tried to "*intimidate*" the suffragists not to submit a resolution to the state convention. Clark felt the "benefit of publicity" outweighed the risk of failure. The "politicians are bluffing," he counseled, and "if their bluff is called, they generally back down."[29]

Gertrude was caught between Catt's and Clark's conflicting advice. A telegram arrived from NAWSA secretary Nettie Shuler: "Follow Mrs. Catss [*sic*] directions explicitly." Catt wrote that Clark was "an ardent and good friend," but as she later observed, "Judge Clark is often more optimistic than facts warrant." An ESANC delegation attended the Republican convention, which adopted a suffragist plank without opposition. The plank cited the justice of granting women the vote as taxpayers and honored their "patriotic and unselfish service to our country."[30] NAWSA saw possibility in North Carolina with its large—for the South—Republican Party and its hardworking suffragists.

For Democrats the women's vote became a racial "wedge issue." Senator Simmons, the machine boss, staunchly opposed woman suffrage. Now in his sixties, he had been the architect of violent white supremacist campaigns in the 1890s. His Senate colleague Lee Overman built a political career on race- and red-baiting. Their candidate for governor, Cameron Morrison, a former racist Red Shirt, warned that black women's vote would lead to socialism, trample on states' rights, and return the state to black rule. Challenging the Democratic machine was the young, charismatic Lieutenant Governor O. Max Gardner, a lawyer and industrialist. Gardner eschewed race-baiting and heartily endorsed women's vote. Male politicians were experiencing their own generational conflict on woman suffrage. In the gubernatorial primary campaign, the Simmons camp distributed handbills of Gardner locking arms with a black woman.[31] Nowhere was racist propaganda more effective than in Gertrude's eastern North Carolina.

The Democratic convention, Gertrude informed Catt, declined the suffrage resolution by voice vote. Later, Catt responded by observing that "our question is continually set aside and thrown down by the men whose personal ambition rises above any question, problem and principle." Excepting "an ardent and good friend" like Justice Clark, Catt assured Gertrude, North Carolina men like those of other states lacked "a very high political ideal." The senators of the "extreme South," she suspected, conspired to stand united in opposition. Still, Justice Clark was confident that the Senate would pass the amendment in the coming month. Senator Simmons's daughters, he noted, had signed the suffrage petition. Clark lobbied his fellow lawyers and distributed a pamphlet, "Votes for Women." Momentum was gaining as resolutions of support came not just from the General Federation of Women's Clubs but also from a host of farm, labor, and women's groups.[32]

Attending the NAWSA convention in 1918, Gertrude reported on North Carolina's progress. "War activities" had stifled the movement. Although the state had but eleven local affiliates, there was much "growth in unorganized suffrage" as petitions and letters, especially from campuses, flooded the senators. Increasing numbers of professional and religious bodies endorsed it. "Notwithstanding the patriotic and efficient work of the suffragists," she noted, the U.S. Senators were opposed. The state senate did pass municipal suffrage, but it failed in the house, which Gertrude nonetheless regarded as progress. More women were appointed to state boards.[33]

In April, the NAWSA Executive Council, meeting in Indianapolis, launched a "mobilization of our suffrage army" to convince the U.S. Senate to follow the House's lead. Catt wired Gertrude to inform all state workers that "no effort should be spared to secure flood of telegrams from influencial [sic] constituents." That month a bulletin announced "a nationwide protest campaign against further delay in passing the Federal Amendment."

Gertrude wrote to "every suffragist.... The Call comes from Washington." Catt informed Gertrude, "We are putting quite a little expense" into North Carolina. Nonetheless, both Simmons and Overman remained adamant. In the Senate the amendment failed by two votes to secure a two-thirds majority in September 1918, and four months later it fell short by one.[34]

In January 1919, Gertrude was elected president of ESANC at its conference in Raleigh. Her ascendancy involved some suffragist politics. Harriet Elliott, a professor at Woman's College and disciple of Anna Howard Shaw, wrote Gertrude confidentially seeking support for Cornelia Jerman's candidacy. Contrarily, a Greensboro activist insisted that "this is a young woman's movement" and wanted a Miss Clark. Whatever the intrigue, Gertrude was elected president and Jerman vice president and chair of the Legislative Committee. "Miss Weil is the best answer to the politicians' objection that southern women do not want to vote," the *Greensboro Daily Record* commented. Charlotte attorney Julia Alexander wrote her cousin Walter Clark that Weil "seems to be a very capable person" and will give "impetus to the work."[35]

At the Raleigh conference, as a show of political might, the state suffragist infantry summoned its artillery, progressive Democrats of national repute. Adelaide Daniels, whose husband Josephus was now secretary of the navy, was elected honorary president. Before a crowd of three thousand, with Governor Thomas Bickett, Lieutenant Governor O. Max Gardner, and Justice Walter Clark seated on stage, William Jennings Bryan delivered the keynote. Reviewing the growing numbers of entities—not just states but entire countries—adopting women's suffrage, Bryan admonished, "You can't keep it from coming." Again, he noted women's loyalty in reelecting Wilson in 1916 and pronounced "shame" on Democrats for ceding the issue to Republicans.[36]

Gertrude's ESANC colleagues were formidable. Cornelia Jerman, who led legislative lobbying, was a Women's Club veteran and politically well connected. In the 1920s she was thrice delegate to the Democratic National Convention and was mentioned as a gubernatorial candidate. Harriet Elliott was a professor of history and political science at Woman's College, who held national posts in the Democratic Party and federal government. Treasurer Laura Weill Cone was an intellectually accomplished, progressive woman married to a textile magnate. ESANC stationery listed an advisory board of ninety-six men. It included not just old suffragist hands like Clark and Henderson but also business plutocrats. Although weighted toward the progressive wing of the Democratic Party, they crossed boundaries that conventionally divided pros and antis, as they were popularly known. General

Julian S. Carr was a Civil War veteran who led Confederate revivals. "I am heartily disposed toward equal suffrage," wrote Rev. A. A. McGeachy, D.D., of Charlotte. "The privilege of the ballot to women ... will operate to the best interest of our country," added Lionel Weil, merchant of Goldsboro.[37]

Gertrude, in all her causes, believed education was the means to the ends. Political opponents were sent Walter Clark's pamphlets "Some Few of the Discriminations against Women in North Carolina" or "Women in the Home." She spoke of her principles as if they were self-evident. "I wondered why people made speeches in favor of something so obviously right," she reflected. "Women breathed the same air, got the same education; it was ridiculous, spending so much energy and elocution on something rightfully theirs."[38] The college student who studied Kant expressed her political ideals categorically as universal principles. In contrast to her opponents, who spoke their prejudices, she justified her positions with reason.

In 1919, while the U.S. Congress debated a federal amendment, the North Carolina legislature once again considered municipal suffrage. Gertrude could hardly have felt edified by the Bible-thumping debate that refought battles between Old and New Souths. Hallet Ward, a state senator and later a congressman, claimed that women's suffrage "had no place in the sunny South," that with women in the general assembly, "one box of mice" could break up the legislature. Greensboro senator A. M. Scales responded by citing biblical Deborah and Joan of Arc. He read the roll of nations and states that had adopted suffrage. Rodents aside—Ward's speech was widely derided—the state senate passed municipal suffrage thirty-five to twelve and sent it to the house.[39]

As suffragists crammed the gallery, the house session began with the "singing of old time Camp Meeting tunes." House "Evangelists" again prevailed as municipal suffrage was rejected forty-nine to fifty-four. Gertrude wrote to "My Dear Suffragist" that what "looks like a defeat" was actually encouraging as the "legislature shows so decided an advance in suffrage sentiment." The total suffrage vote of both houses exceeded the rejectionist sum. Gertrude asked for renewed effort and predicted that a federal amendment would secure the ballot in 1921.[40]

When Gertrude went to the 1919 NAWSA convention in St. Louis in March, soon after recovering from influenza, she found a movement so confident—with twenty-eight states having ratified—that it was debating whether to dissolve or continue. At this Golden Jubilee convention, commemorating its fiftieth anniversary, NAWSA organized a successor League of Women Voters for states that had achieved full suffrage. While North Carolina was still fighting for women's municipal vote, fifteen states had fully enfranchised women and were turning their suffrage associations into League chapters.[41]

Gertrude returned from St. Louis and mobilized a statewide campaign: "Our Aim: To gain equal suffrage for men and women. How? Through passage of the Federal Suffrage Amendment by Congress and ratification by the State Legislatures." She laid out seven steps. First, convince congressmen and legislators that the "a majority of white women of North Carolina" favored equal suffrage. She sent blank petitions, encouraging workers to collect signatures of "ALL the white women of your town and country." They were to proceed "AT ONCE!" in time for special sessions of Congress and the state legislature. "Prominent, influential men" in each county were asked to send telegrams to congressmen. She ended, "FINISH THE FIGHT." Gertrude added a postscript, "Please let me hear from you."[42]

Gertrude asked each local league to enlist labor unions at a time when such organizing was widely suspect as red and radical. "The platform and aims of the Equal Suffrage League and Labor Unions being the same," she noted, they supported "fair living wages," compulsory schooling of children, "fair and honest elections," and equal suffrage from men and women. The platform was printed on the letterhead of the Raleigh Central Labor Union, which resolved to a "joint effort" with ESANC. The sudden death of Anna Howard Shaw in July checked their momentum. Shaw only months earlier had spoken in Greensboro at a Woman's College commencement. Gertrude felt "a deep sense of personal loss as of a dear friend," and ESANC passed a resolution on its "irreparable loss." Gertrude sent flowers.[43]

Gertrude's facts and reason were less persuasive than were inherited prejudices. Writing her congressman Sam Brinson in May 1919, "even at the risk of seeming over-persistent," Gertrude again urged his support. She found "astonishing" his argument that enfranchisement would be "bad for the women themselves." Brinson observed that in western states where full suffrage had been adopted women devolved into "profane liquor-drinking creatures." Gertrude, ever the southern lady, assured him that "North Carolina women will be true to their own type" and that, to the contrary, liquor interests were the "strongest, most active" opponents to equal suffrage here. She conceded that the "NEGRO WOMAN's vote . . . is a problem. It is one phase of the larger negro problem." She had "faith in the feasibility of its solution," but "OTHERWISE THAN AT THE COST OF INJUSTICE AND DISCRIMINATIONS AGAINST THE WHITE WOMEN." She noted the anomaly of permitting women to hold appointive offices but not elective offices. To Justice Clark, she wrote that Brinson "was possessed to the end with the fear that women will leap from their pedestals if allowed to vote."[44]

Gertrude confronted another political obstacle. Catt, perennial president of the International Woman Suffrage Alliance, had been a noted antiwar activist. Suffrage became tied to Woodrow Wilson's support for a League of Nations, an initiative that won Gertrude's heart. For Gertrude, who would chair international relations committees and attend global peace conferences, garnering political support for the League of Nations was both a motivation and a complication. The linkage alienated politicians like Senators Simmons and Overman who advocated "Americanism" and bitterly opposed "internationalism."[45]

Nineteenth Amendment

While North Carolina dithered, the nation moved swiftly forward. Both political parties eyed the 1920 presidential election. With populous states already granting equal suffrage, women's vote could prove decisive. Republicans weighed whether it would be to their electoral advantage to have the "perfect 36" state be Vermont, Tennessee, or North Carolina. President Wilson called a special session of Congress again to pass the amendment. Gertrude asked women—*at once*—to "rain" letters and telegrams on representatives. The amendment sailed through the House with a forty-two vote margin, although supported only by Zebulon Weaver of Buncombe County among the state's seven representatives. In the Senate, however, both Simmons and Overman remained opposed. They spurned intense lobbying from Democratic National Executive Committeemen, who urged loyalty to the party platform, as well as from their fellow Trinity College alumni and from state leaders, including the governor.

At Walter Clark's insistence, Gertrude pressed petition drives on state campuses, despite resistance from trustees. Some 575 signed at Woman's College and 200 at Meredith. President W. P. Few at Trinity would "interpose no objection" but doubted the "wisdom" of such "propaganda." Over eight thousand North Carolina college and high school students signed petitions of support. Yet, as Gertrude wrote Mrs. T. D. Jones of Durham, "Simmons seems perfectly impregnable to any kind of influence." He wanted to know student feelings at men's colleges, not just at women's. Simmons declared, "I cannot support this amendment." Overman acknowledged that "a great number of the best people" favor woman suffrage, but he could not endorse it until "convinced that a majority of the white people of North Carolina" did so.[46]

On 4 June 1919, the federal woman suffrage amendment passed the Senate by a two-thirds majority with "two votes to spare," with wide Republican and narrow Democratic support. The *News and Observer* telegraphed the North Carolina Federation of Women's Clubs convention in Hendersonville, and Gertrude brought the news to the cheering women. That very night, Walter Clark wrote Gertrude proclaiming it "the greatest triumph for genuine democracy since 4 July 1776." He proposed strategy for the special session of the state legislature to be held next spring, warning that it will take "intensive cultivation."[47]

North Carolina was not among the states rushing to ratify. Gertrude went on the road. Speaking before the United Daughters of the Confederacy, she told this "splendid body" that between ESANC and the UDC there existed "a feeling of real sisterhood." (Although eligible, Gertrude never joined.) Both were "striving to raise the standard of patriotic living." She knew UDC members were wary of "politics," but politics meant not "partisanship" but the "science of government." If women could serve their nation in war, why not in peace? Had not the UDC lobbied the legislature on behalf of the Old Soldiers Home? By September, under Gertrude's leadership, ESANC held public meetings in twenty-nine towns across the state. Gertrude asked each district director to prepare a plan and forward it to her.[48]

ESANC struggled with funding and staffing. In March 1919 NAWSA sent Maria McMahon as a fieldworker—national paid her salary, state her expenses—and in April Mary Pidgeon, a field secretary, arrived for a month. Gertrude lamented the lack of grassroots support. She could not find a leader in High Point and found it "discouraging" that Oxford did not answer her letters. She wanted to hire a state organizer for the year, although she doubted the organization could afford the two-hundred-dollar monthly salary and had difficulties finding a qualified candidate. She discovered her in Mary O. Cowper, a native Tennessean, who had moved to Durham in 1918 when her husband joined Trinity College's French department. Cowper, a doctoral candidate in sociology at the University of Chicago, shared Gertrude's leftist politics. Women's vote would be the "great moral force" to break the stranglehold trade and industry held on government.[49] Gertrude mentored the younger Cowper, as she herself often had been, and the women bonded.

While ESANC was pursuing "sane, law-abiding methods," the National Woman's Party engaged in a militant campaign. In Washington women were chaining themselves to the White House gates and subjecting themselves to mass arrest. They went on hunger strikes that prison guards ended with brutal forced feedings that repulsed the nation. Gertrude issued a statement dissociating ESANC from "undignified demonstrations." The National Woman's Party's strength in North Carolina was "nil," the statement read, and ESANC was "in no way connected . . . nor is it responsible for its so-called militant methods."[50]

When ESANC met in Greensboro in January 1920, suffrage momentum was growing. After a memorial for Shaw, the convention held a banquet for three hundred. Carrie Chapman Catt sent glittering speakers from NAWSA headquarters. Alexander White of the British Parliament praised American women for their "plucky fight." Adelaide Daniels described suffrage as the "latchkey" to the future. At the business meeting, attended by one hundred, Gertrude was reelected. Filled with hope, Gertrude went to Chicago in February for NAWSA's Victory Convention. By month's end, thirty-three states had ratified. The convention featured a Ratification Banquet and the First Congress of the League of Women Voters. A School of Education for Citizenship, directed by Catt, followed. In her convention report Gertrude noted the state's growth to twenty-four local branches. North Carolinians served on five league national committees. She regretted that the U.S. Senate had passed the federal suffrage resolution too late for North Carolina's biannual legislature to consider.[51]

Such was the optimism that women began preparing for citizenship. Cochaired by Gertrude, the North Carolina Federation of Women's Clubs offered a course in American citizenship through the University Extension Bureau. In March, with Washington ratifying and Delaware poised to vote, victory seemed so imminent that Gertrude invited chapter presidents to Raleigh for a "TREMENDOUS celebration." Those not in Raleigh could party locally. "Let everyone know how rejoiced we are that our goal has been reached," she exulted.[52]

As Carrie Chapman Catt waited "breathless" for Delaware to vote, she cautioned Gertrude. She was finding it "difficult to keep up with the procession" of states, but "everybody who writes us from North Carolina says that of course the Legislature will ratify." Yet Catt remained skeptical: "Now it will do nothing of the kind, unless it is persuaded to do so by different tactics than those which have yet been used." North Carolina may be more "progressive" than sister states, but the "prejudice of Southern men . . . is very bitter and deep seated."[53]

Party invitations were indeed premature. Delaware's senate passed the amendment, but its house refused to consider. North Carolina was thus the next candidate for the "perfect 36." Governor Thomas Bickett responded to calls for ratification by stating that he intended to put the issue before the legislature. First, he wanted the Democratic Party to act at its April convention. Gertrude wrote Catt a frank political assessment. She "was hopeful of success" in North Carolina with a "decided change in some of our erstwhile anti influential politicians." Senator Overman conceded suffrage's inevitably but was still opposed. ESANC twice polled North Carolina legislators, but few replied. It planned a lobbying effort by organizing counties whose representatives had voted in "favor or mildly opposed" municipal suffrage last winter.[54]

Catt held doubts about Gertrude's southern strategy. "People are so terribly touchy about an 'outsider' interfering and have an aversion to being pushed," Gertrude warned. NAWSA had tried to send only southern women to North Carolina, and Gertrude asked that Catt not come "unless it proves absolutely necessary." She continued, "We have made a strong point of conducting our campaign ourselves, without the importation of strangers making the contrast to the disadvantage of the anti-suffragists" who have imported "out-of-the-state workers." She added, "The men keep urging us not to have any one come into the State from outside." Speaking to chivalrous southerners, Gertrude wrote the next day to Senator W. L. Long of Roanoke Rapids asking him to "work" on his colleagues by appealing to their "gallantry and loyalty" as North Carolinians. The plan, Gertrude wrote, was to have the suffrage amendment "introduced early in the session and go through with acclaim."[55]

Gertrude anticipated a "safe majority" in the special session with pro-suffrage legislators influencing others. The senatorial and two of the three Democratic gubernatorial candidates supported ratification. Josephus Daniels was "doing all in his power," and his wife, Adelaide, was moving to Raleigh for the special session, taking a house to entertain legislators. Republicans, who were fielding a strong ticket, were "solidly for it." Gertrude's poll indicated that in the 50-member state senate, thirty-two were favorable and two "favorably doubtful." In the 120-member house, 57 were favorable and 3 favorably doubtful. Still, she tempered optimism. Gertrude confessed that the "situation here has become so confused" that her poll was unreliable. "Mr. Everett [chair of the house's Woman Suffrage Committee] tells me that bitterness in some quarters is so bitter ... that it might be fatal to Democratic success in the State election." Many state Democrats opposed their presidential nominee, James Cox, and Warren Harding, the Republican nominee, was running strong. Both Governor Bickett and T. D. Warren, an antisuffragist who chaired the North Carolina Democratic Committee, hoped that Tennessee would ratify and save North Carolina from the "necessity" of considering the issue. Gertrude noted, too, that suffrage was not the only question factionalizing Democrats. A bill to revaluate property was also divisive, and a "hot newspaper controversy" had erupted among party leaders. Governor Bickett read to Gertrude "in confidence" his intended speech to the legislature on suffrage. He expressed his "own personal unfriendliness to woman suffrage" but would advocate it on the "ground of its inevitableness."[56]

The tide-turning battle was to be fought at the Democratic state convention. As the date approached, state suffragists quietly planned what NAWSA headlined as "The Coup d'Etat of Tar Heel Women." Democratic practice was to allow any male who would be twenty-one by election day to participate in precinct meetings. Declaring that they would be eligible to vote in the forthcoming election, women marched into precinct gatherings—in Raleigh, fifty strong. Some precincts welcomed them, even cheered them. Six counties sent women to represent them at the state convention.[57]

When state Democrats convened in April 1920, thirty-five states had ratified. North Carolinians were still hedging. The platform committee recommended that the legislature reject the federal amendment but submit a state constitutional amendment. While a member of the CU from Tennessee harangued delegates, two women were seated. One minority report asked for a vote on ratification of the federal amendment, while another asked that all references to woman suffrage be removed from the platform. A floor fight erupted. Despite powerful opposition, the suffrage resolution was adopted 585 to 428. Jubilant suffragists saw victory coming in the legislative session. In May NAWSA flew the North Carolina state banner from its New York headquarters.[58]

Gertrude worked closely with sympathetic legislators plotting strategy. A. M. Scales of Greensboro wrote letters to his fellow senators on 21 May soliciting their positions. The results were not heartening. Senator James Gray spoke for many when he said that his sympathy for women's suffrage was "theoretical" and not "practical." He argued, "First, my constituents are opposed almost to a man to woman's suffrage. Then again, there is hardly one out of ten women in our city who wants the ballot." Many legislators made similar arguments. As Gray wrote, "The most powerful reason of all is that it would bring on race problems." He predicted "trouble" if the Negro, removed from the vote in 1900, were brought back into politics. It was still not clear if a special legislative session would be called in August. Victory was uncertain. On 21 June NAWSA sent Gertrude the results of two polls showing fifty-one or fifty-two favorable votes in the state house and twenty-one in the senate, with decisive numbers doubtful or not responding. NAWSA would need to fight with its treasury drained. An "S.O.S." was sent to raise another ten thousand dollars to finish the campaign.[59]

A report in the New York "'highbrow'" magazine *Forum* that Senator

Overman had reversed himself brought elation, but after he strenuously refuted it—he remained convinced suffrage was a states' rights question—"the ladies," as one headline put it, "now look upon Mr. Overman as a horrid, ugly thing."[60]

The Rejectionists

Within days of the Democratic convention, antisuffragists rallied. Mary Hilliard Hinton, a plantation lady of Wake County, invited the prominent antisuffragist Carrie Preston Davis from Richmond to organize a North Carolina affiliate of the Southern Women's Rejection League. Hinton would chair. Its advisory board included an "aristocratic line-up": Episcopal Bishop J. B. Cheshire, Democratic activist and historian Samuel Ashe, and leading bankers and mill owners, some with histories in black disfranchisement. In May the antis held a rally that packed the Senate chambers. In June the league opened offices at the Raleigh Hotel at 118 Fayetteville Street only doors from the ESANC office at 116. In the hotel dining room they draped a banner, "Politics are bad for women and women are bad for politics." On 21 June, forty men organized the States Rights Defense League.[61]

Antisuffragists, like their opponents, took guidance from a national movement, The National Association Opposed to Woman Suffrage. It published the *Woman Patriot*, a newspaper battling feminism, socialism, and women's suffrage. By 1916 six southern states had formed rejectionist organizations, though, as typical, North Carolina lagged. In contrast to their combative northern sisters, southern antis remained ladylike. Yet antis so mimicked suffragists with their lobbying, petitioning, and letter writing that opponents accused them of disingenuously practicing the very politics that they claimed to disdain. In June 1919, with the passage of the federal amendment, antisuffragists began a last-minute campaign to prevent state ratification.[62]

Mary Hinton and Gertrude Weil were very much representative figures. Hinton was an Old South aristocrat, a plantation lady educated at St. Mary's and Peace Institute. Heraldic artist of the Daughters of the American Revolution, she was a Colonial Dame and niece of a former governor. Like many antisuffragists, she belonged to the Episcopal church. Gertrude, by contrast, arose from the New South. Her family, like that of many suffragists, was urban, mercantile, and middle class. Her southern roots traced only a generation or two. As a Jew, she was an outsider. Graduate of a northern college, she was educated not in agrarian ideals like Hinton but in the science of progress. Suffragists were disproportionately college educated, and professionals were also overrepresented. In age, too, the two women personified popular perceptions that younger women—Hinton was ten years older—wanted the vote. Suffrage was one locus of a struggle of opportunity for women in education, politics, and profession.[63]

Both pros and antis argued that their positions were the best guarantors of women's domesticity. Gertrude, unmarried and childless, was vulnerable to the charge that suffragists would undo home life. The Raleigh suffrage league publicly stated that its members were mostly married. In fact, despite arguments about marriage and generational gaps, pros and antis differed little in either age or marital status. The conflict was not simply between southern ladies and New Women. One in five anti leaders, like Hinton, was unmarried, slightly less than the pros. Yet rejectionists continued to allege—often in cartoonish ways—that women's vote would unravel families.[64]

Bound by a "moral conservatism," both sides agreed on the primacy of woman's role in the home. "What will we do with the vote?" Gertrude asked at the 1920 North Carolina Federation of Women's Clubs convention. "We shall use it in our old, time-honored business of housekeeping, of making life fair and clean and sanitary and beautiful for our families." As journalist Nell Battle Lewis recalled, "Woman suffrage effort in North Carolina was always very well-behaved. The leaders frowned upon militancy." In 1917, to the consternation of ESANC, two CU suffragettes stood on a Raleigh street corner haranguing a crowd, but the hunger strikes and mass arrests that erupted in Washington were inappropriate for North Carolina.[65]

Typical of pro and anti leaders alike, both Weil and Hinton were well-bred southerners from privileged backgrounds. Both women knew well the plutocrats of the Democratic Party and shared membership in the North Carolina Literary and Historical Association. Its president, James Sprunt of Wilmington, a southern aristocrat, responded to Gertrude's solicitation with his "unqualified approval" of her "splendid" humanitarian work, which inclined him toward suffragism, but his late wife was "a good friend" of Miss Hinton, who also asked him "for moral and financial support." He resolved his conflict by refusing both. Social lines were not sharply drawn. Suffragist Julia Alexander was the first woman in the state to have her own law practice and served as president of the North Carolina Federation of Business and Professional Women, but she was also from an Old South family—Judge Clark was her cousin—and held high office in both the Daughters of the American Revolution and the UDC. She was hardly unique as a southern lady embracing progressive politics and a professional career.[66]

Both Weil and Hinton came from eastern North Carolina, where antisuffragist sentiment was strongest. That region with its plantation legacy was the birthing place of black disfranchisement under Governor Charles B. Aycock, a Weil family compatriot. In 1915, when the North Carolina legislature voted on women's suffrage, members from districts that were more than 40 percent black were three times more likely to vote against. This pattern intensified on voting for the federal amendment. Gertrude complained that suffragism received scant support in her native Wayne County, which was heavily African American.[67]

Gertrude struggled to win the argument that public opinion supported women's suffrage. In a letter to Catt, Gertrude described a local primary election that pitted pro- and antisuffragist candidates against each other. The anti candidate dwelt on the "negro woman's vote." As Gertrude observed, his opponent then backed down and disavowed his suffragism. She added, "Great bitterness was aroused." Politicians apologized to Gertrude that they personally supported women's suffrage but could not vote against "the expressed wishes of their constituents." In Mecklenburg County a straw vote on woman suffrage was defeated handily. State legislators cited this example in explaining their reluctance. Antisuffragists argued, with evidence, that women who wanted the ballot were not representative.[68]

Pundits observed closely the comings and goings of every politico at the nearby prosuffrage and antisuffrage Raleigh headquarters, noting whether he wore the suffragist yellow ribbon on his lapel or clutched the rejectionist's red rose. Planters, industrialists, railroad executives, political bosses, and liquor advocates united against the suffragists' larger reform agenda. Women's vote, they feared, would bring Prohibition, an end to child labor, minimum wages, maximum hour laws, and health and safety regulations that would hurt their finances and upset social hierarchies.[69] The prosuffragists, they claimed, deserted homes and children. Antisuffragist women waved hankies and red roses from General Assembly galleries.

Gertrude collected the literature streaming from the antis' headquarters. One antisuffrage league broadside read "A Vote for Federal Suffrage Is a Vote for Organized Female Nagging Forever." Flyers warned of abandoned babies. By July, Gertrude conceded that the flood of anti literature was exerting its effect. Although they claimed to represent popular sentiment, antis lacked the grassroots organization of the pros. By 1920 ESANC claimed a thousand members, while the Southern Women's Rejection League had perhaps twenty active. Unable to create local affiliates, the Raleigh headquarters remained the league's sole statewide presence. In contrast to the suffragists, whose movement was years in the making, the antis pursued an "'eleventh hour' mobilization."[70]

NAWSA sent four fieldworkers and countered with a propaganda barrage. Newspapers were sent twice weekly columns as "plate," or copy ready for publication. ESANC distributed NAWSA's national publication *Woman Citizen*, founded by Catt, which featured inspirational articles like "For the Honor of Tarhelia." As the legislature opened, the pros answered an issue of the anti's newspaper *State's Defense* with "A Special Session Edition" of *Everywoman's Magazine*, which included a lead editorial by "Mrs. Josephus Daniels," as well as testimonials from Justice Walter Clark and Republican gubernatorial nominee John Parker. More powerfully, it profiled recent converts to the suffrage cause, among them Senator Simmons and Governor Bickett. Simmons explained that he had earlier voted against the suffrage amendment, thinking that women "did not want it," but "it seems now that they do." The "practical question" was not "whether" women would achieve suffrage but "when." Bickett remained opposed in principle but conceded its inevitably. Philosophically, he had learned to accept what he could not change. Democrats were obligated to sacrifice their own interests in loyalty to the national candidate and platform. In a handbill Gertrude reiterated America's first principles: Women were subject to "taxation without representation." Government derives its just powers from the consent of the governed. Women were citizens with responsibilities for education and sanitation. Therefore, it was inconsistent to allow them to hold public offices but then deprive them of the vote.[71]

The Race Question, Again

Behind the partisan politics and desperate tactics were arguments that persisted in the South generally. Even in the suffrage camp, legislative director Cornelia Jerman needed convincing that a federal amendment was preferable to state legislation. Debating points raised reflexively were white supremacy, states' rights, local government, biblical authority, biological capability, and the inevitability of woman suffrage. Of these, race dominated southern campaigns. Indeed, the Raleigh branch of the Southern Women's Rejection League began its statement of principles, "The women of North Carolina fully alive to the danger which threatens white supremacy." With black men removed from the ballot, white politicians opposed reopening the franchise question. Suffragists "downplayed" race, knowing that they would lose if it became focus of the debate.[72]

Gertrude's predicament on race and women's suffragism had a long history, at least since the Seneca Falls women's rights convention in 1848. NAWSA, too, walked the race line. When the "negro question" arose at its 1903 meeting in New Orleans, NAWSA's board responded, "The association as such has no view on this subject," adding that its members held "all shades of opinion." NAWSA affirmed the "doctrine of State's rights," and each state association was free to act "in harmony with the customs of its own section." Southerners could thus exclude black women and work for state amendments. NAWSA did, however, reject proposals by southerners to work only for white suffrage, and it held that principled position even after southerners threatened to cut financial aid. Southern suffrage associations supported NAWSA's position that a federal amendment was not incompatible with states' rights.[73]

North Carolina suffragists had advocated black education and economic uplift without endorsing political enfranchisement. Gertrude's colleague Delia Dixon-Carroll joined interracial panels, and her friends Laura and Julius Cone endowed and served as trustees of black colleges. Gertrude actively participated in the North Carolina Conference for Social Service, which in 1919 featured Dr. A. M. Moore, an African American physician and insurance executive from Durham, speaking on "The Proper Basis of Race Relationship." A year later the conference listed "favor justice for negroes" in its Declaration of Principles. The 1920 state Women's Club convention heard pioneering African American educator Charlotte Hawkins Brown lecture on "The Negro Problem," calling for the black women's vote.[74]

ESANC responded to the racial argument with press releases and broadsides that demonstrated women's suffrage would not change the racial status quo. If not written by Gertrude, they were produced under her command. "Woman Suffrage and White Supremacy in the South" offered statistical refutation of anti claims. It began, "The Federal Suffrage Amendment will not affect the negro situation in the South." Since whites outnumber blacks 70 percent to 30 percent, it followed that women's vote would only increase white majorities. "If white domination is threatened in the South, it is, therefore, DOUBLY EXPEDIENT TO ENFRANCHISE THE WOMEN QUICKLY IN ORDER THAT IT BE PRESERVED." The flyer then added endorsements from Josephus Daniels, Walter Clark, Woodrow Wilson, and Furnifold Simmons, "who waged the successful fight for White Supremacy in North Carolina in 1898." A second flyer headlined "Woman Suffrage Amendment Raises No Race Issue" argued that women's suffrage added nothing to the Fifteenth Amendment "so far as the negro is concerned." The federal government left voting qualifications to the states. "Just as the East allows the West to regulate the Jap problem," the handbill concluded, "so the North has accustomed itself to hands off in the negro question." A third statement, related to the race issue, refuted arguments on the "19th Amendment and

States' Rights." It noted that North Carolina had previously ratified eighteen amendments, and granting woman suffrage presented no challenge to constitutional principles.[75]

In defending the racial status quo ESANC did not employ race-baiting rhetoric or advocate black disfranchisement. Facts spoke for themselves. The statistical justification was commonly made, and it dated to abolitionist times. Significantly, Gertrude assumed that black women would vote. As historian Glenda Gilmore observes, "Concocting an argument that dared speak of the deployment of 336,000 African Americans to the polls represented a departure from political rhetoric of the past." But suffragists also needed to win influential white supremacists like Senator Simmons. Gertrude wrote another legislator, "The menace of the negro woman's vote is a figment of the Anti imagination." Rumors had spread that black women would be exempt from the education qualification that had largely succeeded in eliminating black men from the ballot. Gertrude accused "imported," out-of-state rejectionists of making "capital of race prejudice" in North Carolina. NAWSA and Catt personally assured southerners that women's suffrage would not upset white supremacy. The *Woman Citizen* headlined "Makes for White Supremacy," in which state bureaucrat Josiah Bailey argued that woman suffrage "is the only way to guarantee the existence of two parties in North Carolina pledged to white supremacy."[76]

In letters to legislators, Gertrude defined her position. She admitted that the illiteracy of African Americans was indeed a "problem . . . one phase of the larger Negro problem." She believed its "seriousness is so generally recognized that it will be successfully handled." She had "faith in the feasibility of its solution and OTHERWISE than at the cost of injustice and discrimination against the white women of the state." She drew a distinction: "Equal suffrage does not necessarily imply UNIVERSAL suffrage. It does not forbid the limiting of the franchise right, but simply that the limitations be NOT ON LINES OF SEX. I, myself am strongly in favor of demanding higher qualifications for voting than at present. To my mind it is the only way to cope fairly and effectively with the Negro problem."[77] Though Gertrude echoed popular rhetoric in speaking of black people as a "problem," she did not defend black disfranchisement but did argue that the vote ought to be qualified on the basis of education. No doubt, given the greater prevalence of black illiteracy, even a "fair" test "effectively" and honestly administered, as Gertrude advocated, would ensure the continued suppression of the black vote. In contrast to a "liberal" like Walter Clark, Gertrude did not expressly disparage blacks.

Gertrude always acknowledged that she had been raised with prejudices, and she fervently believed education was the means to overcome them. Her view of education as the agency for full citizenship was a progressive precept. Governor Aycock, an ideological white supremacist, saw black disfranchisement as a temporary expedient until blacks were sufficiently educated to vote. In its founding "program" of March 1919, the national League of Women Voters had called for compulsory schooling, higher standards for citizenship, and "an educational qualification for the vote in all states." Catt had spoken of the "ill-advised haste" in enfranchising the "foreigner, the negro, and the Indian." Considering the spectrum of racial positions in southern suffragist debates, Gertrude Weil's views were racially moderate.[78]

The Final Battle

In the summer 1920, as the special session date neared, Gertrude urged ESANC members to put their "shoulders to the wheel and make one strong final effort." Her advice was "THINK RATIFICATION, TALK RATIFICATION, WORK FOR RATIFICATION." North Carolina was to be the "PERFECT THIRTY-SIX." She cautioned, "Time is short." Ratification rallies were held in towns across the state, and petitions were distributed. Allied organizations issued resolutions. Gertrude pushed local workers to collect signatures, distribute literature, pass resolutions, lobby senators and representatives, and write newspapers. President Wilson telegraphed Governor Bickett of "the critical importance" of the state in adopting the amendment. Bickett replied that he hoped Tennessee would ratify and render North Carolina superfluous. Fears rose of a "double-cross" from Senator Simmons. Gertrude enlisted F. P. Hobgood, a state senate suffragist leader, to write Simmons to confirm his commitment.[79]

North Carolina was doing what it could to avoid becoming the deciding state. Not wanting to call a special session before Vermont and Tennessee voted, Governor Bickett played a game of political chicken. As Catt wrote in a 1 July joint letter to Gertrude and Cornelia Jerman, "We can no longer count on any state until the vote is actually taken." The "big contest for advantage" was between Vermont Republicans and North Carolina Democrats over who would gain an electoral advantage. The NAWSA board had voted to send a "large deputation" of Democratic women to North Carolina. As she boarded a ship for the International Woman Suffrage Alliance conference in Geneva, Catt spoke to Josephus Daniels, who was confident that "North Carolina would surely ratify." She did not share his "over-optimism," believing, as she told Gertrude during a New York visit, that the antis would go far in arousing "hostility." Reports coming to her "seem to spell Discouragement and Pessimism." Though not entirely convinced that the state was lost, Catt nonetheless lamented, "It is unfortunate that North Carolina stands in line as a decisive state." After a conversation with Gertrude, Catt expressed concern that the North Carolina campaign employed a "soft pedal," without "bold advertising" or mass meetings. NAWSA field organizer Maria McMahon suffered an accident, limiting her work, and the Democratic Party "gobbled up" women so that they were "no longer available for suffrage." Women were so "overjoyed to think the political parties are taking them in," Catt wrote Gertrude, that they "are content to play away off in the corner of the back-door yard."[80]

Perhaps sensing her futility and exhaustion, Catt bucked up Gertrude for the final round. If leaders "lose courage and faith," how can they inspire others? "All the world loves a good fighter and a good fight!" Catt exclaimed. "It must be bold or there is no hope." Catt—and Walter Clark, too—expressed frustration that ESANC relied too much on reason and persuasion as if the legislators were rational men. The cause would be lost if dependent on the "eventual enlightenment" of southern men, Clark warned. Gertrude, Catt noted, had focused on meetings. "Agitation is helpful," she advised, but to move suffrage forward meant "getting the political leaders to fight for you." Governor Bickett was, as Cornelia Jerman confirmed, no more than "a weak friend." Catt recommended that Adelaide Daniels be brought into the fray. She expressed impatience. Moderation was more than a reflection of Gertrude's personality. In 1914 ESANC had declared that it was "opposed to any form of militancy and goes on record as desiring to gain the vote by an appeal to reason and fair play." NAWSA had flooded Connecticut with Democratic activists from forty-seven states, but North Carolina persistently warned against intruders.[81]

In response Gertrude confessed that she was not "disheartened" and felt the "impatience," too. She reminded Catt of North Carolina's political realities. Given popular feeling, even supportive legislators had warned against agitation like mass meetings. In calling a special legislative session the governor's priority was a revaluation of property, and he was "jealous" of any issue that detracted from that. Gertrude thought the best hope lay with the National Democratic Party and state leaders returning from the San Francisco convention who considered the national political interest. Gertrude needed time to address Catt's call for a "stronger, more robust campaign."[82]

Leading Democratic Party progressives offered last-minute political advice. Josiah Bailey, a crusading reformer, suggested that Gertrude solicit testimonials from each member of her advisory committee and invite them to Raleigh for the special session. The request should come from Gertrude to make it seem as if each "were the only man of whom the requests were being made." He offered to "be of any service." Gertrude solicited the endorsements and published them in the *Raleigh News and Observer.* Angus McLean, a future governor, favored women's suffrage "unhesitatingly." O. Max Gardner declared his loyalty to the Democratic Party platform. Always reliable Walter Clark urged North Carolina and Tennessee to share the honor of ratifying jointly. At the University of North Carolina thirty-three of forty professors wrote in favor. Frank Graham said the "right to vote was a human right."[83]

North Carolina's newspapers rallied to the cause. At a meeting of the North Carolina Press Association in Waynesville in early August, NAWSA sent publicist Marjorie Shuler, a journalist, to work the crowd. Only one of more than twenty editors surveyed questioned whether North Carolina would ratify. Editorial pages challenged anti arguments on the fitness of women for politics or the alleged violation of states' rights.[84]

As July ended, Gertrude lacked funds to mount a robust campaign. To employ organizers, print literature, hire secretaries, and maintain the Raleigh office required $4,000. She sent appeals. Mrs. Jones was asked to raise $1,000 in Durham. Would she solicit mill owner Julian S. Carr, who should be good for at least $500, Gertrude thought, or perhaps the whole $4,000? Or maybe ten people could give $100. "This is the psychological time," Gertrude advised, and she "shudder[ed]" to think of a deficit. Though "National has helped considerably," Gertrude wrote, "we cannot pay the expenses we have incurred.... It is the self respectful thing for us to do." Given her retiring personality, Gertrude was not a forceful fundraiser. A correspondent had described her as "anxious."[85]

In June 1920 Gertrude embarked on a breathless travel schedule touring several dozen small towns across eastern North Carolina. By July 29 she had left Goldsboro and moved to Raleigh, establishing herself at suffragist headquarters. "We are some busy people here—all day long," she wrote a Durham sympathizer. A photograph shows Gertrude seated at a desk, typewriter before her, desktop cluttered with papers. On the wall is a state map. Although ESANC president, she took the smaller desk. Legislative chair Cornelia Jerman and volunteer chair Sallie Dortch worked the office with her. Among those "hanging around" was aspiring journalist Nell Battle Lewis, ready for an errand. A generation younger than Gertrude, Lewis, a Smith alumna, was an "unabashed feminist." Unlike the ladies at the Yarborough Hotel, she believed heckling, parading, smashing windows, or perhaps a "little arson here and there" might help the cause. Boldly, Josephus Daniels hired Lewis as a cub reporter for the *News and Observer.*[86]

However lacking resources, pros and antis fired barrages of propa-

Gertrude (at far left) at Raleigh suffragist headquarters.
Cornelia Jerman sits at the desk on the right, with Sallie Dortch beside her.
Courtesy of the State Archives of North Carolina.

ganda. Well-worn issues were rehashed—race, domesticity, states' rights, scripture, suffrage's inevitability. One ESANC broadside listed eight reasonable justifications on why the state legislature "should ratify." They ranged from "democratic justice" to "it makes white supremacy absolutely sure." The United States was the last English-speaking country not to enfranchise women. ESANC appealed to state pride "as an advocate of freedom and human liberty." Both political parties as well as labor, farm, and women's groups endorsed it.[87]

The antis "in a dire need of argument" blasted new salvos that were petty, contrived, unfair, and often baseless. The rejectionists distributed literature ripping Shaw's and Catt's words from context and reprinting incendiary quotes from reds and blacks. "They don't seem to have let Dr. Shaw alone, even in her grave," Gertrude wrote in the margin of one inflammatory report. Late in the campaign the antis raised the issue of the *Woman's Bible*, published a half century earlier by Elizabeth Cady Stanton. Its title alone was provocative even beyond the women's liberation theology it espoused. The antis charged that Shaw and Catt were its authors. Gertrude wrote a rebuttal titled "THE SO-CALLED WOMAN'S BIBLE." Catt and Shaw "had NOTHING to do with the authorship of the book," she asserted. State suffrage leaders "knew nothing of its existence until told of it by the anti-suffragists."[88]

In late July rejectionists circulated a letter sent to the Tennessee governor allegedly written by one Annie Bock of Los Angeles, who identified herself as a "prominent" California suffragist. Now, she "shall do penance forever." Politics taught her that "women are intolerant, radical, revolutionary, and more corrupt ... than men." Furthermore, "their so-called reforms lead to the Socialist Co-operative Commonwealth." California had experienced "an alarming increase in immorality, divorce, and murder." Ninety percent of women do not want suffrage, she added. Antis had distributed the Bock letter nationally since 1913, but it proved more effective in the urban North than in the rural South. Gertrude countered that the Nineteenth Amendment entailed "no radical or revolutionary overturning of our political and social institutions."[89]

Gertrude kept busy refuting charges, however outlandish. She assured one legislator that "contrary to certain scurrilous reports, the leaders of the suffrage movement, national and State, have been and are women of unimpeachable moral character." To the repeated charge that women were not interested in suffrage, Gertrude answered, "the women of North Carolina DO want the vote," and she listed endorsing women's organizations. Both sides played the old North Carolina political game of alleging their opponents were outsiders. The struggle was drawing "nation-wide attention," and the taint of northern money was suggested. Swatting a late rumor that "ten thousand dollars has been subscribed and hordes of outsiders are en route to our State to urge ratification upon the Legislature," Gertrude assured that, apart from "a small group of National Suffragists," ESANC was "entirely" of, by, and for "North Carolina women." She noted that "imported" Maine and New York women started the state antisuffrage organization.[90]

Predictably, the final blast was a racist fusillade. On 16 August, days before the vote, the *State's Defense*—rejecting any "desire to fan the fires of race antagonism"—extensively quoted Dr. A. M. Moore's speech that past March in Goldsboro at the North Carolina Conference for Social Service. Moore described how the breakdown of slavery had led to the sexual subjugation of the Negro woman by her "white overlord."[91] The antis played to fears of miscegenation and sexual violation that underlay southern anti-black racism.

As North Carolina and Tennessee legislatures prepared to vote, Catt traveled to Nashville while NAWSA sent Maria McMahon to lobby North Carolina. Catt described McMahon to Gertrude as the kind of "charming and sincere woman" who "will appeal to the Southern men." Lavinia Engle had also returned to the state, but Catt advised that the work be "conducted as far as possible by North Carolina women." Adopting the national strategy, women lobbyists were assigned to specific legislators and were "expected to know exactly where they were at all times." As each session closed, the lobbyist was to ensure that her solon held true to his position. Catt handwrote Gertrude a letter the following day. North Carolina should "not excuse herself from action" since Tennessee's ratification might be challenged as illegal, and the Supreme Court would then not decide the issue until October. "It would mean a lot of anxiety," she felt. "Therefore we want N.C. also.... I fear Tenn will not ratify," Catt added. Gertrude was "quite right in your decision to do the work yourselves. I am relieved that I shall not be needed."[92]

A day before the session opened Gertrude received a telegram from Asheville warning about stolen and bogus suffrage petitions. As the legislators arrived Cornelia Jerman counted twenty-nine votes certain in the senate, but only twenty-eight in the house. At least twenty-five legislators had not committed either way. In the "thick of the fight" urging "yea" votes were U.S. congressmen Clyde Hoey and Zebulon Weaver and secretary of the navy Josephus Daniels.[93]

A Hot Vote

The North Carolina legislature opened in "unspeakable heat" on 10 August at the very moment that Tennessee was considering ratification. The next day, even before Governor Bickett submitted the amendment to the legislature, 63 of the 120 members of the North Carolina house, including four Republicans, sent a surprise "round robin" telegram to Nashville declaring that they "will not ratify" and urging Tennessee to reject. Rumors flew that representative W. W. Neal went to Nashville as a rejectionist "ambassador." The "immortal 63," as Gertrude sarcastically labeled them, wrote that they stood in defense of states' rights. They were opposed to "interfering with the sovereignty of Tennessee" and "most respectfully request that this measure be not forced upon the people of North Carolina." Anti leaders in the senate pronounced the fight for the amendment in North Carolina "finis." Suffragists were stunned that some putative supporters signed the petition, but they pressed forward, believing that national Democrats—most notably Daniels and Simmons—could pressure them into repudiating their "solemn pledge." Telegrams flew from Catt in Nashville to Gertrude in Raleigh. The

North Carolina round-robin did not sway the Tennesseans, and two days later its senate ratified, passing it to its house.[94]

Walking into the statehouse to hear Governor Bickett address the special session, Gertrude Weil and Mary Hinton met by chance at the door. "One was the quiet, capable idealist" who led the suffragists, a journalist observed, "the other the equally decorous president" of the rejectionists. "They both paused . . . took a long look at each other" before the reporter intervened to introduce Miss Weil to Miss Hinton. They shook hands, and "verbally exchanged the customary civilities." The reporter speculated on the lack of "outward perturbation visible in either." Were they measuring each other? Did they mutually respect the other's "loyalty to a deep, inherent conviction?"[95] In Gertrude's case preserving the demeanor of the southern lady was essential to her argument and political success. Though capable of a sharp tongue, she was acting in character.

Events moved swiftly. The day was hot, the hall so packed an order was made to clear the galleries. Crowds blocked the windows. The governor entered the chamber accompanied by suffragists Fanny Bickett, Adelaide Daniels, and Cornelia Jerman. Speaking to the joint session, the governor at first encouraged the rejectionists. Slowly and deliberately, he predicted that suffrage would be bad for women and "unfortunate" for race relations. However, he conceded, woman suffrage was coming. At best the state could delay it a month or so. He was "profoundly convinced that it would be the part of wisdom and of grace for North Carolina to accept the inevitable and ratify the amendment." On 17 August the senate began debate. Proponents argued that women's suffrage was both just and right. R. D. Fisk of Franklin County pointed an accusatory finger at liquor interests for backing the antis. D. F. Lovill of Boone, the senate's last Confederate veteran, recalled the dutiful service of women in the war. Others urged loyalty to the Democratic platform.[96]

Lindsay Warren of Washington led the opposition. Home and hearth were praised once more. Warren evoked states' rights and warned that the "overwhelming sentiment" of the people was against women's vote. He drew a line between "expediency" and "principle," noting that when suffrage had come before the U.S. Senate, Simmons had opposed it. Now Simmons as well as Bickett supported it as politically necessary. "I denounce such an insidious appeal from Governor Bickett to our base natures," Warren declaimed. "Expediency is a word not found in my dictionary." Warren then caught suffragists off guard—he asked the senate to postpone consideration of the amendment until the regular session of the legislature, to be held in 1921, and substituted a resolution to that effect. The 1920 election would thus become a referendum on women's suffrage. Warren's move for postponement passed twenty-five to twenty-three. Some pro-suffrage senators supported postponement to escape a political predicament. Suffragists were stunned by Horace Stacy of Lumberton, hitherto a supporter. His vote in opposition would have forced a tie that pro-suffragist Lieutenant Governor Gardner would have then resolved in their favor.[97]

With this vote North Carolina became not a chapter but a footnote in the history of women's suffrage. On 18 August, newsboys on Fayetteville Street shouted, "Tennessee's ratified." Seemingly, the woman's movement had its long-sought "perfect 36," but before victory could be declared, the Tennessee house speaker moved to reconsider. Catt wrote Gertrude an urgent, handwritten letter that though the law was on the suffragists' side they were in "the usual condition of doubt as to what will happen next." She explained, "The opponents are hanging the amendment up in order to give N.C. time to kill it there." Catt despaired for Tennessee: "Our side is not so well led." In her long life, never had she seen such "excitable men anywhere" or so much "drunkenness." She felt "intense anxiety." She offered to come to North Carolina if Gertrude wired her that it was "necessary." The letter ended, "Keep up your courage. God is with us. Lovingly, C. C. Catt."[98]

A day later, 19 August, the North Carolina house continued fighting a lost cause. The house considered resolutions to ratify and to reject. Rumors flew. Gertrude telegraphed Catt, "Report circulated on floor of House here that Tennessee has reversed decision. Wire truth immediately." Catt responded, "No truth in statement. Suffragists have gained in additional votes." The North Carolina house voted down a motion to postpone ratification forty-one to seventy-one. It then tabled a resolution to reject the amendment. Meanwhile, from Tennessee, Catt wrote Gertrude, thirty-eight men "fled in the darkness of night" to deny the legislature a quorum, but this delaying tactic failed. Catt feared that antisuffragists might win a court injunction to delay suffrage for another year. Two days later, with opponents hiding, the Tennessee house voted forty-nine to zero not to reconsider, and the Nineteenth Amendment became the law of the land. On 26 August Catt wired Gertrude, "Ratification accomplished proceed with state wide celebrations disregard all litigation news." On the session's last day, the North Carolina General Assembly voted to amend the Consolidated Statutes to allow women to register and vote—but it did not ratify the amendment.[99]

On behalf of ESANC Gertrude issued a statement: "We are very much humiliated that our men have not shown confidence enough in us to entrust us with a share in the government. But we are not at all downcast, because we shall be enfranchised anyway. However, it will always be a source of shame that we had to receive the ballot at the hands of men of other States."[100] A southern lady scolded southern gentlemen that they had failed the test of chivalry. On 23 August, Gertrude addressed "My dear Friend Suffragist." She confessed that they had been "unsuccessful"; suffrage had been given to them as a "gift." However disconsolate over North Carolina's failure, Gertrude responded with her typical resilience. After offering "appreciative thanks," she wrote, "I beg you to hold together whatever local organization you have. We shall need it to carry out the work that lies before us."[101]

Letters and telegrams flowed to Gertrude consoling her and offering tributes. Mina sent congratulations, but then, of course, wanted to know when Gertrude would come home. Others urged her to "enjoy a nice rest." A typical message read, "Our own state failed, but we all rejoice in the victory." Catt wrote that she was not "surprised at the result in N.C. but I was disappointed for your sakes. Cheer up." Georgia, Delaware, and Tennessee suffragists offered thanks. For her part Gertrude sent congratulatory telegrams to Tennessee. Despite North Carolina's failure, four southern states had ratified the federal amendment. "I guess I never was a politician," Gertrude later reflected. "I never could tell after I talked with a lawmaker whether he was for us or against us."[102]

Suffragists celebrated at a victory banquet at the Yarborough Hotel, which featured a woman impersonating Governor Bickett. Antisuffragist legislators sitting in an anteroom booed and hooted. Wayne County resident L. J. H. Mewborn wrote Gertrude replaying every Old South trope. "Can't help being surprised at you," he wrote, "you being a Jew and knowing the Jews were God's choosen [sic] nation to be a light to the gentiles.... And knowing that the children of Ham the negro was cursed and made servants to Shem." Because of woman suffrage "the negro will be put back in politics, then woe to our free South land." He claimed that Miss Gertrude did "not think half as much of your own sex as I do." The thought of "two negro women" beside a white woman at the polling place gave him "cold chills." He ended by invoking the God of Abraham, Isaac, and Jacob.[103]

Mary Hilliard Hinton did not look back. Though suffrage had been unwillingly imposed on women through "no action nor fault" of their own, Hinton wrote in a public appeal, they should yield to "stern reality" and register.[104] She did not want to cede the political ground to reform-minded suffragists. Hinton was exactly right in her fears. For Gertrude Weil women's suffrage was not an end but a means to change society: social justice in North Carolina, democracy in America, and, to a war weary-world, global peace.

{ 7 }

HOW SHALL WOMEN VOTE
League, Council, and Conference

Gertrude Weil had been home but a month after the exhausting suffrage fight, but she was eager to start a new day. In September 1920 she announced that the Equal Suffrage Association of North Carolina would meet next month at the Greensboro courthouse to organize a "STATE LEAGUE OF WOMEN VOTERS." Subjects to discuss included "How and why shall women vote. How shall women prepare for the vote. What kind of state and national legislation shall women work for."[1]

With the vote Gertrude saw opportunity to realize her ideals. Joined by progressive allies, she would lay the groundwork for a welfare state. Yet, as Gertrude learned in the suffrage campaign, her ideals did not accord with those of a conservative society or a corrupt political system. She would need to temper her visionary views with reason and pragmatism. She struggled not merely in the civic marketplace but within herself. She aspired to be effective as well as virtuous. She became, in modern terms, a community organizer working through the electoral process. Education would create an enlightened citizenry that would end war and poverty.

In contrast to suffragists who had a clear, single focus, voting women confronted questions of how and what. Carrie Chapman Catt set a grand example. Not only had she led the national suffrage campaign, but she had founded a woman's international peace movement. Gertrude, too, felt herself a citizen of both Goldsboro and the world, attending local school board meetings as well as global disarmament conferences. In the postwar years, the economy was depressed and the national mood uncertain. The cost of living spiraled higher, farm prices fell, and destitute industrial workers struck. A national clamor for Americanism led to disengagement abroad and nativism at home. President Warren Harding's call for "normalcy" was an argument against reform. North Carolina governor Cameron Morrison, a machine Democrat, embarked on a progressive program of road and school building without addressing labor inequities. North Carolina remained a contending ground for business elites who benefited from its rapid industrial growth versus rural and working poor whose well-being continued to erode. Its labor strife drew worldwide attention as a microcosm of problems besetting newly industrial societies.

Back Home

Gertrude back on Chestnut Street cultivated her garden literally and figuratively. Citizen and neighbor, she taught Sunday school, sponsored Girl Scout picnics, and led the Goldsboro Woman's Club. She headed the campaign to move the club from rooms above a Chinese laundry to its own building.[2] She was president of the Charity Organization Society and continued in that post as it evolved into the Goldsboro Bureau for Social Service. When the Goldsboro Community Chest organized in 1928, she sat on its board. She immersed herself in antituberculosis casework and directed the county drive for Christmas Seals. She planted flowers for city beautification and joined societies devoted to historic preservation.

Gertrude shared the house with Mina, now in her sixties, still active as a charity worker and generous host despite ailments that sent her to spas and sanitariums. Gertrude's aspiration for independence yielded to a deepening devotion to her mother. Mina found purpose providing "constant care" to her elderly mother Eva, now bedridden in their home. Mina's charities extended from the African American hospital in Goldsboro to the Zionist scouts in Jerusalem. After a visit in 1927, Raleigh author Hope Chamberlain wrote that "breathing" the home's "atmosphere ... I feel a deeper desire for the greatest good of the greatest numbers, a restoration of a new sense of worthwhileness of spiritual things." Another houseguest, journalist Nell Battle Lewis, wrote Gertrude, "I think your mother is just one of the very best things we have in North Carolina."[3] Gertrude followed her mother's example.

Supporting students with scholarships was a Weil family avocation, all the more necessary as the Depression crushed hopes. Henry Weil Fellowships aided students at the University of North Carolina at Chapel Hill and Woman's College in Greensboro. A Goldsboro friend teaching in Brevard asked Gertrude if she "had a scholarship up your sleeve" for Anna Mottsman, a high school student from a rabbinic family whose "poverty prevents ... further education." Another college fund, administered by Gertrude, supported "worthy" Wayne County students. Gertrude wrote tuition checks to the Pineland School for Girls in Salemburg and sent several students five-dollar monthly stipends. She extended a two-thousand-dollar loan to keep the school open after a "crop failure" prevented students from paying tuition. In 1920 Gertrude sent two thousand dollars to the Smith College Fund. Beyond tuition, Mina and Gertrude mailed suits or dresses for graduation. Mina required recipients to send her report cards, examined their grades, and dispensed advice. "Although my grades did not show up so well," a Woman's College student wrote, "I appreciate what you have done for me, Mrs. Weil, not only in loaning me money, but in making me see my weak points."[4]

Local social welfare was another priority. Mother and daughter supported patients at the state sanitarium and paid hospital bills. Periodically they wrote three-hundred-dollar checks to the Charity Organization Society to pay for the county public health nurse. Hundreds more went to the community chest. Gertrude's annual donations encompassed Jewish, educational, and progressive causes. Jews, jealous of their public reputation and not wanting to burden the larger society, took pride in caring for their own. Gertrude continued her father's and uncle's fealty to the Hebrew Orphans' Home in Atlanta. Her largest donations went through cousin Lionel to the United Palestine Appeal and Joint Distribution Committee, which served overseas Jewry. She also kept membership in the National Consumers League, American Association of University Women, and Women's Trade Union League. Hundreds of her dollars underwrote publication of the *Women Citizen*, Catt's suffrage journal now dedicated to political education. Annual dues were paid to the North Carolina Folklore Society and the North Carolina Literary and Historical Association. Smaller donations supported labor reform and the abolition of capital punishment. A reflexive writer of thank-you notes, Gertrude habitually gave gifts. Table mats went to Frances Towers Doggett in Washington and Christmas greens to Frederick Peterson in New York, a noted psychoanalyst whom the family consulted.[5]

The generational tide was turning. Grandmother Eva died in 1924, followed three years later by Gertrude's beloved uncle Joe Rosenthal, who lived across the street. Like his sister Mina, Joe was quietly generous to the farmer seeking credit, student wanting tuition, or needy widow, and publicly he supported the hospital and schools. For seventeen years he was a trustee of Woman's College, which named its gymnasium for him. Aunt Sarah next door, a fount of ideas and initiatives, died in 1928, her children bequeathing her home to the city as the public library.

Now in her forties, Gertrude stepped forward as head of household. After her grandmother's death, she redecorated the home. In her garden she cultivated roses and Japanese irises. The house—served by maid, cook, and butler—testified to southern grace. Guests were welcomed to dinner with fine china and crystal. She ordered glassware from Corning and considered Chippendale from a New York dealer. Her purveyors were the finest: B. Altman, Saks, Tiffany, R. H. Macy, and John Wannamaker. Her youthful fad for fashion faded, although as photographs show, she remained elegant in a simple dress, accented with a broach or string of pearls. Petite, fair skinned, and crystal eyed, her hair neatly if not stylishly coiffed, she always looked younger than her years.

Gertrude busied herself with her crowd of Weils, Rosenthals, and Oettingers. She played favorite aunt to Leslie's five children, as well as to Janet's four, who resided in Wilmington. Nieces and nephews adored their aunt, who arrived as surrogate mother when parents traveled, sometimes for weeks. After a nephew suffered a breakdown, he wrote his aunt tenderly, and the two shared stories, exchanged political views, and discussed the Weil "nervousness." Family gatherings at the Bluethenthal cottage at Wrightsville Beach were recalled nostalgically. Ruth Weil, Lionel's wife, joined Gertrude's organizations, as did sister-in-law Hilda on occasion. Janet followed Sister's activist footsteps in Wilmington. Leslie and Lionel served as civic leaders, organizing scout troops, guiding the temple, and heading municipal campaigns. Leslie remained Gertrude's male confidante.[6]

As a Weil, Gertrude was welcomed when she solicited donors, lobbied politicians, or approached professors on behalf of her own causes. "You are loved," an admiring mill owner wrote Gertrude. Congressman Charles Abernethy remarked, "I value your friendship very much indeed, and I shall never forget the very fine service that you rendered me when I first came to Congress." He thanked Gertrude for turning out the vote.[7]

Gertrude's passion for travel remained insatiable. A Massachusetts friend wanted to know, "Isn't it about time for you to be taking a trip northward? That is your custom, n'est-ce pas, every year?" To and from conferences, she visited Baltimore and New York to see friends and family. Summers found her in the mountains calling on the Cones at Blowing Rock or attending folk and workers schools. In 1926 she traveled to New Orleans and as far west as the Grand Canyon with Harriet Payne. In 1929 she sailed again to Europe, accompanied by her ten-year-old niece Mina Bluethenthal, touring Switzerland, Austria, Germany, and France. Mina heard *Rigoletto* at the Paris Opera, "feeling like a companion, not a child in tow." With family and friends abroad the Weils remained cosmopolitans. When Florie Altmeyer traveled to Florence, Italy, her Goldsboro cousins arranged an invitation to Bernard Berenson's fabled Renaissance Villa I Tatti. Table talk centered on Janet's family and Gertrude's work. When Berenson's nephew enrolled at Chapel Hill, Gertrude paid visits. Weils and Berensons kept each other up-to-date.[8]

Harriet Payne remained vividly present, visiting Goldsboro whenever she could and, when she could not, writing of her "tremendous" desire to be with "peerless Gertrude." Whatever the adventure, Gertrude was invited to the "party." Even as Harriet despised her own mother, she revered the "unique" Mina. Harriet pressed Gertrude with books to read. Like Gertrude, Harriet was a peripatetic soul, and the two planned trips, few of which were undertaken. Short of cash, Harriet borrowed five hundred dollars from Gertrude in 1927, only to depart two months later for Paris, her third visit in three years. Her finances were so dire that she prepared to auction her home, a guest house, asking Gertrude for a ten-thousand-dollar bridge loan. The family was outraged, but Gertrude appeased her with kind words and a smaller loan. When Mina told Harriet she was "crazy," she felt "doomed."[9] Gertrude and Harriet complemented each other: the flighty one who needed to be grounded and the grounded one who would fly.

Southern Reform

Gertrude's causes were entangled in North Carolina's cultural wars. After a postwar depression, North Carolina boomed, its industries—textiles, tobacco, furniture—leading the Southeast. Corporate paternalists employed entire families over generations. A worker's life in a mill village was carefully controlled from home to school to church to store to factory. Wages were still half the national average, yet industrialists felt assured of their benevolence. They endowed church-related colleges like Trinity College (renamed Duke University in 1924) and Wake Forest College north of Raleigh. Governors underwrote public universities for both blacks and whites that were the envy of the South. A massive bond campaign built "good roads" to link farmers to markets.

Gertrude was tied personally and professionally to the University of North Carolina at Chapel Hill, where her father, brothers, and cousin served as trustees. Faculty wives like poet and suffragist Barbara Henderson became friends and colleagues, and professors were guests in the Weil home. Frank Graham and the Weil family formed a mutual admiration society. Carolina Playmaker founder Frederick Koch was another favorite of the theater-loving family. Gertrude had an open door at the Chapel Hill home of Louis Graves, a well-known journalist, whose wife and mother were Goldsboro natives. Her brother Leslie's devotion to his alma mater was so extensive that the university dedicated the 1926 yearbook to him. Leslie was an incorporator of the University of North Carolina Press. When

it was attacked for publishing books on chain gangs, black life, and other allegedly radical topics, editor W. T. Couch appealed personally to Gertrude as a "liberal citizen" for funds and support.[10] Their challenge was to ensure that social justice kept pace with the state's economic progress, to defend a liberal university under perpetual conservative attack.

Nationally, the war effort had unleashed a patriotic fervor. The immigrant flow roused nativist calls for 100 percent Americanism. Newcomers brought not just "alien" languages and cultures but ideologies like anarchism, socialism, and communism. As a Red Scare swept America, enflamed by labor strife and anarchist bombings, Attorney General A. Mitchell Palmer unleashed raids that resulted in the arrest of thousands and the deportation of hundreds without regard to guilt or innocence. Jews were especially suspect as radicals, personified by the infamous immigrant anarchist Emma Goldman. Jews were distrusted not only as reds but also as capitalists, supposedly seeking world domination through their international cabals. The Weils cut from the *New York Times* articles reporting Henry Ford's publication of the anti-Semitic *Protocols of the Elders of Zion*, a tsarist forgery that alleged a global Jewish economic conspiracy, as well as his retraction. Though the state had the nation's smallest percentage of foreign born, nativism became a rallying cry. Across North Carolina fundamentalist preachers like Mordecai Ham held tent revivals, declaring war against modernism and blaming Jews for all kinds of sins from Wall Street to Tin Pan Alley. Those wanting to bring North Carolina into the twentieth century contended with a society ranked last in library books and near last in newspaper readership. By contrast, Gertrude's household subscribed to the *Atlantic, New Republic, Menorah, Nation*, and *Saturday Evening Post*. The *New York Herald Tribune* arrived daily, and the *New York Times* arrived on Sundays.[11]

A resurgent Ku Klux Klan, more anti-Catholic than anti-Semitic, enjoyed popularity in rural areas and small towns. In 1923, as a courtesy, G. B. Morris, a Goldsboro physician, sent Gertrude a copy of his acceptance speech for Klan membership. He rebutted anti-Semitic accusations thrown at Sol and Henry Weil that they "improve the town ... to improve their property" or "have made all of their money" out of the people and "ought to give SOMETHING" back. Dismissing anti-Semites, Morris lauded Sol, Henry, Mina, and Joe Rosenthal as Lions of Judea who gave from their pockets without anyone knowing. He took "off my hat" in tribute to the "One Hundred Per Cent American, THE AMERICAN HEBREW." He then launched into a viciously antiblack and anti-Catholic screed and extolled the lynch mob. He spoke to "help keep down fanaticism." Gertrude's brother

Herman warned Harriet Payne of "a movement afoot" about which he felt "gloomy." Visiting France, Payne dined with two British officers who pressed upon her the anti-Semitic *Protocols* and *The Bolshevists of Ancient History (the Jews)*. When Payne defended her Jewish friend as "the nicest girl in America" and lauded her family's "consistent kindness," they warned that Jews were deceitful.[12]

Gertrude would have seen the headlines in 1925 when Klansmen in nearby Williamston castrated a Jewish salesman, Joseph Needleman, for allegedly seducing a local woman. Unlike ten year years earlier in Georgia, where a mob lynched Jewish factory manager Leo Frank wrongly convicted of murdering a working girl, public sympathy in North Carolina, starting with the governor, went to Needleman. The perpetrators were arrested and sentenced to hard labor. The Klan, though strong in Gertrude's Down East, was otherwise weak in North Carolina. Gertrude almost never spoke or wrote of religious prejudice. Nativism expressed itself mostly as anti-Catholic, climaxing in 1928 when Al Smith ran for president.[13]

Gertrude's avoidance of party politics was explicable given the grip of the Democratic machine. Reflecting on the suffrage campaign, she laughed heartily at her own political naivety. Courthouse cronyism dominated politics, and elections featured marked ballots, stuffed boxes, and backroom vote counting. Ward heelers posed as poll watchers. According to one journalist, politics consisted of little more than a blowhard candidate standing on the courthouse steps shouting "nigger," damning the Pope, railing against Wall Street, and espousing Prohibition before a crowd tipsy on bootleg. Without irony, the North Carolina League of Women Voters titled one conference session, "Political Nuts to Crack."[14]

The North Carolina League of Women Voters

The vision enunciated by Carrie Chapman Catt at the National American Woman Suffrage Association Jubilee Convention to "Finish the Fight" set the agenda for a "non-partisan and non-sectarian" League of Women Voters. In 1920 Gertrude appealed to women from every county and every women's organization to come to Greensboro. There, she declared that the "Equal Suffrage Association of North Carolina ceases to be" and announced its successor, the North Carolina League of Women Voters. Suffrage leadership moved to the League, with Gertrude remaining chair, Laura Cone treasurer, and Nell Battle Lewis publicist. The women who gathered on 7 October were exclusively white, well educated, and mostly middle class. The state's first families were well represented. Gladys Tillett, daughter of a state supreme court justice, led an active Charlotte League. Fannie Bickett was a governor's widow. One meeting was held at Adelaide Daniels's home, where guests met Eleanor Roosevelt. The advisory board grew to include the grandees of the North Carolina Federation of Women's Clubs. Some, like Sallie Southall Cotten, had been reluctant suffragists. "I believe strongly in the work of the League," wrote Cotten, now eighty-two, in 1927, enclosing a donation.[15] The League's social welfare agenda drew from the Women's Clubs' maternalism in advocating legislation to protect women, children, and public health.

"The organization and work of our League is in accordance with those of the National League," Gertrude wrote four days after that initial meeting. The League as a whole was a hierarchy: the national office issued directives, which state affiliates endorsed at an annual convention. Staff, departments, and committees developed expertise, publishing an array of study guides and educational programming for the membership. The state League, in turn, asked each county to form a local affiliate. Gertrude sent a "model constitution" to local Leagues that recommended a threefold program to interest women in registering and voting, educate women in the "ideals and processes of government," and invite them to study "social conditions" and then propose "progressive legislation." Insisting that this program was "patriotic" and "practical," Gertrude well knew that merely organizing women as a political body would arouse a popular backlash, viewed as radical at worst or naive at best.[16] The League's voter education programs preempted unthinking partisan loyalty, threatening the political parties. In a place where localism and states' rights shaped political culture, submitting to a national program proved contentious.

For her part Gertrude saw the need for the League of Women Voters as self-evident, "so simple, so logical and compelling" that anyone who understood it would be "convinced." Though the legislature never ratified the Nineteenth Amendment, she noted, it had "graciously" provided legislation for women's vote. Some 120,000 North Carolina women registered for the November 1920 election, and both political parties welcomed them at precinct meetings. Sixteen went to the Democratic state convention as delegates, and Cornelia Jerman attended the national convention. In some western counties, the total vote in 1920 more than doubled, although Gertrude's Down East showed the lowest increases. Democrat Lillian Exum Clement was elected to the state house from Buncombe County, the first woman in the North Carolina General Assembly.[17]

Politically, the League also had to contend with Alice Paul's National Woman's Party, which in 1921 launched a campaign for an Equal Rights Amendment. This conflict was philosophical as well as partisan. League proposals on labor and health offered women special protections, but the amendment prohibited gendered safeguards. Feminists argued that the League's social reforms assumed women's inferiority. Gertrude explained that the "League believes that women are a distinct element in the electorate, but does not believe in a separate woman's political party; rather that women and men have a common stake in civilization." League women were acting "for the public good as well as for the protection of their own rights."[18] Woman's difference did not imply inequality.

From the start the national League had encouraged citizenship schools, usually in collaboration with state colleges. At the League's founding, Gertrude had attended one at the University of Chicago. In July 1920, eight hundred women came to a summer course at Chapel Hill, where they held a practice election. Two years later Gertrude assisted a citizenship program at the Appalachian Training School for Teachers in Boone that attracted students from thirty-eight counties. Questions were raised regarding whether the schools were to limit themselves to the mechanics of the electoral process—how to register, how to mark a ballot—or to provide a broader civic education into the principles of government. Given the antisuffragist sentiment, inspiring women simply to register at the courthouse was challenging, but the schools proved popular and became part of the state League's annual meetings.[19]

In planning citizenship schools, developing educational literature, and devising legislative strategy, Gertrude worked closely with sociologists at the University of North Carolina at Chapel Hill. In 1922 the university extension division under League auspices published the booklet "Problems of Citizenship" and then a series on parent-teacher relations, school nutrition, playgrounds, and rural education. The Chapel Hill southern regionalists— directing their studies to race, labor, and the rural economy—were prophets of yet another New South. They redeemed southern folklife from its hillbilly stereotypes and accorded dignity to African Americans. Howard Odum, founder of the Institute for Research in Social Science at the university and its journal *Social Forces*, conducted pioneering studies in race, class, and gender relations. For the journal's first issue Gertrude contributed "The Social Program of the National League of Women Voters." Rural economist E. C. Branson wrote Gertrude, "Our civic structures were built by men, they must be renovated and perhaps disinfected by women." He added, "Men are not cruel by nature, they are just stupid."[20]

Legislative Lobbying

In 1920 the North Carolina Federation of Women's Clubs organized the Legislative Council of North Carolina Women. Again, the model was the national League of Women Voters, which had proposed a Women's Joint Congressional Committee of "liberal" women as a lobbying agency. The council's purpose was to present a "united front" of women's organizations to the state legislature, with the state League setting the agenda. Cornelia Jerman took leadership, with Gertrude as recording secretary. Offices were opened on Fayetteville Street, near the state capitol. The council's proposals focused on education, political corruption, reform of delinquents, and working women and children.[21]

The League responded to a newly empowered state government. In the postwar years localities yielded control of school, welfare, and public health programs to the state as centralized, bureaucratic governance was firmly established. State spending increased exponentially. The League pressed to have women placed on boards and commissions. In 1921 Kate Burr Johnson, a former president of the North Carolina Federation of Women's Clubs, was appointed state commissioner of charities and public welfare, the first woman to hold such a post in the nation. Politicians who assumed that Johnson would be cowed and compliant were quickly disabused as she committed her agency to progressive policies. Johnson, Gertrude's friend, became a political target. Gertrude worked closely with bureaucrats under her jurisdiction on infant and maternal issues. Dr. Charles Laughinghouse, the state health officer, wrote Gertrude that he shared her "ideals" and lobbied Congress on maternal and infant health programs. Dr. W. S. Rankin of the North Carolina Board of Health held "out a strong helpful hand," instituting free health care services to blacks and whites equally.[22] Public health programs gave the state its progressive reputation.

The League's earliest program focused on domestic issues that reflected traditional municipal housekeeping. In December 1920 Gertrude presented a sixfold "legislative program" for the 1921 North Carolina General Assembly. The age of consent was to be raised to sixteen, and provisions were to be made for mothers' pensions. Moving pictures needed censorship. The League also wanted adequate funding for the Stonewall Jackson Manual Training and Industrial School for white boys and Samarcand Manor, the State Home and Industrial School for white girls, and a school for "delinquent colored boys." Gertrude thought that all women could support this agenda "without controversy." Ever the organizer, she liked numbered lists and outlined a threefold procedure, as directed by the national League, to study the issues, lobby legislators, and report back to state legislative chair Cornelia Jerman. This format—education followed by legislation—was embedded in League culture. Speaking at the 1922 convention, Gertrude explained, "We want knowledge based on facts, convictions founded on painstaking investigation." Second was "POLITICAL ACTION." That meant "keeping in close touch" with officials. The "urgent duty," Gertrude insisted, was "intelligent, conscientious, active citizenship."[23]

The women did not succeed in enacting their agenda, to the relief of their many detractors. The age of consent was not raised. Rather, women were urged to "go forth" to bring culprits to justice. Their fight to censor "immoral or obscene" motion pictures ended when the state house tabled the bill. But the League did succeed in funding schools for delinquents, black as well as white. In response to a League request for town surveys, Gertrude prepared a four-page report on Goldsboro in 1922 detailing the "WHOLE town"—planting trees, garbage collection, the water supply, mosquito eradication, and much more. Abandoning their civic textbooks, the women met with town officials and attended council meetings. Study moved to action.[24]

Social issues inspired women, Gertrude included, more than politics. The League, although nonpartisan, encouraged women to join parties. A legislative agenda proposing sixty-nine measures led to complaints that the organization lacked focus, especially for politically inexperienced women. Clarifying its mission with but two goals, the state League adopted as a motto, "to foster education in citizenship and to support improved legislation." While serving as state League president, Gertrude worked to enlist Women's Clubs in the League's agenda. She headed the civics department of her local club and the citizenship committee of the state Federation. At a district meeting in rural Gates County she urged 350 Women's Club members to participate in government, particularly in the county, which she labeled the "plague spot."[25]

The League agenda challenged foundational principles of American government. Gertrude, now socialistic in her views if not in party affiliation, was fighting to create a federal welfare state. The national League's first legislative campaign after women's enfranchisement was to have Congress pass the Sheppard-Towner Maternity and Infancy Protection Act. Federal aid to the states was not yet an established principle, and Sheppard-Towner was a first foray into social security. States' righters protested federal intervention, while conservatives warned of creeping socialism. With League lobbying, the bill passed Congress in 1921, but its renewal was annually contested. The public viewed Sheppard-Towner as the League's signature victory. Gertrude fought rumors that it would forcibly remove children from their mothers and institutionalize them. Opponents charged "too much being done for mothers today."[26]

To build a "store of fact and opinion" that would convince legislators, League president Belle Sherwin wrote Gertrude requesting a North Carolina health survey. In 1927 she made a detailed inquiry to the North Carolina Board of Health on financing county nurses and physicians, classes in home hygiene, and pediatric dental care. Registering midwives was critical in a state where one physician was found, on average, every twenty-three miles. On a checklist Gertrude reported programs reaching 8,348 expectant mothers and 18,746 preschool children. Sheppard-Towner was not renewed, but North Carolina created a Bureau of Maternity and Infancy.[27]

With the vote, women saw unlimited possibilities. Catt had envisioned a national organization that could mobilize the grassroots, and Gertrude, who loyally attended League conventions, worked to enlist the state's congressional delegation. The League lobbied, with less success, to give women equal guardianship rights to children and to ensure that courts would admit women's testimony in rape cases. It advocated for the World Court and treaties to resolve conflict through arbitration. It argued for women's right to sit on juries, countering claims that women were too emotional to be impartial or that domestic duties would either bias them or prevent them from serving. In 1922 the state League endorsed programs to reduce adult illiteracy, house delinquent women, and aid impoverished mothers so their children would not need to be institutionalized. Women's vote would put an end to political corruption.[28]

By the 1922 state League convention Gertrude admitted that in its sixteen months the League had "but begun to work out the big, comprehensive program before us." Experience taught that the "average group of women" was not easily persuaded of the "urgency" for "training for citizenship." Letter writing did not work. The only way was through "personal visits." In early 1922 the national League sent organizer Doris Graves to the state. Over four weeks she visited six towns, establishing three chapters. Graves found an "embryonic" organization with Gertrude personally carrying the workload. She thought Gertrude "timid," which expressed a Northerner's impatience with southern ways. But Graves also affirmed her formidable challenge: "It is going to take nothing short of an earthquake to put the LWV over in some sections of this state."[29]

For an organization that advertised itself as nonpartisan, it took stands on labor and social welfare that were decidedly liberal. Conservatives scorned them as reds. Men condescended politely. When Governor Angus MacLean sent personal greetings to the 1924 state convention, he counseled, "There is only one infallible test of any state or of any individual, and that is faithful adherence to ... the 'homely virtues.'"[30]

Gertrude was not alone among southern progressives in urging moderation as the most politically effective course in a conservative society. Surely, her suffrage campaign had chastened her. Lillian Exum Clement, the first woman elected to the North Carolina General Assembly, described herself as "by nature a very timid woman, and very conservative too, but I am very firm in my convictions." Then she added paradoxically, "I want to blaze a trail for other women." Politically active women like Cornelia Jerman and Gladys Tillett were also southern ladies, too well bred to confront, accuse, or contend but winning their way through persistence and by outflanking rather than assaulting their opponents.[31]

Voting Women

At its 1922 national conference in Baltimore, the League of Women Voters retreated from its ambitious social welfare agenda in response to criticism from other states, too, that its program was expensive and bureaucratic. Catt provoked debate when she suggested that the League drop "Women" from its title as she urged women to participate in government. The League was divided between those like Catt more interested in the machinery of efficient government regardless of gender and those like national League presidents Maud Wood Park and Belle Sherwin who advocated welfare reform reflecting women's social concerns.[32] Gertrude had a foot in each camp.

Gertrude was among those who saw ballot reform and government efficiency as "the chief feature of League work," issues beyond women's traditional concerns. In 1923 the state League convention had as its theme "practical politics." The women wanted a single, short ballot to replace the multiple slips that intimidated novice voters and opened opportunities for fraud. The 1920 gubernatorial primary between progressive O. Max Gardner and machine candidate Cameron Morrison was widely believed to have been stolen when ballots were tabulated in backrooms. A year later Gertrude joined the fight for the secret ballot, and state house member Lillian Exum Clement submitted a measure for private voting booths.[33] Without privacy, how could women vote freely with husbands or party hacks looking over their shoulders?

Gertrude's outrage at the polls in 1922 drew national headlines. When she went "to vote her own ticket" in her Goldsboro precinct, she encountered a ward heeler who naively handed her a ballot marked for the Democratic machine. After tearing it to shreds, Gertrude saw more marked ballots stacked on a table. She ripped into those. "The corrupt political heelers were dumbfounded," the newspaper reported, "and the fellow who was marking ballots challenged her to send a man to do her fighting." Wire services "traveled" the news. "Soon she was front page stuff on the papers throughout the nation," the *Goldsboro News* reported. Weil's "annihilation of marked ballots" left Democrats "ill at ease," especially with Republicans endorsing the secret ballot. "What has happened to my old friend '*gentle little Gertrude Weil?*'" Sallie Southall Cotten wrote her. "Is it she who 'purifies politics' by forcibly destroying *marked ballots*?"[34]

Gertrude's sudden notoriety inspired a delegation of Republicans and independent Democrats to launch a "propaganda" campaign to draft Gertrude for Congress. Republican county chairs meeting in Raleigh were told only "folly" could prevent Miss Weil's nomination and election. With the party's blessing, the Republican nominee volunteered to withdraw in her favor. Justice Walter Clark pronounced her fit for office. The *Raleigh Times* suggested that a "considerable time" had passed since Down East "had as much brains at Washington as it would have were Miss Weil to go." Gertrude quickly squelched the "groundless rumor." The *Goldsboro News* reported, "The enterprise has no encouragement from Miss Weil who always has been regarded a more or less, mostly more, unmanageable Democrat." She wrote the newspapers "definitely that I am not considering—nor have I ever considered—running for Congress on the Republican, Democratic, Farm-Labor, Socialist, Independent, or any other ticket."[35] Gertrude wanted to maintain the League's nonpartisanship. The rancor and chest-beating egotism of electoral politics did not suit her retiring character. She rarely campaigned for candidates, and then only when she felt personally invested. Politicking and public office, too, would have taken her from home, which was not possible given her domestic duties.

Organizing Women

Creating a political culture among women proved daunting. Women generally did not show interest in the vote as the League anticipated. Gertrude was disheartened to see lower women's turn out in the 1924 election despite get-out-the-vote campaigns. The expectation that women would vote as a progressive bloc in support of a woman's agenda was also dashed as they voted no differently than men. At the national League convention, state presidents analyzed their failure. Gertrude observed that the absence of a short, secret ballot—the "Australian plan of suffrage"—kept women from the polls. Before the state primaries she wrote Women's Club presidents suggesting a renewed effort by appointing precinct chairs and block workers who would knock at every door. She hoped for a 75 percent turnout.[36]

Visiting communities, Gertrude spoke frequently at teas and luncheons, conferences and meetings, even chapel services, to inspire women to register and vote. As a speaker, Gertrude described herself as "scared" and "feeble," but despite her usual self-effacement, she was much in demand. Her innate modesty charmed. Speaking in Rocky Mount, she confessed her inability "to compose a SPONTANEOUSLY WITTY speech." Her brother had given her an opening joke, but then she forgot it. She spoke more seriously on women's political "ignorance and unsophistication" and their need for the secret ballot to ensure an independent vote. After a 1928 speech in Chapel Hill, she felt "discomfiture" when the Associated Press wired for a copy. Her "speech"—she qualified it with quotes—was widely reprinted, and the Chapel Hill League asked for a return engagement.[37]

Timidity was not the League's reputation in the state. A politician observed, "The Federation of Women's Clubs passes a resolution, then goes to a garden party while the League of Women Voters passes a resolution and then goes out to fight like H____ [*sic*]."[38] Preferring the background and leading by example, Gertrude was not a driver of women. Yet Gertrude also had a reputation for candor and expressed privately what she would not publicly. In the 1922 election, she warned that one candidate will "deliberately lie" and that he tried to get a Goldsboro legislator so soused that he could not cast a vote. When the county superintendent of schools eliminated funds for a supervisor, Gertrude stood on the courthouse steps declaring the only waste was that "jackass upstairs." One aspiring citizenship school speaker she dismissed as "bright" but "boring."[39]

The League lacked staff and resources. The task was beyond voluntarism. Gertrude called upon the League to fund a "permanent field worker" or "Executive Secretary" to provide "expert guidance" and coordinate local Leagues. Otherwise, she feared that county Leagues will be "sporadic and ephemeral." This ambition was large. In 1921 treasurer Laura Cone reported but $521 on hand. Gertrude and Cone reached into their pockets to meet deficits. In 1923 Gertrude sent $500, followed by $200 a year later, the total pledged from Goldsboro. Gertrude confessed that "I am utterly incapable" of raising money. One of her far-fetched ideas was to bring Irish tenor John McCormack for a benefit concert at the state fair.[40]

The funding crises reflected widespread apathy. Creating a cohesive organization was daunting in a state five hundred miles long, notable for bad roads and remote swamp and mountain towns. The League was most successful in western North Carolina, with its libertarian mountain culture, where suffrage sentiment had been strongest. Her native east, as Gertrude put it, "is in some respects not as advanced—I am thinking now of mental, not railroad development." In 1922 Gertrude had passed the presidency to Greensboro attorney Louise Alexander, demoting herself to third vice president. She struggled to organize a League in her native Wayne County. Maria McMahon, hired as an organizer, wrote Gertrude in early 1923 that the state League "lacked enthusiasm" and was in a "bad way." She called for an emergency board meeting and an "aggressive campaign." At best, a "few" Leagues were "semi-active." This situation was not North Carolina's alone. Carrie Chapman Catt wrote of a national League that was "drifting."[41]

Gertrude confessed that their "accomplishments may seem meager," but she reminded the women that "we are still at beginning of our career." A contending issue was reconciling the League's educational and legislative ambitions. Gertrude aligned herself with Belle Sherwin, national president from 1924 to 1934, on the need for study. Sherwin recruited a research staff. The original thirteen-point platform was reduced to four. In 1928 Sherwin asked Gertrude to serve on a national committee "to consider the results of the program-making procedure."[42]

The hiring of Mary O. Cowper, a suffrage veteran, as state organizer proved critical. From 1923 to 1931 Cowper edited the League's *Monthly Bulletin*, which became its public face. Cowper rose in the hierarchy and in 1925 became regional director, representing southeastern states, and was appointed to the national board. She fought to enact the League's liberal national agenda in a resistant North Carolina. While the older "Miss Weil" was temperate, the younger Mary Cowper was "brimming over with ideas." Each had a reputation for frankness. "Please don't apologize, even inferentially, for writing to me, ever," Gertrude once wrote her. "I realize that I grew too confidential with you." Importantly, Cowper was not rooted in North Carolina, and though southern born, she was rumored a Northerner.[43]

Gertrude and Cowper traveled the state seeking leaders and seeding new chapters. With a paid administrator, the state League grew in both members and chapters. At its 1924 state convention, which featured Belle Sherwin, the League received greetings from a spectrum of women's organizations, not just progressive ones but also the Daughters of the American Revolution, United Daughters of the Confederacy, and National Society of the Colonial Dames of America. New Leagues were announced in Salisbury, Monroe, and Rutherfordton. The Asheville Citizenship School of 1924 drew 1,000 attendees. In 1925 the state League claimed ten local Leagues and 600 members, then 700 in 1927, and 800 in 1928. North Carolina uniquely among southern Leagues boasted a headquarters, a regularly published bulletin, and, with the hiring of Cowper, a staff.[44]

The League's legislative efforts brought little success. Though Cowper was a diligent student of the legislature, reporting to Gertrude, not one bill that the League supported in 1925 passed, although several that it opposed were defeated. Gertrude rode to Raleigh to attend sessions or testify before committees. The League set the agenda for the Legislative Council, the lobbying agency of women's groups, but its "openness," its stand on moral high ground, could not counter the "hidden activity" of deal making that passed for political process. "Yes, politics is *dirty*," Cowper underlined.[45]

Changing Times

Chapel Hill historian Guion Johnson recalled that in North Carolina joining the League was "not the thing to do." After the patriotic sacrifices of the Great War, the Roaring Twenties was an era of indulgence. Gertrude's Progressive Era moral uplift was discordant with these material times when the nation was about making money. Flappers, not League lobbyists, became symbols of a jazz age. Motion pictures, bootleg alcohol, dance crazes, sexualized fashions, and the automobile all encouraged new freedoms that an older generation found licentious. Feminism pressed for women's liberation. Women driving, flying, or smoking upset Victorian pieties of home and hearth. Socialists, anarchists, and communists threatened to overthrow a society ordered on hierarchies of class. The League's appeal remained with white middle- and upper-class women. Indeed, Legislative Council members were mostly women of means who were professionals, married to prosperous husbands, or, like Gertrude, independently wealthy.[46]

Now in her forties, Gertrude was amused to be out of step. She received an inquiry from Hollywood artist Penrhyn Stanlaws, who was surveying "the American woman on fashion" concerning, as Gertrude responded, the "weighty subject of bobbed vs. neatly netted hair." She confessed to not being a "woman of fashion" and wondered just who was. If Stanlaws's models were drawn smartly enough, she wrote, why she just might buy a hairnet herself. After seeing a stylish young woman in a "slit skirt" enter a street car, Gertrude complained that women were slaves to fashion.[47]

With business plutocrats ruling state and federal governments, Gertrude quarreled with the times. In 1927 Mrs. Walter Crowell of Monroe wrote to ask, "Are American politics deteriorating?" In response Gertrude recalled "the good old days when our politics were run by statesmen" who would have been shocked by "fraud or dishonesty." Back then, she observed, the franchise was limited and politics was confined to the "educated, intelligent class," and, "by implication," the "unfit" did not participate. "It was NOT a democratic government, or democratic only in name," she recognized. With suffrage now extended to "practically the whole population," the proportion of "educated, intelligent participating citizens" seemed small among "the majority of unthinking, untrained electors." She lamented, "This is the price we pay for democracy." Her prescription was that "until ALL the people get educated"—not just literate but "trained in ideals and governmental methods"—"we shall run the danger of government by the unfit and irresponsible." The result was a loss of "political efficiency and morals." The public, distracted by luxuries and pleasures, was incapable of sustaining the "zeal and idealism" of the war effort. She called for "change upward" through "influence exerted by a comparatively few leaders who will nobly, think clearly and act courageously."[48]

Gertrude's call for an educated elite—of which she was clearly one—reflected upper-class bias. Her "good old days" evoked eras when women, blacks, and poor whites were excluded from the political process. Questioning democracy, Gertrude recalled nostalgically those progressive days earlier in the century when benevolent hierarchies prevailed. Frustrated in their political ambitions, many activists felt similarly disillusioned. The revolutionary W. E. B. DuBois called for educating an African American "Talented Tenth" of "exceptional men," a concept that originated with white progressives. In North Carolina women's suffrage itself had been elitist, given its unpopularity. The lament over contemporary times and nostalgia for a golden age were perhaps legacies of Gertrude's *Bildung*, her classical education.[49]

Many League policies were forms of social control that would mandate middle-class values into law. Although Gertrude had misgivings, the League endorsed Prohibition and movie censorship. Both would stifle working-class pleasures. Raising the age of consent and strengthening marriage laws addressed promiscuous behaviors that were allegedly vices of blacks and lower classes. Eugenics and birth control responded to feeblemindedness, which was thought prolific among immigrants and the poor. Juvenile courts and reform schools corrected antisocial delinquency, and social workers would have authority to remove children from neglectful parents. Education requirements for voting had both class and racial biases.[50]

Social Work

Gertrude's local efforts as a caseworker with impoverished families informed her worldview and inspired her League work for state and federal legislation. The evolution of the Ladies Benevolent Society to the Charity

Organization Society and then to the Goldsboro Bureau for Social Service reflected the recognition that social welfare needed to move from private charity to civic agency and then to government intervention. In the early 1920s Gertrude chaired the society's Anti-Tuberculosis Committee. There she led educational campaigns, directed the county Christmas Seal drives, and served as a liaison to state and federal agencies. She took practical steps to stem contagion and to care for the infected. As was her method, she collected technical literature on tuberculosis and consulted authorities for best practices. In 1921 she reported over three hundred cases in the county, with seventy-two deaths. She advocated for patients, both black and white, and wrote the state sanitarium director to find them spaces. She fell short in her ambition to raise funds to build a local facility in a nearby pine wood. She urged neighbors to adopt a patient and intervened in the case of Winnie, a child incurably infected, offering to pay her expenses. Of an eleven-year-old with tuberculosis in one lung, she wrote, "If anyone should see this beautiful little girl he would have no hesitancy in investing money in her behalf."[51]

With her friend Annie O'Berry, who succeeded her as Goldsboro Bureau for Social Service president, Gertrude worked intimately with people who seemed incorrigibly poor, some whose families she knew personally over generations. Syphilis was a recurrent problem. A county health department, organized in 1921, systematized dental care and vaccinations for both black and white communities. Gertrude recognized the need for a public welfare program, arguing that "promiscuous giving, without investigation," only exacerbated poverty. With children begging in the streets, several families were "treading upon the sympathy of the public and refusing to help themselves in any way."[52]

Gertrude and Annie O'Berry served on the bureau's Decisions Committee, reviewing who was deserving of aid. Her pleading was for the "friendless in distress, widowed mothers, orphaned children, disabled workers, the unemployed, the sick, the transient" She and Father Freeman of Goldsboro's Catholic church formed a two-person subcommittee that mediated with the county public welfare officer. She appealed to the superintendent of the Children's Home Society of North Carolina, a foster-child placement agency, advocating for Jimmie, eight, and Katie, ten, whose father had been murdered and whose mother and sisters worked as prostitutes. The Goldsboro Bureau for Social Service paid grocers for flour, lard, meat, potatoes, cabbage, and rice. It became an agency of the Goldsboro Community Chest, with Weils and Rosenthals heading or joining its board. Gertrude also served on the board of the Children's Home Society.[53]

One solution that Gertrude saw to poverty was birth control. In her 1927 report as president of the bureau, she observed, "So far we have for the most part let the feeble-minded go on procreating, increasing the number of their own kind, and consequently increasing social problems for this and the next generation." That was neither "intelligent" nor "constructive," Gertrude argued. "It is not enough to eliminate one case of poverty after another but to eliminate poverty itself."[54]

Race and Welfare

In the 1920s Gertrude had yet to commit to racial justice, although she was becoming aware of its urgency and connection to poverty. After their war service, African Americans became more confident and assertive. The Great Migration recast southern racial demography, demonstrating to southern whites that their assumption of docile, contented black folk falsified the indignities of living in a segregated society. Interracial efforts to ameliorate the impact of segregation were frequently Christian, through the Young Men's Christian Association or Protestant churches, all outside Gertrude's precincts. Julius Rosenwald, the Sears, Roebuck, & Co. magnate, had provided seed money to build schools for African Americans across the South, predicated on local communities matching the funds. Like Gertrude, Rosenwald was a child of German Jews. Other Jews prominently helped found and lead the National Association for the Advancement of Colored People. The Jewish and black alliance provided fodder for anti-Semites, who accused Jews of being racial mongrelizers. With 813 Rosenwald Schools, including a dozen in Wayne County, North Carolina had more than any state.[55]

Typical of progressives, Gertrude advocated education as the stepping stone of black uplift. The North Carolina Federation of Women's Clubs maintained a Committee on Promotion of Negro Welfare and, joined by the League, supported remediation through schools for delinquent black boys and girls. The League cooperated with Colored Women's Clubs, which had built a home for black girls in Efland. Black women, who were registering in large numbers, were a potential constituency for the League, but it was indifferent to them. When a Commission on Interracial Cooperation invited the national League to affiliate, it took "no action" beyond "informal co-operation." The state League focused on white working women and children, despite the exploitation of African American women as domestic workers and tobacco laborers. Gertrude was preoccupied with the League's survival, and the race question was not her priority.[56]

In 1924 the national League created a Special Committee on Interracial Problems that included states with a threshold of black population. Asked to report, Gertrude contacted Clara Cox, a Quaker worker for the Young

Women's Christian Association (YWCA) who chaired the state committee, asking to be informed on "definite activities in the state that are for the benefit of the negro and that make for a better understanding between the races." Gertrude wrote that she knew that the state had a director of Negro schools, training facilities, and public welfare but was unsure if an interracial conference had been held and, if so, where. In 1925 the League board agreed to study the black women's vote and to discuss citizenship training at black institutions and cooperation with black women's groups.[57]

In Cox's absence, Gertrude represented North Carolina at a national League interracial conference in 1928. She wanted "to be specific when I say that N.C. is doing significant work toward interracial harmony." She reported, "We think we have a unique situation here in the happy, harmonious relations between the races, and, of course, we are working consciously and positively to improve this relation all the time."[58] Yet blacks were leaving the state in the tens of thousands.

Southern whites commonly expressed racial goodwill, oblivious of African American sentiment. The good relations that Gertrude reported did not address social equality, political rights, or economic opportunity. However, Gertrude was correct—in relative terms—in observing that in the 1920s North Carolina was making racial progress. The state had a regional reputation for moderation. North Carolina made the most expansive commitment to black education of any southern state, building high schools and colleges. On her seventy-fifth birthday Mina was honored for "her benevolence and generosity which knows no bounds of race or religion." Weils supported black schools and a hospital. C. Dillard, principal of the black high school, turned to the Weils for help with his "constructive work in the Negro churches in Wayne County."[59]

With Gertrude in the leadership, the Charity Organization Society twice invited to Goldsboro Lt. Lawrence Oxley, an African American who supervised the Bureau of Work among Negroes in the State Board of Charities and Public Welfare. This board was unique in the South and became a national model. The society wanted to create a companion organization in Goldsboro. Oxley spoke at black churches and schools. "The basic motive," Gertrude explained, employing racial stereotypes, "is to supplant the idle, mischievous and often vicious habits of the negro youth with occupations that will lead to orderly and useful habits." She asserted that "white friends" should take "practical interest" in supporting such a plan.[60]

In the 1920s Gertrude increasingly directed her philanthropy toward African Americans. Starting in 1925 Gertrude wrote checks annually to Allen Young, an African American who was principal of Wake Forest Normal and Industrial School, a boarding school for blacks. Other donations went to Annie Fort, who operated a "training school for colored girls." In 1927 and 1928 Gertrude contributed two hundred dollars to the Goldsboro Bureau for Social Service, which she served as president, for "work among Negroes." That gift was exceptional in a state that a year earlier had counted but thirteen black social workers.[61]

At various forums, notably the North Carolina Conference for Social Service, where she was an officer, Gertrude heard prominent African Americans like Charlotte Hawkins Brown, a Wellesley graduate who founded Palmer Memorial Institute, describe her humiliation traveling on Jim Crow railways. The conference, too, called for reform schools for blacks and maintained standing committees on the so-called Negro problem. Supported by the Young Men's Christian Association and northern philanthropists, the national Commission on Interracial Cooperation (CIC), founded in 1919, formed a North Carolina affiliate two years later. This biracial committee recruited the "'better' classes" of both races, but the educated elites did not represent the black and white working classes who more often interacted. Local CICs tended to act only when violence threatened, and with a charge to change white attitudes, their achievement may have been little more than to hold meetings.[62]

Although hardly integrationist, the CIC still tested racial limits even among progressives. In 1923 the North Carolina Conference for Social Service executive committee—including Gertrude—unanimously voted to accept the CIC as an affiliate, although one member threatened to quit, feeling that it would be "most dangerous, insidious, and wholly unwarranted" to cooperate with an interracial group. Others welcomed the "legitimate" step forward. Still in 1928 when an African American attempted to register for the conference, the application was marked "Colored—Not accepted," and the dollar enrollment fee was returned. Few African Americans joined or attended conference meetings.[63]

Gertrude supported interracial efforts but was not yet fully informed or actively engaged. In the late 1920s and early 1930s she would become a committed benefactor and participant. In 1931 Gertrude was a member of the North Carolina Interracial Committee Woman's Section. In 1932 she was among the five hundred "best leadership of both races" that Governor Gardner appointed to the CIC. In the midst of Depression the state director of Negro relief asked Gertrude if she would personally finance his visit to Goldsboro for a "big meeting" on unemployment.[64] Gertrude's racial awareness was gradually growing beyond the paternalism of the white progressive to an appreciation of black agency.

In 1930 Gertrude traveled to Atlanta to attend the Anti-Lynching Conference for Southern White Women, convened by Jessie Daniel Ames, founder of the Texas League of Women Voters. Until then, the cause had drawn black women and white men. From that meeting came the Association of Southern Women for the Prevention of Lynching. Some forty thousand women in thirteen hundred southern counties joined the campaign. Clara Cox and Bertha Newell invited Gertrude to attend a state meeting in Greensboro in February, 1931. North Carolina was not conspicuous for anti-black violence; the association listed 204 lynchings in southern states from 1922 to 1930, with but one in North Carolina. Its program was to educate the public to prevent lynchings and prosecute mob members. By providing statistics proving that rape of white women was *not* the main motivation for lynching black men, the association challenged southern chivalric traditions. Gertrude joined white women stepping off their pedestals to confront publicly the racial and sexual anxieties that underlay white supremacy.[65]

Gertrude also worked closely with the sociologists at the University of North Carolina at Chapel Hill, notably Howard Odum, whose studies emphasized not innate racial differences but environmental factors that could be ameliorated through education, public health, and economic policy. Yet neither black nor white progressives saw the time as propitious to push integration. The labor movement, especially in the South, neglected African Americans. Odum gave qualified support for segregation, arguing that it allowed blacks to develop independently. Though Frank Graham personally defied racial customs, he rejected black applicants to Chapel Hill, apologizing that he was bound by law. Southern progressives went no further than gradualism. Gertrude shared a sensibility with other southern ladies who later became known for racial liberalism, Lillian Smith and Virginia Foster Durr among them. They were initially circumspect on race before assaulting Jim Crow.[66]

World Citizen

A dedicated student of foreign affairs, Gertrude promoted antiwar and global justice activities. Carrie Chapman Catt, with Jane Addams, founded a Women's Peace Party, forerunner of the Women's International League for Peace and Freedom. The League's victory convention in 1920 featured speakers denouncing war and endorsing a League of Nations. Gertrude responded enthusiastically. Starting in 1925, she traveled to Washington annually to attend Conferences on the Cause and Cure of War that included marathon roundtables with diplomats and academic experts. She passionately and extensively took notes and collected publications addressing peace and disarmament issues.

In 1926 Gertrude went to St. Louis where the League's Department of International Co-operation to Prevent War presented experts advocating arbitration, security, and disarmament. It was an issue, she noted, that is "felt most poignantly by women." To the state League of Women Voters she reported, "Our national welfare cannot be separated from international welfare."[67] The League of Nations, however, proved as divisive in the national League of Women Voters as it did in American political parties. At its Cleveland convention the League passed resolutions supporting arms reduction but rescinded its endorsement of the League of Nations. Not until 1927 did it endorse a World Court. To fight isolationism, the League maintained overlapping committees on international cooperation and the cause and cure of war.

As chair of international relations committees for both the League and North Carolina Federation of Women's Clubs, Gertrude served as a foreign affairs reporter to North Carolina. As usual, her first step was "a carefully planned educational movement." She worked tirelessly to enlist groups, ranging from her temple Sisterhood to the state League, to lobby Congress in support of the League of Nations and World Court. In 1926 a coalition of women's organizations meeting in Greensboro passed a resolution of support. A conference of college students followed at Duke. In 1927 the School of Citizenship held in Chapel Hill focused on international cooperation to prevent war, with Frank Graham as speaker. A year later Gertrude spent nine days in Baltimore and Washington at an international conference that featured Latina delegates. She then brought speakers to Goldsboro to explain "Our Pan American Relations." She called for American neutrality and arbitration of disputes with Mexico and Nicaragua. At the 1929 conference she heard liberal theologians Harry Fosdick and Reinhold Niebuhr and a year later General Jan Christian Smuts of South Africa advocate for the League of Nations.[68]

Jewish and secular movements affiliated in common cause, and Carrie Chapman Catt and Lillian Wald jointly attended world peace conferences. Jews especially, with their immigrant legacy and foreign family ties, retained a cosmopolitan perspective. No less than the League of Women Voters, the National Council of Jewish Women, and National Federation of Temple Sisterhoods advocated global peace and disarmament as integral to their social justice agenda. Gertrude's hand can be seen in a resolution sent to Senator F. W. Simmons in 1925 expressing the gratitude of forty

Goldsboro Jewish women for his support of the World Court. Three years later Gertrude summarized—in religious terms—her credo in a report to the state Federation: "As women are the producers of the race, they would naturally be the conservers of the race.... Viewed from any standpoint, we can find no justification for war.... We find that war abrogates the teachings of all religions. There is nothing in war compatible with the doctrine of human brotherhood and the universal law of love." She then asked for a resolution to support the Paris Peace Pact that renounced the use of war to resolve conflict. A year later Gertrude was pleased to observe that the U.S. Senate, including both North Carolinians, ratified the treaty on the very afternoon that the women lobbied.[69]

Labor Rights and Wrongs

Gertrude felt in her heart the plight of southern children and women workers, typically white families pushed by poverty from their farms to the textile and tobacco mills. With her penchant for fact gathering, Gertrude had first proposed a survey of working women and children at the North Carolina Federation of Women's Clubs convention in 1916. The U.S. Department of Labor had conducted such surveys in Alabama and Virginia, resulting in improved workplaces if not shortened hours. Working mothers were a traditional home-and-hearth issue, especially with children laboring at their sides. When the national League of Women Voters convened in Washington in 1921, no more than six of the four hundred delegates held union cards. Nonetheless, it adopted a pro-labor platform calling for collective bargaining, work and wage laws, and an end to gender discrimination.[70] Following the national model, the state League maintained a Women in Industry Committee. Labor reform proved contentious. In advocating labor rights the state League—along with the YWCA Industrial Clubs for workers—confronted the business plutocrats who exercised ruthless political and economic control.

Gertrude's persistence on the labor survey was part of her larger effort to strengthen government's role in social welfare and to improve its efficiency. The League had worked to replace partisan policy makers with scientific experts. Legislation required facts. As Kate Burr Johnson put it, "All we know about the condition of women is that we don't know anything." Johnson, as director of Charities and Public Welfare, was attacked politically as the women sought to expand the department's mission and increase its funding. In 1923 the Federation resolved, with Gertrude leading, that the Women's Bureau in the state Department of Labor conduct a survey, but the women were warned that investigatory powers lay with the Child Welfare Commission, another state agency. Women's organizations pushed to extend the survey beyond factories to stores, hotels, offices, laundries, and restaurants.[71]

In 1923 the Child Welfare Commission's executive secretary, E. C. Carter, assured the League that two thousand workplaces would be inspected before its 1924 meeting. The survey that he special delivered to Mary Cowper belied that promise: it was an outdated, inch-long clipping from the commission's yearly report. The women were irate. When a delegation met with Carter, he seemed unaware that state law limited woman's workday to eleven hours. They found his ignorance and contempt insulting. Manufacturers supported Carter, fearing a women's survey would open a front on labor itself. In 1925 David Clark, editor of the *Southern Textile Bulletin*, blasted Cowper—"a northern woman and the wife of a professor at Duke"— as "very radical and is known to have carried on an active correspondence with Russia during the period when Levine [*sic*; Lenin] and Trotzky [*sic*] were trying to spread sovietism [*sic*] over the United States."[72] Gertrude doubtlessly recognized Clark's insinuation of Jewish Bolshevism.

The labor survey fight dragged for years. Secretary Carter informed newspapers that the women wanted out-of-state inspectors, and industrialists raised the specter of federal interference. The Child Welfare Commission declined to conduct the survey by a vote of two to one, with Kate Burr Johnson dissenting. The survey battle turned to the governor and legislature.[73]

Governor Angus MacLean, a mill owner, summoned his Industrial Advisory Board to hear "what THAT League of Women Voters wanted." The governor expressed skepticism over any commission that would "go into the mills and tell them how to run their business." The men demanded to know who in the League requested the survey, warning that they "knew who had done it in other organizations and expected to make it hot for that person." The League president, whose husband's business depended on the mills, soon resigned. The governor leaked a report that some women did not want any survey.[74]

The manufacturers were unrelenting. When Mary Cowper, with the YWCA's cooperation, brought millworkers to testify on their work hours, YWCA chapters found their industrial committee secretaries fired and fundraising stalled. For its support of a child labor bill, the Legislative Council confronted charges of radicalism and then resignations. Rather than have the women's choice, Kate Herring Highsmith, a Trinity College graduate and state Board of Health publicist, conduct the survey, the governor left Carter in charge. Gertrude, League first vice president, responded in fury, writing an open letter—in capitals—to the governor. A women's committee wrote a more measured petition to "His Excellency." Carter, the women declared, had neither "training nor the experience." An "unscientific incomplete survey" was a "waste of the taxpayers' money," a challenge thrown at the tightwad governor. Carter, Highsmith learned, had been vetting her surveys. She resigned, followed by Kate Burr Johnson. The governor canceled the survey, blaming the women.[75]

The governor's response to the women was an "Insult," headlined the *Raleigh News and Observer*. Gertrude was asked to make a statement. She rebutted charges that the women intended to indict any corporation or that anything but "competence" was the issue. She "blush[ed] to discuss" allegations that northern manufacturers had "paid, subsidized, or instigated" the women to ask for the survey. They acted in "interest in their working sisters," not for "northern gold." Gertrude wrote League members that their "only weapon" was "unfavorable publicity." That was the "one thing the Gov. seems to hate and fear." She continued, "It is bad enough to be beaten, but he must know that we know how it was done." Gertrude sent a letter to MacLean, who wrote back that he found it "impossible to reconsider" and advised the women to go to the General Assembly.[76]

In 1927 the women pushed forward again. This time they spoke more loudly, with Nell Battle Lewis promoting the issue in her widely read newspaper column. The press generally spoke for the manufacturers, and Lewis, whose brothers were textile executives, found herself denounced as a Bolshevik. The Legislative Council concluded the wisest path was to press for legislation on women's work hours. The national League had advocated an eight-hour day, forty-four-hour week, and minimum wage, while North Carolina's laws set limits of an eleven-hour day and sixty-hour week.

In a 1928 letter Gertrude outlined why a state survey was needed: North Carolina had "the longest legal working hours of any State." The protective laws had "no standards," nor was any legal agency entrusted with enforcement. The commissioner of labor was "not in sympathy with protective laws." Moreover, "the Executive of the Child Welfare Commission, Mr. E. F. Carter, who has assumed the duty of enforcing the law simply conceals bad conditions and does not report violations," she alleged. Therefore, the League wanted an "impartial and trained agency" to conduct the survey. The League now called for a nine-hour workday and fifty-four-hour week, not ideal but the best Gertrude could hope.[77]

Working Children

Beyond the League's advocacy for women workers, it also confronted children's labor, a pervasive practice in mills across North Carolina. Its availability pulled industry southward. In 1920 some 16 percent of state youth between ten and fifteen years worked. The industrialists begrudged reforms, hoping to stave off comprehensive legislation. Reformers also contended with working parents, especially from families disabled by death or illness, who needed their children's wages.[78]

At the 1923 national League convention, which Gertrude attended, Julia Lathrop of the U.S. Children's Bureau moved delegates with a speech endorsing the Child Labor Amendment to the constitution. Despite horrific reports, protective laws were weak. In 1918 and 1922 the U.S. Supreme Court had ruled that Congress lacked authority to enact child labor legislation. Conservative groups like the U.S. Chamber of Commerce railed that such laws were "communistic."[79] Southern textile interests were especially vocal, and reform-minded women could not be insensitive to their arguments.

The League lobbied Congress for passage of the federal amendment. Gertrude joined a state committee in support, but public opinion opposed it. In part, this opposition reflected discomfort with the League's broad, variegated program. Other states, too, complained that the national League was unfocused and overly ambitious. Rather than address child labor, the state League responded to an appeal from Kate Burr Johnson and voted to push instead for a survey of the juvenile court system. Gertrude herself had worked with juvenile courts since her return to Goldsboro from Smith College.[80]

In 1924 the federal Child Labor Amendment passed Congress and was sent to the states for ratification. In North Carolina Gertrude's attitude was "pivotal" in both the League of Women Voters and the North Carolina Federation of Women's Clubs. She had been loyal to the national League's agenda and counted its leaders as friends, but its advocacy of the federal amendment put her in a bind. Her personal view had to be tempered against local political realities. When Sarah Matthews of the national League visited Gertrude and Mina in 1924, she reported to headquarters that they held views "current in Cotton Mill and Cotton Field circles":

> They assured me among other things that it was better for children to work in the mills WITH THEIR MOTHERS than to run wild on the streets; also that children under fourteen do not work in the North

Carolina mills; that it is fun for them in the cotton fields; that North Carolina has a compulsory education law to fourteen years and that it is enforced 100%, which they challenged me to contradict. They said that they favored protecting children, but lots of them would be better off working; that you couldn't keep them in school. They did not doubt that Congress would set 18 as the limit in all fields, and asked how I could say it would not. They "did not want Minnesota to dictate to North Carolina" and said I was quibbling when I said Minnesota took the same chance. In short, we grew so heated, that the butler rolled his eyes in fright until only the whites were visible.[81]

Even as they berated Matthews for deprecating North Carolina, both women had long histories fighting for protective legislation. Mother and daughter had for decades experienced the workers' plight as volunteers in a mill town, and they resided in the farm belt of one of the nation's most agrarian states. The poor had sat in their parlor, and they had visited their homes. Gertrude lectured on "The Cry of the Children." Southern child labor reformers argued that seasonal outdoor farm work was physically beneficial and did not interfere with schooling, in contrast to the deprivation of the mill.[82]

Mina and Gertrude's assurances of the state's goodwill expressed the maternalism that middle- and upper-class women brought to their work among the poor. Sarah Matthews thought them confused and uninformed, yet beyond personal experience, Gertrude was a meticulous student of facts. Their "paradoxical stance" likely owed to an "extreme southern defensiveness" that was a typical response to what they likely perceived as northern aggression.[83] Nothing rankled a southerner like a presumptuous outsider passing judgment. Gertrude closed ranks with her elderly mother, who was affronted. Both women stood on North Carolina's fault line of contradiction. They were traditional southern ladies defending states' rights and the agrarian ideal, as well as progressive New Women arguing in support of compulsory education and efficient government.

The suffrage struggle had taught bitter political lessons. Many League women were wives of industrialists who did not tolerate having their goodwill questioned. Farm folk flocking to their mills attested to the prosperity they brought to an impoverished and declining agrarian society, textile interests argued. Unmarried, Gertrude was not answerable to a husband, and her family was financially diversified, not wholly dependent on industry. Laura Cone wrote Gertrude that she was retiring from labor advocacy in respect to her husband, Julius, a mill executive. Few were as daring as

Gertrude's Goldsboro friend Annie O'Berry, who handed flyers to workers at the gate of an overalls factory where her husband was president. Mary Cowper asked national League president Belle Sherwin to come to Durham to mollify her husband, a French professor at Duke.[84]

At its 1924 convention the state League considered endorsement of the federal Child Labor Amendment. Few spoke in support of "federal interference." The convention voted to endorse state legislation, the result that Gertrude had anticipated. North Carolina created a Child Labor Board to administer laws and inspect factories, but it was poorly funded, under-staffed, and beholden to manufacturers. Rather than authorize unannounced inspections, it relied on manufacturers to self-report.[85]

The state League adopted a gradualist approach focused on incremental revisions of state laws. Legislative chair Cornelia Jerman formulated an "entering wedge" strategy that employed quiet persuasion and avoided confrontation, thus deflecting accusations of radicalism. Mary Cowper still wished that the League would be "forceful," less deferential to the manufacturers. She was dismayed at this "retreat" from the national agenda. Although Gertrude opposed the federal bill, Cowper was "stating my private opinion and reasons for it, everywhere I go." North Carolina typified industrial states where federal legislation was "anathema." The amendment—never ratified—was also defeated in the textile state of Massachusetts. The League recognized that child labor was a "stumbling block" to its progress in North Carolina.[86]

The League continued its battle for state reform. In 1927 Gertrude experienced again the magnitude of political opposition when the League lobbied for a law limiting children under sixteen to an eight-hour day. A League report—likely by Gertrude—bore a heading "Vicissitudes of Social Legislation." The report observed, "The bill got one vote in [a General Assembly] Committee and a tirade of abuse against its proponents, who were accused of being the tools of Russian 'Reds.'" Singled out for attack were "active workers of the League of Women Voters." People feared being identified with such an "unpopular cause." The bill was introduced late in the session and sent to one "antagonistic committee" after another. Defeated, it was brought back, tabled, and then called back again. An amendment forbade employment of children between fourteen and sixteen for more than eight hours daily, but only if they had not completed fourth grade. At midnight, with the clock turned forward to create the fiction of a new legislative day, the amended bill passed, the assembly's last act.[87]

The League victory was qualified. According to the attorney general, the fourth grade exemption allowed children to work an eleven-hour day and sixty-hour week. As a newspaper observed, the stipulation offered a "prize for mental inactivity." Gertrude met with Wiley Swift of the nonprofit National Child Labor Committee to plan its repeal.[88]

Progress on labor reform was painstaking. In 1927 the women again reintroduced a bill to provide an eight-hour workday for women. Mary Cowper lobbied incessantly. To their surprise, it passed the state senate and then the house even as it was attacked as "futile and dangerous." The federal Child Labor Amendment was rejected, but the General Assembly closed a loophole allowing boys under fourteen to work in mills during school vacations. The legislature also forbade children from working in dangerous occupations, but it did not end the fourth-grade exemption.[89]

Organizational Worries

As Gertrude fought for labor reform, she was entangled in League politics that tested both her principles and her friendships. Gertrude and Mary Cowper remained cordial and mutually supportive, despite their conflicting strategies. After the failure of the labor survey in 1926 Gertrude had written her, "I certainly would like to have a good old — heart-to-heart talk with somebody who ... is agitated as I." She added in longhand, "In other words, I long for you." But Gertrude had to strike a balance. Cowper was often described as abrasive or radical, and as a nonnative she lacked natural allies. As she traveled the state, Cowper wrote national, "It seems impossible for the League to grow here."[90]

Six years after the state League's founding, its *Monthly News* still asked, "Why a League in North Carolina?" Gertrude and Cowper struggled to identify local leaders and inspire them to act. They kept lists, checking or crossing off names of who might head a committee or serve as an officer. New Women were consumed with professional careers; others were beset by domestic duties tending children or, like Gertrude, caring for an aging parent. Pregnancies and miscarriages led to resignations. A European excursion pulled some away. When recruiting, the League also had to counter misperceptions that it was a political party.

League struggles were hardly unique to North Carolina. Of the forty-four states with Leagues, only twenty-four had boards. Membership numbers were unreliable, and finances were precarious. With the federal Child Labor Amendment's defeat, women's organizations nationally suffered a decline as women gravitated to political parties or groups that included men. The League held its last annual national conference in 1926, thereafter meeting biennially. After one state League president resigned, not in "sympathy" with the program, and another quit abruptly, Gertrude in 1927 took the euphemistic title of "acting president." In the annual report, Gertrude apologized, with her usual wit, for the "boring monotony" of having her president again "just when you thought you had got me safely shelved in an inconspicuous and innocuous vice-presidency." Now here she was on "stage wearing the ermine robes." She reaffirmed the League's "goal of trained, intelligent, thinking citizenship" within the "recognized, orderly processes provided by our government itself." She observed, "This hardly sounds like the red and frightful terror that we have sometimes been called."[91]

Gertrude intended to step down as president and instead chair the Committee on Organization, but just then Cowper fell near fatally ill. After surgery at Johns Hopkins, she sailed to Europe for treatment. In Cowper's absence, Gertrude assumed her administrative duties, primarily editing the monthly bulletin.

In midst of this personal crisis Gertrude faced political attacks from left and right. Once again the League found itself outflanked by Alice Paul's National Woman's Party, which in 1927 renewed its campaign to pass what the League labeled the "so-called equal rights amendment." The state League questioned whether Congress would allow itself to be "influenced by the sudden agitation of a small group while the great majority of women" were opposed to it. In rebuttal the League published "Equal Rights—How Not to Get Them."[92]

The old antisuffragist coalition resumed its assaults on progressive women. In 1927 the national Daughters of the American Revolution (DAR) launched a furious campaign accusing fourteen organizations of plotting world revolution. Army general Amos Fries produced a "spider chart" linking women's and radical groups, alleging that Sheppard-Towner had been drafted in Moscow and that disarmament was a communist plot. In North Carolina DAR regent Margaret Overman Gregory, Senator Lee Overman's daughter, publicly attacked the League as a communist tool. Some DAR members quit the League. In 1928 Gertrude bravely spoke at the DAR state convention. She identified the League with the cause of American independence and encouraged the women not to listen to the "howlings of the mob, the sophisms of the demagogue, or the orders of the bosses higher up."[93] She was making thinly veiled reference to the red baiting, fundamentalist fulminating, and machine politics that passed for political culture in North Carolina.

The League courted controversy in challenging the Democratic machine and in raising disputed issues like labor justice. In 1927 Gertrude wrote the national League that the North Carolina General Assembly either tabled, rejected, or failed to introduce bills reducing women's hours in industry, limiting the workday for children, and requiring an eight-month school term. The nation paid attention. Paul Blanshard, then field secretary of the League for Industrial Democracy, reported for the *New Republic* on "labor conditions in the Southern cotton mills." He organized a conference in Greensboro in December 1927 "for the shorter work day in cotton mills" and invited several dozen prominent southern reformers. At Cowper's recommendation, Gertrude attended.[94]

The League still adhered to quiet diplomacy, but Gertrude, as Frank Porter Graham observed, was "sometimes caught in the crossfire of the conflict." Returning from Europe, Cowper was ready to fight. The League was not. Cornelia Jerman, League legislative chair and president of the Legislative Council of North Carolina Women, was a gradualist. Cowper and Jerman were strong-willed and clashed. Gertrude was left consoling hurt feelings. Cowper wrote the national League expressing impatience with Gertrude. She bristled at the League's incrementalism and Gertrude's unwillingness to confront politicians. For her part, Gertrude complained that she was tired mending Cowper's fences. In a 1927 letter to Gertrude, Cowper freely assessed the leadership qualities "very *confidentially*" of candidates for state League office. Cowper protested when Gertrude proposed that treasurer Laura Cone become president, fearing "we'll go bust." In all frankness Cowper was "suggesting that I be elected."[95] As Gertrude mediated among personalities, she felt contrary pulls within herself, once again tempering her idealism and personal loyalties against political possibilities.

League regional director Huldah Moorhead spoke of Gertrude as the one person who could make a local League successful, noting "all the nice things that were said" about her. In asking that Gertrude accompany Mary Cowper on a tour, Moorhead acknowledged that "Mrs. Cowper does not appeal to many of the women." In 1927 Gertrude and Cowper were off to mountain towns—Franklin, Bryson City, Murphy, Spruce Pine—to rally women "to promote education in citizenship, efficiency in Government and international cooperation." After attending an antiwar conference in Washington, Gertrude went to Salisbury and Statesville. Sometimes she was warned that the "small number" did not justify a visit, and one local League "can't get up a meeting." In Rutherfordton, women debated "for and against disorganizing." Eleanor Mosher wrote from Chapel Hill in 1928, "Even here in this university community, we are meeting with much opposition. This will have been the third attempt in the last seven years to organize a chapter." That year Gertrude lamented that she would attend the Chicago national convention alone and that "all my efforts have been unsuccessful to collect another delegate." Still, the state claimed fifteen local Leagues.[96]

Gertrude worked tirelessly, writing letters to members and releasing statements in support of the national League's agenda. She updated League members on the legislative progress, recommended amendments to bills, and urged all to lobby their congressmen. One cause was the cost of living, the subject of a 1927 Chapel Hill conference. An economic issue, it led women into new political realms beyond maternalism—tariffs, federal budget, utility regulation. Even before the stock market crash, Gertrude was calling for a regulated economy. The festering national issue for a decade concerned the Tennessee River dam at Muscle Shoals, Alabama. The League wanted the government-built dam, constructed to produce military explosives, to be developed as a public utility rather than leased to a profit-making corporation. Conservatives cried socialism. In 1928 Belle Sherwin wrote Gertrude arguing that it was a women's issue since the cost of electricity affected the "consumer in the home."[97] Muscle Shoals, like Sheppard-Towner, was a stepping stone to a welfare state.

Welfare Politics

If Gertrude took moderate positions publicly, in her personal writings she expressed socialistic views that indeed justified the suspicions of the League's enemies. In a 1928 article on "Adult Education in Citizenship" Gertrude questioned capitalism and the inequities of free markets: "Of special interest to women is the relation between government and human welfare." Do "our laws provide . . . health and happiness?" She continued, "In short, is it enough that we pile up wealth, that we have an enviable record for the payment of large income taxes each year, without considering the distribution of that wealth?" A friend wrote her excited to hear socialist Norman Thomas at Woman's College and recommended books on the Soviet Union. In 1932 when Harold Glasgow, North Carolina organizer for the Socialist Party of America, needed ten thousand signatures to put the party on the ballot, he spent an afternoon with Gertrude planning the petition drive. He warmly recalled her "splendid aid."[98] With Thomas running for president, Gertrude added her name, yet she remained a nominal Democrat, too independent for a party or an ideology.

Both Carrie Chapman Catt and Maud Wood Park, League founders, had encouraged women to join parties, but national left it to states to set policy. The North Carolina League of Women Voters remained resolutely nonpartisan, supporting issues, not candidates. When Gertrude asked Democratic convention delegates to endorse the 1928 League platform, only one replied in support. Despite the League's lobbying, the legislature failed repeatedly to enact secret voting, although it did simplify and shorten the ballot. The women wanted to clean the state's "dirty" politics, and the Charlotte chapter pioneered "meet the candidate" forums and political debates.[99]

Al Smith's presidential candidacy in 1928 roused Gertrude to partisanship. She wrote League members that she was "feeling at this time the urge to take part in the present political campaign." She offered to resign or withdraw temporarily from the presidency, whichever the board desired. When the *Greensboro News* wired to confirm her resignation, Gertrude responded, "I look upon Governor Smith as an honest fearless intelligent leader to free us from the disgrace at home and abroad to which the present Republican Administration has brought our country." The Smith campaign wired Gertrude to organize the state, but she responded that she knew "no Democratic or Independent women in North Carolina who are interested in the election of Governor Smith." She would volunteer at Democratic headquarters in Raleigh and try to organize college Leagues.[100]

Gertrude stumped for Al Smith. She found Herbert Hoover "full of meaningless generalities & platitudes" and no "impeccable saint." Smith, by contrast, spoke out "clearly & courageously." She dismissed Smith's vulnerability as a "liquor head." Prohibition was driven by "POLITICAL expediency," she argued, and had proven "scandalous and notorious and futile." She attacked Republican "corruption and treachery" on issues like public utilities, in contrast to Smith's "zeal for the public welfare." Her chief concern was "MORAL RESPONSIBILITY ... in the field of INTERNATIONAL RELATIONS," and she excoriated the Republican Party for the failure of the League of Nations.[101]

Once more, Gertrude was out of step. Many League women backed Hoover, who endorsed the World Court. In 1928, Belle Sherwin sent "sailing orders" for the League to support Prohibition, a refutation of Smith. Gladys Tillett, who shared Gertrude's politics, wrote her distressed at "the fanatical religious zeal exhibited by the woman vote in general." A board member forwarded anti-Catholic literature from a patriotic society. Gertrude took Smith's defeat bitterly. As a Jew, she would have felt sensitive to religious prejudice. Smith won almost three-quarters of the Jewish vote nationally, which thereafter became reliably liberal and Democratic. Jews, including Gertrude, shared Smith's opposition to Prohibition and immigration restrictions. The new liberalism eschewed progressive moralizing. With the election past, Mary Cowper welcomed Gertrude back to the League. Cowper thought that by taking an "active part with the leaders of The Party," Gertrude "will sorter [*sic*] remove the curse from the League." By the same token, Cowper's nonpartisanship will be an "advantage" as she toured western counties where anti-Smith "feeling runs high."[102]

Conference Colleagues

Gertrude's foray into partisan politics demonstrated the limits of an exclusively female lobby. Gertrude as a social feminist focused on welfare and women's interests, but she was always willing to cross gender lines. She found allies in the North Carolina Conference for Social Service, whose board she had joined. In 1928 Frank Graham was its president and Gertrude first vice president. Graham wanted to create a new social order for North Carolina, and he selected prominent progressives for a Central Committee on Code to refocus the organization on research. Gertrude was the only woman among its six members. Gertrude also served on the influential Committee on Industry, which Graham chose "with the greatest care." Graham pressed the conference to take up the cause of labor and the poor. Although by 1928 forty-three states had workmen's compensation laws, North Carolina had been its usual dilatory self. The industry committee drafted legislation, supported by new governor O. Max Gardner, that led to the South's most generous law.[103]

The labor struggle drew Gertrude and Frank Graham closer. Their friendship was deeper than common politics or interests. Graham was on spinster Gertrude's short list of people whom, she quipped, she could have married. Both shared temperaments that were modest and democratic. Firm in their beliefs, the observant Jew and staunch Presbyterian were, as Graham described her, "steeped in the Bible," their values grounded in "spiritual rootage." Physically even they were alike: short, athletic, exuding energy. Interested always in others, they led by example and were thrust, often unwillingly, into leadership. Their kindly demeanor, upright character, and good humor disarmed opponents. "Not to do anything Miss Gertrude tells me to do is a real failure to me," Graham wrote Mina. Graham's admiration extended to the Weil clan. Graham's wife, Marian, assumed her husband needed rescue from political trouble whenever she saw Leslie approach their door. Recalling Leslie, Graham became emotional.[104]

Despite Smith's failed bid for president, Gertrude and Graham could take hope from a turn in state politics. In 1928 the conservative Democratic machine of boss Furnifold W. Simmons was overthrown as O. Max Gardner, leader of the party's progressive wing, won the governorship. As early suffragists, Gardner and his wife, Faye, were well known to Gertrude. Gregarious campaigners, Gardner and his wife socialized with Franklin and Eleanor Roosevelt. Although a textile manufacturer with an industrialist's interest in labor peace and social order, he maintained a well-kept mill village and, as a lawyer, defended injured workers. With brother-in-law

Clyde Hoey, he ushered in the Shelby Dynasty, named for their hometown. Gardner was the League's guest of honor at its ninth annual conference, and Faye, a League advisory board member, hosted a tea at the governor's mansion. With Gardner's support, the Australian secret ballot passed in 1929 after thrice failing. In a death blow to the machine, in 1930 Josiah Bailey, another pro-suffragist veteran, defeated the venerable Simmons in the Democratic senatorial primary. Gertrude was "inclined to believe" that Bailey will bring "an attitude of intelligent liberalism in the Senate."[105]

Labor Conflicts

Gertrude would have been only too aware from the headlines that the textile industry was in crisis. Synthetic rayon, shorter hemlines, and foreign cotton led to cutbacks. Manufacturers imposed a "stretch out" that required workers to service more machines at the same pay. Workers responded with walkouts and strikes. Mills hired scabs to replace them, provoking violence. In 1927 the Loray Mill in Gastonia laid off nearly a third of its force and cut wages. Evicted from their villages, workers took to the streets. The National Textile Workers Union, affiliated with the Communist Party, sent organizers.

In 1929 violence exploded in Gastonia. In April, newly elected Governor Gardner called out the National Guard. While the militia sat blocks away, a masked mob destroyed union headquarters. In June events escalated. When police attempted to disarm guards at the strikers' tent city, gunfire erupted. The sheriff was shot dead and two deputies lay wounded. Sixteen strikers—among them three women and labor organizer Fred Beal—were arrested. After a mistrial, a mob chased down a truck loaded with workers and shot dead Ella Mae Wiggins, a labor balladeer and union organizer. Gertrude was hardly alone in clipping from the newspaper the photo of Wiggins's nine children at her graveside, which became an icon of the labor movement. Nell Battle Lewis organized a Fair Trial Fund, and Gertrude sent $25. Wiggins's assailants were acquitted, but Beal and sixteen union members were convicted as agents of a foreign power. Several defendants, led by Beal, jumped bail for the Soviet Union.[106]

The 1929 strikes, with young women in the lead, traumatized the state. Gertrude saw around her the predictable, disheartening consequences of labor reform's failure. From Gastonia and then to smaller towns, strikes spread, often stimulated by union radicals. In spring 1929, workers at two mills in Marion walked out. Sherwood Anderson and Sinclair Lewis publicized the strike in *The Nation* and *The New Republic*. As strikers demonstrated, police opened fire. Six workers fell dead, some shot in the back, and dozens were wounded. Governor Gardner rejected union calls for an investigation. The strike ended. When union activity stirred at Cone Mills, management fired and evicted the organizers from the mill village.[107]

As labor wars raged, Gertrude, Harriet Payne wrote, had "worn herself out." Aunt Sarah had just died. At home Gertrude contended with illness and a steady stream of guests. After the deaths of Grandmother Eva, Uncle Joe, and Aunt Sarah, Gertrude had to comfort a widowed mother who "finds it hard to read and sleep," who "feels she has nothing to do now." Gertrude confessed, "It is hard to speak my mind of anything with any degree of concentration." The Smith election, League politics, and failed survey campaign took their toll. In April 1929, while labor violence percolated, Gertrude traveled to Washington as a delegate to a League "Fireside Conference," an executive council meeting. The League still struggled to define its mission.[108]

In July 1929 Gertrude sailed to Europe with aunt Lizzie Rosenthal, who was seeking medical care and a sanitarium. Gertrude herself wanted a rest cure not just from her exhausting public duties but from the emotional fatigue of home. The League bulletin noted, "Her mind is always on the work," but she needed a vacation. Gertrude promised upon her return in September, "I'll visit all the Leagues." Back from Europe, she headed west, speaking in four mountain towns, lecturing on the World Court in Charlotte, and attending a meeting at Woman's College. She closed one letter to Mary Cowper, "Yours hurriedly—as usual." By March 1930 Gertrude had "visited all the local Leagues," as well as "old suffragists."[109]

Gertrude returned from Europe just as bullets were felling Wiggins and the Marion workers. In October the League asked how it could "think clearly ... when there is so little real information?" Once again, it demanded a "*competent* and *unbiased*" survey of women's working conditions. On 5 October Gertrude met with Frank Graham and Clara Cox in Chapel Hill to plan a legislative agenda weighted toward labor reform.[110]

With the violence, Nell Battle Lewis could write, "Told you so!" Yet the manufacturers proved too powerful and the workers too disorganized and downtrodden for unions to gain a foothold in North Carolina. The public remained unsympathetic even as wages dropped and workplace conditions worsened. The Legislative Council, as a coalition, was constrained by its conservative members, and Women's Clubs were less daring than the League of Women Voters or YWCA.[111]

Gertrude was again caught in the crossfire between her labor sympathies and pro-business public sentiment. The League passed a resolution commending the governor for "condemning the mob violence" but also for demanding an "investigation" to apprehend and punish "guilty parties." The League questioned whether troops were called to "keep order"—protect strikers—or to safeguard mill interests. The League's *Monthly News* conceded that northern communists had misled native southerners. Yet the newsletter writer, an anonymous League member living near Gastonia, wrote sympathetically of workers who have "grievances which are real and not imaginary ones created out of the brains of Communist agitators." It reported a front-porch conversation with a working woman wanting "sumpin' to eat" whose "chillin don't go to Sunday school. They ain't got no clothes fittin' to wear." Another striker added, "No'm they ain't no law for us—the law's for the comp'ny."[112] Such stories motivated Gertrude more than statistics or ideological posturing.

The Red Scare dominated headlines. The strikers had little sense of ideology—their rallies resembled camp revivals—but communists did infiltrate the National Textile Workers' Union. The *Gastonia Gazette* warned that the union would overthrow the "established social order," that it respected no religion or color line, that it advocated free love. Other reports expressed outrage that white and black communists danced together.[113] The Depression intensified passions, and fears arose that labor strife would scare away northern investors and cost jobs.

To sympathize with labor, as Gertrude did, was to risk opprobrium. Josephus Daniels's *News and Observer* was a notable newspaper exception to antilabor public sentiment. Columnist Nell Battle Lewis blasted the manufacturers for their "arrogance, pig-headedness, and general social blindness." As strikes spread, the League's *Monthly News* kept the labor flame burning. The Legislative Council lobbied the General Assembly, fending off the manufacturers' efforts to kill or weaken proposals. Gertrude, at the council's behest, joined Mary Cowper to appear before the state House Judiciary Committee. Their testimony was disregarded, but the legislature did pass an eleven-hour workday and a fifty-five-hour week, as well as the workmen's compensation law. In late 1929 Gertrude joined Lewis and Cowper in Greensboro to organize a committee to educate the public on the need for legislation to curtail women's work hours.[114]

Responding to public appeals, Frank Graham drafted a statement on labor rights, and Gertrude was among the first he solicited. As Graham wrote Gertrude in December 1929, he wanted the statement to come from "our own home folks" and not from "any other organization or agency." The statement enumerated four rights, guaranteeing free speech and assembly, collective bargaining, a national labor survey of the textile industry, and "social adjustment" of working hours and conditions. Graham thought it "presumptuous" for the statement to come from one person, but he feared "getting others into trouble." He asked Gertrude to join an "informal" leadership committee that succeeded in enlisting four hundred prominent men and women.[115]

With the state in depression and the labor movement defeated, reformers regrouped. In 1930, at the instigation of Graham and Hugh MacRae, a Wilmington entrepreneur, Gertrude went as state delegate to the Southeastern Economic Conference in Atlanta and served on its Resolutions Committee. This conference, a joint meeting of farmers and businessmen, was held to create a regional organization dedicated to economic policy. Graham asked Gertrude about holding a similar conference on agriculture in eastern North Carolina. The state, despite its industrialization, was second in the nation in the number of farms, although last in acres per farm. MacRae wrote Gertrude that the conference should shift focus from industry to the "great problems of agriculture." With crop prices falling, the poverty of the tenant farmer pressed urgently forward. Gertrude suggested to Graham that the conference reorient from a "reform agency"—which is "a most serious handicap" because of the "deep seated prejudice against reform"—into an "independent, impartial investigator of facts," a Society for Social Research.[116] In focusing on research and agriculture rather than on reform and industry, Gertrude was conceding to political reality. More often she urged direct action, expressing impatience with academic approaches that ended with more studies and discussion.

Gertrude was still unwilling for the League to abandon the labor fight. Bulus Bagby Swift, whose husband, Wiley, was executive of the National Child Labor Committee, had joined Mary Cowper to form a Committee on the Working Child. The women toured the state, distributing leaflets and newsletters. The 1930 League convention, pushed by Cowper, was dedicated to women and children workers. Meeting in Goldsboro, it held a School for Citizens in cooperation with the University of North Carolina's extension division. Speakers included Frank Graham. The League, compromising, agreed to lobby for a ten-hour day and fifty-four-hour week and end night work for women and children.[117]

Though Cowper had a reputation as a firebrand, she and Gertrude worked together respectfully. Over the years, Gertrude had sent Cowper money to supplement her meager salary. Now, Gertrude declined to support Cowper for League president, complaining again that she was exhausted defending her. The formidable Cornelia Jerman succeeded in having Cowper and Swift removed from leadership of the Committee on the Working Child. Gertrude diminished her own role in the League, as well as financial support, but continued her labor advocacy. Her philanthropy revealed her sympathies. In 1930 she sent Swift one hundred dollars for labor causes. She annually contributed to the Women's Trade Union League, which supported federal legislation. In the mid-1930s she sent small sums to the Tom Mooney Defense Committee in support of a socialist labor militant jailed for his alleged involvement in a bombing. His case became a cause célèbre among intellectuals and Hollywood personalities.[118]

Excepting dedicated activists like Mary Cowper and Bulus Bagby Swift, League women largely abandoned labor reform during the Depression. Laura Cone wrote that she would return to the League only if "industrial problems" were no longer on its agenda. Even the avid Nell Battle Lewis advised that, with the Depression, working women should feel grateful for a job and not demand higher wages.[119] Former ladies of leisure sought employment, crimping the culture of voluntarism.

The League's Decline

Labor advocacy exacerbated the League's decline. By 1929 state Leagues had shrunk from twelve to eight, and membership fell. New leadership failed to emerge. By 1930 the League was largely spent. Gertrude reflected in the *Monthly News*, "In trying to evaluate our growth and development during these ten years ... I admit that we seem to have grown rather slowly, and at times there has been a temptation to discouragement." She added, "Political education is not an objective that has so far thrilled our women generally with a feverish enthusiasm and activity." She doubted that it would appeal to "great numbers" for a "long time" but called on those of "us who have caught the vision of the ideal to work with continuing faith and zeal."[120]

The North Carolina League's struggles mirrored the national picture. With Depression women had more pressing needs for their time and money. Rather than plan for the future, the national League at its 1930 convention in Louisville recalled nostalgically the suffrage crusade. It ceased publishing its *Woman's Journal*. In March 1930 the *Monthly News* "expressed regret at the decision of Miss Weil that she could not continue as President." She remained a committee chair but was rethinking her activism. In May the bulletin reported an enlarged Committee on the Working Child that included not just women—Gertrude, Cornelia Jerman, and Fannie Bickett—but also men: Frank Graham and Rabbi Iser Freund of Goldsboro. Ten professional, educational, and religious organizations endorsed this committee.[121]

The 1931 League meeting was contentious as the Legislative Council backed away from labor reform. Mary Cowper and Bulus Bagby Swift wanted the League to quit the council, believing it too timid. To the contrary, Cornelia Jerman, council president, and Elsie Riddick, League president, wanted the League to abandon the labor fight and join the North Carolina Federation of Women's Clubs as a political education agency. Women further divided on the Equal Rights Amendment.[122]

Schooling Working Women

Gertrude, withdrawing from League politics, found other forums for her labor activism. She had a lifelong interest in alternative education, particularly for the poor and working class. In 1927 she had visited the Pine Mountain Settlement School in Harlan, Kentucky, and she donated to the John C. Campbell Folk School, a Scandinavia-inspired crafts center in Brasstown, North Carolina. In a handwritten note Gertrude described the Southern Summer School for Women Workers in Industry as a "project I am working on." Modeled on a program at Bryn Mawr and inspired by YWCA industrial study clubs, the school, driven by precarious finances and local hostility, relocated from Virginia to the North Carolina mountains in 1928.[123]

The school brought together women across class lines, with middle-class women mentoring millworkers. At the school, Gertrude heard firsthand of long days and nights in sweat-inducing factories, of lint heads and brown lungs, of working without meal breaks, of wages that perpetuated poverty over generations. Gertrude joined its advisory board in 1933 and arranged for her college-age niece Mina Bluethenthal to intern there. The school, a training ground for union workers, inspired proletarian consciousness. For poorly educated textile and tobacco workers, the school offered a curriculum emphasizing English and economics.[124] Beyond study, Gertrude would have enjoyed seeing young millworkers hiking and swimming.

Gertrude's association with the summer school was a risk as it was targeted for its alleged radicalism. David Clark's *Southern Textile Bulletin* attacked the school for "Teaching Socialism and Communism to Textile Workers." Clark listed members of its advisory board and wrote sinisterly, "It would be interesting to know who finances it." Gertrude numbered among its annual donors. Clark assailed Frank Graham for speaking at its conferences, serving on its board, and contributing to its scholarship fund. The YWCA, which provided students, was denounced as communist. Clark had no evidence, but the charges echoed in newspapers and were widely believed. Students worried that they would lose their jobs. Thirty-six workers attended in 1929, which dropped to twenty-six in 1930, after strikes hit the mills, and eighteen in 1931. In the late 1930s it boldly admitted black women. Damned as radical, its finances declined, and it expired.[125]

A Changing State

Political and economic developments in both state and nation changed the tenor of the labor struggle. The election of O. Max Gardner as governor and his friend Franklin Roosevelt as president put liberals in power. As the League wrestled with labor advocacy, the legislature in 1931 finally removed the fourth-grade exemption and limited children under sixteen to an eight-hour day and a forty-eight-hour week. Night work was forbidden for girls under eighteen. This belated legislation marked the high point of the League's and council's efforts to enact labor reform. After taking an anti-union stance, Gardner responded to recurring labor strife by calling up mediators rather than the militia. At a 1932 High Point strike, he sent state troopers home and sat down personally with labor and management to negotiate a settlement. The governor has "redeemed" the "dark blots" of Gastonia and Marion, Nell Battle Lewis rejoiced, and "we are learning, slowly learning."[126] Gertrude, too, saw hope in the Gardners. With New Deal labor codes — an eight-hour day, forty-hour week — working women as well as men found some relief from exploitation.

"And yet more was expected of us," Adelaide Daniels declared at the 1928 state League convention, a comment taken as a judgment on "what women accomplished with the ballot." In 1928 Gertrude, writing in the *Monthly News*, lamented, "It was the high hope of some of us, that the enfranchisement of women would sound a gong whose ring great masses of women would rise to political interest and act." She now recognized, "It was a hope founded on desire and not a knowledge of psychology. We had too long formed a habit of political inactivity; we had found it too easy to 'let George do it.'" Experience had taught that "the idea of political education has not yet popular appeal."[127] In the 1920s the League's progressive ethos clashed with the times. Professor Woodrow Wilson with his idealism yielded to businessmen Warren G. Harding, Calvin Coolidge, and Herbert Hoover, ready to veto legislation that in their minds smacked of socialism. In North Carolina the business plutocracy had its political way. After the violence of 1929, the industrialists conceded but limited reform.

Like other southern progressives, notably Frank Graham, Gertrude had taken gradualist positions, tempering her idealism on such issues as labor rights and race relations. Yet, as her activism and donations indicate, she held principles on labor and politics that were left of the consensus. League politics exhausted her. The personal crises of family deaths and her mother's decline wore on her. By the mid-1930s hardly any local North Carolina

Leagues remained active, and the national League removed the state from its registry. The Legislative Council of North Carolina Women merged with the North Carolina Conference for Social Service as a North Carolina Legislative Council, and, with male leadership, ceased to be a women's lobby. Lacking funds, its primary activity was letter writing.[128]

Gertrude always said that social welfare, rather than a specifically feminist agenda, was her primary interest. Middle-class women attending League meetings and working women leading walkouts did not cross class lines or bond as a feminist sisterhood. To Gertrude's disappointment, women's vote was not consistently progressive. Southern soils were not fertile for such activism. A nonpartisan League was less able to influence politicians to pass legislation. Despite the fearful rhetoric of her opponents, Gertrude, whatever her personal views, was hardly the radical leader of a socialist revolution. She had her sympathies but was not ideological. On occasion she would speak of her feminism or socialism, but she did not subscribe to a party. She remained an "unmanageable Democrat."

As Frank Graham observed, Gertrude always felt that she had not done enough. Her feeling of failure was relative to her idealism. She had been given to inspirational, utopian rhetoric on the grand themes of justice and democracy. An end to war and poverty and clean and efficient government were hardly realizable, but the decade did see incremental advances on numerous fronts: reduced hours for working women, the decline of child labor in manufacturing, improved living conditions in mill villages, and greater expenditures and more stringent standards in schools. The secret ballot was secured, and state government was reorganized, with patronage yielding to expertise. From municipal housekeeping women now addressed issues concerning the national economy and international relations. The Democratic Party ended its efforts to disfranchise its opponents as it once had with blacks, poor whites, and women. The race question, which white supremacy had supposedly suppressed forever, was resurfacing. Liberalism moved beyond the social controls of early twentieth-century progressivism to emphasize civil liberties and economic security. A New Deal would enact a welfare state. In foreign affairs, Gertrude heard Carrie Chapman Catt reflect that the past ten years were notable for the "growth in the supplanting of war by peace," with a League of Nations, World Court, Pan-American Treaties, and Paris Peace Pact. In the coming decade, with depression and crises abroad, Gertrude found new battles to fight and would become ever more fully the woman citizen of her ideal.[129]

{ 8 }

MEETING THE NEEDS

The Struggle for Economic and Social Justice

With the women's vote Gertrude had envisioned an ideal society, but in the 1930s she confronted a state and nation mired in the Great Depression. A champion of peace and disarmament, she looked helplessly at a world marching toward war with her own Jewish people the primary victim. Gertrude was still committed to working within the electoral system, especially now that liberals had power in Raleigh and Washington, but around her were reasons for despair. Beyond the failing economy, labor strife, and portending war, she dealt daily with a weakening mother who demanded her attention. Then, in fall 1932 Gertrude found a new and unwanted cause pressing upon her. She had been feeling unwell and a "questionable chest X-ray" drew her, accompanied by her sister, Janet, to Johns Hopkins in Baltimore. The distinguished surgeon J. M. T. Finney Jr. sent a report to her brother Leslie that did not comfort:

> The X-ray examination of Miss Weil's chest showed that the suspicious area of metastasis in the right lung, is now very definite and at least one-third larger than it was six weeks ago.... We have talked things over with Miss Gertrude, as well as Mrs. Bluethenthal, and they decided that she would stay here and have the course of X-ray treatment.... This will involve probably around about 16 to 18 exposures during a period of three weeks.... Of course, her ultimate outlook is bad, but I still believe that at least for awhile we will be able to control things by X-ray. But you must realize that each time there is a recurrence it will be more resistant to X-ray treatment than before.[1]

Gertrude, as was her nature, deflected concern, scribbling a note to Leslie and Hilda: "I hate to be away just now, when there are so many things to do at home. Also, and most of all, I hate to miss seeing your children.... There is nothing in the above med for treatments to worry about. They are just very cautious indeed."[2] She sent her love.

Gertrude would live nearly forty years more. Always a private person, she kept the cancer prognosis largely to herself as if her imminent demise was but an inconvenience. The news was apparently concealed from her perpetually worried mother, whose letters to her in Baltimore report local gossip but not anxieties over her health. Perhaps illness explains her declining activism in the League of Women Voters. Whatever break Gertrude took was brief indeed. Returning home, she resumed a busy social life. Her friend Martha Boswell grew concerned that constant "friendly visitations" were exhausting Gertrude and that she should call a "closed season." Boswell advised, "Those who nourish any independent life in this crowded day are obliged to protect their spiritual freedom from the onslaughts of bridge and blaah—and who blaahs so unrelentingly as the contented guest." Boswell expressed "contrition" for her own visits when she and Gertrude "talked till 2 A.M." Guests recalled a host so stimulated by conversation as to be oblivious to the clock. In spring 1933 she was traveling again. When Rachel Berenson Perry met her old Smith friend in Chapel Hill, she found "perennially youthful Gertrude."[3]

A wide circle surrounded Gertrude, many describing her as dearest of friends. Harriet Payne's relations with the Weils were soured by her constant indebtedness to them, but Gertrude wrote tenderly, assuring her that her admiration stood. Where others found Harriet flighty and unreliable, Gertrude respected her "original standard of behavior unaffected by the usual considerations of self interest or practical expediency." Harriet and Gertrude remained intimate friends, but the distance between them ensured that Gertrude could maintain her privacy and independence. Bookish, erudite Martha Boswell was an engaging houseguest and correspondent. Boswell, from Goldsboro, taught English to poor Appalachian youth at a mountain high school. Gertrude's friendship also blossomed with Harriet Elliott, an eminent political scientist at Woman's College and a national Democratic leader. Her closest friends were all learned women committed to social justice. They visited, wrote familiarly, and planned travel together but lived apart, following their careers.[4] The youthful effusions of love that had passed between Gertrude and her women friends yielded to more sober reflections on aging mothers and social and political issues. Gertrude remained within the bosom of her loving family, gratified emotionally as daughter, sister, aunt, and cousin.

Daily life revolved around local friends and family. "Gertrude and her

Gertrude's resilience was tested by war, Holocaust, and family deaths.
Courtesy of the State Archives of North Carolina.

mother were the most hospitable people," recalled cousin Kala Rosenthal Herlands. At mealtimes the large dining room filled with company. A new lawyer, doctor, or businessman in town was at once invited. Gertrude became companionable with Dr. Samuel McPheeters, the city and county health supervisor, the two working closely and traveling to meetings together. McPheeters, according to one expert, was "one of the best qualified health directors" in the state. Joined by his wife, Virginia, they enjoyed dinners, movies, or walks in the woods. She met childhood friend Julia Thompson regularly for teas, luncheons, or bridge. Always there were dinners with cousins and siblings at their homes or hers. Weil siblings, a friend observed, were "an unusually harmonious and sympathetic group." She was especially close to Leslie, a "delightfully modest" person. Like Gertrude, he was valued as wise and kindly, with the Weil penchant for whimsical humor. Her African American help, Haywood Spearman and later Mittie Exum, who remained with her for decades, became, in the southern lexicon, almost family. Exum cooked while Spearman—a tall, slim, fair-skinned man—was house servant, yardman, and sometimes chauffeur. Among the pleasures of home life was her beloved garden. With friends she drove country roads looking for wildflowers to replant in her yard. She kept meticulous notes of her plantings, studying catalogs of varietal roses and amassing a collection of lilies.[5]

The cocoon of security that the family created on Chestnut Street was threatened by illness, death, war, and the Depression. Adding to Gertrude's distress were financial losses that the family suffered in 1930 and 1932 with the failures of the Wayne County banks in which Weils were investors and officers. At the end of December 1932, after the Wayne National Bank collapsed, Frank Graham wrote them caringly of the "crushing despair of these times," but he foresaw "the beautiful personal and civic spirit of all the Weils shining through." Mina lamented that she could no longer help her Greensboro cousins, and Eli Oettinger responded by commiserating over her "troubles" and "heartaches." Gertrude began budgeting personal expenses, listing the nickel she spent on peanuts and the fifty cents for a Chapel Hill trip. Her habitual twenty-five-dollar annual donations were now five or ten dollars.[6]

In 1933, New Deal programs, notably the Emergency Banking Act, restored banks to solvency. Lionel Weil stepped forward to rebuild Goldsboro's banking system and was named president of the Bank of Wayne's holding corporation. He also served on local and state boards concerned with finance and agriculture. In 1935 a woman named Augusta, whose hospital bills the Weils had paid, sent a letter praising them. "The Money of the

Bank is doing very well I suppose thanks to You and Your People," she wrote, "as otherwise it would have ben a great loss to many People."[7]

Gertrude's brother Herman, nephew Henry, and cousin Emil managed her finances, sending her checks as banks settled claims and buying and selling bonds and stocks in her name. The Weils were diversified, with holdings beyond the department store, in real estate, farmland, the rice mill, a brickyard, and a fertilizer factory, as well as mortgages. On the map was a farming community called Weil. By 1933 the family apparently recovered. In that year Gertrude ordered an antique silver service from Richmond and sent the Persian silk rugs for cleaning. Gertrude and her mother vacationed in Canada, and a year later Gertrude was off again to England. From Chester she shipped home Chippendale chairs. Philanthropies resumed at generous levels, and she traded in the Studebaker for an Oldsmobile.[8]

Less amenable to recovery was the family's declining health. Mina's heart was failing. She had fallen ill in spring 1934 and was soon bedridden, her mobility limited to a wheelchair. Visitors found her perpetually cheerful. Gertrude postponed her trip abroad until she felt assured, but in subsequent years as her mother became increasingly dependent she stayed near her side. "I don't want to undertake anything just now that will take me away from home," she wrote the North Carolina Conference for Social Service president in 1936, explaining that her mother could barely sit up in bed.[9] Gertrude, now in her fifties, soon suffered devastating personal losses.

The desperate times tested her idealism. Ambitious to eradicate poverty, she now confronted growing numbers of "ill-clad, ill-fed beggars" walking Goldsboro's streets, knocking on her door.[10] Daily Gertrude read of Europe rearming for war. Nazi anti-Semitism abroad echoed at home in the radio ranting of Father Coughlin, isolationist rhetoric against Jewish immigration, and calumny against Roosevelt's "Jew Deal." Gertrude's calamities were personal, familial, communal, and global.

Tar Heel Depression

North Carolina was heading toward a crash even before the stock market cataclysm of 1929. State government was bogged in $560 million debt, largely from a road-building frenzy, and its per capita debt ranked second among states. Farm income fell nearly two-thirds from 1928 to 1932. The South's leading industrial state ranked forty-fifth in per capita income. By the end of 1932 towns and counties were declaring bankruptcy.[11]

Sharecroppers, hungry and looking for work, flocked to towns like Goldsboro, although they found prospects little better than the countryside. The problem of rural poverty, especially among African Americans, became urban. "The poverty is so overwhelming I often feel I cannot face it another day," Martha Boswell wrote Gertrude, "and all the diseases of poverty physical and spiritual, have me down in the depths." She felt as if she were looking "straight down into the heart of the sixteenth century." One fall day in 1932, Goldsboro hosted a Hoover Cart rodeo. Some fifteen thousand onlookers watched a parade of three hundred cars pulled by mules.[12]

As president of the Goldsboro Bureau for Social Service, Gertrude knew firsthand the Depression's deprivations. In 1931 she chaired the bureau's Decisions Committee, personally reviewing cases to judge if applicants qualified for aid. Committee members were drawn from the town's churches, Salvation Army, and municipal health and welfare departments. Such public and private collaboration was the North Carolina way. In its 1931 report, the bureau listed 7,506 calls for help but only 1,261 assisted. Just sixty-two secured jobs. The Decisions Committee described the Goldsboro situation—children begging on the streets, a waiting list at orphanages—as "disheartening." The bureau's files reported a father of five too ill to work and a widow with six children. A year later the committee complained of "diminished funds" and the "promiscuous begging making it impossible for our office to keep track of the real condition of families." Even "the self-respecting workman" finds himself "exhausted and no job in sight." To combat hunger, the bureau placed food collection barrels in grocery stores and encouraged planting of private and community gardens.[13]

"Times are tragic," lamented Governor O. Max Gardner. He asked folks to "live at home," to feed themselves from gardens and personal livestock. In 1930 on recommendation of the liberal Brookings Institution, Gardner reorganized state government. Defying conservatives, Gardner appointed his University of North Carolina classmate Frank Graham to head the newly consolidated University of North Carolina system. Gardner selected a committee of distinguished citizens to revise the state constitution. Gertrude was invited to join. She wanted public welfare included in its provisions. Stalemated by warfare between progressives and conservatives, the committee's work never went as far as a public vote.[14]

Gertrude looked to reinvigorate the progressive movement. Seeking advice, in 1932 she wrote Lucy Randolph Mason, the Virginia blueblood and noted social activist who would succeed Florence Kelley as president of the National Consumers League. The two wrote familiarly. The question was whether to join a "ready-made organization" like the National Consumers League or whether, as Mason put it, "to get different organizations into some one cooperative movement." Even as Mason bemoaned "our low standards in the South," she complimented Gertrude: "You have in North Carolina the best organized and most effective group of women that I know of in any Southern state." Gertrude rebutted, "Our own momentum seems to have slackened—we've grown tired." Mason suggested organizing a Southern Council on Industry, including both men and women. Gertrude feared that any "advertised or known connection between organized groups in the South" with liberal societies "would be a detriment in public opinion." Kelley's "name aroused suspicion," Gertrude warned, and even the National Child Labor Committee bore "the stigma of a sinister organization." Gertrude thought that "the most practicable plan" was, quoting Mason, "working through 'independent existing organizations,'" which focus on specific legislation acceptable to the state.[15]

Gertrude joined efforts to expand the Legislative Council of North Carolina Women by including men. In 1932, by coincidence, Frank Graham and A. W. McAlister, a Greensboro insurance executive, had both independently conceived the idea of forming, as Graham put it, "a federated council of elected representatives of all the organizations interested in the human side of North Carolina legislation." McAlister enlisted Gertrude, addressing her as "Guardian of the Flame of our social altar." Two years later the Legislative Council included men, among them Graham, Howard Odum, and dramatist Paul Green. The council advocated for family and juvenile courts, against the death penalty, and for children's legislation.[16]

At the council's formative meeting in Chapel Hill, Gertrude represented the North Carolina Association of Jewish Women (NCAJW). She was committed to moving Jewish organizations beyond parochial concerns, although some women were reluctant. At the 1930 NCAJW meeting she "called attention to the conditions of North Carolina's child workers," and a motion passed to endorse the League of Women Voters' legislative program. Gertrude remained NCAJW representative to the council, attending a conference on "Women's Work in Relief" in Raleigh.[17]

Gertrude also remained secretary of the North Carolina Conference for Social Service, working closely with its leaders. Annie Bost described Gertrude as "efficient, thoughtful, considerate." In organizations, Gertrude preferred the secretarial post, where she won the affection of presidents for her cheery willingness to undertake the tedious but necessary tasks of ordering stationery, enlisting committee members, scheduling conferences, or printing programs. Gertrude served on its influential Committee on Code, chaired by Harriet Elliot, and the Committee on Industry. She rose to vice president in 1935, a post she held for three years. The organization studied subjects from pellagra to motion pictures, bank deposits to child labor, flogging in the prisons to parent-teacher relations. Whatever her title,

Gertrude was part of the conference's inner circle, its executive commit-tee. "After the meeting adjourned, and most of the folks had left," A. W. McAlister wrote of a 1932 meeting, Gertrude Weil, Frank Graham, W. C. Jackson, and Dr. Hobbs remained to discuss themes and strategy. Gertrude worked closely with McAlister, "Father of the North Carolina Conference." A kindly southern gentleman seventeen years her senior, McAlister became Gertrude's trusted friend.[18]

A New Deal

Although Gertrude kept distant from politics, she was a Roosevelt Demo-crat. She would have assented to Governor O. Max Gardner's advice: "If I were Roosevelt, I would become more liberal. I would march with the crowd, because I tell you the masses are marching." We must, Gardner ar-gued, "discard . . . our preconceived ideas and formulas."[19] Roosevelt was popular in North Carolina, although the New Deal roiled the state's politi-cal currents. In 1932 bumptious mountain populist Robert "Our Bob" Rey-nolds won a U.S. Senate seat over the establishment candidate by posing as a New Dealer, but he shed his liberal garb once in office.

Despite hard times North Carolina remained wary of federalism. The millions flowing into the state led to accusations of waste and corruption and that New Deal programs were make-work projects for the lazy and un-worthy. Governor John C. B. Ehringhaus, Gardner's successor, professed loyalty to Roosevelt but gave priority to budget cutting. The debate was "how little, not how much" the state could do to combat poverty.[20]

North Carolina responded to the economic crisis by encouraging co-operation between charities and public agencies. In July 1932 the economy bottomed, with some 175,000 Tar Heels applying for assistance. Gertrude applied herself to local relief. At an organizational meeting in November with Gertrude and Wayne County officials, Annie O'Berry, now a supervi-sor of public welfare, apologized, "At present the funds of the Bureau are exhausted." A Central Relief Council formed, with Rev. A. J. Smith as chair and Gertrude in her usual post as secretary. Some three thousand regis-tered for one thousand jobs available. In the city one hundred men went to work at ten cents an hour digging drainage ditches, cutting wood, trimming trees, and building a boat lake for children. Cloth and flour were distributed to "grade mothers" in the schools, both black and white. The superintendent of public welfare issued cards to shoeless children directing them to the Weil store, often with the note "charge to Mrs. Mina Weil."[21]

In May 1933, "to avert the collapse of state and local relief," Congress created the Federal Emergency Relief Administration. Grants were available to the states provided that they create their own agencies under federal standards and match funds by one-third. Rather than just coordinate programs, the agencies now doled out money directly. Governor Ehringhaus established the North Carolina Emergency Relief Agency (NCERA) and appointed Annie O'Berry as state director. Annie and Gertrude were old friends and colleagues, succeeding presidents of the Goldsboro Bureau for Social Service. In August 1933 the board of alderman appointed Gertrude chair of the City Emergency Relief Committee, which allocated federal funds locally. Completing the projects, an official report noted, "required the exercise of considerable ingenuity and close supervision" to match relief cases with the work available. Among Gertrude's challenges were finding construction materials, identifying "worthwhile projects ... accessible to the relief clients," and hiring competent supervisors. Gertrude had to negotiate with O'Berry to obtain money and then oversee city administrator Eva Giddens to spend it.[22]

The NCERA struggled with delays and bureaucracy, but its severest challenge was underfunding. The state contributed but $700,000, 13 percent of the federal funding, well below its mandated one-third. Annie O'Berry warned that federal grants for unemployment relief did "not absolve state and local communities of their responsibility to see that the necessities of life were assured" destitute citizens. Towns and counties were left footing the bill. With the state abdicating, O'Berry advised Wayne County that "THE STATE WILL BE SERIOUSLY AFFECTED" unless money was raised locally. Wayne County, including Goldsboro under chair Gertrude Weil, did contribute its fair share, pledging $4,150 but paying out $5,688.[23]

Budgetary uncertainties made it difficult for Gertrude to implement a program. Gertrude asked O'Berry, "What will be our allowance of funds for the next month or two or three?" The director could not assure funding and issued an order to discontinue projects. Gertrude pressed forward: can she give the unemployed relief work doing roadside planting, paying them as if they were farm labor? O'Berry encouraged her to move ahead but again cautioned that she could not guarantee funding for another month.[24]

In Wayne County, Gertrude was caught between the conflicting needs of town and country. "The city has a constant influx of people from the county," the Goldsboro Bureau for Social Service reported. As a stopgap for the winter 1933, Roosevelt created a Civil Works Administration under the Federal Emergency Relief Administration, which put the unemployed to work on construction projects at a minimum wage. With some 120,000 migrants in North Carolina searching for work, camps were built to house them. A local reforestation camp supported 429 men on its payroll, 296 black and 136 white. By April Gertrude convened the Central Emergency Council to discuss suspending city work for a "short time" to discourage county residents from overburdening the town. "There appears very little work to be had," the bureau reported. When a local box factory started hiring two weeks later, thirty "Colored men" were dropped from the rolls to encourage them to seek work there. Town dwellers were advised to feed themselves from gardens, and 368 town plots were reported.[25]

Under Gertrude's chairmanship Goldsboro had fifteen projects in operation, including typical public works: roads, airport, and sewers. The city's white and "colored" cemeteries were restored. Privies were built or repaired. City cattle pens were erected, and manure was stockpiled. Gertrude's committee selected projects that filled her long-held ambitions for the town, including cottages for tubercular patients. As chair of the Wayne County Recreational Council, she worked to create healthier environments for children. A pool was built at the Wayne County Memorial Community Building, where Gertrude served as a board member for forty years, and Herman Park was beautified. Schools added new gyms, and playgrounds boasted new equipment. Recreation supervisors were hired for parks, nurses for schools, and assistants for the public library. A community garden was planted.[26]

The New Deal caught Gertrude in a familiar political dilemma between her ideals and political realities, between federalism and states' rights. Annie O'Berry, responding to Washington, wanted to centralize relief efforts under NCERA, but the state Board of Charities and Public Welfare under Annie Bost resisted, wanting to preserve the traditional system of county boards. The two Annies were both Gertrude's friends. Bost's public welfare chairman was another colleague, Howard Odum, a proponent of regionalism. Where Bost and Odum saw effective county institutions sensitive to local needs and independent of federal control, O'Berry found entrenched interests and partisanship. This conflict required Gertrude to choose among friends but, more critically, confounded her efforts to implement the New Deal.

To the consternation of Democrats, Annie O'Berry appointed acknowledged experts rather than party loyalists. Gertrude was sympathetic to O'Berry's struggle to resist fraud and cronyism. "Speaking of corruption," Martha Boswell wrote Gertrude, "I certainly do not envy Mrs. O'Berry her present troubles." She asked Gertrude, "Does she feel she has dropped into a mammoth pool of graft or does she think our state is conducting its relief very decently?" In undated notes for what was presumably a public speech, Gertrude warned, "To be effective welfare work must be made secure against the evils of petty politics." She added, "public opinion" must govern, but "offices must not be bestowed for any other reason than actual efficiency."[27] As usual with Gertrude, when caught in a crossfire she positioned herself pragmatically in the middle, affirming both Bost and Odum's localism and O'Berry's expertise. On the one hand was populist democracy; on the other, elitist technocracy.

The New Deal benefited North Carolina. The federal programs brought over $40 million from Washington, serving some three hundred thousand people monthly. The textile industry prospered, and the devastated furniture manufacturers returned to pre-Depression levels. After the Supreme Court ruled the National Industrial Recovery Act unconstitutional, Roosevelt, facing the 1936 elections, launched a Second New Deal that expanded welfare programs, including Social Security. Governor Clyde Hoey, who took office in 1937, declared that he had "no intention of letting this Washington crowd dictate to me how to conduct the affairs of North Carolina."[28] The state's senators worked to frustrate social welfare spending while the representatives, with whom Gertrude maintained a steady correspondence, remained loyal to Roosevelt's agenda.

Gertrude felt heartened to see the labor movement revive. In 1934 American Federation of Labor workers packed in "flying squads" of cars and trucks traveled the state, shutting down some 150 mills. The governor called out the National Guard. Herman Weil drove to Greensboro to witness the spectacle. By 1935 more than a third of the state's textile workers had joined a union, although southern working-class culture remained more agrarian than proletarian.[29]

The New Deal industrial codes succeeded in establishing many labor reforms that Gertrude and her allies had failed to achieve. The manufacturers agreed to a twelve dollar weekly wage in the South, a forty-hour week, collective bargaining, and an end to child labor, yet anti-union sentiment remained entrenched, and industry dominated regulatory agencies. Farmers and businessmen clamored that America was becoming a land of charity rather than of free enterprise. Recovery stalled in 1937, the nation slipping into recession. North Carolinians looked to Raleigh, not Washington. Governor Clyde Hoey increased school funding and conceded some reform but resisted New Deal measures. Tobacco support was sound economic policy, business plutocrats argued, but relief for the poor was socialism.[30]

Gertrude's focus remained social welfare. In 1938 she addressed the local Kiwanis club "On Knowing, Coordinating, and Developing our Social Resources in Goldsboro." She left "economic and industrial progress" to the Chamber of Commerce but was concerned with "progress in well-being, in human happiness." Her interests included health, education, food, and housing. She called upon the town's social service agencies to pool resources and conduct a survey on "meeting the needs of our unfortunate fellow citizens." Are beggars being cared for? What are the wages of Works Progress Administration workers? Can the streets be beautified?[31]

Gertrude's liberalism ran against the political tide. Max Gardner, now a presidential adviser, relocated to Washington, where he abandoned his New Deal salesmanship and became a spokesperson for business. She had anticipated that Senator Josiah Bailey, a suffragist supporter, would be liberal, but he instead authored the anti-Roosevelt "Conservative Manifesto."[32]

A Racial New Deal

Still unaddressed was race. African Americans welcomed the New Deal even as they benefited ambivalently. As federal administrators pushed state relief agencies to hire blacks, politicians like Bailey scorned "that pack of northern liberals." The National Recovery Administration (NRA) had pushed for equal pay for equal work, helping workers, mostly black women, by raising their incomes to subsistence levels. Still, African Americans disdained the NRA as the "Negro Removal Act," as unemployed whites took jobs that had been traditionally relegated to blacks. Segregation confined blacks to menial, unskilled work, especially in tobacco, and NRA wage codes exempted farm and domestic service. Even as New Deal programs succeeded in controlling crop production and raising crop prices, black farmers suffered.[33]

At a time when blacks were underserved, the Goldsboro Bureau for Social Service employed a "colored case worker." Gertrude reported to Lawrence Oxley, an African American federal bureaucrat, that local blacks were "more than usually active organizing themselves." An African American committee supplemented the caseworker's salary. The North Carolina Conference for Social Service, with Gertrude serving as an officer, took tentative steps to secure economic justice for blacks but pointedly did not confront segregation and systemic inequality. At its 1931 meeting in Goldsboro, the conference went no further than to advocate buses for black public schools and extend school days for blacks equal to whites. In 1934 it created a Committee on Race Relations. Gertrude did not join, but close colleagues did. In 1936 the conference, with Gertrude serving as vice president, held an interracial meeting featuring addresses on "Race Relations" by University of North Carolina professor Guy Johnson and "The Negro and the Administration of Justice" by North Carolina College for Negroes president James Shepard, an African American. The conference weakly resolved to urge "upon the white people of the State the importance of according to negro citizens a large share of participation in the rights, duties and benefits of the government under which they live." A "large share" hardly implied equal. The conference also "favored a law to make cohabitation of the races a crime."[34]

Gertrude was certainly aware politically as well as personally that the "race question" was inseparable from considerations of economic justice. Franklin Roosevelt had commissioned *A Report on the Economic Conditions of the South*, which labeled the region "the nation's number one economic problem." On 20 November 1938 twelve hundred liberals—one-third African Americans—met in Birmingham at the Southern Conference for Human Welfare. Frank Graham spoke stirringly and was elected chair. Eleanor Roosevelt came and at first sat in the "colored" section but then, unwilling to either endorse or violate segregation laws, moved to the front facing the audience. The conference was an epiphany of southern liberalism, yet it was too overtly biracial for southern gradualists. The presence of avowed leftists provoked allegations that it was a communist front. Gertrude did not attend but collected literature and later joined its North Carolina affiliate.[35]

At the 1939 state Conference for Social Service, N. C. Newbold, state director of negro education, spoke on "Race Relations in North Carolina," reporting his survey of nine prominent African Americans. They demanded equity in wages and education and fuller participation in the political process. Three years later black leaders meeting in Durham called for integration. In 1942 Newbold "firmly" told the conference board of directors, with Gertrude attending, that "he did not believe we could escape much longer" addressing the unmet demands of "colored people." The board "unanimously agreed" that the question needed attention, perhaps by "possibly" holding a program on "minority groups" at its next conference. A year later Gertrude attended another board meeting at which Howard Odum suggested equivocally "we might also include a discussion on race problems." With the war foremost, the race issue receded. The progressive response was more talk, more committees, a remedy that often frustrated Gertrude. Social service organizations like the conference confronted the choice of whether to remain forums for study and discussion or to engage in direct action. "Unfortunately, it was composed mostly of professional people," Gertrude later reflected. "I was always trying to get laymen into it."[36]

After responding to the economic trauma, the New Deal was too exhausted to cure the pervasive rural and urban poverty that had always been Gertrude's ambitious ideal. To enact his New Deal, Roosevelt needed the consent of industrial and farm interests whose enterprises were regulated. Giving them a place at the table sustained rather than challenged the existing political order. In 1935 Martha Boswell wrote Gertrude, "The New Deal has reseated all the good old Democrats at the expense of the nation."[37] Sentiment in North Carolina remained opposed to unions, regulation, racial equality, and social welfare.

In 1940 with fascism and communism offering competing ideologies here and abroad, Gertrude proposed that the conference dedicate its annual meeting to "Democracy and Social Welfare." "The time has come when we can no longer take our own democracy for granted," Gertrude fretted. "Other systems ... sometimes seem to offer strongly competitive attractions, and we are not as sure as we used to be that our democracy is working." She was impatient with the political process. A year later Gertrude attended a legislative appropriations hearing in Raleigh, finding it a "long, drawn-out and exhausting waste ... but necessary." In 1941 she was dubious that the conference could accomplish anything in the realm of "Good Government" when the League of Women Voters achieved only "controversial results." Indeed, among states with social work conferences, North Carolina ranked among the smallest, with fewer than three hundred members, fewer than in 1913. Public interest in the conference was waning even among progressives. It no longer held yearly meetings.[38]

Better Children in Better Environments

Under the rubric of "Mental Hygiene" Gertrude was a driving force in having the conference adopt birth control. This cause had gathered momentum nationally in the 1920s and 1930s as clinics opened and court challenges loosened regulation of contraceptives. Eleanor Dwight Jones, national president of the American Birth Control League, wrote Gertrude in 1930 asking whether she thought that North Carolina was ready for a state affiliate. Like Gertrude, Jones was concerned that poor mothers needed information.[39]

In contrast to other states, North Carolina did not prohibit physicians and hospitals from obtaining birth control supplies or dispensing information. The state regarded birth control as part of its maternal and infant health program. However, distribution of these materials involved the U.S. mails, which under federal law subjected the offender to a five-thousand-dollar fine and five years in jail. Margaret Sanger, national champion of birth control, organized a national lobbying campaign to change the law. Her legislative director, Hazel Moore, an old North Carolina friend of Gertrude, wrote her, "Please come to Washington. I need tar heel news and your brain." In 1931 Moore planned to accompany Sanger on a southern tour that included Charlotte. She wanted to visit Goldsboro and have Gertrude join them. Sanger was willing to waive her speaking fee, though Moore was not sure that North Carolina was ready for her. "She is a charming little woman," Moore assured Gertrude. Sanger canceled, but not before Gertrude had daringly brought experts to Goldsboro to lecture on birth control.[40]

Like her mother and aunt, Gertrude had joined organizations and collected literature dedicated to maternal health, mental hygiene, and eugenics. Like suffrage, birth control was popularly disdained as another "violation of the natural role of women as mothers." To the public it bore the stigmas of feminism, anarchism, socialism, and communism, not to mention free love and pornography. Margaret Sanger, with an arrest record for distributing contraceptives, was marginalized as a radical. Seeking to dissociate birth control from leftist politics, Sanger enlisted medical professionals to make its case on scientific merit. In February 1932 Gertrude wrote Sanger again, inviting her to speak before the Wayne County Medical Society. Sanger replied that her schedule was too busy but recommended several authorities.[41]

Gertrude advocated birth control as a social welfare issue and did not address the feminist argument of women's self-determination, her right to control her own body. With the Depression, reducing the tax burden of welfare proved a popular and convincing argument. Gertrude saved a newsletter with the headline "Relief Families Need Birth Control." It reported that "birth rates among families on relief are becoming the concern of governmental agencies," with twenty million on the rolls. To "feed so many folks (who ought never to have been born in the beginning)," Moore wrote Gertrude, was futile. She added that "relief giving" did not get "down to the fundamentals" of "mothers already overburdened with too many children."[42]

At the behest of Sanger and Moore, Gertrude lobbied the state's congressmen to open the mails to birth control material. She enlisted her League network, soliciting grassroots contacts across the state. While southern politicians, unlike Northerners, did not face significant numbers of Roman Catholic opponents to birth control, they did contend with churchgoers who could find no biblical justification for it. Moore observed that among religious groups "Jewish people ... have the most intelligent and broadest attitude" on birth control. In 1931 the National Council of Jewish Women resolved to legalize contraception and permit its distribution.[43]

The North Carolina representatives, Moore noted, held influential congressional posts. She wanted Gertrude to "come on up and lobby with them."

Carrying an introductory letter from Gertrude, Moore visited her congressman Charles Abernethy in 1931. Moore found an "ignorant bigoted" person who "raved" that she was "bringing damnation to the country by even mentioning the subject." He only gave her the courtesy of a visit "because you were a friend of a lady I admire." The congressman argued that after thirty-six years of marriage he knew women better than Moore did. Birth control "was interfering with the business of the Lord," he told her. (So did his eyeglasses, she responded.) The congressman calmed and changed his tone, fearing that she would write Gertrude. Gertrude was asked to intercede. Could she find a clergyman to write the congressman?[44]

At its 1932 meeting the North Carolina Conference for Social Service endorsed birth control despite W. A. McAlister's fears that it would "come crashing upon our heads." In 1934, with the theme of "The Child," the conference invited Margaret Sanger to be keynote speaker. At the last moment she canceled, and Hazel Moore took her place. As Moore observed, the birth control movement was New York led and largely ignored the South. She was pleased that a southern birth control organization at last came to fruition. Gertrude served on a North Carolina Birth Control Committee to raise funds from "citizens of wealth" to institute programs in county public health units. By then, Gertrude had noted, "North Carolina is already sold on birth control," with supporters including Frank Graham and Howard Odum, as well as prominent medical and public health faculty at Duke and the University of North Carolina at Chapel Hill.[45]

In April 1935 twenty people met in Durham, where they "enthusiastically" agreed to form the North Carolina Maternal Health League under the sponsorship of the conference. It claimed to speak on behalf of a public groundswell—farmers, officials, ministers, businessmen, and "leaders of every field"—concerned about the high birth rates of welfare families and the tax burden of maintaining them. Once again, Gertrude became secretary and served as a longtime board member. Although birth control information was readily available to the "better class," the League noted, its duty was to bring it to those on relief.[46]

By the mid-1930s birth control had entered the American mainstream. From its origins as a maternal and infant health program, birth control was increasingly justified on eugenic and economic grounds. North Carolina Conference for Social Service president Ella Willard defined the goal: "A better-born child and every child a wanted child." The state's congressional delegation voted unanimously for the federal birth control bill. In 1936 the courts finally removed restrictions on mail distribution. A year later the American Medical Association endorsed contraception. North Carolina became the first state to sponsor a birth control program, with health and welfare agencies dispensing contraceptives. In 1941 the North Carolina Maternal Health League, with Gertrude as secretary, published its own "Population Program for North Carolina" to "solve the problem of the unwanted child" and to "protect the lives of mothers." Its statement italicized, *"Planned parenthood is a basis upon which a sound population policy can be built."*[47] A year later, a coalition of national birth control organizations united under the name Planned Parenthood.

Eugenics

Eugenics, like birth control, was viewed as a public welfare issue, an answer to poverty. Gertrude wrote Margaret Sanger that she was "most eager" to address the problem "of controlling the reproduction of the unfit." Headlines warned of a "moron" problem in the state. Mina was a fervent believer in eugenics, a member of the American Genetic Association since 1916, and collected popular literature forecasting race suicide. In a 1931 letter to Mina, E. S. Gosney, president of the Human Betterment Foundation, noted that twenty-seven states had laws for "eugenics sterilization," a course recommended by "scientific students of the subject." The goal was to relieve "the burden of organized charity" and the "cost to the taxpayer." He included a brochure, "Human Sterilization."[48]

Responding to a query from an Asheville editor, Gertrude wrote that newspapers were obligated to educate the public on the "importance of decreasing feeble-mindedness in the state." From her experience working with "dependents" in the welfare system, she was concerned about "wastage," the futility of trying to educate those with "mental subnormality." Noting that the feebleminded were "notoriously prolific"—with a propensity toward crime—Gertrude spoke of "the need of segregating, and preventing the increase of, this class of people." She did not think that North Carolina was ready for a campaign, but the place to start was to educate the public with "actual facts." Gertrude knew these facts from her work with the Goldsboro Bureau for Social Service, which reported in 1933, "The same problems of drink, immorality, 'laziness,' and unemployment make the solution of family problems difficult." These conditions were "exaggerated in some cases by sub-normal mental equipment." In 1929 the legislature had passed a eugenics law that established a procedure to sterilize the "feeble minded" and other "defectives," subject to review by a five-member board of health and public welfare commissioners. Courts declared the law unconstitutional, but a new eugenics board replaced it in 1933. The overwhelming majority sterilized were institutionalized women diagnosed as feebleminded.[49]

Progressives, citing the authority of science, endorsed eugenics. Academic experts like Howard Odum and Gertrude's cousin Etta Spier, a professor of rural education at Woman's College, advocated it at conference meetings. When A. W. McAlister suggested that the 1931 conference choose as its theme the "Child First," Gertrude explained her thinking on the perpetual issue of nature versus nurture: "First, the better child, and secondly, the child of better environment. To my mind the very most fundamental objective is getting a better average child in the world, through eugenics and birth control. For with a stream of mentally and physically unfit constantly pouring into our population we can make no progress no matter how favorable an environment we may furnish in the way of schools, playgrounds, psychiatrists, institutions, and welfare systems." She was not abandoning efforts to create a "favorable environment." She still advocated for an eight-month school law and limits on child labor, but she also saw the need for "headway" on controlling births. A 1931 conference resolution urged "leaders (negro and white) to encourage negro farm tenants to seek a higher level of life." The conference called "for a sane, scientifically based eugenic marriage law." In 1934 Gertrude—a self-described shy maiden—was asked to chair a special committee to restore laws dealing with the "Physical Examination for Marriage" that would require a Wassermann test for syphilis to "protect marriage against venereal disease."[50]

North Carolina's sterilization program was among the nation's first and longest lasting. Some—of all races, genders, and ethnicities—volunteered, not wanting more children, but the poor also faced involuntary sterilization. Doctors, social workers, and health officers referred women on welfare rolls or in state institutions. Legal and technical professionals aligned with the North Carolina Eugenics Board intimidated poor, uneducated women labeled "feebleminded." For the poor, the lure was an opportunity for health care.[51]

To a modern sensibility, the Weil women's position seems unenlightened, but their views expressed the progressive thinking of the day, most notably in the advocacy of Margaret Sanger. Jane Addams also supported it. George Bernard Shaw, whom Gertrude admired, blended eugenics into his socialist program. Liberal justices Louis Brandeis and Oliver Wendell Holmes joined the U. S. Supreme Court majority in ruling in favor of forced sterilization. Gertrude did not yet discern eugenics' link to racial extremism, immigration restriction, and anti-Semitism. Sanger had once suggested that East European Jews were a case study of "overpopulation" and was accused of anti-Semitism, which she vigorously denied. Nazis cited American eugenics programs as models. In the American South eugenics has borne the stigma of racial bias—with whites acting from fear of high black birth rates—but nowhere in Gertrude's writings on the subject does she target black people even when lamenting "laziness," a racist stereotype.[52] She repeated the popular argument that sterilization would reduce poverty and end undesirable genetic traits like feeblemindedness.

North Carolinians associated with eugenics, notably Howard Odum, were—relative to the times—racial progressives. In her report advocating birth control, Gertrude asserted the need to "create an interracial relation of friendliness and cooperation." She continued, "The time is past when one believes that when two races live side by side the welfare of one is not affected by the welfare of the other." While two-thirds of the counties had birth control clinics by 1939, those largely African American were less likely to have one. Health care generally underserved blacks. More commonly, blacks at first welcomed birth control and reproductive health services, not yet seeing them as forms of state control. Some African American women spoke the language of eugenics. Blacks were also less likely to be on welfare rolls or institutionalized in asylums or hospitals that were sources of sterilization candidates. Of the seventy-six hundred people the state sterilized over forty-five years, 60 per cent were white and 77 per cent were women.[53]

After World War II sterilization rates in the state increased dramatically. In 1947 Clarence Gamble, a Procter & Gamble heir with a Harvard medical degree, wrote Gertrude about his concerns for the feebleminded in state institutions. Due to a physician shortage, "sterilizations had been impossible at the Goldsboro State Hospital." Could Gertrude make an inquiry? Gertrude agreed that children who were wards of the state were a problem, but the hospital's doctors did not see it as a priority. She welcomed the publicity of the Human Betterment League, sponsored by the socially elite textile magnate James Hanes of Winston-Salem. Perhaps, she thought, it could bring the issue to public awareness. Neither Gamble nor Gertrude mentioned that the Goldsboro hospital served African Americans. In the 1950s blacks began constituting a decisive majority of those being sterilized, rising to some 60 percent in the late 1960s. Forced sterilization shifted from the alleged feebleminded to poor, unmarried African American mothers stereotyped as promiscuous. Racial bias grew ever more significant in North Carolina's eugenics program as the civil rights movement threatened white hegemony. By then Gertrude was no longer an advocate.[54]

On eugenics Gertrude's idealism led to utopian thinking that overlooked social and racial consequences. Her arguments reflected the rationalism, the necessity of applying scientific principles to social problems, with which she approached reform generally. Nazism discredited eugenics as a tool of

the totalitarian state. By the late 1940s most states had ended forced sterilization, but in North Carolina it expanded. Objections to sterilization on
grounds that it violated personal rights were less likely to be made in the
1930s and did not press forward until the late 1960s.[55] The North Carolina
Eugenics Board endured until 1977. If Gertrude's position reflected prejudice, it was class bias, not a racist ideology or program. Eugenics exemplified the control that the powerful exercised over the powerless rather than
the program to promote social welfare that Gertrude thought it to be.

A Better Environment

In Goldsboro Gertrude joined civic organizations that worked to create a
healthier environment. She brought her avocations into the public sphere.
Athletic since her college days, an avid swimmer, Gertrude in 1935 helped
draw a constitution for the Wayne Recreation Council and served as its
chair. Her calendar was packed with meetings to plan parks, and she enlisted the Works Progress Administration to conduct cultural and "leisure-
time activities" for both children and adults. The recreation council spawned
troops of Boy Scouts and Girl Scouts, which Gertrude and her brothers
supported personally and philanthropically. The council was responsible
for both the white and black communities, listing in 1939 six playgrounds
for whites with eleven workers and three for "colored" with six workers,
two of whom were paid by the Works Progress Administration. The Wayne
County Memorial Community Building, which served as the white recreation center, replete with a gym and pool, was supplemented by a Colored
Community Center. Gertrude headed City Beautiful campaigns, using New
Deal funds to put people to work on roadside plantings. She held no greater
love than flowers and regularly attended the garden club. Widely read, she
joined the North Carolina Literary and Historical Association and worked
with the State Library Commission to bring its services to Wayne County.
An art lover, she enjoyed exhibitions of the state art society. Her engagement books note Parent-Teacher Association meetings, theatrical produc-
tions of the Wayne Players and Carolina Playmakers, and equestrian shows
by the Goldsboro Horse Association. She joined the boards of the Red Cross
and the Goldsboro Community Chest, with a Weil or Rosenthal often chairing the fundraising campaigns.[56]

Gertrude was especially dedicated to the state Farm Colony for Women
(later Dobbs Farm) in nearby Kinston. She had served as secretary at least
since the late 1920s. She was convinced of the farm's effectiveness, noting
that over 80 percent of the women were successfully paroled; of the thirteen
who were failures, twelve were "mentally defective." With its barred rooms

and lack of training facilities, the farm colony lacked the homelike quality "through which a delinquent girl could be reclaimed to a normal life," she wrote. Gertrude thought that "it would seem economic good sense as well as sound sociological procedure" for the state to increase its funding to train the girls in "useful and productive occupations." In 1938 she lobbied state government to match federal funding for an industrial building. She traveled to Kinston to meet with the architect. The Weil Building honored her advocacy and philanthropy.[57]

Always Gertrude's social welfare focused on the individual. Public health officer Helen Martikainen, armed with a Yale doctorate, arrived in Goldsboro in 1944 to organize a countywide tuberculosis prevention program. Martikainen's task was to educate the public, the federal government wanting to protect soldiers from contagion. She saw that Gertrude was "very highly appreciated." On her first day "Dr. McPheeters asked if I had a place to stay and I said I was living in a hotel," she recalled. "He picked up the phone and made a call and the next I knew a lady appeared at the door said very simply, 'Come with me.'" Gertrude rented her an upstairs room in her home and invited her to dinner. For years thereafter the two ate together nightly, followed by hours of conversation. Gertrude became her "orientation to living in the South. She knew everyone." Traveling the county, Martikainen "could not have done without the blessing of Gertrude Weil's presence," whether in white or black communities. Gertrude had been "very focused on organizing the county for tuberculosis," Martikainen saw. Though Gertrude was nearly forty years senior, the two highly educated women bonded.[58]

The world seemed to come to Gertrude's door, including officials and legislators, Martikainen noted. "She didn't avoid anybody." Later, as state health education director, Martikainen observed that Gertrude and Frank Graham were especially close. Working intimately with both, she noted similar qualities. Gertrude was "focused on people"; she would "empower local people to become responsible rather than do things for them." Graham shared a passion for public health education and traveled the counties delivering motivational speeches. "I never saw Dr. Frank minimize the value of a single person no matter who they were," she added. "He gave a high regard to the dignity and worth of every human being." Martikainen helped found the World Health Organization and served as its chief of health education in Geneva. She cited the "community focus in North Carolina" as an inspiration, using her Goldsboro experience as a model for the organization's international programs.[59]

Gertrude, now in her sixties, approached the age of laurels. In 1946 W. C.

Jackson, chancellor of Woman's College, wrote that she had been selected for an honorary Doctor of Laws. Gertrude responded in shock: "O, Mr. Jackson, how did you all happen to think of such a thing? ... I wouldn't consider letting you do it." She had a ready answer whenever honors came her way: "I have never done anything in my long life-time to merit such a distinction." An award to a person of her insignificance would embarrass the college, she insisted. The faculty voted unanimously, Jackson replied, and her refusal only confirmed her worthiness. He would have Frank Graham speak to her. Gertrude would have none of it and declined.[60]

How does one account for such humility, for moral principle carried to such an extreme? Gertrude measured herself by her ideals and found herself lacking. After all, her suffrage campaign had failed, and war and poverty remained persistent. Such modesty was deeply rooted in her psychology—as a schoolgirl she had declined an honor in favor of a friend—and it went beyond the inbred courtesy, the self-effacement, of a southern lady. She seemed to feel always inadequate, a syndrome common to children of powerful parents. Her father's rise from immigrant peddler to business magnate and public citizen and her mother's endless generosity implanted in their children feelings of never having done enough. They were especially humbled to measure themselves against their venerated mother, whom more than one observer described as Christ-like. Still in Gertrude was the adolescent who despaired of ever being as good as her mother. Mina's "moral strength and love sustained us every hour of every day," Gertrude wrote, and their only hope was to live by her example.[61]

In the family such modesty was hardly unique to Gertrude. Janet was similarly silent about her activism. Nor was it only feminine. There was also the Weil "nervousness," an anxiety that sent family members, most notably Mina, to specialists and sanitariums. When the University of North Carolina at Chapel Hill awarded Leslie an honorary doctorate in 1941, he, too, at first declined as "undeserving" until prevailed upon to accept. A houseguest at Frank and Marian Graham's home for the ceremony, he was "miserable," his wife observed, at being the center of attention. Brother Herman wrote his own self-deprecatory eulogy, letting his fellow University of North Carolina trustees know that "his record was in no way outstanding." When Gertrude donated three thousand dollars to Woman's College in 1946, she corrected Chancellor Jackson that the scholarship for a student in social sciences would be named for Mina Weil, not Gertrude. On the Greensboro campus, which had the Rosenthal Gymnasium named for Uncle Joe, rose the Mina Weil Residence Hall. Gertrude sent another three thousand dollars to Chapel Hill in Leslie's name.[62] In Mina's household selflessness was both a religious commandment and a matter of family honor. In speaking of her mother at the dormitory's dedication in 1941, Gertrude might as well have been speaking about herself: "She was never so absorbed in institutions and organizations that she lost sight of the individual.... I think her passion and ruling motive was Duty; but it was so integrated in herself as to be an organic element in her being and behavior.... It was her nature to do right."[63]

A Woman of the Left

Gertrude's rectitude was integral to her character, and as it did for Frank Graham, it won her respect even from those who were politically unsympathetic. Gertrude's politics over her lifetime moved leftward, and by the 1940s she described herself as a socialist. "Wealth should be more equally divided," she explained to an interviewer. "People are wrong in thinking that the best incentive is competition. Competition is good, but only as an instrument for the common good." She was unabashed about her affiliations during a time when communism and race mixing were intertwined in the public mind. *Progressive* now denoted a radical, more extreme than a New Deal liberal. In 1945 the left-leaning, integrationist Southern Conference for Human Welfare sought to create state affiliates and hired Mary Price, former secretary to journalist Walter Lippmann, to form a North Carolina Committee. Gertrude joined the organizing conference in Raleigh and edited its proposed constitution. Drawing no more than fifty people, it was the first racially integrated meeting held in the city auditorium. Among the speakers were Clark Foreman, president of the Southern Conference for Human Welfare, and Junius Scales, a communist party organizer.[64]

Although the North Carolina Committee was among the most active of eleven state affiliates, it struggled to attract even liberals because of its ties to organized labor. Its educational efforts through radio, pamphlets, and public forums failed to inspire a mass movement, and its legislative record in support of labor justice, public spending, and higher pay for teachers and state employees was at best mixed. Gertrude read the conference newspaper *Southern Patriot*, which in October 1947 began a campaign against segregation.[65]

The House Un-American Activities Committee labeled the Southern Conference for Human Welfare "perhaps the most deviously camouflaged communist-front organization." Certainly, Gertrude was putting her good name at risk during this fervidly anticommunist era when guilt by association ruined reputations. Clark Foreman, a civil libertarian, was red-baited when he refused to conduct "heresy hunts" to weed out communists. Despite pressures from liberal groups, he insisted that the "the communist party has had a positive role in the South with respect to the Negro problem." Junius Scales became state Communist Party chair, and Mary Price was accused of being a Soviet agent.[66]

Gertrude sided with the broadly tolerant Frank Graham, who argued that political association was no more a disqualification than racial or religious affiliation. Gertrude's niece Mina Bluethenthal, a socialist—the family jokingly blamed Gertrude for it—often discussed with her aunt the role of socialists and communists in liberal causes. "I felt she was politically naïve in this respect and told her so," she recalled. Gertrude "felt strongly that so long as a person was an activist in what she considered a good cause, it was o.k. with her." Indeed, some conference members were communists despite their denials. Gertrude seemed not to have been targeted, although red-baiters opened fire on Graham, who habitually lent his name to causes. The House Un-American Activities Committee judged that he was "not a communist" but had a "predilection."[67] Gertrude was thus at least a fellow traveler with a fellow traveler.

As the 1948 election approached, the North Carolina Committee was bitterly divided on whether to endorse the Progressive Party and its presidential candidate, Henry Wallace. Gertrude admired Wallace, who spoke before desegregated audiences across the South, the first presidential candidate to do so. Courting North Carolina's black vote, Wallace was pelted with eggs and tomatoes, and his bodyguard was stabbed. With its membership declining and its finances in disarray, the Southern Conference for Human Welfare effectively died with Wallace's defeat.[68]

Through the University of North Carolina's annual Weil Lecture on American Citizenship, endowed in memory of her father and uncle, Gertrude met statesmen of the left. Although lecturers for the three-day event ranged across the political spectrum, speakers in the 1930s included British political theorist Harold Laski, Harvard historian Charles Beard, Roosevelt adviser Felix Frankfurter, and Henry Wallace. Later came Eleanor Roosevelt. Both Wallace and Roosevelt were, as she described the former, Gertrude's "favorite heroes." Gertrude also admired Laski, a socialist who was, in her words, "keenly analytic and puts his finger on weaknesses."[69] The university in Chapel Hill, with Frank Graham likely on the podium, was the ideal setting for a Weil Lecture, under the seal with the university's motto, Light and Liberty.

Gertrude's lifelong work, as she often said, was to realize her ideals. Her reality in the 1930s was tatterdemalion children begging in the streets, her family finances imperiled, tuberculosis widespread, a recalcitrant state government, and a world preparing for war. Without losing sight of her ideals, she struggled toward a political consensus. She believed in socialism but acted as a Roosevelt Democrat. In race relations she moved gradually toward an unambiguous stand for integration. Her advocacy of eugenics, shared by progressives of her day, led her to an unfortunate paternalism. It was a cause she ultimately abandoned. Incremental progress was the best to be achieved.

Undimmed was her relentless energy to do more. A week in the life of Gertrude Weil in the 1930s and 1940s might find her in Kinston for the board of the state farm for delinquent girls, driving to Chapel Hill to hear journalist Drew Pearson, chairing a Wayne Recreation Council meeting, judging a Girl Scout flower show, sitting in at a Rat Control meeting, and attending an evening symphony, an art society gallery opening, or a lecture on birth control. Her social calendar was crowded with teas and dinners with old friends or visiting family. And always there was gardening. And letters to write and gifts to send. And Sabbath at the temple and then Sunday school to teach.

Gertrude rarely expressed the toll that her activism cost her inner being. She was, after all, a woman in her sixties fighting cancer while caring for a dying mother. Those who knew her recalled that her interest remained with others, always wanting to know about their lives and not wishing to speak of herself. She seemed congenitally good natured, an optimist by nature, curious. In the early 1930s she joined a local PEN Club (focusing on poetry, essays, and novels) where townspeople—a journalist, housewife, editor, rabbi, civil servant—all gathered to share their creativity. Through art, among friends in community, she expressed conflict, unwilling to shirk duty but longing for release. A first poem suggested her exhaustion and impatience:

> Oft in my hours of scurrying here and yon
> On drives, campaigns, to conferences and such,
> Intent on this or t'other serious cause
> Oft have I sighed for some surcease of struggle
> And freedom from the heavy obligation
> To hurry on the world's slow evolution.[70]

Her world was evolving, and not for the better, or in ways that freed her from heavy obligation. Her German cousins were desperate for American visas to escape Nazi Europe. The peace activist now confronted another world war. For Gertrude the global became personal.

{ 9 }

THE TERRIBLE NEWS IN
EACH MORNING'S PAPER
The War Abroad and at Home

In September, 1939, the eve of World War II, Gertrude wrote a letter to old Goldsboro friends, a retired minister and his wife. "Civilization's suicide," she feared, seemed at hand: "I do nothing but waste time hovering around the radio lest I miss something of the world's happenings.... It is wicked to feel as exhilarated as I do at the firm stand of opposition to Hitler on the part of Poland, England, and France when the result can only be war. I had sunk into a state of despair that he would ever be stopped in his mad career of ruthless conquest.... It looks as if the conscience of the world has finally been awakened."[1]

The Weils could not be insensitive to Hitler's anti-Semitic ranting or to the echoing domestic voices. In the 1930s Mina subscribed to the *Jewish Daily Bulletin*, a newspaper overflowing with graphic stories of Jews beaten, disappeared, or murdered in Berlin, Vilna, Vienna, Warsaw. In May 1940 Gertrude declined travel to a Greensboro meeting since her "mother seemed so depressed ... largely due to the terrible news in each morning's paper."[2] The world at war was at their doorstep. Out their window they could see servicemen crowding Goldsboro's streets, their wives and families seeking housing in the teeming camp town.

More personally, foreign affairs entered the household in increasingly desperate letters from German cousins. Across the years they had remained in touch. The postwar depression ravaged the European family, and Nazism threatened not just Jewish livelihoods but lives. Relatives, some unknown, wrote anxiously for funds and sponsors to emigrate. While struggling to save her family abroad, Gertrude contended with domestic crises at home. Her mother was bedridden, and she lived with the threat of recurring cancer.

The approach of war and Jewish persecutions in the 1930s tempered

Gertrude's idealism and optimism. She had not been especially reactive to anti-Semitism. If she had felt it personally, she rarely spoke or wrote of it. Yet North Carolina Jews, like Jews elsewhere, were not immune to social discrimination and to occasional outbursts of vitriol or even violence. In the 1930s anti-Semitism was rampant, arousing both Jewish insecurities and defenses.

Social Discrimination

Small-town southern Jews often denied any experience of anti-Semitism. At worst, they spoke of ambivalence. Thus, Gertrude's Sunday school student Amy Meyers Krumbein could say of her native Goldsboro that "I felt no anti-Jewish feeling" and "I never felt that the Christians accepted the Jews." Yet Jews, including Krumbein, quickly named friends and neighbors who were understanding and kindhearted. Having a Jewish friend next door was not inconsistent with a general prejudice against mythic Jews. This attitude can be seen in a letter protesting the growing Jewish enrollment at the University of North Carolina at Chapel Hill that Kemp Battle, president of the North Carolina State Bar, sent Frank Graham in 1936. Battle served with Gertrude on the North Carolina Conference for Social Service, and he joined Leslie on university alumni affairs. His wife had hosted Gertrude for a suffragist talk in Rocky Mount. Battle warned Graham, "The native North Carolina Jew is an entirely different personality from those in the large cities." He enclosed a statement from a noted southern "liberal." It advised that northern Jews were from Poland and Russia and "show the vices but not the virtues" of southern Jews who were "Sephardim [sic] Jews" from Spain, England, and Germany. The former were "known vulgarly as … Kike[s]" and ought to be excluded. His anthropology was nonsensical, but such an "exception mechanism" allowed an elite southerner like Battle to befriend and admire successful, acculturated Jews like Leslie and Gertrude Weil without abandoning his broader prejudice.[3]

Chapel Hill was the site of a celebrated case of anti-Jewish discrimination that drew national headlines in 1933. With the Weils' personal and institutional ties to the University of North Carolina—Leslie was a trustee—they knew campus affairs intimately. Under President Frank Graham, the university, more than southern colleges generally, had a liberal admission policy at a time when Jewish quotas were common. In 1936 some 15 percent of its freshman class was Jewish, while the state's Jewish population constituted about one-quarter of 1 percent, lowest in the nation. Nonetheless, Dean Isaac Manning maintained a 10 percent Jewish quota at the medical school, although he claimed to exempt North Carolina Jews. A northern Jewish student who was denied admission complained about the quota to Graham, who summoned the dean and ordered the student admitted. After a vigorous public debate, the dean resigned. At a time when Nazi propaganda was deprecating Jews, Graham became a national Jewish hero. The one medical school faculty opponent of Manning's quota was pharmacologist William MacNider, a Weil friend from Goldsboro. He jotted "bless your heart" notes to "Mother Weil," who sent him home-baked cakes. In one Easter letter he compared Mina to Christ as "an ideal of goodness and fairness and kindliness." Such personalism did much to alleviate prejudice, and southerners frequently spoke of their admiration for a Jewish neighbor whose rectitude had disabused them of bigotry.[4]

North Carolina Jews more commonly encountered the gentlemanly variety of anti-Semitism that was not spoken out loud but expressed behind closed doors. Such discrimination limited the Jewish presence in the professions and corporate board rooms, imposed quotas at universities, and closed elite societies like country clubs. Leslie Weil received a letter from a cousin asking him to "pull strings" to get her daughter into Chapel Hill. "It is extremely difficult for a Jew," she wrote, "much less a woman to get into medical schools." Given their prominence in Goldsboro, the Weils confronted less exclusion than Jews in places like Wilmington or Winston-Salem, where Old South social hierarchies ruled. Weils were founders of the Goldsboro country club. Gertrude frequented it, and the Oheb Sholom Sisterhood held luncheons there. A 1946 national survey revealed that anti-Semitism was weaker in the South than in the North and in small towns than in cities. That profile described North Carolina generally and Goldsboro specifically.[5]

Domestic Warfare

Although the Weils rarely suffered anti-Semitism personally, its noise was unavoidable in the 1930s, though it was not as loud in North Carolina as in northern metropolitan areas. Gertrude collected literature from national Jewish defense agencies refuting blood libels, debunking the link between Jews and bolshevism, and exposing the *Protocols of Elders of Zion* as a forgery. When Oheb Sholom celebrated its fiftieth anniversary in 1933 the keynote speaker, Rabbi Edward Israel of Baltimore, "made a strong appeal for the united cooperation of Jews in combating Nazi activities in North Carolina and the United States." In 1938 the doors of Wilmington's Temple of Israel, Janet's congregation, were defaced with swastikas.[6]

As Nell Battle Lewis noted in her newspaper column, when it came to pro-Nazi organizations North Carolina "has had very little knowledge of their contemptible and dangerous goings on," but she warned of "two persons of local interest," William Dudley Pelley and U.S. Senator Robert Reynolds. Both were nationally known Nazi sympathizers. Pelley, the self-anointed American Hitler, established headquarters for his Silver Shirts legion in Asheville from 1932 to 1941, spewing anti-Semitic propaganda. "Our Bob" Reynolds was a virulent isolationist who hired a Nazi agent and alleged international Jewish conspiracies. The North Carolina Association of Jewish Women (NCAJW) in 1938 warned that "Reynolds is sponsoring legislation providing for the deportation of aliens," although North Carolina had the smallest percentage of foreign born of any state.[7]

North Carolina did not welcome anti-Semites. Pelley was denounced from church pulpits, and, assisted by local Jewish activists, the Asheville sheriff drove him from town. The Wilmington mayor personally supervised cleansing of swastikas from the temple doors. And Senator Our Bob, hounded by the press, was so unpopular that he did not seek reelection in 1944. North Carolina also was home to well-known philo-Semites, the two most notable of whom were Weil family friends. Josephus Daniels aided Jewish refugees as U.S. ambassador to Mexico and was a leading Christian Zionist. Frank Graham was the most prominent southerner in the National Conference of Christians and Jews, lobbied to ease immigration of European Jews, and endorsed a Jewish homeland in Palestine. Treasury Secretary Henry Morgenthau wanted Graham to lead the War Refugee Board formed to aid Nazi victims.[8]

Jewish Defense

As Jews confronted discrimination at home and persecution abroad, the religious indifference of the 1930s yielded to a growing affiliation. In 1935 at an NCAJW convention Gertrude introduced national Hillel director Abram Sachar, who spoke on "Crises in Jewish History." He urged Jews to return to Judaism to counter the Nazi challenge. North Carolina Jews, like those nationally, unified and organized across Zionist, ethnic, and movement divides. Lionel Weil had led separate local campaigns in Goldsboro for the United Palestine Appeal and the Joint Distribution Committee for European relief. In 1932, responding to the grass roots, a unified National Council of Jewish Federations and Welfare Funds organized. As Nazi persecutions intensified after the Kristallnacht pogrom and the British restricted immigration to Palestine, a United Jewish Appeal for Refugees and Overseas Needs formed. Gertrude contributed generously.[9]

The Jewish penchant for organization was felt even in small communities like Goldsboro, which boasted a plethora of societies. Local women supported the Sisterhood, Hadassah, ncajw, B'nai B'rith auxiliary, and Union of American Hebrew Congregations. Gertrude observed that historically Sisterhoods financed the synagogue, decorated its interior, supported the choir, and educated children. As the local president, Gertrude asked a fundamental question: "Why do we have a Sisterhood?" Her answer was that it nourishes and develops "the Jewish spirit in our community" and encourages "a feeling of loyalty to our group." In 1931 its thirty-seven members maintained fifteen committees and sponsored twenty-five events. For women, excluded from synagogue ritual and leadership, these societies created opportunities for community status. They held card parties, a fancy dress Purim ball, school picnics, and a Chanukah festival.[10]

The crises of the 1930s renewed and intensified Jewish education. In 1931 Hebrew instruction was reintroduced into the Sunday school. As school superintendent, Gertrude taught the sixth grade on the history of Jews since the destruction of the Temple and "elements of the Jewish faith." She insisted that children consider the big questions and relate ancient times to current events. As she put it, "What our past may mean in enriching our lives and binding us together as Jews." In 1935, with Hitler's rise, Gertrude directed the temple's Young People's Group in "Haman of Today." She asked, "In the face of this anti-Semitism, *What shall Jews do about it?*" One answer was Zionism, and she had the students "discuss present conditions of Palestine." She organized formal debates on whether America, too, had anti-Semitism. Students had to develop premises to their arguments and acknowledge the merits of each side.[11]

Gertrude's ambition was to move the Oheb Sholom Sisterhood beyond a philanthropic auxiliary by "looking beyond our own local borders." Her interest was to strengthen both Jewish solidarity and ecumenical outreach. She advocated for the National Federation of Temple Sisterhoods' progressive agenda, which she knew from her frequent attendance at regional and national conferences. In the Depression, she appointed a committee to investigate sponsoring free lunches in the public schools. The women contributed to the rehabilitation of Abyssinian Jews, the so-called Falasha. The Sisterhood maintained a Palestine Garments Committee, and in 1931 it sent four delegates, including Gertrude, to a Regional Zionist Organization Conference in Newport News, Virginia.[12]

Like other Jewish organizations responding to the global Jewish crisis, the ncajw intensified its efforts. In 1930 it formed the North Carolina Association of Jewish Men as an auxiliary. In 1933, as ncajw program chair, Gertrude introduced Rabbi James Heller of Cincinnati, who warned that the world was heading toward "calamity," and a year later she presented

Tony Sender, a former member of the Reichstag, who described "the persecution and sufferings of the Jews and their exile." The 1937 NCAJW conference in Winston-Salem reported record attendance. In 1941 political scientist Max Lerner pled for democracy.[13] For the war effort the women hosted
dances, served on United Service Organizations (USO) boards, sold war
bonds, and worked with the Red Cross.

In response to rising Jewish enrollment on state campuses, the NCAJW
took a lead in establishing a Hillel Foundation. A 1935 NCAJW survey revealed one hundred Jewish students at Duke, which had a 3 percent Jewish quota, and over three hundred at the more liberal University of North
Carolina at Chapel Hill, of whom 189 were North Carolinians. As chair of
the NCAJW Student Activity Committee in 1935–36, Gertrude helped raise
funds and hire a director. The mission was not merely to bond Jewish students but to bring "proper training, a better understanding" to the "Northern Jewish student who not being accustomed to the ways of the South
finds many difficulties in his path, and through misunderstanding, creates
many more." In these fraught times, Jews wanted to avoid social tensions.
When the Hillel House was dedicated in Chapel Hill in 1936, Frank Graham
presided, asking students to take strength from their Jewish heritage, to be
"a part of, and not apart from, the University."[14]

Brotherhood

The 1930s and 1940s witnessed increasing ecumenical outreach in response
to the rising racist and anti-Semitic voices. The 1933 NCAJW conference
held a Protestant-Catholic-Jew Three Faiths Dialogue, a popular national
format. Brotherhood Weeks were announced by gubernatorial proclamation, and rabbis broadcast morning prayers on radio. At the NCAJW conference in Raleigh in 1940, Governor Clyde Hoey praised the Jewish leadership
in the state, pledging that intolerance would never be tolerated. Gertrude
frequently appeared before church groups "Explaining Judaism," as she put
it, echoing a term popular among practitioners of outreach. Often in small
communities, a Jewish leader filled the role of ethnic ambassador to the
Christian community, a spokesperson at interfaith forums. Various Weils,
including Gertrude, stepped forward frequently, sometimes as a radio voice.
Such interfaith efforts would not have been necessary if prejudice were un-
common. The forums often involved elites who expressed civic pride in their
own tolerance and praised their community's exceptionalism.[15]

Gertrude did not react to anti-Semitism. Her response was not unlike
that to illness: she neither yielded nor obsessed, but improved herself.
Similarly, she did not join confrontational feminist groups to combat gen-

der discrimination but worked to bolster women's self-worth and assert their rights. From small-town life she had learned to accommodate, and her ethic was to look for the good. Gertrude had no warmer friend than A. W. McAlister, her longtime colleague at the North Carolina Conference for Social Service. He once wrote her, "I want you to know that the 'shy, maidenly affection' with which I have been so highly favored is balanced by a Platonic devotion whose flame has grown brighter and warmer with every passing year." McAlister, a devout Presbyterian, led Christian-Jewish interfaith efforts in Greensboro, but even he saw each Jew as representative of "The Jew." In 1934 McAlister wanted to produce a conference pageant to dramatize "Social Welfare in its various phases," beginning with "The Child." He sketched a storyline to Gertrude: "If I have my history right, it was a Jew who first gave us the exalted conception of childhood," alluding, of course, to the Christ child. "It would be a right and noble gesture to select a Jewess for the part of the Mother of Jesus," McAlister continued, and "the first person I thought of in that connection was yourself." Gertrude responded politely, "You take my breath away!" At McAlister's insistence, she interceded with University of North Carolina dramatist Frederick Koch and composer Lamar Stringfield, pioneers of the folk play, but nothing came of the project. Years later McAlister still addressed Gertrude fondly as "Mother of God."[16]

Whether Jews constituted a race or religion created confusion and dissonance. Awareness of Jewish difference was present if not always expressed, and "belief" still presented an irresolvable conflict. In 1938, A. W. McAlister wrote journalist W. T. Bost congratulating him on his column on "that old concept of 'chosen people.'" He believed that it was "the key to the Jewish problem" and the source of "their undoing," though the Jews "have set so much store" in it. "I yield to none in my interest in the Jews," wrote McAlister, "and so great is my respect and affection for them that I am unsympathetic with the self isolation which they have imposed upon themselves, and which I believe has invited the retaliation which the world has visited upon them so cruelly and so unjustly." The solution was "their amalgamation with other races" to the "enrichment of both." Jews might want "religious separateness," but he saw no reason for "racial separateness."[17] McAlister was writing at the moment when Gertrude was struggling to save her German family from the Nazis, who defined Jews by race rather than by religion. Domestic social discrimination was not motivated by Jewish clannishness, nor, as McAlister argued, did Jews, especially Reform Jews, put "so much store" in chosenness.

Gertrude likely had Bost's column in mind when she spoke to a Jewish audience in Danville in 1941. She addressed "the accusation of clannishness, of exclusiveness, among us." She noted that in ancient times "rights & privileges & duties" were not exclusively Jewish but were extended to the "stranger within his gates." In modern times Jews were "willing and quick" to "cooperate in any community undertaking" once given the opportunity. Beyond the racial ideology that led to social discrimination, Jews and Christians still contended with religious differences. She indeed recognized "two types of persecution," the first on "*belief*" and the second on "*race*." She still held that "the old idea of a *Chosen People*, a people with a mission, may still have something of a meaning for us even to-day" in "bearing the torch of monotheism and of individual and social and ethical standards." As "ancient Israel stood superior to the ancient peoples around them," so too modern Jews can lead by "precept and example ... a confused world into a surer way of social righteousness and brotherly love."[18] Chosenness implied an ethical mission, not divine election. Gertrude resisted any suggestion that Jews were culpable for their persecution. However much Jews presented themselves as modern, progressive Americans, southerners, steeped in the Bible, romanticized Jews as People of the Book, later-day matriarchs and patriarchs.

Peace and War

Gertrude had wholeheartedly embraced the progressive women's global peace and disarmament agenda. She followed the leads of Jane Addams and Carrie Chapman Catt, who inspired the Women's International League for Peace and Freedom. In the North Carolina League of Women Voters Gertrude chaired the Department of International Cooperation and reliably traveled to Duke or Chapel Hill to attend International Relations Institutes or to Washington for Catt's National Committee on the Cause and Cure of War. When the North Carolina Peace Action Committee organized in 1934, she was invited to its executive board. She assiduously attended "Round Table" panels of foreign policy experts and exhaustively collected foreign affairs literature.[19]

Peace advocacy was also on the agenda of the National Council of Jewish Women and the National Federation of Temple Sisterhoods. Gertrude had pushed her own Sisterhood to pass resolutions on internationalism. For progressive Jewish women like Gertrude, Hitler's rise was soul wrenching. She abandoned her customary optimism when it came to Nazism. When a cousin argued that "nobody would bother" a Smith alumni group touring Germany, Gertrude snapped, "If you think that, you're a damn fool." In her speech before a Jewish audience in Danville, Virginia, in 1941 Gertrude confessed that "the pacifist in a warring world finds the principles espoused in the vacuum of peacetime in embarrassing conflict with policies and a code of conduct acceptable in the present actual situation."[20]

Gertrude's antiwar advocacy ended. In 1940 she added her name to the southern division of the Committee to Defend America by Aiding the Allies. Its traveling secretary was her friend Martha Boswell, and Frank Graham was its chair. The committee organized lobbying campaigns in support of America's military rearmament, restraining Japan, and aiding Britain through Lend-Lease. The intent was to counter the anti-interventionist America First Committee, whose spokesman Charles Lindbergh warned of a Jewish war policy. Gertrude also joined Boswell in working with the United Nations Association. In November 1940 Gertrude attended Catt's Woman's Centennial Congress in Washington. A half century earlier Catt had been an immigration restrictionist. Now she led the Protest Committee of Non-Jewish Women Against the Persecution of Jews in Germany that urged America to open its doors.[21]

European Family

The immigration issue was foremost in the Weil household. Mina habitually sent Jewish New Year's letters to her European cousins, and the families exchanged visits and were warmly familiar. Max Oettinger had escorted Weils around London, and his brother Emil had been not just their hosts in Frankfurt but, in spring 1929, a guest in their Goldsboro home. Emil returned to a changing Germany with the Nazis winning nearly 20 percent of the vote in 1930. He observed, "Interior politics are more confused than ever and as usual in bad times the jews [sic] are held responsible by many stupid people." But, he assured Mina, "I do not believe that there will be very devious trouble." A year later, a cousin in Bielefeld, Fritz Herzberg, a corn dealer impoverished by inflation and bank failures, wrote Mina, who hardly knew of him, pleading for help. As a Jew, Herzberg could not find work. She arranged foreign bank transfers and began sending him monthly remittances of $25.[22]

The German cousins' ambition was America. "It must be wonderful to have a country where one can live in peace," cousin Grete Oettinger wrote, "since 15 years we have nothing but persecution, abuse, and humiliation suffered and since 6 years we had hell." Her brother-in-law Emil Oettinger had taken a post with the Jewish Colonization Association, which required travel to Paris and London to resettle refugees. Though as a banker he had sufficient wealth to fend for himself, his "jewish [sic] obligations" pulled him back to Frankfurt. Like Mina, Emil was a compulsive letter writer. Like

Gertrude, he was a public servant, and the two shared a love of political discourse whether on Germany, America, Russia, or Palestine. The extended family in France and England was "worried for Emil and his wife ... who will not abandon his self-chosen duties" in Germany. As a Jewish official, he risked being taken hostage.[23]

The Weils' experience assisting their European family affirms the broader indictment made not just against Nazi Germany for its anti-Semitic policies but against the allies themselves—most notably America and Britain—for their failure to provide haven. Mina when she was able and then Gertrude worked relentlessly and generously to rescue their pleading relatives. It took determination. The bureaucratic hurdles placed by the American government were formidable. National quotas had been imposed in the 1920s, made all the more stringent as unemployment led Americans to be less receptive to newcomers. Both North Carolina senators Josiah Bailey and Robert Reynolds opposed open immigration of Jews from Nazi Europe. Assistant secretary of state Breckinridge Long advised American consuls to "put every obstacle in the way" of those seeking to emigrate. A whistleblower in the treasury department titled a report, "The Acquiescence of This Government in the Murder of the Jews." By July 1941 doors shut tighter just as the Germans began an anti-Jewish campaign of mass deportation and murder. Grete Oettinger wrote, "I read that in the next 2 years America won't be able to receive any new immigrants. That means for many thousands vanishing last hope." Grete and her husband Albert fled to Paris.[24]

Gertrude wrote numerous agencies—Hebrew Sheltering and Immigrant Aid Society (HIAS) and National Refugee Service among them—seeking advice. She received a 1937 Department of State information sheet outlining requirements. As the American sponsor Gertrude had to submit notarized documents of her income, property, and other assets to provide evidence that the alien applicant would not "become a public charge." Moreover, she had to present notarized affidavits from a bank officer attesting to her deposits and withdrawals and certified copies of her tax returns for two years, property tax receipts, and a statement verifying her good credit. A letter of support was to detail the relationship between sponsor and applicant.[25]

Gertrude swore in an affidavit that the Oettingers were "persons of high principles and exemplary conduct" of whom she was "personally fond." She also swore that she had never been a member of any group advocating the violent overthrow of the U.S. government. "I have known Miss Gertrude Weil, of Goldsboro, N.C., all her life," the postmaster wrote. "I know her to be one of the finest citizens of the State." The sheriff labeled her "a citizen of Wayne County of the highest type." A bank officer verified that she was worth over fifty thousand dollars and "has ample income for her own requirements and substantial surplus," enough to support dependents. Other documents confirmed that she owned four properties and had paid real estate taxes. Mina had to validate that Gertrude was born in Goldsboro. These forms had to be updated with each new visa request. The immigrant then had to brave long lines at an American consulate—in Berlin, Hamburg, or Stuttgart—with thirteen items of documentation, difficult for Gertrude's cousins, who like many Jews fled their homelands as persecutions intensified.[26]

By 1938 the German government no longer permitted immigrants to take out money, yet potential host countries demanded substantial deposits to ensure that they would not become public wards. With many Weil relatives now destitute, the Nazis having robbed their possessions and forbidden them work, Mina and Gertrude sent large sums to satisfy these guarantees. Gertrude also had to purchase rail and ship tickets and show receipts. Mina arranged for a New York bank to forward marks to cousin Fritz Herzberg in Bielefeld and six hundred dollars to Buenos Aires where a friend agreed to sponsor him. America was all but closed for an unskilled, single man without English. As Mina was increasingly bedridden, the German cousins turned to "Gertrud." Heartrending appeals also came from elderly cousin Anna Rosenbaum stranded in Vienna with her daughter's family of four, the Lederers.[27]

"The struggle against Jewish existence is as fierce as ever," Emil Oettinger wrote in late 1937. Jewish shops were boycotted and "economic possibilities" closed. "My resolve to stay is still the same," he continued, "firstly on account of my obligations to my customers & secondly because of my many engagements in jewish [sic] affairs." A San Francisco cousin, Henry Gundfinger, traveled to Germany in September 1938 to investigate. He brought out five family members, found them jobs and apartments, but could not convince Emil and Marie Oettinger to leave. In November 1938, Kristallnacht rampages left Jews beaten, murdered, and arrested in the tens of thousands. Synagogues burned.[28]

Just prior to the September 1939 outbreak of war, Emil and Marie Oettinger escaped to Paris, always keeping their Goldsboro cousins informed. Emil's "hope" was that from the "outside" he could still help the "many people we cherish or esteem" stranded in Germany. Daily he offered his services at the HICEM agency—a coalition of French, German, and American Jewish refugee organizations—but, as he wrote Mina, he despaired of finding haven for cousin Fritz Herzberg. Other extended family members had settled in France or England or were awaiting visas to America. By 1937 second-generation English Oettingers were in the army or nursing corps while Emil's son, a student of Oriental languages, served with the French army in Morocco. After two wars, Max Oettinger in London had enough of being German and changed his name to Osborne.[29]

Fritz Herzberg's letters now came days apart. Mina continued to send him money by way of Argentina and Holland. Other checks went to distant relatives. Letters arrived from cousins Hans and Alice Fischer who were stranded in Vienna, surviving on furniture they sold, awaiting American visas. To assist their admittance to England, Mina sent $300 to London, only to be informed that the government required $1,000, plus another $150 for their child. Alice and her son Erich made their way to London, but her husband Hans was arrested in Germany. He entered Britain on condition that they all leave for America. Booksellers in Germany, they were stranded, unable to find work even as a maid or farm worker. Mina learned that funds she had sent to London were being held in escrow to pay for their ship tickets.[30]

While Mina bankrolled expenses, Gertrude handled politics and bureaucracy. Just when success seemed imminent new obstacles both here and abroad were thrown in their way. "The regulations, however, are getting stricter and stricter every day," Olga Fortgang advised them from London, "and more money is required." They at last obtained visas for the Fischers but not before their teenage son Erich was deported to Canada, where he languished in an internment camp as an enemy alien. "Without your great kindness and generosity," Alice Fischer wrote Gertrude, "we should still be in Vienna and in great misfortune." Mina succeeded in getting her cousin Otto Birnbaum to America, followed in 1939 by his mother, Mizzi, who entered Britain on 27 August, one day before the frontier closed. A letter arrived from another relative, Walter Oppenheim, recalling Mina's and Leslie's visits thirty-five years earlier and asking help to get his mother out of Germany. Ever more letters arrived from Fritz Herzberg in Bielefeld with new schemes to fund him and to facilitate his immigration to Argentina.[31]

Beyond family, Gertrude struggled on behalf of Marta Rosy Goldschmidt, an employee and friend of Emil Oettinger, still in Frankfurt. In May 1939 Emil asked Gertrude to help get her an affidavit, but Goldschmidt's case as a single woman of forty-two, without family in America, was difficult. Nonetheless, Gertrude, who had no personal acquaintance with Goldschmidt, applied herself, filling out affidavits, writing refugee agencies, appealing to her congressmen and the state department.[32]

Painful Losses

Gertrude's distress about how to save her family occurred as her mother was slipping away. In December 1938, Mina wrote Gertrude a letter that read as a deathbed blessing: "I want to tell you what you have meant to me since you came into my life; this past twenty four years you have shielded & cared for me, and your devotion during these past three years has been measureless and constant ... from the depths of my being I value your love and every attention and utter unselfishness. God bless you my daughter."[33] In late 1940 Mina died. Sympathy letters recalled her "cheerfulness during her bed-ridden years" and how she "remained the youngest mentally and the most elastic in her outlook in life." Friend Margaret Norwood offered consolation by quoting Gertrude's very own words to her: "We are never ready to let our mothers go."[34] Any sense of freedom, of having a burden lifted, could not compensate for such a profound loss.

Gertrude now shouldered the burden of her European family. More frantic letters came from the Rosenbaums, who, after Hitler's invasion of Austria, fled to Paris. With the German onslaught into France in 1940, they escaped to Marseille in Vichy France. While awaiting American visas, they received permission to enter Brazil, but the British diverted their ship to Dakar, Senegal. They were confined to harbor for four months until directed to Casablanca, where they were interned in a camp, sleeping on straw mats in tropical heat with malaria rampant. They would not be released until Gertrude obtained American visas. Hans Lederer, the Rosenbaum son in law, wrote Gertrude begging her to intercede with "Senators or other influential personalities." In July 1941, the U.S. government changed the visa procedure, and Gertrude had to begin anew not only for the Rosenbaums and Lederers in Morocco but for the Oettingers in France. She wrote the Department of State to obtain new forms. Now two sponsors were required for each applicant. She and Elizabeth Rosenthal requested sixteen copies of one form and thirty-two of another on behalf of three parties. She would need to provide over twenty items of biographical data, typed and notarized, for each of the visa applicants.[35]

The Weils were less successful with Marta Goldschmidt and Fritz Herzberg. At each step new bureaucratic obstacles were thrown at them. In October 1941, Herzberg wrote his "liebe Cousine" that "one speaks of the transports of Jews to the East." His last letter, dated 16 November 1941, ominously reports, "I am greatly upset that I must make ready to evacuate to Poland." After sending affidavits for Goldschmidt, Gertrude received new requests from the state department for a canceled check confirming her payment of income tax and a new statement of support. Gertrude wrote the U.S. consul in Frankfurt that "I am more than willing to take Miss Goldschmidt into my home as a member of my family." When she notified the American consul in Stuttgart that she had placed three hundred dollars in escrow for Goldschmidt's benefit, it was returned with a request to send a new document with more satisfactory financial terms. In July 1941, Gertrude purchased a ticket for Goldschmidt on a Portuguese steamer from Lisbon, but the next ship was not available until December, by which time her permit to leave Germany would have expired. By September 1941, the state department informed Gertrude that the American consulates in Germany had closed, and Goldschmidt's only hope was emigration to a neutral country. American bureaucratic delays no less than the advent of war sealed her fate.[36]

With France invaded, Emil and Marie Oettinger were torn whether to remain in Paris with his brother Albert or to follow their children to Vichy France. Their daughter Lise and her husband had successfully embarked on a Spanish steamer from Bilbao to New York and soon appeared in Goldsboro. By autumn 1940, the Vichy government began promulgating anti-Semitic measures, and as aliens they were at greater risk than native French Jews. In July 1941, Emil and Marie decided to flee "again" to Aix-en-Provence to await visas that Leslie secured for them through Lisbon. "We are no longer wanted here," Emil wrote Gertrude, gratefully acknowledging her "kind invitation" to her home. That letter was written on Pearl Harbor Day. Still, their possibilities were better in the countryside of southern France than in Nazi-occupied Paris, where deportations in July 1942 led to Auschwitz.[37]

American Sponsors

Altogether, Mina and then Gertrude sponsored to America some dozen relatives. Once they escaped Nazi-occupied Europe, their reliance on the Weils' largesse continued. The Weils had succeeded in getting their Fischer cousins from London to New York, and Gertrude took responsibility for their resettlement. With their Birnbaum cousins, they joined the German Jewish enclave on New York's Upper West Side. Gertrude was besieged with letters as they struggled to find even sweatshop labor. Their seventeen-year-old son, confined to an internment camp outside Montreal, was sinking into depression. His desperate parents—"Erich is all we have in this world and our only hope"—wanted him with them in New York, but the United States, under pressure from the American Legion, opposed admitting Canadian internees, even to reunify families. Gertrude contacted her friend Amy

Jacobs, widow of a Canadian member of Parliament and chair of the Canadian Division of the Council of Jewish Women, who agreed to sponsor him. To satisfy the Canadian government, Gertrude placed twenty-five hundred dollars with the Central Committee for Interned Refugees in Montreal. In March 1942 Jacobs brought Erich—"very nervous and a changed boy"—to her home. The Fischers themselves lived on stipends from the HIAS office, unaware that Gertrude was underwriting them.[38]

And then there were her cousins, Anna Rosenbaum and the Lederer family, still stranded in the Moroccan internment camp. They, at last, got their Brazilian visas renewed, while Gertrude worked for their admission to America. They set sail in September 1941, only to have their ship refused entry first in Rio de Janeiro and then in Buenos Aires. Anna's daughter Mizzi in New York begged Gertrude for help. Their ship would return the family to Nazi-occupied Europe unless Gertrude could arrange for the American consulate in Trinidad to present them visas when their ship stopped there. Three passengers had already died aboard. Gertrude appealed to her congressman, Graham Barden, who contacted the State Department. It forwarded visas, and Gertrude paid six hundred dollars for fare.[39] The family arrived in New York.

In mid-October Gertrude—still recovering from cancer treatments and still mourning her mother—escaped to Chicago, Wyoming, and San Francisco for two weeks. Travel always revived her. Upon her return she found telegrams from Goldschmidt in Frankfurt demanding instant reply. A local German friend warned Gertrude that "all Jews have been ordered out of Frankfurt immediately, and they will probably be put in a concentration camp." However, he thought, the Germans might permit her to remain in Frankfurt if Gertrude sent a cable that Goldschmidt was immigrating to Cuba. Gertrude hastily wrote Jewish agencies. She sent inquiries to the American consulate in Havana for help finding a lawyer. She forwarded $650 to Cuba to secure the visa and another $2,000 for a letter of credit. With war declared in December 1941, the Portuguese steamship line ceased sailing. On 15 December Gertrude received a letter from HIAS regretting to inform her that Cuba no longer issued visas. Hope ended. In January 1942, Gertrude requested refunds for train and steamship tickets.[40]

As for Emil and Marie Oettinger in France, Gertrude succeeded in obtaining visas, but they had waited too long. The State Department wrote her in January 1942, that "developments incidental to the war have made it necessary to reexamine" the "immigration visa case of Emil Oettinger of Marseille, France." Emil sent his "dear cousins" a letter from Aix-en-Provence in April 1942, that "it may be that this is the last opportunity to write to your country." Gertrude turned again to Congressman Barden, who agreed to appear personally at a hearing to challenge the "disapproval" of the Oettinger visa. She herself would travel to Washington to attend. Nonetheless, the hearing ruled unfavorably. In the unoccupied zone the Vichy government had interned Jews in camps, and in August 1942 rounded up more than ten thousand foreign Jews who were handed to the Germans. Three months later the German army moved in. Still the possibilities of survival were greater in Vichy France where relief organizations, like Emil's HICEM, operated, and the populace was unsympathetic to the Jewish round up.[41]

Camp Town Lady

While the Weils labored to save their European family, they also had duties on the home front. In North Carolina the war was not far away. Off the coast from the Bluethenthal cottage at Wrightsville Beach German submarines torpedoed freighters. Burning ships lit the night sky. Depth charges rattled windows. Bodies of seamen washed ashore. Rumors of German landings or escapes from local prisoner-of-war camps spread fear across eastern North Carolina. At Van Eeden, an agricultural colony an hour or so away, the family visited German and Austrian Jewish refugees, artists and professors turned dirt farmers.

Challenges abroad always inspired Jewish solidarity at home. The Weils were hardly alone among North Carolina's Jews in their exertions to save family trapped in Nazi Europe. National refugee agencies distributed immigrants across the state. In 1941 Benjamin Cone convened in Greensboro a state conference of the North Carolina Resettlement Committee. The Weils joined a global rescue effort. From Jerusalem Henrietta Szold led the Youth Aliyah campaign, which saved more than twenty thousand children. Noting the Weils' ability to obtain visas for their European family, Szold wrote Mina, "You are successful, and I, alas, must confess inability to help in the dozens upon dozens of cases that apply to me." Emissaries arrived to organize North Carolina Jews, and fundraising campaigns were held for Youth Aliyah. With more Jewish refugees arriving in Miami the National Refugee Service wrote Gertrude's cousin Emil Rosenthal asking him to raise his commitment to employ immigrants in the Weil store.[42]

Local Jews also felt responsible for soldiers at nearby camps. Responding to a national program, Lionel Weil chaired the state Jewish Welfare Board, which provided social services for servicemen. In 1942 Seymour Johnson Field opened in Goldsboro as an air training base and depot for overseas deployment. When the base reached its peak in 1943, as many as twenty-five hundred Jewish soldiers were stationed there. Soldiers from nearby Fort Bragg in Fayetteville and Camp Lejeune in Jacksonville came on leave. With anti-Semitism loud at home and abroad, local Jews were sensitive to tensions between townies and Jewish soldiers, many of whom were brash, ungenteel northerners raised in urban Jewish ghettos.

Gertrude, Leslie, Herman, and her nephew Henry opened their homes to Jewish soldiers and their wives for Sabbath and Passover dinners. Gertrude as chair of the Wayne County Recreational Council served on the Goldsboro Operating Committee for the USO. The temple vestry, with the USO banner hanging next to an American flag, was turned into a rec room for soldiers regardless of religion. Saturday nights and Sundays soldiers gathered for darts or ping pong while the women served snacks and sandwiches. Gertrude led the temple Sisterhood, which joined the United Council of Church Women in a lecture series, "Youth and Family Life in Wartime." A community seder for Passover in 1944 drew nearly one thousand soldiers, guests, and officials, the meal cooked by Oheb Sholom women.[43]

As restless young soldiers prowled camp towns for women, local girls found themselves in a precarious position. The North Carolina Conference for Social Service was so concerned that it appointed Gertrude to chair a committee dedicated to "The Adolescent Girl in the War Camp Area." The committee addressed the "demoralizing influence of war." Older, uniformed men, with money in their pockets, were luring "adolescent girls" whose protective fathers and brothers were called away. Though admitting that "the girl who has poise, self-control, and sophistication" constitutes the "largest number," the committee was concerned with "the girl who gets into trouble (usually sexual) or outside court jurisdiction."[44]

Typical of camp towns, housing was scarce. Gertrude offered room and board for soldiers on leave from Seymour Johnson and Fort Bragg, as well their spouses and parents. A friend, after visiting her home, inquired, "Is it still full of soldiers and their pregnant wives?" In 1941 she hosted a half dozen soldiers for the High Holidays. In 1943 she wrote Seymour Johnson military chaplain Alexander Goode that she would take five for dinner on Yom Kippur eve and scribbled a note inviting them to break the fast the next day. (Rabbi Goode, son of a Kinston rabbi, later became a national hero as one of the Four Chaplains martyred on a sinking troop ship in the North Atlantic.) The distinguished Rabbi Stephen Wise wrote from New York wanting his great-nephew stationed at the air field "to have the privilege of meeting all the Weils." Besides the "delicious" food, the allure of Gertrude's home for Passover was the chance "to meet your lovely niece" or "most attractive cousin." She assured one soldier that he could marry at Oheb Sholom and offered rooms for his girlfriend and mother. Altogether the rabbi or post chaplain conducted a dozen Jewish weddings.[45]

Some soldiers were college boys, graduates of Harvard and John Hopkins, whom Gertrude engaged in heady discourse. "I especially enjoyed our discussion after lunch, a stimulating experience in which I seldom have the opportunity to indulge," wrote Sgt. Paul Kessler. She loaned him a book by Harold Laski, the British socialist. Others appreciated not only the "palate so pleasantly titillated" but also the host's "infinite humor & hospitality." Letters continued from foreign posts, and grateful Jewish mothers wrote Gertrude thanking her for the tender care of their sons so far from a mama's loving arms.[46]

Home Front

In 1943, with the allies now advancing, the war had reached its turning point, but whatever relief Gertrude felt was countered by personal setbacks. At least one friend wrote Gertrude, now sixty-four, worried about her "poor health." While her house filled with guests, while her European cousins beseeched her, while she was still coping with her mother's death, Gertrude confronted a recurrence of her malignancy. In 1942 and then annually for the next several years she was back at Johns Hopkins for the X-ray regimen. She underwent periodic treatments locally, returning to Dr. Finney in Baltimore for consultations.[47]

If cancer alone could not break her resiliency, Gertrude was struck a devastating blow. One afternoon in 1943 her brother Leslie, stopping to visit his grandchildren, suffered a fatal heart attack. Letters of condolence described him as "one of the very best citizens of our state," one who "did more for charity than any man in Goldsboro & never allowed it to be publicized." He was remembered for his "warm sympathy," "his gentleness and understanding," "his absolute sense of fairness and justice." Another lamented, "What a friend." Minister M. G. Canfield wrote Gertrude, "I had long since sensed the deep bond of affection existing between you two. Of course the break tears one's heart into shreds."[48]

Gertrude, so private in her feelings, overflowed with emotion. She wrote a confessional letter, so very rare for her, to the avuncular A. W. McAlister: "I need pity now though my own self pity in its unbridled profusion should be enough. May be after awhile I shall be able to rise to the heights of a philosophic calm, but now I can only feel the sharp pangs of a terrible separation. . . . In addition to his impersonal traits of tolerance and a judicial fair-mindedness he was the most tender and sympathetic and consider-

Sister and Brother, Gertrude and Leslie, in their youth.
Courtesy of the State Archives of North Carolina.

ate friend. He always understood . . . part of philosophy is to be grateful for much that has been given. After a while that may come, but just now I feel lonely."[49] Friends inquired about her well-being. Martha Boswell was unsure whether to believe Gertrude's reassurances: "You always down your own illness to such a point that I don't trust you." In her midsixties, she confronted myriad challenges personal, local, and global. Hope Chamberlain, too, was concerned: "I hope your own health is holding out under the strain of grief, of change, and of the growing anxiety this war must bring to us all." With her mother's example before her, Gertrude carried on still dedicated to the welfare of others. Her buoyancy was irrepressible but at a cost that she kept to herself.[50]

At war's end, Gertrude busied herself with new dependencies, her German family. Erich Fischer, emaciated after internment in the Canadian camp, returned to his music lessons and with funds from Gertrude enrolled in an engineering program at McGill. Gertrude also sent his mother a monthly stipend. For cousin Mizzi Burnham—she changed her name from Birnbaum—Gertrude purchased Pine Tree Lodge, a boarding house in the Catskills, which became a summer gathering place for the cousins and a largely Viennese Jewish clientele. Nothing was heard from Emil and Marie Oettinger for several years, but in 1946 they surfaced in Queens, New York, "bewildered" by "numerous emotions" but feeling "mutual joy" in being re-united with their daughter Lise. Gertrude visited that August, and Emil de-lighted in seeing how "well & young" she looked. The following spring they sat at Gertrude's table celebrating Jewish liberation at a Passover seder. Annually into the 1950s they visited Goldsboro for month-long stays. Fritz Herzberg was never heard from again. The name Marta Goldschmidt of Frankfurt appears in a Holocaust directory of murdered Jews.[51]

Now approaching seventy, with Depression and war behind her, Gertrude renewed her optimism. Tearing at her spirit had been the debilities of war, Holocaust, cancer, and, deepest of all, the deaths of her beloved mother and brother. She still took pleasure in life, retaining her youthful curiosity and enthusiasm for good deeds. She made time to walk in the woods and see movies. One journal note reminded her to listen to the UNC–Oklahoma football game on the radio, another to visit a neighbor in the hospital. Her old friend Harriet Payne visited, and she traveled often to Baltimore to re-new ties to her Jewish crowd. Weekly her brother Herman's family came for supper. Every summer found her at Janet's cottage at Wrightsville Beach for a week with nieces and nephews. In 1946 she escaped to Quebec, Gaspé, and Halifax.

Engrained in Gertrude was a lifelong commitment to self-improvement. She had worked for the redemption of her own family, and she approached with ardor the revival of the Jewish people in the wake of Holocaust. Her urgent cause became the restoration of her global Jewish family to its an-cient homeland.

{ 10 }

MY KINSHIP WITH
ALL OTHER JEWS
Jews, Judaism, and Zionism

After world war and Holocaust, Gertrude's torch of idealism became a beacon of survival. She dedicated herself with renewed fervor to rebuilding
her North Carolina Jewish community and to establishing a Jewish state in
Palestine. As was typical, she brought a global perspective to her local commitments. Having postponed domestic concerns during the war, America
was enjoying a postwar religious revival, with new churches and synagogues
arising. That movement was felt among North Carolina Jews as soldiers
returned home to start families and new industries, especially textiles,
pulled more Jews southward to open stores or factories. Agrarian Goldsboro, with a Jewish population of 135 in 1948, did not enjoy the dramatic
Jewish growth of urban centers like Charlotte, Greensboro, or Raleigh, but
Gertrude was dedicated to sustaining its community. Israel would create a
new Jew in America as well as in Palestine. She embraced the Zionist enterprise as a donor, organizer, and public advocate.

Typical of her paradoxes, Gertrude remained in religion both southern
lady and New Woman. In a 1941 speech in Danville, Virginia, she extolled
"the good old Jewish virtues of charity, cooperation, and neighborly kindness." Three years later in Raleigh she explained that "it is no accident that
Jews are to be found among the most advanced social thinkers today." She
read into ancient Jewish texts "a broad democratic social outlook," observing that "it is a traditional interest, this of social justice."[1] She held a modern
worldview without abandoning her Victorian pieties.

Gertrude was a well-read student of religion. She educated herself until
her dying day, studying Jewish texts and attending Bible classes at churches
as well as synagogue. The Bible was familiar to her as it was generally to

religious southerners, and she could cite chapter and verse to defend her positions. Her library included the classics of Jewish literature, as well as the canon of Western civilization. At critical life junctures she turned to William James's *The Varieties of Religious Experience*, which took a broadly comparative view of spirituality, emphasizing not metaphysical truths but, as its title suggests, religion as a felt, living reality.

Temple Lady

However her beliefs evolved, Gertrude remained a temple lady. That was her lifetime avocation. With Leslie's widow, Hilda, she was honored as a congregational matriarch. Community dynamics were changing. With the passing of the immigrant generation, Orthodox Jews ceased holding separate services, and the few remaining joined the Oheb Sholom fold. In the late 1950s the congregation at forty-nine households enjoyed modest growth as new families arrived. Gertrude invited them to her home and congregation. Following national trends, the newcomers, often second-generation Jews of East European background, tended to be more conservative than the established Reform community. Rabbis came and went, and for several years there was none. Hebrew Union College students visited. The congregation struggled financially. Gertrude paid $350 a year, although dues were but $50.

Gertrude remained involved with youth groups, serving as religious school superintendent into the 1940s and then substituting or teaching Sunday school. She attended teacher conferences and reported back to the congregation. Gertrude corresponded with pedagogical authorities until she amassed "a rich collection of autographs." Her library of Jewish educational material included *Your Child and You: A Pamphlet Series for Jewish Parents* by Azriel Eisenberg. After his lecture at a Jewish education conference in High Point in 1952, Gertrude began an eleven-year correspondence on his initiatives to create and distribute material appropriate for small towns. Holding personal fulfillment to be the educational "ideal," Eisenberg founded his program on modern developmental principles. Gertrude wrote Eisenberg that she has "been giving a good deal of thought" to his project and probed him on his plans to get materials into households. "To help make it possible," she sent two thousand dollars.[2]

On a 1962 educational brochure, Gertrude scribbled "Ethics—the Central Idea in Jewish thought." One study text in the 1940s was "Seek justice, relieve the oppressed," an admonition from Isaiah. Students learned more from her "living example" than any explicit lesson, recalled David Weil, her great-nephew and Sunday school student. "You always felt that what she had to say was so right and proper, so human and positive about everybody." He added, it was "always a liberal view." In 1957 pupils brought fruit to the Negro Old Folks Home and the white Wayne County Home. Children discussed verses on the "obligations to the stranger from Exodus."[3]

True to her character, Gertrude was a model of both decorum and unconventional thinking. A loudly praying girl at temple was admonished to "tone it down." Not that Miss Gertrude discouraged girls from speaking up: her egalitarianism countered the patriarchy of both Jewish and southern cultures. "I had been around so many women who were so subservient," reflected Muriel Kramer from the rural market town of Wallace. Pursuing higher education or a career beyond nursing or teaching "was just not the way to be in the little towns in the South." Recalling how Miss Gertrude challenged her intellectually, she added, "I had never been exposed to that kind of education." Elder Jewish women, like Kramer's mother, had often received scant religious training. "She let us know it would not be easy for women," Kramer recalled. Gertrude encouraged her as a girl "to learn, speak up, be active." She "made you think." Miss Gertrude, Kramer realized, "was more interested in helping us find where we belong in this world." Gertrude urged Kramer to attend a women's college—she suspected Gertrude interceded to have her admitted to Smith—and inspired a career in public service where she became the first Jew to hold statewide office as secretary of revenue.[4]

Gertrude nurtured friendships with local rabbis, who were frequent dinner guests. Several were European émigrés, including a Holocaust survivor, but more typically they were recent seminary graduates for whom a small congregation was a stop on a rabbinic career. She enjoyed the company of these educated, cosmopolitan men and their wives. As rabbis left for larger communities, they wrote her affectionately. They shared her liberalism, particularly on race relations. Rabbi Iser Freund, who served in the early 1930s, published academic articles on North Carolina Jewry and joined her on the Commission on Interracial Cooperation. In 1955 former Goldsboro rabbi Solomon Herbst wrote from his new pulpit in Arkansas, "Just watching you has given me more wisdom of the heart (*Herzensbildung*) than all the years I spent—maybe wasted—in school.... I shall try to pattern my life accordingly." He called Miss Gertrude his "most cherished teacher." She remained friends with Rabbi Julius Mayerberg's daughter Florence, a local schoolteacher, and son Samuel, a Reform rabbi in Kansas City nationally known as a crusader for civic, racial, and social justice. When Oheb Sholom observed its seventy-fifth anniversary in 1958, Gertrude chaired the celebration committee and invited Samuel Mayerberg to speak. Rabbi Herbst wrote to Hebrew Union College nominating Gertrude for an honorary degree: "Her life is a Kiddush Ha-shem," a sanctification of God's name.[5]

An Organized Woman

In Goldsboro Hadassah and the temple sisterhood were so intertwined that they met jointly, discussing Zionist affairs before turning to the temple's needs. In small communities, in contrast to urban areas where such societies were fiefdoms, women belonged to all organizations. Gertrude was a lifelong Sisterhood board member and its three-time president and a regional Hadassah officer. Monthly meetings rotated among members' homes, and Gertrude was happy to host a card party. Extolling domestic virtues, she described Sisterhood as "a little local Household of Israel united and harmonious." She volunteered for small, ladylike tasks like selling cheery Union grams for Hebrew Union College scholarships, planting ivy on the temple grounds, arranging flowers on its altar, or hanging a curtain for a Purim play. She represented the Sisterhood to the local Council of Church Women. For a Hanukkah bazaar she advised the women to sell aprons, not potholders. She was also intellectually engaged, leading Bible study, book reviews, and discussions of current events. She regularly attended regional Sisterhood, Hadassah, and NCAJW conventions, traveling in her seventies to Norfolk, Roanoke, or Washington.[6]

In her Jewish activism, Gertrude negotiated tensions between her universal and parochial concerns. She wanted her local Sisterhood to withdraw from Goldsboro's interfaith society since its "purposes are to further the causes of Christianity solely," but she then called for continuing support of the Salvation Army's lunch fund for indigent children. In 1942 Gertrude pushed the North Carolina Association of Jewish Women to help build a chapel at the Dobbs Farm, a training school for delinquent white girls, although some members opposed supporting a cause not specifically Jewish. Her ideal remained social welfare. In 1950 Gertrude introduced as an NCAJW keynote speaker Frank Graham, now a U.S. senator. Citing Rabbi Leo Baeck, she hailed Graham for applying Judaism's "ethical monotheism ... in the practical business of living ... securing to all men fair treatment and equal opportunities." By 1957 the NCAJW's Sophie Einstein Loan Fund supported African Americans with interest-free college loans.[7]

In the postwar years, Gertrude as NCAJW Projects Committee chair worked to revive the organization by focusing on education and interfaith efforts. She was concerned that public schools adhere to the Supreme Court ruling that forbade the teaching of religion, a battle her father had fought before the state legislature decades earlier. The NCAJW continued to be vibrant in Gertrude's eastern North Carolina, where isolated Jews welcomed opportunities for Jewish association, but it languished in the more resourceful cities of the Piedmont, where local community building held a higher priority. In 1950 the seventy-year-old was asked once again to serve as president. "Despite her age," wrote outgoing president Irene Miller, "the name 'Weil' will do much to rejuvenate the Association." She had "drawing power," another member agreed. "Age" was a needless concern, as Gertrude's October report made clear: "So far I have made visits in Gastonia and Charlotte and had meetings in Hickory and Roanoke Rapids. I go to Wilmington tomorrow. After that, Kinston and Chapel Hill."[8]

What Judaism Meant to Her

As a student at Horace Mann, Gertrude had been a questioning adolescent. At Smith she exercised her independence away from home, worshiping at synagogue infrequently but attending vespers regularly and accompanying friends to church occasionally. In her twenties she had a "live issue" about Judaism and had explored Unitarianism and later Christian Science and Ethical Culture. These loosely doctrinal movements appealed to assimilationist Jews who were reluctant to join denominational churches. At home she returned to the bosom of Jewish family and congregation. In the 1930s she defended a Judaism under challenge and threat. As a teacher and communal leader, Gertrude made public creedal statements explaining Judaism. Like many Americans, she was reassessing the possibility of belief in wake of war and Holocaust. In the 1940s she began committing her thoughts to paper.

Although she adhered to a religion that values the collective above the individual, Gertrude expressed views that she described as her very own. In the postwar years especially, American Judaism, responding to a culture of freedom and individualism, had given rise to personalism. Religious authority waned. Many different religious narratives can be read from—or into—Jewish history, and Gertrude exercised that liberty. Her emphases changed over time, but the consistent theme was her grounding Judaism in ethics and in religious experience. "In the field of ethics," she wrote in 1941, "I find greater satisfaction in the Jewish ideal of justice and righteousness in human society here on earth than in the familiar idea of a 'kingdom of Heaven' in some nebulous world to come."[9]

Gertrude's credos largely expressed the tenets of Classical Reform Judaism as articulated in the 1885 Pittsburgh Platform. Drawing from the prophets rather than the priests or rabbis, Classical Reform emphasized moralism, rationalism, and universalism. Absent from Gertrude's consider-

ations were the assumptions of traditional Judaism that regarded obedience to the commandments of Torah as the pathway to God. Judaism was
not generally given to theological speculation. The Pittsburgh Platform
spoke of a "God-idea as the central religious truth for the human race." In
its 1937 Columbus Platform Reform Jews added to "the Lord of the universe" the idea of a loving God, "our merciful Father," but Gertrude in her
credos did not consider the possibility of a personal God who answered
prayers and responded to petitions. She found irresistible the concept of a
"Creative Essence ... manifest in all of life." She thought that Shakespeare
"might have truly said *God in everything*" when in *As You Like It* he wrote
of "sermons in stones, and good in everything." At some points she spoke of
pantheism, although she recognized that it is "generally applied as a term
of derogation."[10]

As did the nineteenth-century German advocates of Jewish Reform,
Gertrude adhered to the positivist school, affirming that Judaism was a
historical phenomenon. The 1885 platform asserted that Judaism was not
antagonistic to "modern discoveries of scientific researches in the domain
of nature and history, . . . the Bible reflecting the primitive ideas of its own
age." In asking "Survival for What?"—in undated notes—Gertrude composed a Jewish apologia on "what do we find of real value" in Judaism's
"historic past." If the Greeks contributed philosophy, reason, and beauty
and the Romans, law, "what," she asked, is "our contribution to western
civilization?" Her answer was that "Jewish civilization as expressed by the
prophets is *the source of Western ethics*." The prophets presented "an ethic
unconfused by any impossible or childish dogma, a rule of living free of
superstition, supported by idealistic conceptions of world unity & a universal creation" compatible with science. A "sense of social responsibility," she
observed, was "engrained" in Jews as they evolved from a family to a tribe.[11]

A historian of religion may take issue with Gertrude's generalizations—
the prophets were hardly free from mystical visions or magical thinking—
but the application of ethics to the "everyday business of living" was her
constant concern. She did acknowledge that Jewish metaphysicians and
philosophers indeed had speculated on the "future world" and the "mysteries of the occult," but they have "not diverted the attention from the main
interest," which is to be lived "amid a society of men and women." If ethics
was the Jewish contribution to civilization, then it followed that the "obligation of Jews today, the inheritors of these ideas," is to live exemplarily. That
was her answer to both the question of Jewish chosenness and survival. "I
do expect Jews to be morally superior," Gertrude wrote, "to be an example
of obedience to moral laws because these laws were given directly to us &

long ago in our history." She ended, as she often did, by quoting her favorite verse from Deuteronomy that the law of God is here and now and not in the heavens or beyond the seas.[12]

Although hardly a systematic philosopher—her temperament was more poetic and spiritual—she was broadly read and deep thinking. Visitors recalled the classics of philosophy on her bookshelf. Gertrude's religious speculations trace to the Smith undergraduate who wrote her senior thesis on Immanuel Kant. "We cannot know reality in its essence (noumena)," Gertrude reflected in 1952, but only "in part, as it appears to us." She cited the example of Moses who, according to Exodus, could not see God's face, only his back. Three years later she expanded that theme, sounding again like a Kantian: "Being finite ourselves, we human beings cannot know God directly, but only through the phenomena, or manifestations of God in our universe."[13]

Beyond her personal study, German philosophical thought filtered to Gertrude through Reform Judaism. She regarded her personal principles as clear and self-evident truths consistent with reason. Reform Judaism emphasized moral action, the autonomy of the individual, and the universality of religious faith. Gertrude's own creed embraced those principles. In scripture she sought proof texts of her own moral reasoning. At the heart of Gertrude's lifelong pursuit to achieve her ideals was the culture of *Bildung*, as in her definition of sin as a failure to achieve the ideal, a shirking of duty. She confessed to "little interest in history," but like a Hegelian, she found there a "meaningful" dialectic of "Great *Ideas*." Thus, Adam and Eve discovered morality and the "birth of Conscience." Abraham's "obedience to conscience" expressed "duty." The prophets synthesized these ideas by espousing "social justice," that the path to God was through "prayer and good deeds and not by sacrifice and ceremonials."[14]

"Through the centuries of Jewish experience," she observed in undated notes, "there was a moral evolution, leading up to the prophets, whose teaching represents the highest conception of spiritual and moral attainment." That theme was consistent across her creedal statements. She cited Isaiah's impatience with iniquity and solemn assemblies, Jonah's responsibility to Nineveh, and Micah's walking humbly with God. "Our prophets and teachers are absorbed in the idea of righteousness as the ideal," she wrote, "and only through righteous behavior can they obtain blessedness." This idea was not "highflown," she cautioned, but included enumerated duties such as honesty in business, treatment of slaves, and care for the widow, orphan, and stranger.[15]

With the rise of Nazism, and the loud, violent, constant disparagement of Jews abroad and even at home, Gertrude recognized that Jews needed to reaffirm their self-worth. "Especially to us Jews this time of crisis means a reexamination of many things that affect our life, of our position in the world in which we as a small minority have suffered painfully and tragically," she asserted in 1941 to a Jewish audience. Jews, even those who had escaped to Ethical Culture or Christian Science, were still in the "mesh of 'belonging,'" still beholden to an "inescapable self-consciousness" that "glows with pride" at the mention of a Brandeis or a Cardozo.[16] In her talks and writing Gertrude instilled Jewish pride.

Gertrude rarely addressed anti-Semitism—she would not let others define her—but emphasized Jewish agency. In 1941, as Nazi persecutions turned murderous, she spoke publicly of anti-Semitism as the "same" as *the problem of any minority.*" Gertrude universalized anti-Semitism at the very moment when it was particular and disproportionate as she would have well known from headlines and correspondence from her German cousins. Three years later, in a Raleigh talk, she noted that it was "easy" with social discrimination, professional obstacles, and business competition to fall into the "too absorbing consciousness of anti-Jewish prejudices." She did not advocate "escaping" from those problems, but she thought the answer was "knowing our past" where Jews would find strength to meet present challenges "with a true sense of proportion."[17]

To Jewish audiences, Gertrude spoke of the "burden" to *respect ourselves.*" She urged upon her audience that *"the first duty of the Jew is to know himself. Why is he a Jew?"* After study and research, Gertrude did "declare my findings of superiority in Judaism over the current creeds and declared ethics of our neighbors." She explained, "Our creed is simple and elemental—a belief in the unity of God." She reveled in the liberty of conscience that Judaism gave her: "We are free, each to the limits of his spiritual capacity, to interpret God in our interrelated world."[18]

In 1944, at Raleigh's Temple Beth Or, she expounded on peoplehood. "I like to think of us as a people, united not only by the ties of kinship and of a common history, but as sharing in the development of religious experience." That experience included "political organizations" and "social institutions." From the Sabbath prayers she was able to derive the universal "social ideal . . . to secure fair labor laws providing decent working conditions and fair wages." She also felt obligated to share religious experience through interfaith programs, which grew popular in postwar America. "Brotherhood" became America's civil religion. The setting for a Jewish-Catholic-Protestant panel might be a Presbyterian Church, the Society of Friends, or even a

Jewish forum like the Sisterhood or an NCAJW convention. Increasingly the nation's heritage was described as "Judeo-Christian."

During the war years, Gertrude was bold in asserting Judaism's superiority to Christianity. More typically, southern Jews were circumspect in expressing religious views and emphasized commonalities. In handwritten notes, Gertrude wrote that "my greatest quarrel with Christianity is its terrible emphasis on Sin." Rejecting Christian dogma, she could not accept that the "sin of our first progenitor" carried to succeeding generations or that "an inherited sin ... demands Redemption." She understood that the "life and teaching" of Jesus could lead toward a better life and that believers found meaning in the mystical identification of Jesus with the "source of Life." But she adhered to "the Jewish teaching ... that men should look into their own lives." She reflected, "I find it not only more realistic but more ethical that man should be responsible for building a better, happier civilization than that man be 'saved' from his inherited sinful state by the vicarious sacrifice of a person who lived 2000 years ago."[19]

Elaborating on "what is sin?" Gertrude in a 1952 statement thus looked beyond denominational religion. She defined sin as "the conflict bet[ween] a highly developed class of humans with a less highly developed class." She explained parenthetically, "As the human race has evolved & adopted high ideals of thought & behavior, failure to live consistently w[ith] these ideals results in 'sin.'" Those with a conscience are "offended by humans with a less highly developed conscience" and view them as "sinful." As with eugenics, idealism led her to think in terms of hierarchies, but she did not define her "highly developed class of humans" by race, gender, or religion. One writer she cited was George Bernard Shaw, who argued for a benign, superior ruling caste. In emphasizing the will as the faculty of transformation, she seemed influenced, too, perhaps through Shaw, by Friedrich Nietzsche's *Übermensch*. As the earth evolves, she wrote, man, endowed with a conscience, will "use his ideals, his will, his determination, his efforts to make the world according to his desires."[20]

Gertrude's desires, however, were grounded in a morality of good and evil. The persistent message across Gertrude's religious meditations and public life was her faith in human agency. Responding in 1954 as her temple's ritual chair to an inquiry from the journal *American Judaism* on what constitutes an ideal sermon, Gertrude wrote that "one of our most common topics" that did not interest her was anti-Semitism. She wanted sermons to stir the emotions, to be "positive and constructive," to inspire "aspirations toward a nobler life."[21]

As Gertrude aged, she continued to set her calendar by Jewish time. "She never fails to attend services, even if she is alone on Saturdays—the show goes on," recalled Rabbi Solomon Herbst, who served Oheb Sholom in the 1950s. That story grew into legend: how Gertrude Weil, although the lone worshiper, once demanded that the rabbi conduct the entire service and deliver his sermon. Another story tells of her at first declining the Goldsboro Woman of the Year award since it was to be presented on a Friday night, which was her Sabbath. Gertrude would apologize for having to miss this meeting or that conference but would explain that it conflicted with her Jewish New Year. A visitor invited for a Sabbath dinner recalled rushing through the meal and then struggling to keep up as she hurried the few blocks to temple. They were the only two there. Gertrude took her customary seat in the second row—no one sat in the first—with her feet propped on a stool. In her old age she had hearing aids—sometimes they emitted a buzz—but she also relied on an old-fashioned ear trumpet to amplify the service. On Sukkot (Tabernacles) house servant Haywood Spearman built a temporary booth, and on Passover he set up tables for a community seder. In her ninetieth year she hosted eight at her Passover table. Before the spring festival of Shavuot she decorated the temple for a flower service. She told her niece Betty Weil, "If my generation doesn't attend regularly, why would we expect the younger generation to attend?"[22]

Like her parents, Gertrude maintained her Jewish crowd. Her neighbor Emma Edwards was well educated and civic minded, a companion at secular and Jewish women's societies. A community historian, Edwards penned tributes to Gertrude for publication. Gertrude had a deepening friendship with Nell Hirschberg, a Smith alumna who had come to Raleigh in 1942 with the U.S. Public Health Service. A biologist, Dr. Hirschberg was a cultured woman, a newspaper music critic, and an art adviser to the schools who ended her career at North Carolina College for Negroes (later North Carolina Central University), where she was honored as professor emeritus. Like Gertrude, Hirschberg was a loyal temple member who served on national Jewish boards. She traveled with Gertrude to NCAJW and Sisterhood conventions, and the two vacationed together.

Gertrude continued her excursions to Baltimore, New York, Cincinnati, Montreal, and London to visit her dwindling crowd. Traipsing the world, she sought the Jewish connection. In Edinburgh she sat in the women's balcony of an Orthodox synagogue where she heard the Torah read in a Scottish brogue. In the Rome synagogue she stayed for a service although not one hymn or prayer was familiar. In Cochin, India, she observed white and black Malabar Jews going to separate synagogues. Twice she visited Israel—the last time in her eighties—exploring both ancient archeology and modern kibbutzim.

Although Gertrude was well integrated socially in the larger community, she would not go so far as an assimilation that would melt Jews in the American pot. Family intermarriages with Christians had begun with her uncle Joe, and they became more common in the third generation, a typical immigrant pattern. It was not the case that Weils who intermarried did so to escape Judaism, since some with Christian spouses continued as congregational and community leaders. Several raised their children as Jews at a time when intermarried Jews often faced ostracism in traditional communities. Several Goldsboro residents observed, "If a Christian married into the Weil family, they would have been considered Jewish," even if the children attended church. Gertrude's brother Herman, who had intermarried, was a once-a-year Jew, appearing on High Holidays, but he managed the temple's finances and donated to the United Jewish Appeal. Her nephews Henry and Abram led the temple. Intermarried Jewish women joined the Sisterhood and taught Sunday school, and one was eulogized as a "true woman in Israel."[23]

In the 1950s Gertrude began attending B'nai B'rith Institutes held at Wildacres, an ecumenical retreat in Little Switzerland, North Carolina, endowed by the Blumenthal family of Charlotte. For Gertrude Wildacres' hilltop setting with its scenic overlooks was a religious experience in itself. At the institutes Gertrude heard leading Jewish intellectuals. Like the NCAJW conferences, the institutes kept the provincials connected to the cosmopolitan Jewish world. Gertrude took notes avidly. In 1955 she met Trude Weiss-Rosmarin, the advocate of women's equality in the synagogue and Jewish-Arab coexistence in Palestine, as well as Nathan Glazer, the Harvard scholar of race and ethnicity and author of the 1957 book *American Judaism*.

Gertrude's Bible study, including Hebrew lessons, intensified in her later years. Rabbi Solomon Herbst, who knew her in her seventies, observed, "As to her general knowledge, including the fields of Religion and Judaism—I wish I had it. She has a brilliant mind." A month after her ninetieth birthday, a lunchtime visitor found Gertrude in her parlor preparing a book review for the Sisterhood. Before her was *My People: The Story of the Jews* by Abba Eban, the Israeli diplomat. Pulling volumes from her library shelves, she was poring over tomes on ancient Israel by the German scholars Emil Schurer, a Christian, and Joseph Klausner, a Jew. She was fact-checking and drawing comparisons to Eban's work.[24]

Gertrude also joined the larger effort to write women into the Jewish narrative. When addressing a Raleigh Sisterhood Sabbath in 1944, Gertrude spoke from the viewpoint of "we feminists"—a label that she had resisted in other contexts—pointing with "pride" to Deborah, the Israelite judge. She cited Beruriah of the Talmudic era, who offered Jewish women a model of nobility, learning, and "unflinching faith." For a later generation of Jewish feminists Beruriah's story provided both a model and a cautionary tale. Yet, when enumerating opportunities for women, Gertrude could only cite traditional roles in home life, motherhood, synagogue voluntarism, and religious education. Not given to ideology, Gertrude was straddling eras, identifying with the rising feminism but still habitually domestic.[25]

What Judaism Means to Me

In the late 1960s, a few years before her death, Gertrude wrote a final creedal statement, "What Judaism Means to Me." She prefaced her apologia with a disclaimer: "This is a statement of my personal experience, which may be egotistical. I make no apologies: it *will* be personal." It is indeed a statement of "Gertrudism" as much as of Judaism. Gertrude began by tracing the "anthropomorphism" of the early Jews whose "conception of God was a god made in their own image, with human emotions: love, hate, jealousy, etc." Now, by contrast, God was seen as "the impersonal creative power, the universal cause." She could only conceive of God in "this universal cosmic sense" as the "Cosmic Cause, the Cosmic Law, or the Cosmic Force."[26]

"What is religion?" she asked, as always, questioning fundamentals. She rejected conceptions of religion as theology, doctrinal creed, or obedience to divine law. She neither hoped for heaven nor feared hell. She pointedly rebutted criticism leveled against Raleigh's Rev. W. W. Finletter [Finlator], a Baptist whose social activism had drawn criticism. "In my definition," she wrote "religion includes the *whole* of life: one's beliefs, one's attitudes to society, one's behavior." What "our prophets and priests—enjoined on their people not only a belief (faith) but an ethical code of behavior." She would make no distinction between sacred and profane, or "the things that are God's and the things that are Caesar's.... All things are God's." She opposed the "modern tendency to divide life into compartments.... Life is one and whole." Her religion demanded that she be honest, fair, and reliable "in *all* one's relations," whether in charity, commerce, employment, or humane care of animals.[27]

The most "extreme example" of an institutional commitment to "moral behavior," Gertrude explained in her credo, was the Society of Ethical Culture, founded by "Rabbi Felix Adler." Adler, a neo-Kantian, was not a rabbi—

although his father was—and the Jewish establishment regarded his move-ment as a challenge to Judaism. If not mistaken, Gertrude, with her broad views, was including him in the Jewish fold. Her library contained Adler's *Ethical Addresses* dating to the early 1900s. "But is ethics the whole of reli-gion?" Gertrude asked in the way of a critique. In fact, Ethical Culture did not claim to be a religion but left that question to the believer. More off-putting to Gertrude was its neutrality on spirituality. As she wrote, Ethical Culture lacked "another element, something that raises our spirit above the level of duty." She found such feeling in the Hebrew psalms: "The heavens declare the glory of God, and the firmament showeth His handiwork." Each of us, she believed, "felt certain moments of exaltation, a sense of wonder … something beyond the physical phenomenon." Here she quoted Words-worth on the sublime.[28] She retained a southerner's sense of romantic reli-gion, and throughout her life she spoke of finding religious experience not just in worship but in art, music, poetry, flowers, and mountain views.

Gertrude's quest for religious experience carried her beyond the limits of reason alone, beyond even science. A poetic sensibility balanced her ratio-nalism. She rooted in the religious imagination finer feelings of beauty and sublimity. Her handwritten notes on religion included copious citations from Gandhi, Thoreau, and Einstein, who described himself as "deeply reli-gious" in his feelings for the "radiant beauty" of an "impenetrable" reality "only accessible to our reason in their most elementary forms." In analyz-ing the "cause of our awe, wonder, gratitude, and worship," Gertrude noted that modern physics explains that all colors are "waves of light in various lengths," but then she asked, "What are these waves to us?" Her artistic re-sponse was "the gorgeous colors of the sunset sky … the pageantry of the flowers' procession, this gift of appreciating beauty." She felt the emotion of religious experience. Attempting poetry of her own, she had written of "The mystic gleam of moonlight, / That lift man's spirit toward divinity." Gertrude had read Thoreau's *Walden* carefully, her notes reveal, and al-though she did not cite Emerson, there was much of the romantic imagi-nation in her impatience with religious creed, her belief in the unity of the soul, her feelings of spiritual awe, and her sense of an impersonal, transcen-dental, cosmic force. Here again, she was bringing the light of the cosmo-politan world into Judaism's sanctum.[29]

The "third element" of her Judaism was "my relation to the Jewish people." She found tedious the debate on whether Jews constituted a race, a tribe, or an ethnic group, nor did she claim Jews to be the chosen people. She preferred the biblical explanation that Jews were "descended from one family" tracing to Abraham. Beyond "blood kinship, there is an identity of

Jews as Jews." Without justifying it on reason, she affirmed "a kinsman's responsibility for other Jews." That explained fundraising campaigns for the United Jewish Appeal, the purchase of Israel Bonds, the gifts to the Atlanta Hebrew Orphans' Home. That was why Diaspora Jewry rushed to Israel's defense when it was threatened in 1967. In speaking of an "obligation based on our kinship," Gertrude was again expanding on her own home truths, extending devotion to family from the local to the global.[30] Building a synagogue, teaching children, rescuing her European cousins, creating a Jewish state in Palestine all were "kinship" values passed from a beloved mother to a dutiful daughter.

As with kinship, Gertrude did not scrutinize her feelings of Jewish pride. Even those detached from other Jews share "an automatic reaction" to the Jewish best-selling author, Nobel Prize winner, or World Series hero. Such feelings heightened in the postwar years. After the Holocaust, Jews had rejoiced in Israel's rebirth. American-Jewish culture enjoyed an extraordinary flowering in the mid-twentieth century, and Jews asserted themselves as a proud people. Gertrude felt that.[31]

Like William James, who concluded *The Varieties of Religious Experience* by enumerating five reasons for religion, Gertrude ended by summarizing her own four reasons "in which I feel my identity as a Jew." First, she had the "freedom to find God as a creator and ruler of the universe without a prescribed theology from outside myself"; second, in "our traditional inclusion of morals"; third, "in my sense of an informing, super sensuous spirit in the universe"; and fourth, "in my kinship with all other Jews."[32] Gertrude was approaching her ninetieth year when she penned this credo. It is a remarkable testimonial to the clarity of an organized mind and the centrality of Judaism as she engaged in a life review. Her Jewish credo reflected the amalgam of reason and spirituality, idealism and pragmatism, morals and aesthetics, localism and universalism that had marked her lifetime endeavors. Curiously, for a woman who was a faithful worshiper, she omitted any discussion of prayer, nor for a congregational and organizational activist did she reflect much on institutional Judaism. Yet, even when describing herself as a humanist, she would not transcend the bonds of Judaism and Jewish community. Gertrude's focus on "identity" anticipated a concept that would achieve growing significance as Jews become an increasingly secular, acculturated people.

Rebuilding Israel

The founding of Israel in 1948 made whole the spiritual, familial, and communal values and feelings that lay at the heart of Gertrude's Judaism. Zionism bonded Gertrude to her mother and affirmed her kinship with Jews as a people. Rebuilding the lives of refugees addressed her social welfare aspirations. Gertrude also wrestled with the ethical questions of a state at war as it struggled to realize the prophetic call for a just society.

With the rise of Nazism and dire consequences of Jewish homelessness, American Jewry moved resolutely into the Zionist camp. Reform Judaism, historically unsympathetic to Jewish nationalism and Palestinian longings, reaffirmed Jewish peoplehood, opening a door to Zionism. Goldsboro women, with their rabbis' blessings, organized for a Jewish state. With Weil women leading, the NCAJW oriented toward Zionism. That was indeed significant at a time when American Jewish organizations fractured on the issue. Gertrude sent four hundred dollars in 1938 to cousin Lionel, who managed competing campaigns for both the Joint Distribution Committee, which provided European relief, and the United Palestine Appeal. After Jews nationally organized a United Jewish Appeal in 1939 for both European and Palestinian relief, Gertrude donated seven hundred dollars annually, her largest single donation among her dozens of charitable contributions.

Organizations like Hadassah, the Zionist Organization of America, and the United Jewish Appeal sent emissaries to Goldsboro to raise funds and enlist political support for a Jewish state. Frequently they were guests in the Weil home. In 1931 Gertrude, as NCAJW program chair, arranged for Hadassah founder Henrietta Szold to speak at its conference in Wilmington. On her way Szold stopped at the Weil home in Goldsboro to visit her old friend Mina. Some three hundred greeted Szold in Wilmington. In 1933 Szold moved permanently to Jerusalem. When she met a Zionist envoy returning from North Carolina, her unprompted response was, "How is Mrs. Weil?" Another guest, Bernard Berger, of the Palestine Maritime Lloyd shipping line, wrote Gertrude from Palestine in 1938 to update her on "the real truth" beyond newspaper headlines. The Great Arab Revolt against Jewish immigration and British mandate rule had erupted, with massacres and rising death tolls. Compared with European Jews, who "hide or run away from persecution," Berger argued, to see Palestinian Jews "imbued with the spirit of self-defense" was justification enough for Zionism. Berger observed that the Palestinian Jewish fighter upset Diaspora Jews more comfortable hearing "beautiful sermons" on the "people of the Book." Though Goldsboro may need no Jewish "self-defence army," Berger observed, "Palestine is not North Carolina."[33] American and Palestinian Zionists diverged. As a disciple of Henrietta Szold, Gertrude was likely discomfited by Berger's militarism and Jewish statism. Among the men of Zionist politics, Szold was outspoken in her pacifist outlook and support of a binational Jewish-Arab state. Szold's social welfare approach, serving Arab as well as Jew, was not always appreciated. Gertrude shared Szold's peace advocacy and unease with militarism.

Gertrude's Zionism followed her usual modus operandi: first study and then action. Like Szold, Gertrude rooted her Zionism in Jewish spirituality rather than political ideology. Mina and Gertrude collected literature on the so-called Jewish Question and Arab-Jewish relations in Palestine. They were familiar with Israel Zangwill's plans to find alternative sites for a Jewish homeland in Africa. They kept material on the new Hebrew University in Jerusalem, including its 1925 dedicatory program. They saved issues of the *New Palestine* magazine, containing essays by philosopher Martin Buber on Zionism and addresses by Justice Louis Brandeis on economic development in Palestine. Although not aligned in the fierce partisanship of Zionist politics, Gertrude's sympathies were leftist. Their copious collection also included articles by philosopher Hannah Arendt and Hebrew University president Judah Magnes, who argued that any state should be predicated on Jewish-Arab coexistence. Hadassah and the Zionist Organization of America sent her public relations material, which she avidly read, scribbling marginalia. In an "integrated kit" from Hadassah she underlined once every mention of "disarmament" and twice "our program is for peace through strength." She also studied literature from the Zionist lobbying group American Israel Public Affairs Committee, as well from agencies dedicated to Israel's economy. She purchased Israel Bonds to underwrite Israel's industrial growth and attended fundraising dinners.[34]

Hadassah linked Jews in a southern mill town to global Jewish destiny. Goldsboro women sewed infants' kimonos to send to Jerusalem. Gertrude traveled to Newport News, for Hadassah conventions, rising in the hierarchy until she was vice president of the multistate Seaboard Region in 1931, the only officer not from a metropolitan area. By 1937 the state had a dozen Hadassah chapters. The Goldsboro chapter, consisting of nineteen members, created settings—picnics, showers, bazaars, cake sales—that bonded women socially across Jewish ethnic lines. During the war years, Mina and Gertrude supported Youth Aliyah, Szold's program to rescue children from Nazi Europe. In 1939 Henrietta Szold, now seventy-nine, wrote Mina apologetically that she lacked time and strength to acknowledge all her letters and contributions.[35]

In 1951 Gertrude, joined by her Canadian friend Amy Jacobs, visited Israel for the first time, sailing from New York to Haifa, for a three-week sojourn. Israel, after just three years of statehood, was a society in crisis.

Hundreds of thousands of refugees crammed into camps where they lived primitively in tents, shacks, or former British barracks. Unemployment was in double digits, and inflation stifled development. Back home, Gertrude sent a bundle of clothing to Haifa through Hadassah. Returning to Israel in 1962, Gertrude observed that "the contrast is incredible." By then German reparations and the sale of Israel Bonds to Americans had spurred what was labeled an economic miracle. "A tremendous flow of immigration (mostly from eastern Europe)" was still arriving, she noted, and she was impressed how the "socialist democracy" was responding. The immigrant refugee camps yielded to housing estates. Every week a new kibbutz (communal agricultural settlement) arose. She spent a month touring the country, from the Red Sea resort of Eilat to Safed in the Galilean hills. Archeologists were excavating ancient sites underground, she observed, even as new cities were being built above. She visited a dressmaking factory and toured a kibbutz, admiring its "democratic atmosphere." Gertrude reflected, "It is still a poor country, with tremendous needs pressing upon it, so that one still feels a sort of exalted sense of purpose." Attending the Independence Day parade in Tel Aviv, she contrasted it with the modest affair she had witnessed in Haifa in 1951. She observed the "powerful engines of war" on show. Though the military display dismayed her, she held a "corresponding appreciation of ever threatening danger" that Israel faced.[36]

As owner of Israel Bonds, Gertrude was courted by officials. Once again she sought the experts. She went to the Knesset to hear a debate on finance and enjoyed dinners and evenings with Joseph and Sarah Bentwich and their son Zvi, Anglo-Jewish aristocrats of Zionism's founding families. Friends, like Ruth Roth Rypins of Greensboro, gave her lists of relatives to visit, some tied to North Carolina, who constituted her Israel crowd. Altogether, she found Israel to be "a constructive development of individual and communal living."[37]

Enthused, Gertrude returned from Israel as an emissary of Zion. She spoke on Israel thirty-five times before almost anyone who would listen, Christian or Jewish, church society or civic club, from the Daughters of the American Revolution to the Faison Garden Club. Her mission was to both raise funds and enlist political support. She conveyed her own enthusiasm for Israel, which she pronounced "the most exciting and thrilling thing happening in Jewry, each person there is a story of heroism." At one statewide benefit dinner for Israel Bonds, attended by Governor Kerr Scott, she heard Israeli minister of labor Golda Myerson (later Prime Minister Meir). Scott became so accustomed to the Zionist ladies that he referred to them fondly as "Hadassies." In 1955 Gertrude stood beside Eleanor Roosevelt at an

Eleanor Roosevelt signs a Zionist proclamation in Charlotte while Gertrude Weil and Morris Leder, a Goldsboro Jewish leader, look on. Courtesy of Arnold Leder.

Israel Bond event in Charlotte, where she and nine Goldsboro Jews signed a Zionist proclamation. Gertrude was impatient with those who were indifferent: "I hold no license for the Jews of the American Council for Judaism who seem to want a Judaism without Israel." All such Jews had was a "theology," and, she questioned "who can believe in theology these days?" Though wary of militarism, she noted Arab intransigence, the refusal to negotiate with Israel. In 1956 Gertrude and Hilda Weil hosted an Israeli soldier, Yael Dayan, daughter of the Israeli general Moshe Dayan, who later became spokesperson for the Israeli peace camp.[38]

When the Six-Day War erupted in 1967, Goldsboro responded as did American Jewry generally, rallying in support of the Jewish state. Fears for Israel's survival yielded to pride in its seemingly miraculous victory. Gertrude, eighty-eight, was asked to serve as honorary chairman of the Goldsboro Jewish Charities, the fundraising agency for the United Jewish Appeal. Nationally, Jewish philanthropy reached record levels. In 1967 Goldsboro collected $21,758; the following year that sum more than doubled to $44,059. Gertrude gave fifty-five hundred dollars. "Israel," said prime minister David Ben-Gurion in a speech Gertrude marked "read," "enhanced the dignity and prestige of every Jew wherever he lives."[39]

In the words of a Passover song, if Gertrude Weil had confined her career to Jewish causes alone, "it would have been enough." Yet, while she was heading the NCAJW, she was also leading the North Carolina League of Women Voters and serving on myriad civic boards, committees, and conferences. As she wrote in her credo, she would not compartmentalize her life. Rescuing her German cousins and improving the welfare of southern millworkers arose from a single, ethical imperative that she rooted spiritually in Judaism. Though her methods were founded on scientific principles, she drew inspiration from the Hebrew prophets, whom she idealized. She justified her ethics in biblical text. In a personal way she was reconstructing Judaism, inventing a religious ideology consistent with her humanist principles and, like many American Jews, picking and choosing those rituals that fit her values. The family covenant expanded into a sense of duty that she carried forward to her community, state, and nation—indeed, to the world itself. Her "one big purpose," as she told Jewish women in 1926, was to uphold "the torch of idealism."

Now in her seventies, Gertrude had new fires to kindle. War and Holocaust had focused awareness on the baneful consequences of exclusion and racial hatred. With her Jewish people resettled in their ancestral homeland, she saw more clearly her neighbors and fellow citizens seeking redress of their historic injustices. In a brochure of the North Carolina Commission on Interracial Cooperation, its president-elect wrote, "Hitler has placed this question of racism squarely before us." It was time, she read, to make a "real effort" to be friends with Negroes.[40]

{ II }

TREAT PEOPLE EQUALLY
From Gradualism to Integration

Gertrude Weil constantly enlarged her sympathies. For a southern lady who believed in the good of social convention, confronting racial segregation meant violating custom where it was most sensitive and volatile. White privilege, from the household help to segregated public schools, was assumed. Within the confines of segregation, sympathetic whites could enjoy friendly if unequal relations with African Americans. Gertrude, like many white southern progressives, was committed to black uplift, but that embraced a paternalism that did not breach segregation. Now the challenge was to dismantle segregation itself.

Gertrude always acknowledged that southerners of her generation had inherited racial prejudices. At Horace Mann and at Smith she met African Americans who dispelled her southern assumptions. During the women's suffrage campaign she radically affirmed black enfranchisement but pragmatically acknowledged the white supremacist status quo. In the 1920s she was not a leader of interracial relations, although she endorsed such efforts and provided financial support. She did not yet seem wholly informed or committed. During the 1930s and 1940s Gertrude's public health and social welfare work led her into more personal, egalitarian relationships with African American clergy, educators, and professionals. She increasingly joined committees and organizations dedicated to racial justice. Her engagement books list her presence at commencement exercises and glee club concerts at Dillard High School, meetings of the Colored Eastern Star, performances by a black theater group, and home demonstrations at the Colored Community Center. At one ceremony at Dillard to celebrate the community drive, Gertrude Weil was named from the podium among the "white friends . . . who so zealously worked to make the drive the very great success it was." Nearly half the twelve hundred dollars collected came from these friends.[1]

When Helen Martikainen arrived in Goldsboro with the federal Public

Health Service in 1944, she and Gertrude talked long on southern racial ways. Gertrude had impressed upon Martikainen, a New Englander, the "need to have contact with people of all colors." Gertrude told her that she had been "working with a very fine group of women, and they were black." She introduced Martikainen to these educators and health workers. "Blacks in Wayne County were very receptive to her," she saw, observing that Gertrude had a personal history with them. The respect was mutual. "Don't fail to call on me any time you need me to help in any way," Nannie Frederick, principal of Goldsboro Colored Schools, wrote Gertrude in 1944.[2]

The war had deflected attention from the race question. When discussing the "Jewish problem" in 1941, Gertrude thought that what Jews suffered was typical of "any minority," but the peoples that she listed as "objects of obloquy" and "vile names" were the pacifists, Quakers, and progressives, not blacks. To arouse the nation, African Americans embarked on a new militancy, notably A. Philip Randolph's March on Washington Movement in 1941, which led to the desegregation of defense industries. Younger blacks, especially returning war veterans, were less patient than the older generation, who had improved their position by accommodating to segregation. In 1942 African American leaders at a Durham conference resolved to oppose "compulsory segregation." A year later, a gathering of mostly white liberals responded by proposing a new regional organization. The two groups met in Richmond to form the biracial Southern Regional Council, with Howard Odum as president and Guy Johnson, a sociologist at the University of North Carolina, as executive director. Charles Johnson, president of Fisk University, chaired its executive committee. Gertrude joined.[3]

The Southern Regional Council was mostly white and male, and its members included both gradualists and militants. With academic leadership it was oriented toward research. In the 1940s the council debated whether to support segregation as the law of the land. To the consternation of liberals like Lillian Smith, it did not endorse integration until 1949, and when it did so, nearly half its members resigned. Gertrude stayed.[4]

Gertrude had served with the North Carolina Commission on Interracial Cooperation (CIC) as a member of the local chapter and the state executive committee. With the governor as honorary chair, the North Carolina CIC was devoted to "good neighbor" dialogue rather than to action, nor did it challenge the segregated status quo. Its energy was exhausted. A 1946 report indicated that, among its listed seven hundred members, "many have not been contacted in several years." A year later the CIC executive committee, with Gertrude attending, debated whether to continue but then decided to reconstitute itself as the new North Carolina Commission on Interracial

Cooperation and invite a general membership. Its statement of principles declared carefully, "We believe that compulsory segregation is incompatible with Christianity and democracy and that it must eventually be eliminated from our way of life." The CIC conceded that "'separate but equal' ... rarely, if ever" existed. "Segregation has been practically synonymous with discrimination." The CIC called for "new thinking" but not "wholesale or sudden abolition ... in terms of the ultimate elimination of segregation." Places to start were public transportation and graduate and professional schools at state universities, issues already on the Supreme Court docket.[5]

The CIC would neither engage in "political activity" nor sponsor legislation, believing that "the problem of race relations is primarily a moral problem and that sound progress in solving it depends upon change of heart and change of mind." This statement, signed by Guy Johnson and black insurance executive C. C. Spaulding, affirmed the gradualism that was then the common stance of the southern liberal. Frank Graham had advocated integration of the University of North Carolina at Chapel Hill in 1940, but even he believed that segregation could be ended only through changing hearts by the slow process of education. In 1948 Gertrude attended an integrated conference of twenty-four teachers at Duke University to develop curricula and materials on "Knowledge Helps Understanding." A Committee on Colleges encouraged interracial programs, and six hundred ministers were sent literature for Race Relations Sunday. When Governor Kerr Scott took office in 1949 on a progressive "Go Forward" campaign, the CIC executive board appointed Gertrude to a committee to meet with him on creating a state agency dedicated to interracial relations. As a candidate, Scott, a cigar-chomping dairy farmer, said that he would rather lose than race-bait, and once in office he took the then radical step of appointing a black to the State Board of Education.[6]

Gertrude had been reassessing her own racial attitudes along with the nation. She kept a copy of "To Secure These Rights," the 1947 report by Harry Truman's presidential commission, one of whose members was Frank Graham. The report referred to a "tremendous awakening of the American conscience" on race relations. President Truman issued executive orders desegregating the armed services and federal workforce. Gertrude also read the *Southern School News*, which included state-by-state updates on desegregation. She continued membership on the executive committee of the North Carolina Council on Human Relations.[7]

As was her custom, Gertrude read the literature and sought authorities. For years she had been reading Lillian Smith's articles in the *North Georgia Review* and the *South Today*. Through her publishing, writing, and educational programs Smith had been an outspoken southern voice on racial and gender equality. In 1944 Smith's best-selling novel *Strange Fruit* had scandalized much of the country with its depiction of interracial romance. Gertrude had attempted but failed to meet Smith at her home near the North Carolina state line in Clayton, Georgia, where she ran a progressive summer camp. Finally, in 1953 Gertrude phoned Smith but then had to apologize for having reached her in a hospital. She appreciated Smith, as she wrote her, for her "clear & unequivocal stand on the side of justice and human decency in our race relations." She admired Smith's "honesty and courage" in advancing the "cause of these ideals. You have made the most complaisant of us think of our attitudes toward our Negro neighbor."[8]

Gertrude's views had evolved since the suffrage campaign when she had carefully parsed the race issue. Now she would say, "I felt the same about suffrage as I felt about the interracial problem. I have never understood why we must talk and talk about it. It seems not a question for people to grow eloquent about. It is so obvious that to treat people equally is the right thing to do."[9] Indeed, "talk about it" had been the response of her conferences and committees.

Gertrude was moving from the gradualism of the southern moderate to the activism of the integrationist, although not so far as civil disobedience—despite her copious reading notes on Thoreau and Gandhi. Southern progressives often held traditional views on social order, fearing a violent white backlash as had occurred in the 1890s. Gertrude was still committed to the changing-hearts strategy. Though she continued to work within the political system, she was increasingly willing to confront it. When Carl Braden, a white Kentuckian with a history of racial and social justice activism, was arrested for violating an injunction against demonstrating in Alabama, Gertrude contributed to his defense fund. Gertrude also supported Rev. Charles Jones, pastor of Chapel Hill's Presbyterian Church. In 1947 a multiracial group of "freedom riders," led by pacifist Bayard Rustin, had been arrested in Chapel Hill for testing segregation laws in interstate bus travel. After a hostile mob had manhandled and pursued the riders, Jones invited them to his house. Visiting Goldsboro, Jones requested a meeting with Gertrude, and she in turn met him in Chapel Hill. Any public association with Jones carried risk. A delegation confronted the governor to protest UNC president Frank Graham's membership in Jones's church. In 1952 the regional presbytery accused Jones of heresy and expelled him. Gertrude wrote in his defense. He and Gertrude kept in touch.[10]

The North Carolina Way

North Carolina's response to the 1954 *Brown v. Board of Education* decision was consistent with its historically desultory behavior on racial issues. The state was hailed for its moderation in contrast to the massive resistance that provoked violence and school closings in neighboring states and in the Deep South. State leaders wanted to avoid the extremism that could hamper economic development while forestalling any meaningful integration. In August 1954 Governor William Umstead appointed a Special Advisory Committee on Education consisting of sixteen whites and three blacks, under racially moderate mill owner Thomas Pearsall, which cautioned that "mixing of races forthwith" would provoke violence. To forestall integration but comply with federal mandates, the committee recommended removing responsibility for desegregation from the State Board of Education and assigning it to city and county school systems. In 1955, in a decision known as *Brown II*, the Supreme Court sanctioned this approach, ruling vaguely that desegregation should proceed with "all deliberate speed." That policy assured years of delay as each of the state's 175 school districts now had to be confronted and litigated individually.

New governor Luther Hodges appointed a second committee still chaired by Pearsall—but this time all white. It recommended that local boards be permitted to close schools rather than be forced to integrate. Students could attend private schools with $135 vouchers. The legislature scheduled a public referendum. The Pearsall Plan was "the middle way," deflecting potential violence from arch-segregationists while appealing to white moderates reconciled to gradual integration. The plan also responded to an increasingly militant National Association for the Advancement of Colored People (NAACP), which was not appeased.[11]

Nor did the Pearsall Plan appease Gertrude Weil. She traveled to Raleigh to attend the special session of the legislature that debated and passed the plan. She studied the arguments. As the referendum campaign heated, she wrote a scathing letter to the editor in August 1956. "My own opinions have become clarified," she wrote. "The statesmen have talked high-mindedly of recognizing the 'law of the land' and of 'acting in good faith,' as well as 'preserving the public school system.'" Upon examining the proposals "carefully and conscientiously, I see no honesty in them." She continued, "The plan seems to me to be built on the flimsy foundation of pretense and double talk." She warned that the "destruction of our public school system" was a "greater calamity" than any benefit the Plan could accomplish. She preferred genuine good faith, declaring "I shall vote AGAINST the proposed school amendment."[12] She thus aligned with the integrationists.

Gertrude hardly spoke for North Carolina. A few courageous editors, like Gertrude's friend Jonathan Daniels of the *Raleigh News and Observer*, opined against the Pearsall Plan but to little effect. Also against were leading church bodies, including the newly organized North Carolina Board of Rabbis, which twice passed resolutions giving "its whole-hearted support" for "a swift end to segregation." The Pearsall Plan, however, passed by a four to one margin—ten to one in Gertrude's Down East. Eschewing the massive resistance that closed Virginia schools, North Carolina became the least integrated state while the most compliant with federal mandates. The Pearsall Plan's defenders—including a rising young politician from Fayetteville, Terry Sanford—regarded it as an expedient to buy time. The schools remained open, and integration was impeded but not stopped. All knew that the state had neither sufficient private schools nor adequate money to fund a voucher program. Gertrude had seen through the bad faith. In her letter Gertrude asked, "By the way, what is 135 dollars' worth of education? And where is it to be had?"[13]

National Jewish defense agencies like the Anti-Defamation League, American Jewish Congress, and American Jewish Committee had joined judicial challenges to segregation, and Jews were disproportionate in the ranks of activists and Freedom Riders. Southern Jews feared a white backlash. A delegation of Charlotte Jewish leaders traveled to New York to express their "grave concerns" to the American Jewish Congress for filing desegregation briefs. After the National Council of Jewish Women endorsed the *Brown* decision, its executive committee exempted southern members from having to "identify" with integration.[14]

Gertrude had a naïve expectation that Jews should be liberally disposed to black civil rights simply because they were Jews. Both peoples shared a history of oppression. Surveys revealed that southern Jews were more sympathetic than other southern whites but less so than northern Jews. Jews in Gastonia, Weldon, Greensboro, and Wilmington, among other places, served on biracial councils or school boards where they mediated between white and black communities in effecting peaceful integration. Jewish mayors, notably E. J. Evans of Durham, sought to desegregate but also to maintain civic peace. Goldsboro rabbis, like those across the state, sermonized in support of integration, but their local tenures were often too brief to commit meaningfully, nor would they cross into civil disobedience. Jewish women, in contrast to their businessmen husbands, could commit to civil rights without jeopardizing their livelihoods. Jewish women did take leadership among southern whites in desegregating schools in Miami, New Orleans, and Little Rock. Like Gertrude, these women tended to be middle and upper class and commonly cited as inspiration the ethics of Reform Judaism.[15]

Segregationists targeted Jews. In 1957 dynamite was planted at a synagogue in Charlotte, and a year later at one in Gastonia. In Durham a Klansman alleged that mayoral candidate E. J. Evans was part of an international Jewish conspiracy. Laura Cone in Greensboro was threatened, too, when she donated to build a memorial statue of Dr. Martin Luther King Jr. Harry Golden, publisher of the *Carolina Israelite* newspaper in Charlotte, heard death threats and anti-Semitic rants for editorializing in favor of integration. Gertrude doubtlessly knew of these widely reported incidents and would justifiably have felt vulnerable. Eastern North Carolina was Klan country, and segregationist propaganda commonly blamed Jews and communists—the two were often conflated—for stirring up blacks, who, racists charged, would otherwise have been complacent. In Goldsboro Gertrude seemed not to have been targeted, nor did she express fear of the Klan.

While campaigning for Frank Graham's senate bid in 1950, Gertrude had met Harry Golden, rambunctious journalist and raconteur who remained a wisecracking New Yorker despite his southern address. He had moved to Charlotte in 1941 to advocate first for the labor movement and then for black civil rights. In his newspaper *Carolina Israelite* Golden turned his wit on school segregation, reducing it to absurdity with his comic Golden Plans and winning the admiration of Dr. King. Gertrude wrote Golden that she enjoyed his articles, and the two arranged to meet. In 1955, after the *Brown* decision, he spoke at Oheb Sholom. An unabashed self-promoter, Golden honored Gertrude with a Carolina Israelite Award and profiled her in his 1974 book *Our Southern Landsman*. Golden, who often played the role of Jewish clown, lamented that no one took him seriously.[16] Gertrude never had that concern, although she shared his outrage at racism's absurdity.

Gertrude flashed her own wit to shred the color line. An oft-cited episode occurred in 1963 when tensions ran high after an African American wrote the newspaper protesting the grinning black-jockey hitching posts adorning front lawns about town. One stood before the Weil house. Many white homeowners responded angrily to demands for their removal, but Gertrude resolved the issue with a can of white paint, turning hers Caucasian. When a Democratic gubernatorial candidate invited her to "bring your neighbor" to a political rally at the segregated Goldsboro Hotel, Gertrude led a parade of African Americans into the lobby. "They all looked at me rather strangely, but they didn't dare say anything," Gertrude recalled. "I said I brought my neighbors with me … and we had a lovely time."[17]

As a longtime member and former chair of the Wayne Recreational Council, Gertrude was offended that African Americans lacked facilities. In 1952 she had pushed for a recreation tax levy to support its program. She wanted a survey of town needs and construction of city swimming pools, especially for an underserved black population. The public voted against it by a margin of three to one. "We have no budget," Gertrude complained, and the program was "quiescent." Three years later, writing an op-ed piece in the *Goldsboro News-Argus* on "Ways to Make Goldsboro a Better Place," Gertrude saluted parks and recreation but added, "We are not blind to the fact that such facilities and leadership are sadly lacking of our Colored citizens. We should not rest content until Goldsboro Negro children also have the opportunity."[18]

Town leaders meeting at the Goldsboro Hotel agreed to build two pools but doubted their ability to finance one in the black community. The first potential donor suggested was Gertrude Weil, and newspaper editor Eugene Price was delegated to solicit her. He recalled her response as he stood at her door: "Young man, stop mumbling and chewing your fingers," she advised him. "Come in the house and tell me what you want." Her response was direct: "You tell your group that I will build a swimming pool for the black children." The family donated land owned in a black neighborhood. In 1958 the Weils through the family's Wayne Foundation contributed thirty thousand dollars. Friends wanted to name the park for her, but again, Gertrude would have none of it. When Mina Weil Park was dedicated on a hot spring day in 1963, Gertrude arrived for the poolside ceremony wearing a robe. The eighty-three-year old "stripped down" to an old-fashioned swim suit, Price recalled, and was the first to dive in, inviting the excited children to follow her.[19]

Gertrude attended institutes of the North Carolina Council on Human Relations, which some years brought her onto the campuses of historically black colleges. She saw hope in campus movements, particularly the student mock legislature which she found "much more progressive than the real legislature." The 1945 student state legislature, representing white campuses, voted to desegregate the assembly by a two to one margin. The action, engineered by University of North Carolina student Allard Lowenstein, a Jewish New Yorker, was branded communistic, and university appropriations were threatened, but Frank Graham defended the students' "freedom and conscience." In 1948 Gertrude joined an interracial meeting at the North Carolina College for Negroes with representatives from all state campuses. She traveled to Shaw University in Raleigh, where the Student Nonviolent Coordinating Committee later formed in 1960. Months after the Greensboro Woolworth's sit-in of 1 February 1960, she attended a Council on Human Relations meeting in Kinston to hear president Samuel DeWitt Proctor of North Carolina A&T, the Greensboro protestors' campus, report on "The Sit-In Demonstrations: What Do They Mean?" Legal and moral questions were debated, whether such demonstrations were "good" or merely "stirred up" race relations.[20]

The Goldsboro Way

The Greensboro Woolworth's sit-in marked a new stage of civil rights activism as student-led protests spread to Durham, Chapel Hill, and Winston-Salem. Gertrude inquired at her local Woolworth about its lunch counter practices, but the manager advised her that "headquarters" set policy. A stockholder, she sent a resolution to be voted at the next corporate meeting. "Since the local Woolworth store seems glad to receive the patronage of Negroes in every other department than the lunch counter," she wrote, "it seems inconsistent and discourteous to refuse to serve them there." Therefore, she called upon the company to "adopt the policy of serving ANY customers in ANY department."[21]

Goldsboro's race relations reflected its changing economic fortunes. In postwar years it shared the prosperity that was redrawing the landscape of North Carolina along with that of the nation. As veterans returned to start families, new suburbs sprouted. The growing of corn feed spawned hog and turkey industries. Furniture and tobacco-processing plants arose. Seymour Johnson Air Force Base had closed in 1947 but reopened in 1956 as Cold War politics brought new fighter wings. The base spurred development, and the population grew. Temple Oheb Sholom added an annex. Governor Kerr Scott's "Go Forward" campaign expressed optimism.

The mill and market town did not sustain this growth, and in the 1960s its population began falling. Antismoking campaigns devastated tobacco. Cotton and textile production yielded to foreign competition and synthetic fabrics. As shopping malls and box stores sprouted on new highway loops, downtown went into a tailspin. The railroad tracks, the reason for Goldsboro's creation, were gone. In 1963 the Weil store anticipated record sales, but its prosperity was unsustainable. Like many southern cities, Goldsboro saw its racial demography change as rural blacks, pushed by mechanization and the end of tenancy, moved into town, and whites fled to new suburbs. In 1960 nearly half Goldsboro's urban population was black. Gertrude stayed put as African Americans settled her neighborhood. Once stately houses deteriorated, and fires left empty lots. A gas station and farmer's market replaced residences. When asked if she were scared to live alone in a large house in a declining neighborhood, Gertrude answered simply, "This is my home."[22]

In 1963 the civil rights revolution approached a climax in Goldsboro as it did across the South. Gertrude found the situation "painful." On 11 June Alabama governor George Wallace, pledging "segregation forever," defiantly blocked a university door to black students. The next day Mississippi NAACP field secretary Medgar Evers was assassinated in his driveway. Later that year the Birmingham church bombing killed four girls. In August the March on Washington galvanized public opinion. Gertrude recognized that "it's very difficult to convince people" to change their attitudes. She could understand her generation's prejudices but was disturbed to see youth succumb.[23]

In 1963, Governor Terry Sanford astonished North Carolina—as well as the South and the nation—by declaring a Second Emancipation Proclamation at a journalists' meeting in Chapel Hill. The time had come "to quit unfair discrimination" in employment, he announced. For the state's progress, the people of North Carolina "have come to the point of recognizing the urgent need for opening new economic opportunities for Negro citizens." He appointed a Good Neighbor Council and called upon state agencies to write nondiscriminatory hiring policies immediately. He received an ovation.[24]

Governor Sanford met with civil rights leaders asking them to trust the good faith of his office. The Good Neighbor Council would foster equal opportunities in employment while a Mayors Cooperating Committee identified challenges specific to each community. These gradualist policies were intended to counter the activism of the NAACP and the Black Power militancy of student groups like the Student Nonviolent Coordinating Committee. The *Goldsboro News-Argus* saluted Terry Sanford. The "North Carolina Way" recognized the justice of African Americans' civil rights while affirming the necessity of law and order. Civic and business leaders met with hotel, store, theater, and restaurant owners to enlist, or to pressure, them into desegregating. Integration would proceed city by city. Martin Luther King's celebrated "Letter from Birmingham Jail" was addressed to just such moderates who asked blacks to trust patiently in the whites' goodwill and refrain from demonstrations.[25]

Terry Sanford's popularity plummeted as black leaders intensified their dissent. By mid-1963 protests erupted across the state, starting with marching and chanting students and followed by picketing of stores. In some towns rocks flew as whites and blacks faced off. The state legislature repealed Jim Crow laws but increased penalties on those who violated trespass and contempt of court laws. The Speaker Ban Law, aimed at Chapel Hill, outlawed communists from lecturing on state campuses. Southerners clung to the myth that radical outside agitators, not their loyal black neighbors, were fomenting the civil rights revolution.[26]

Governor Sanford called for an end to demonstrations, promising to sit down with African American leadership. The NAACP announced city-by-city "truce agreements," consenting to moratoriums for good-faith negotiations. While George Wallace stood in a schoolhouse doorway and Medgar Evers lay dead on his driveway, biracial councils in Durham, Charlotte, Greensboro, Winston-Salem, and Raleigh announced desegregation.[27]

The North Carolina Council on Human Relations had sponsored voluntary biracial community committees, with alternating racial leadership, but without real progress. As was typical, the threat of demonstrations moved the city's leadership to act. On 28 May 1963, African Americans organized a Committee to Eliminate Racial Segregation and Discrimination in the City of Goldsboro. It demanded an immediate end to racial bias in employment, public accommodations, and school assignments. Protestors, mostly young, paraded downtown, singing hymns and carrying signs. Curious whites watched from sidewalks. Gertrude, whose home was a block from Center Street, would have had a view from her porch. By early June, demonstrators escalated the protests by picketing movie theaters and drugstores. White bystanders turned into a mob. On 12 June the *News-Argus* warned in a front-page editorial, written by Gertrude's friend Eugene Price, that the "peaceful, inoffensive" parades of the past weeks had turned into "confrontations" with police and taunting whites. The newspaper cautioned, "Our streets today boil on the verge of racial violence." It called upon the city to "move immediately to meet its race crisis." Two days later the biracial council of nearby Kinston announced that city's integration, and dozens more towns like Goldsboro proclaimed similar committees.[28]

The Goldsboro Ministerial Association, responding to "mounting tension in our city," convened an emergency meeting that called upon the mayor to appoint a biracial council. It asked the public to be "Christian in attitude" and patronize desegregated businesses. Black demonstrators agreed to "halt picketing" for five days, recognizing that "tensions had mounted to the point of explosion." On 17 June, at the mayor's initiative, city aldermen created the Goldsboro Bi-Racial Council to "promulgate some work-able program looking to resolving racial differences." The sixteen appointees, divided evenly by race, consisted of ministers, educators, professionals, and executives—including Gertrude's nephew Henry Weil. The council sponsored a Women's Goodwill Committee whose organizational gathering drew 140 women, 60 percent of whom were black. Gertrude joined its steering committee and hosted its first meeting at her house. That gesture, reported on the newspaper's front page, made a public statement to Goldsboro at a time when African Americans customarily entered white homes through back doors. A black participant traced the city's improved race relations to "whites and blacks actually going into each other's homes." She recalled, "We drank coffee, and ate doughnuts, and we talked."[29]

Modeled on a similar committee in High Point, the Goldsboro Women's Goodwill Committee was the second in the Southeast. Henry Weil chaired the Bi-Racial Council's employment committee, and by April 1964 it had written pledges from Goldsboro businesses in support of equal opportunity hiring practices. A public accommodations committee was working for a "break-through" with area businessmen.[30]

Gertrude likely felt heartened by the Goldsboro Bi-Racial Council's 1964 report, which pointed to progress. A year later the Goldsboro City Board of Education announced a "policy of complete desegregation." Wayne Memorial Hospital hired blacks on staff, and the county now had a black deputy sheriff. City parks and playgrounds were integrated. The report noted "certainly at the outset, the white people generally were not ready to accept the idea" of integration in "public accommodation," conceding that "segregation of rooming and eating facilities has been tradition in the South for many generations." Committee members spoke before church and civic groups "to effect change in a peaceful manner." The threat of "demonstrations" was a proven incentive to integrate. Months after this report, the federal Civil Rights Act of 1964 opened doors to public accommodations, rendering the council's actions moot.[31]

Gertrude regularly attended Bi-Racial Council and steering committee meetings, which continued to convene at members' homes, both black and white. She participated in public meetings of Operation Bootstrap, which worked to "break the cycle of poverty" by encouraging "poverty victims to become self-relying." Henry Weil served as Bootstrap leader and headed a biracial effort to utilize federal funds to rehabilitate housing. Gertrude was also a shareholder in the Goldsboro Community Grocery Store, a coop that "some of our Negro citizens" created in 1967 as a self-help project.[32]

One of Gertrude's civic virtues was just showing up, and after many years she was a familiar figure in the African American community. Sitting through a "Panorama of Progress" pageant at Dillard High, she responded to the appeal of tenth-grader Arabia Bunn to contribute to its college fund. She attended as an "honored guest" a meeting of Negro Law Enforcement Officers at Dillard in 1957. To Walter Foster, principal of the East End School, went two hundred dollars to establish a Boy's Club. She and Dr. Foster, along with school principal H. V. Brown, enjoyed a cordial relationship. In 1964 the Alumni Association of Dillard High School presented Gertrude with its Citizenship Award "in recognition of her consistency and faithfulness to all humanity." Returning home from a reunion at Dillard, she found an admirer had left a chrysanthemum corsage at her door.[33]

The response of Goldsboro to civil rights followed the "North Carolina Way." Wayne County had been among a small number of jurisdictions that had begun token school integration in 1959, but it was not until 1964, ten years after *Brown*, that the Goldsboro Bi-Racial Council reported that "approximately one half of Negro students were reassigned to white schools."[34] The federal government at that point had threatened to withhold funding from segregated systems. The schools did not fully integrate until 1970. Yet, relative to neighboring communities, Goldsboro enjoyed the racial peace that the business leadership coveted.

The Help

Throughout the civil rights struggles, Mittie Exum and Haywood Spearman continued to serve Gertrude. She spoke of them often as her family, as was the southern custom. Spearman, married with a daughter, served as deacon at his Baptist church. After he suffered a heart attack in 1960, Gertrude was bedside at the hospital and arranged appointments with her personal physician. She also accompanied Exum to the outpatient clinic at Chapel Hill and was again bedside when she was hospitalized in 1966. As Gertrude aged, the family was concerned about her living alone but compromised by having Exum live in. She confessed to a niece that Exum was "the person closest to being a daughter to her." When Exum remarried a man seven years younger in 1967, Gertrude advised her to wear blue rather than virginal white and attended the wedding. The marriage lasted but days. Gertrude explained, "Can you imagine me being engrossed in the comings and goings of Mittie's no-count husband?" Then she added, "Mittie's life is my soap opera." Exum's devotion to Oral Roberts's evangelism amused her.[35]

Gertrude's niece Mina Kempton recognized vestiges of southern paternalism in the relationship, but the employer and her house workers forged bonds of affection across persisting class and racial lines. "They were both always there for her," Gertrude's niece Joanne Bluethenthal observed. She could not have done without them.[36] Although Gertrude enjoyed a southern lady's privilege, in symbolic ways she breached customs. When chauffeured by Spearman, Miss Gertrude, unlike Miss Daisy, sat beside him in the front seat rather than in the back. She drove herself at night, explaining that she could not "ask Haywood to take me out at night. He has a family to look after." She was generous with wages and bonuses. Gertrude helped prepare Exum's will, which listed both a car and a house. As Chestnut Street changed, Gertrude enjoyed friendly relations with her African American neighbors. Visitors found her in her garden standing with her neighbor, Earl Whitted, who shared her flower passions. "We would go over there to look at the day lilies," Emily Weil recalled, "and she would say, 'I wonder if Earl is home?,' and frequently he'd come over to talk."[37] She would not live long enough to welcome into her family her niece Mina's daughter-in-law, an African American.

An Integrated Town

An interracial team of academics focused on Goldsboro for a case study on the impact of "school desegregation on a southern city." Interviewing ten community leaders, they heard them repeatedly say that Goldsboro had "less racial and religious prejudice" than "in other communities in the region." A banker had a ready answer: "He attributed it to the influence of a prominent Jewish family, descendants of one of the town's founders." Another leader added that Goldsboro's "leadership was more sympathetic to civil rights. He likewise attributed this attitude to the quality of local Jewish leadership." The report observed that the Weils "continued to be the dominant influence in the community" and "have been fully accepted by the social elite." It cited their "statewide reputation in leadership in educational and cultural affairs."[38]

The case study also observed "a lack of militancy within the black community." Its demands were "reasonable," and the white community was able and willing to meet them. The leadership structure of Goldsboro, the sociologists observed, was "monolithic and elitist." It consisted of "one relatively homogeneous set of community leaders—white, upper middle class, highly educated"—who shared social relations. "There are virtually no blacks in the leadership set nor is there any representation of poor whites," it noted. Expertise and "technical competence" were prized above democratic process.[39] Certainly, Gertrude fit the profile of the expert, well-educated, white elite, but her critical contribution was a democratic one, establishing personal relationships that breached racial lines.

Confronting desegregation, Goldsboro thus followed the Atlanta rather than the Selma model. In Raleigh and Charlotte, too, white business establishments were willing to work with African American leaders in effectuating integration. Businessmen preferred to negotiate with moderate black leadership—clergy, educators, professionals—rather than concede ground to younger Black Power militants who might provoke street demonstrations or even resort to violence. Their primary concern was to avoid the disorder and negative publicity that would deter out-of-state investors and impede economic progress.

Civil rights proved Gertrude Weil's last great social justice crusade. For one who lived comfortably and pleasurably in the refuge of social convention, her civic career led her in directions that proved socially disruptive. In her final years came a feminist revolution, an antiwar movement, and a generational youth rebellion. If she were too old and proper to rush to the barricades, she looked on sympathetically. Whatever radicalism she had privately harbored in her struggles had been restrained by her political pragmatism and her own conservative sense of social propriety. As she aged, she felt less inhibited personally and politically to live where her ideals might take her.

{ 12 }

MY SHARE OF RESPONSIBILITY
Citizen and Neighbor

The family had a running joke, Gertrude Weil's niece Mina Bluethenthal Kempton recalled. Her father would ask, who was younger, Aunt Gertrude or her mother Janet? The answer was invariably Gertrude, who was thirteen years older. As she advanced into her seventies, Gertrude's vigor was legendary. Visitors to Chestnut Street—and there were many—left charmed and rejuvenated. Whatever the subject, the conversation was informed and engaging with the added pleasure of a hearty laugh. "Straight-backed, straightforward, but never straitlaced," a biographer observed. One guest commented that "those amazing blue eyes gleamed wickedly." For others they "twinkled" or "sparkle[d] with fun and mischief."[1]

Conscious of the rushing years, Gertrude never retired. Daily there were meetings—the advisory committee of the Girl Scouts, the garden club booth at the fairgrounds, the library or hospital board—and trips to the Weil store to discuss family matters or civic affairs. In her seventies she was still diving into the pool at the country club. She traveled to Raleigh to take voice lessons—she wanted the best teacher. She enjoyed hikes and picnics at the new Cliffs of Neuse State Park on land that cousin Lionel had donated. Her passion for gardening grew as she aged. At the blush of spring, her engagement books exclaimed "First irises!" or "Garden at peak!"[2]

Though she spent a lifetime at 200 Chestnut Street, Gertrude was in constant motion. Returning from ten days in the North in 1950, she left the next day for her annual week with the family at Wrightsville Beach. She came back in time to depart with cousin Edith Eustler for two weeks in the North Carolina mountains, visiting potteries in Biscoe, a folk festival in Asheville, an outdoor Indian folk drama in Cherokee, Brandeis Camp in Hendersonville, and Wildacres Jewish Youth Institute in Little Switzerland. She returned for an intergroup relations seminar and *Twelfth Night* in Chapel Hill. And that fall she attended an NCAJW convention in Roanoke

Rapids, a B'nai B'rith conference in Charlotte, a teacher's institute in Baltimore, and a Zionist convocation in Portsmouth, Virginia. Often she took the bus to Raleigh or Kinston to visit friends, lobby the legislature, or serve on her various boards. A bedraggled stray cat showed up, and though she had not before had a pet, she made a home for it in her garden house. Ragamuffin was always good for a conversation.[3]

As the older generation passed on, Gertrude, if not the matriarch that her mother had been, bonded the extended family. She was among the last who knew how Weils were related to Strausses in Baltimore or Rosenbaums in New York. As had been her mother's habit, she wrote the cousin in London or the niece in Washington. Gifts greeted the birth of the great-nephew named for Leslie and great-niece Trudy named for her. German cousins Lise and Otto Witten, Emil and Marie Oettinger came for monthly stays into the 1950s. Gertrude and Emil dissected United Nations resolutions on Palestine and questioned the reeducation of Nazis in postwar Germany. She helped cousin Mizzi Burnham sell the Catskills resort that she had purchased for her. "You are indeed the pride of the clan," wrote cousin Estelle Ries from Baltimore, the author of eight books.[4]

Her Goldsboro crowd was dwindling. The younger generation, like many of their class, left for opportunities elsewhere. "Doesn't everybody from North Carolina want to go to New York?" quipped her niece Betty Weil. "It's so exciting."[5] Still at the store were Leslie's sons Abram and Henry. The nephews complemented each other, Abram the poetic soul and Henry the civic activist. Gertrude took pride in her great-nephew David's wife Emily, who shared her passion for cultural affairs and community betterment. Gertrude also enjoyed cousins Emil Rosenthal, a lawyer for Weil enterprises, and Miriam Oettinger Rosenthal. Liberal and cultured, Emil served as a trustee and benefactor of Fayetteville State, an African American college, where a classroom building was named for him.

Gertrude's relationship with her brother Herman evoked her childhood when she had bopped him with a croquet mallet and refused to apologize. Though their affection was evident—he managed Gertrude's finances— Herman was as obstinately conservative as Gertrude was idealistically liberal. "Herman and Gertrude probably agreed about nothing in the world," observed cousin Kala Rosenthal Herlans. Their "running battle" enlivened family gatherings. It was fine for her to be generous to Israel, he noted, since she "never had to earn a dime." One skirmish over integration ended when Herman retreated with an angina attack. "Oh, pshaw, now we'll have to stop," Gertrude relented. Another argument closed with Gertrude's rebuke, "It is instructive to observe the deterioration of your mind."[6]

Gertrude also remained close to her sister, Janet, who had inherited the Weil social justice gene. She served on Wilmington's library and hospital boards, "constantly giving her time" to progressive causes. Gertrude enjoyed Janet's children, who shared her social liberalism, staying with her nephew Arthur and his wife Joanne, a civil rights activist, during her Greensboro visits. Her niece Mina, a social worker, married the celebrated, iconoclastic *New York Post* columnist and *New Republic* editor Murray Kempton, and their visits with a brood of children were lively occasions.[7]

Gertrude honored her mother's adage that "she could never understand how one could ever lose sight of one who had been a friend." She held friendships for a lifetime, staying in touch with her childhood crowd, Smith classmates, and suffrage colleagues. Her engagement books list teas with Sallie Kirby Wilkins, dinners at her sister-in-law Hilda's, or theater or country rides with the McPheeters. She reciprocated visits with her old friend Frances Towers Doggett, still full of book talk.[8]

Gertrude's health was a memento mori. An accident in 1947 left "traveling-bitten" Gertrude on crutches. In 1950 and 1951 she was again undergoing x-ray treatments, and four years later she endured several weeks of an intensive regimen. She began attending Cancer Society meetings and donating to the radiology lab at the University of North Carolina at Chapel Hill. In 1957 she was crippled by a lame knee, missing temple for several months. Her great-niece Leslie noticed that Aunt Gertrude was "falling asleep through most of the service." She apologized, "Most things aren't worth listening to anyway." Meetings interspersed with visits to the physical therapist. Few knew of her condition. In a tribute, Frank Porter Graham spoke poetically that when "the judgment of a disease thought to be fatal at the time was pronounced upon her life," Gertrude simply went about gardening "flowers of the soil and flowers of the spirit." There were limits to her forbearance. In a rare outburst she expressed her pique with "two neighbors & sometime companions," who at first treated her "like a feeble-minded old woman, then like an irresponsible child." She was irritated by their "nauseating unctuous solicitude," so much so that her mental "calm" was riled. She felt the great reward of "growing old" was that one had a right to "a standard of one's own."[9]

Certainly, Gertrude, as she rushed to see and do more, was conscious of her mortality. Friends and family were passing away around her. In 1947 a telegram informed her that Harriet Elliott of Woman's College—Gertrude's confidante, colleague, and traveling companion—had died suddenly while visiting family. They had been so close that Gertrude received letters of condolence. Three years later Harriet Payne died. Gertrude rushed to Pennsyl-

A traveling Harriet Payne (left) and Gertrude Weil (right).
The woman between them resembles Carrie Chapman Catt.
Courtesy of the State Archives of North Carolina.

vania for the funeral. "I have never known a more generous person—too generous for her own good ... too generous even for justice," Gertrude eulogized. "Her very goodness, her unstinting generosity in giving herself, her time and her money, militated against her accomplishing anything for herself." She ended, "I loved her dearly."[10] In 1948, the Weil Department Store burned, and three days later cousin Lionel, hospitalized at Johns Hopkins, died. Turning seventy, she was reconciled to her mortality: "As we get older & approach the end of life ourselves, it all seems to hang together in better proportion, & death takes its place in its natural relation to the rest of our lives. This philosophic sense of proportion, however, does little to assuage our painful sense of loss, which just has to be endured until time dims its acuteness."[11]

Ill health did not temper her wanderlust. In 1949 she sailed again to England, where she renewed ties with cousins Max and Fanny Osborne.

She took in theater, toured the South of England, and then headed to Paris, Zurich, Florence, Perugia, and Bologna. In 1951 she was in Montreal, where she set sail with her old friend Amy Jacobs for three weeks in Israel. They flew to Rome for a side trip through Italy. There they visited Bernard Berenson's Villa I Tatti outside Florence. The art connoisseur was not home, but they were welcomed by his sisters Senda and Bessie, old Smith friends. They continued from Italy through chateau country of the Loire and on to Paris. In 1955 she planned travel to Latin America. In 1956 she embarked on her grandest journey yet, a trip around the world with cousins Emil and Miriam Rosenthal. First stop was Hawaii, and then Japan, India, and the cultural capitals of Europe. In England she toured the countryside once more with Max and Fanny. She caught *Hamlet* at Stratford. As usual with Gertrude, she kept a long list of appropriate gifts, whether a kimono for Hilda Weil or a Picasso print for Nell Hirschberg.[12]

Community Worker

However elderly and diminutive, Gertrude Weil exuded "great presence," townspeople recalled. "Initially she terrified me," confessed newspaper editor Eugene Price. "Very soon I respected and loved her more than any person I have known outside my own family." No task was beneath her. "Meetings engage most of her work-day week," the Goldsboro Woman's Club noted in naming Gertrude Weil its 1953 Woman of the Year. A member of the Wayne County Historical Society, Gertrude, eighty, led junior historians at the Goldsboro Junior High School library. She appeared frequently in the town's churches, whether to engage in interfaith Bible study, explain Judaism, or lecture on Israel. She was an active board member of the Wayne Memorial Hospital, which her Aunt Sarah had helped found, and addressed its graduating classes of nurses. Her engagement books listed patients to visit. In 1957 she participated in the Great Books Program, taking copious notes on Antigone, Plutarch, or Tolstoy.[13]

Always her giving was personal. "Frequently I come across young men and women who tell me that they have gone through college with the financial help of Miss W.," observed Rabbi Solomon Herbst. "Negro preachers have informed that their churches receive substantial contributions from her. She visits sick people at the hospital every day carrying flowers, food & radios for patients who are confined for any length of time etc. etc. Whatever the Temple needs—she provides." When she submitted a guest editorial to the *News-Argus*, Eugene Price discovered her "shuffling around a mountain of stuff" on his desk looking for it. "Young man, what kind of system do you have here?" she demanded. "You don't have a system for order," she admonished, "You have a system for a mess."[14]

With her Goldsboro friend Emma Edwards, she represented Jewish women at the North Carolina Legislative Council. She traveled to Raleigh with Virginia McPheeters to lobby and testify for social welfare legislation. In 1953 she was vice president of the North Carolina Literary and Historical Association and a year later organized a Goldsboro meeting for the North Carolina Society for the Preservation of Antiquities. UNC system president William Friday asked her to serve on the committee to nominate a chancellor for Woman's College, after family friend Edward Graham resigned from the post, beset by personal and institutional controversies. She laughed at finding herself the only woman among the "boys." A niece noted, "They took themselves terribly seriously, and she really didn't." When the League of Women Voters reconstituted itself, Gertrude joined but did not resume her activism. She complimented its effectiveness compared with that of her generation.[15]

One cause dear to Gertrude was the campaign to create a statewide home for the Jewish elderly, which the NCAJW had first proposed. In 1954 when an Old-Aged Home Committee organized, Gertrude joined its board. She was listed as a "Grand" donor, for a minimal contribution of one thousand dollars. In 1962 when Governor Terry Sanford dug the ceremonial shovel for the groundbreaking at a site outside Winston-Salem, Gertrude stood proudly beside him.[16]

Gertrude also joined the campaign to restore the birthplace of Governor Charles B. Aycock as a "perpetual memorial to the son of Wayne who set North Carolina on the way of universal public school education." In 1949 the state created a Charles B. Aycock Memorial Commission, and the governor appointed Gertrude to the board, where she took her customary post as secretary. Aycock had been a poor farm boy, educated at Chapel Hill, who rose to such political heights that his statue stood in the U.S. Capitol to represent the state. Beyond Aycock's public reputation, Gertrude felt a more personal calling. Her father had served on the local school board when Aycock was its chair, and she likely recalled Weil men taking a special train to Raleigh for his gubernatorial inauguration. Gertrude discussed the project over many luncheons with Ivor Aycock Darden, whose family donated the farmstead. An 1893 school house was moved to the property, honoring the "Education Governor" during whose term a new school had risen daily.

Gertrude worked on the Aycock commission over ten years helping to raise funds and lobby the legislature. In 1959 the Aycock birthplace was dedicated. Gertrude could then have not known that memorializing Aycock, which seemed uncontroversial, would become more complicated after revisionist historians examined his role in the violent white supremacist political campaigns of the 1890s and his advocacy of black disfranchisement. If not himself a night-riding Red Shirt terrorist, he was hoisted aloft by racist mobs. Yet, to Gertrude's generation of progressives, Aycock was a hero not just of education but also of racial justice. Frank Porter Graham, also a member of the commission, lauded Aycock for his principled stand when he threatened to resign as governor rather than sign a bill that based school funding on each race's tax revenue. Aycock spoke of "universal education" and expressed his intent to franchise literate blacks and disfranchise illiterate whites after 1908. "We see him historically now, more clearly in the context of better relations between the races in the South," Graham said of Aycock. Governor Terry Sanford hanged Aycock's portrait on his office wall.[17]

Political Wars

After years of frustration pushing for progressive legislation, Gertrude, as she aged, moved leftward, describing herself as a socialist. She read *PM*, the leftist New York daily that was a favorite target of red-baiters. Following its demise in 1948, its Washington correspondent, I. F. Stone, published a weekly of his own. Stone wrote Gertrude thanking her for being his first North Carolina subscriber. Stone, blacklisted during the McCarthy era as a former communist, rebuked Cold War warriors, attacked racial segregation, and advocated a binational Zionism. All were positions dear to Gertrude.[18]

Gertrude was well known to the North Carolina congressional delegation as a lobbyist and letter writer on issues of the day. Her campaigns were often quixotic as she was so often out of step politically. In support of her positions, she would send articles from the *Nation* or *I. F. Stone Weekly*, hardly periodicals of choice for the state's conservative legislators. Republican congressman C. R. Jonas responded disdainfully to her that "people generally have long since learned that they cannot rely upon *The Nation* for objective treatment of controversial issues." In 1955 she wrote perennial Republican presidential candidate Harold Stassen, calling for more trade and exchanges to improve Soviet-American relations. That year, too, she urged ratification of the Genocide Convention. On taxes she was "glad to contribute my share to the support of our government" in contrast to the wealthy others who "are not paying their fair share."[19]

Political progress in North Carolina assuaged whatever disappointment Gertrude felt with national politics after Henry Wallace's failed presidential bid. She supported Governor Kerr Scott's Go Forward campaign, writing him complimentary letters and speaking admiringly of his policies. "His administration as governor has shown him to be a man dedicated to the State and its progress & ambitious for the well being of the so-called 'common man,'" she declared in a speech. She especially appreciated his interest in the rural poor. Scott returned the compliment: "I do know what Gertrude Weil has meant to my own generation of North Carolinians."[20]

In 1949, speaking in Chapel Hill, Kerr Scott shocked the state by appointing Frank Porter Graham to an unexpired U.S. Senate term. In 1950 Graham sought election, but at the last moment conservative Democrats pushed forward a candidate, Willis Smith, a corporate attorney. Graham won the primary but fell 1 percent short of a majority. Smith, egged on by radio announcer Jesse Helms, called for a runoff. The 1950 primary became a watershed in state political history, a war between progressives and conservatives unprecedented since the white supremacist campaigns of the 1890s. Graham was pilloried, spat upon as an alleged socialist and "nigger lover." A widely distributed flier urged, "WHITE PEOPLE WAKE UP!"[21]

Gertrude, though outspoken, had rarely involved herself in partisan politics, but she venerated Dr. Frank and joined his campaign. There she renewed her ties with her old suffragist colleague Gladys Tillett, who had resigned as head of the Women's Division of the Democratic National Committee to work for Graham. The two women joined Graham for a speech from the porch at the Goldsboro Hotel. To support Graham publicly was to risk social and political disapprobation, especially in conservative eastern North Carolina where the Klan stood strong. Gertrude recalled visiting "a country woman who had considerable influence in her community." When Gertrude mentioned Frank Graham, the "good church woman . . . flared up." She told Gertrude, "No, I can't vote for him. . . . He'd have our children going to school with niggers." Graham's opponents rightly sensed that in his heart he was an integrationist despite his reluctance to espouse that belief publicly.[22]

Gertrude's defense of Graham erupted into a newspaper war with her old friend and suffragist colleague Nell Battle Lewis. In her "Incidentally" column in the Raleigh *News and Observer* Lewis had excoriated Graham, demanding that he "unequivocally" state "his opposition to Socialism and Communism" and refute allegations that the Communist Party had a branch at the University of North Carolina at Chapel Hill. Once a fire-breathing liberal, Lewis had become feverishly conservative and anticommunist. She began her Easter column citing George Bernard Shaw's Saint Joan, who burned at the stake. Gertrude reprimanded her, "Considering in retrospect what you used to stand for in the early stages of your writing, it seems incredible that it can be you who are now lighting the faggots" at the feet of the saintly Graham. In her 23 April column, "Just an Old Medieval Fagot-Lighter," Lewis replied scathingly to "Dear Miss Gertrude" and published their correspondence. Their political quarrel did not end their thirty-year friendship. Since the 1930s Lewis had battled mental illness, and Gertrude empathized. Lewis continued to write admiringly of "the eminent and public-spirited" Gertrude and Weil clan.[23]

Frank Graham's defeat in the runoff left Gertrude in "anger." She wrote Graham, "I feel embarrassed and ashamed of my own fellow citizens at our failure in this simple test of our clear vision, good judgment & sense of proportion." To Gladys Tillett, she confessed that the election left her "in the depths of depression." Assurances that Graham would secure an "important appointment" brought no comfort. She responded, "They miss the point. I have never felt sorry for him—only embarrassed & mortified for us voters." The downtrodden farmers and workers to whom Graham had dedicated his life had succumbed to racist and illiberal appeals and abandoned him. The election left North Carolina racially and politically embittered for a generation. The rumored author of Smith's dirty tricks, Jesse Helms, would build a conservative Republican Party in the state while Graham disciple Terry Sanford promised to "get even."[24]

The chance for revenge came in the 1954 Democratic primary for Senate when Kerr Scott with Terry Sanford as campaign manager challenged the conservative establishment. Gertrude again spoke out, employing the southern liberal's coded language that suggested but did not openly state that Scott was a racial progressive. As governor, she said in a speech, "He appreciated not only the basic justice of equalizing the opportunities of town and country people, but also the practical truth that a State's welfare and progress must rest on the health and well-being of all its citizens ... equalizing the opportunities of all our people."[25] Scott won the grudge match, although he, like his two predecessors, died before finishing his term. Frank Porter Graham left the South to become a United Nations mediator. Two years later Gertrude found another hero in Adlai Stevenson but was left lamenting again when his presidential bid failed.

An Honored Life

In 1951 Chi Omega sorority at Chapel Hill presented Gertrude its annual award, the second given. Among those offering congratulations to "one of the most unostentatiously useful citizens of North Carolina" was Nell Battle Lewis. At the "tapping" ceremony, Gertrude was asked to speak on

"Women's Responsibility in the World Today." Gertrude demurred: "Perhaps as women we do have special responsibilities, but for the most part, they . . . seem just human." She addressed her lifelong themes: citizenship, moral obligation, and religious duty.[26] To a secular and materialistic generation, she conveyed a timeless, universal, spiritual message.

In 1952 Woman's College again offered Gertrude an honorary degree. This time she accepted. "I see no point in waiting for a third offer of a kindly crown," she wrote Chancellor Edward Graham, however much he was "endangering the reputation of your College." She could hardly refuse Graham, who blessed her heart. His parents were her cherished friends Edward and Susan Moses Graham, who had perished forty years earlier in the flu epidemic. Gertrude could never resist family and community, and the chancellor invoked the "many beloved spirits who in their time were Weils, Rosenthals, Moses, and Grahams" that can now "rejoice." Gertrude was honored as "a beloved member of one of the great families of North Carolina, a Goldsboro Weil in the finest tradition." She was lauded as "a moving spirit in far-reaching social and political reforms."[27]

In 1955 B'nai B'rith honored Gertrude as "one of the outstanding figures in North Carolinian or American Jewry." The organization "can just hear you protesting and refusing" and promised "no flowery laudatory remarks that will embarrass you." Perhaps she agreed to be "present" after learning that Frank Graham would preside. She did not want to "seem mean and unappreciative." She asked Harry Golden for assurances that the event was nothing more than a "routine girl-woman-citizen-gentleman-or-what-have-you of the year." "Greatly embarrassed," she insisted, "I have never done anything of special distinction or usefulness—never anything more than carry my fair share of responsibility." At the banquet, attended by three hundred, Graham needed seven pages to honor her "radiance of spirit" and "nobly useful life."[28]

Gertrude Weil had little patience for those who would eulogize her. She was too alive in the moment to suffer nostalgia or to rest assured. There was a civil rights revolution in the streets demanding her attention, and always friends and family to welcome at her door. She still had much to learn.

{ 13 }

THE WHOLE OF LIFE
Accolades and Aging

Ensconced in her Victorian manse, Gertrude Weil, in her eighties, put her house in order. She was conscious of her impending mortality. In 1961 her brother Herman died, leaving Janet as her lone sibling. In December 1963, her social calendar listed funerals to attend three days running. In 1969 her sister-in-law Hilda passed away, followed the next month by her old friend Dr. McPheeters. Still she looked forward. Committed to ideals that she knew would not be realized in her lifetime, she was dedicated to educating the coming generation. She directed her work and philanthropy to organizations devoted to racial and economic justice, focusing on local groups like Operation Bootstrap. She wanted Goldsboro to have a new public library. She sat young Jewish families at her table, inspiring them to keep the temple alive. Health problems sometimes left her homebound but did not sap her curiosity or energetic spirit. In 1962 she spent a month in Israel. A year later she was planning a freighter cruise of the Caribbean. The days of intrepid world traveling, however, were ending. In 1964 she was hospitalized at Duke for a month for eye surgery, her second. That, however, did not prevent her at eighty-five from enrolling in a pottery-making class. Then there were more hospital stays. She began dispersing her wealth to charities and placing labels on her household goods designating beneficiaries. She would die as she lived, in her own way, respectful of tradition but not beholden to it.

A Southern Salon

On Goldsboro's Chestnut Street Gertrude held an intellectual salon in the grand European style. Indeed, one guest in 1964 was Baroness Vera Nickolic-Podrinsky, an artist exhibiting at a local gallery. "You are very lucky that I am so far away," the baroness wrote her, "because I'd knock very often at your door!" Luncheon at Gertrude's home was a formal affair indif-

Miss Gertrude aged gracefully into her eighties.
Courtesy of David Weil.

ferent to hurried, mid-century America. "Things had to be done the right way," recalled her great-niece Emily Weil. "You waited in the front parlor until everyone gathered," perhaps with a glass of sherry, and then the guests were ushered into the dining room at a table so long it could seat twenty. Ten or twelve might join her for lunch. The lead guest was the manager of a recently opened factory, a new doctor at the hospital, or that night's Woman's Club lecturer. Favorites like Henry Belk, editor of the *Goldsboro News-Argus*, his successor, Eugene Price, and journalist Moses Rountree were regulars. Places were assigned. For family meals children were seated at card tables, graduating as they aged to the formal table. When all were seated, Gertrude rang a bell or stepped on a buzzer under the carpet summoning Haywood Spearman to bring the first course. "Actually the meal was the excuse for the conversation," Emily Weil recalled. "If you were hungry, you stayed hungry a long time." Her great-nephew Louis Weil recalled one luncheon with his fiancée, Cissy. The two hungry college students sat in the parlor for the customary talk. And talk they did, for so long, he recalled, that Aunt Gertrude forgot the meal. Fortunately, Spearman stepped in and whispered, "Did Miss Gertrude invite you all for lunch?"[1]

"Gertrude generally would have a topic for conversation that she would lead off," Emily Weil explained, "and of course it would go in different directions." The subject might be an article or book that she had recently read or the specialty of her guest professor. Duke historian Anne Firor Scott was joined at one dinner by the mayor and town officials, whom, she noticed, listened respectfully to Miss Gertrude's views. Nell Hirschberg dined with several "attractive and intelligent young couples." They discussed problems of non-Orthodox Jews in Israel and considered Emil Fackenheim's book *Quest for Past and Future: Essays in Jewish Theology.* Whoever the guests, adults or children, she wanted to know what they thought, what they were they doing. "Question after question," her great-nephew Louis recalled. "She just loved to talk to people."[2]

Gertrude's aesthetic sensitivities did not extend to culinary arts. Slender and athletic, she never evinced much interest in food. If Spearman and Mittie Exum had not fed her, a niece speculated, Gertrude may not have eaten. Exum was not a great cook. However beautifully set the table with china and silver, the meal was incongruously prosaic. "If you thought that you were going to get a banquet because there was a cook in the kitchen, you were wrong," Joanne Bluethenthal learned. "There just wasn't much food there." Standard fare was cantaloupe, a small portion of overcooked roast beef, roasted potatoes, and vanilla ice cream with a demitasse of coffee to be spooned over it. Butter was daintily molded into florets. When Cissy Weil expressed pleasure in real butter so prettily presented, Gertrude corrected, "It's margarine." Spearman brought platters to Miss Gertrude, who sliced the meat. Service slowed as she talked and cut, sometimes forgetting what she was about. Other times, portions started large but shrunk as she realized that the food was insufficient to feed everyone. Southern manners prevailed, with each new course called by bell or buzzer. Dishes were not cleared until all had finished.[3]

After dessert, adults gathered again in the parlor for more coffee and talk. Gertrude staked out her position and solicited other views. "She had very definite opinions. She knew what she believed in," Joanne Bluethenthal observed. "You couldn't talk her out of it either unless you were awfully smart." The Miss Gertrude luncheon experience took hours. Children were told to play with toys from a back closet. (No television was in the house.) The toy box was an inheritance from her mother, and its contents evoked a bygone era: a beanbag toss, a wagon full of blocks, and an abacus that no one could decode. Gertrude might join the children as they cavorted in the hallway or back room. Miss Gertrude was not the sort to play on the floor but sat on a footstool. One game she taught the children was tiddledywinks. "She didn't have any real understanding about children," not having any of her own, David Weil observed. "I think she thought of children as being just young versions of adults," he reflected.[4]

Gertrude remained the southern lady. When her great-nephew David became engaged, she offered his fiancée, Emily, a wedding gift of twenty-four silver place settings. Emily "about fainted." Gertrude responded, "Well, certainly twelve," and Emily replied, "Eight should be quite enough." For Gertrude, "Eight would hardly do it." She insisted on giving twelve. "Of course, I never entertained like she did," Emily reflected. "This was a different generation."[5]

Public Citizen

Into her eighties Gertrude remained involved in a dizzying array of causes. She lived her moral principle that life was a whole and not to be compartmentalized. She continued to attend meetings of the North Carolina Conference for Social Service. She was often found at city hall or the courthouse arguing for passage of the school budget or library bonds. She appeared before the commissioners to support plantings for city beautification and to protest when it debated whether to deny televisions to welfare recipients. She headed the campaign for the Community Concert Series and the North Carolina Symphony. Its conductor, Benjamin Swalin, was a houseguest. He solicited her to lobby the legislature for an appropriation. In 1963 she provided leadership to create a community arts council. She advised the Boy's Club and sponsored the Girl Scouts, which she had established through the Wayne Recreational Council. She donated funds to construct an annex to the Wayne County Memorial Community Building to house a rec room for teenagers.[6]

In 1968, having served ten years on the county library board, she was appointed to a committee to build a new library. She collected research literature on a library's community role and the implications for design. Scrap paper attested to extensive number crunching. Study, as always, preceded action. In her ninetieth year she still sat on the board of the Wayne County Boys Club and in 1962 donated two hundred dollars to renovate its school rooms. And, as usual, she served the Red Cross, Goldsboro Community Chest, and later the United Fund. In 1968 she was honorary chair of the United Jewish Appeal campaign in Goldsboro and attended the forty-seventh annual NCAJW convention in High Point. "We were all in awe of her," recalled real estate agent Shelley Leder.[7]

Philanthropies flowed with a focus on childhood and education. Funds went to Antioch College, a favorite of her mother. She contributed several thousand dollars to the Herman Weil Memorial Fund and the Medical School at the University of North Carolina at Chapel Hill. A Gertrude Weil Fund established in 1966 held nearly twenty thousand dollars for the purchase of library books. A dormitory at the Dobbs school for women was named in her honor. "Miss Gertrude in a quiet way was instrumental in lots of things that I don't think people knew about" Shelley Leder observed.[8]

Although not a partisan or ideological feminist, Gertrude remained bonded to her sister activists. In 1962 she traveled to Washington to visit Lavinia Engle, who rose from North Carolina suffrage organizer to a distinguished post with the U.S. Department of Health, Education, and Welfare. She resumed correspondence with her League of Women Voters colleague Mary Cowper, still in Durham, where she served as a children's advocate. Historian Guion Johnson at the University of North Carolina at Chapel Hill, another longtime collaborator, recalled a Goldsboro Woman's Club lecture. Gertrude wrote that she wanted to speak with her, but on that March day it snowed heavily. A friend's son braved the storm to drive her. When they arrived at the Goldsboro Hotel, there awaiting her, sitting erectly, was Miss Gertrude. "Although she was probably 86 or 87 at the time," Johnson recalled, "she had got out in the snow to hear me and to talk to me briefly, and all she wanted to say to me was, that 'If there is ever any money that you need for one of your projects, you let me know.'" Gertrude supported Johnson's work to pass legislation "in behalf of mobilizing woman-power in North Carolina."[9]

Gertrude also foresaw that mobility and assimilation would challenge the local Jewish community's future. "She was smart enough at the time to see where everything was heading," observed Shelley Leder, who moved to Goldsboro in 1963 after marrying a local merchant. In the declining mill and market towns around Goldsboro, Jewish communities would expire and die, especially as the founding generation faded and youth left for college and careers. Gertrude gathered a circle of young Jewish couples—the Leders, Korschuns, Kadises, Samuelsons—inviting them for sherry in her parlor and then to dinner. When they had babies, she paid social calls, gifts in hand. "She really tried to keep us all together in the fold," Leder recalled. "It was real important to her. She told me this: 'It's up to you all ... to keep the congregation going.'"[10]

North Carolina's political climate was changing. Race relations made inevitable if incremental progress. North Carolina was still a poor state, with 37 percent of its people living below the poverty line. Rural blacks were disproportionately dispossessed. Gertrude, as well as other family members, had committed to organizations focusing on racial equality and economic opportunity. In 1960, with the election to the presidency of John F. Kennedy, the national spotlight turned toward poverty, and his successor, Lyndon Johnson, declared war on it. North Carolina, too, underwent its generational political change. Governor Terry Sanford embarked on the most ambitious educational program since Governor Charles B. Aycock, established the North Carolina Fund to combat poverty and racial injustice, and allied himself with President Kennedy, whose Catholicism still disquieted many North Carolinians. Gertrude heard Sanford speak at a Goldsboro school and became a believer. In 1967 she dined with his wife, Margaret, and then joined the governor at a museum reception. Sanford was leading the state into the postindustrial Sunbelt. Mill and market towns like Goldsboro were being eclipsed by the rising academic, medical, and high-tech centers.[11]

Eighty in the Sixties

Gertrude's youthful enthusiasm endured, and the times did not pass her by. In the wake of Vietnam protests, the drug revolution, and second-wave feminism, the term "generation gap" entered the popular lexicon. Visiting her sister, Janet, in 1968, the eighty-eight-year-old Gertrude sat before the television past midnight with her niece Mina Bluethenthal Kempton, watching the Democratic convention in Chicago, where Mina's children were demonstrating with their father, Murray. The protests galvanized the nation. Chicago police responded to the Youth International Party's Festival of Life with a violent crackdown. Janet called from upstairs, "What in the world are you all doing up so late?" Gertrude did not budge from the television, not wanting to miss a thing.[12]

Nor did the sexual revolution pass by the nonagenarian. After Mittie Exum's marriage failed after four days, Gertrude quipped to a niece, "People think that I don't know anything about sex just because I never got married." The niece was shocked at Gertrude's frankness. In 1970, great-niece Sally Kempton published a lead article in *Esquire*, "Cutting Loose," that became an infamous, provocative declaration of radical feminism. Writing both a manifesto and confession, Kempton alleged that feminists were neurotic and antisexual. With her "compulsion to seduce men," Kempton admitted that "she screwed a lot of guys I didn't like." She intimately dissected her parents' marriage as well as her own. "My sexual rage was the most powerful single emotion of my life," she confessed. She questioned women's submission to men, which, she argued, cost women their intellect and autonomy. Janet—Kempton's grandmother—hid the magazine, wanting it out of sight. Not so her older sister, the putative southern lady. Sitting on porch rockers at the Wrightsville Beach house, Gertrude remarked, "What an interesting and important article of Sally's, her generation is so much farther along than we were in the woman's movement in my day. They are dealing with sexual politics which we never did." She added with a laugh, "We never even mentioned the word 'sex.'"[13]

When Duke historian Anne Firor Scott interviewed Gertrude in the early 1960s, second-wave feminists were revolutionizing gender relations. Their cause was passage of the Equal Rights Amendment, which in her day Gertrude's League of Women Voters had strenuously opposed as contrary to women's special needs and interests. Gertrude urged Scott to be "realistic" about her own first-wave generation of women. For the most part, women involved in the suffrage struggle, Gertrude explained, "had not been the least bit feminist and certainly most were not radical," although she could name a few who were both. She talked little of herself but implied that her sympathies lay with the militants. Some years later, lamenting the "depressing" state of international affairs, she quipped, "I grow more radical every year. Who knows? I may live long enough to become a communist."[14] As her life came to its close, Gertrude was likely reflecting on her unfulfilled ideals, that her rationalism and liberalism had not brought about the just, egalitarian society to which she had dedicated her life. Though given to moral outrage, Gertrude had lacked the ideological fervor of the revolutionary. She now expressed sympathy for the radicalism of the new generation.

A Woman of Character

Gertrude lived her final years in ways that would not have been unfamiliar to her mother. She remained a welcoming host in her home, an impresario of temple pageants, and a mainstay of civic charities. One day she was overseeing corsage sales for the temple Sisterhood luncheon at the country club; another day she judged flowers at the annual garden club show. She donated her mother's *point de Venise* lace collar to the home economics department at Woman's College and wrote Frank Graham inquiring about some fine china a friend gave to the university. Gertrude had her eccentricities, her great-nephew David Weil observed, but she was not eccentric. Aging accented her character. She grew deafer, and to compensate her voice became louder and sharper. Although she wore hearing aids, she disliked them and sometimes resorted to an old-fashioned ear horn or a rolled-up newspaper. Her townspeople may have regarded her as "quirky," great-great niece Lesley Weil noted, but all knew that she was "acting out of goodness."[15]

Despite her wealth, Gertrude did not enjoy spending money on herself. She arranged travel on her significant birthdays to forestall a fuss being made over her. Her greatest self-indulgence, other than her travels, was her household help. As a young woman Gertrude had enthusiastically decorated the house, but now she was indifferent. "I don't think she noticed," her great-niece Leslie observed. She did collect mortars and pestles, lining her sideboard and bookcases with them, and she kept a display case of Oriental knickknacks. Generations of books covered walls. For an adolescent who had been fashionable, she now hardly cared. On her travels she made do with two dresses, both dark blue, one to wear while the other was washed, which she adorned with an elegant pin. A woman once complimented Gertrude on her broach. "You know I got this at J. C. Penney," she explained. "Why would you spend money on something like that?" Once her great-niece Emily found her in the maternity department of the Weil store. Asked if she were looking for a gift, Gertrude replied, no, she was shopping for clothes for herself. She felt more comfortable in loose fitting dresses.[16]

Miss Gertrude behind the wheel of a car provoked fear, an effect heightened by the sight of a little lady in a large vehicle. To a motorcycle cop who admonished her that "we have to look out for old ladies like you," she responded that she preferred a ticket to being called "old." Another policeman asked, "Miss Gertrude, do you know what you did wrong and why I followed you home?" She answered, "Well, I assume it's because I went through the red light." Since she saw no one in either direction, what was the point of stopping? For a time she drove a modest American Ambassador, explaining that if it were good enough for Walter Reuther, head of the United Autoworkers, it was good enough for her. The car was so humble and battered that when Haywood Spearman chauffeured her to the governor's mansion in Raleigh, he parked around the corner out of sight. She drove until nearly ninety, despite the family's pleas. She professed no concern for her own life, saying that she had lived long enough, but her niece Betty Weil reminded her that her friend Virginia McPheeters had caused a fatal accident. Gertrude handed over her keys.[17]

An Honorable Life

As an éminence grise, Gertrude entertained a steady stream of historians, biographers, and journalists wanting to document her career. All left fascinated and frustrated. "Please make it clear that I didn't start all the organizations I've been credited with," Gertrude cautioned one reporter. In 1964 Anne Firor Scott sought her out. Governor Sanford had appointed Scott to the state Commission on the Status of Women, and Gertrude was curious. A friendship bloomed. In the 1995 edition of the *Southern Lady* Scott recalled talking hours in Miss Gertrude's living room recounting the "galaxy of North Carolina women in her generation." In 1970 Eli Evans, son of the former Durham mayor E. J. Evans, came to interview her for his pioneering book, *The Provincials: A Personal History of Jews in the South*. She warned him not to romanticize the past.[18] To such interlocutors, she was rarely forthcoming and professed not to see the point of their interest.

Journalist Moses Rountree probed Gertrude for a family history. Shown a chapter, she protested that her portrait was "too extravagant." After she crossed out for a third time every "flattering" reference, Rountree protested. He recalled the conversation:

> "You know I can't let you get by with that," I said. "I might as well say nothing about you at all."
> "There is nothing to say," Miss Gertrude professed. "I have done no more than any good citizen."
> "I happen to know better." I said, "What about the young people you helped send to college?"
> "I don't know of any."
> "Didn't you pay a Rosewood's girl's way through a nursing school?"
> Silence.
> "Didn't you pay the salary of a playground supervisor?"
> "The city paid him."
> "Not at first. And don't deny you paid the salary of a public health nurse until public funds were available. I know that to be a fact. I was working in the county auditor's office at the time."
> "Did I? I don't remember."
> "Do you remember leading the fight for school bond issues?"
> "No. I was just one of many. You are trying to give me more credit than I deserve."

Later, when the *Raleigh News and Observer* published a profile, "A Legend in Her Lifetime," she snapped that it "was really too much ... for me of very retiring disposition."[19]

Librarians coveted her papers. Smith College, a repository of the woman suffrage campaign, inquired in 1964 if she had records "of your own valiant battle in North Carolina," to which Gertrude replied, "I seem to have kept none ... that would throw any light on events and movements." She noted that "UNC and also Duke have made futile gestures." Visiting Gertrude at home, Anne Firor Scott was enthralled: "Papers spilled out of drawers and shelves, tantalizing my historian's soul." Gertrude assured her, "Nothing of any value." After Gertrude's death, her niece Betty Weil found stacks of suffragette and League papers in the attic. When the "nonexistent" papers were donated to the State Archives of North Carolina, they filled 101 file boxes, forty-two linear feet.[20]

Gertrude's claim that she held nothing of historical interest is consistent with her modesty and self-effacement. She guarded her privacy. Gertrude had not saved personal material as fastidiously as her mother had. Yet Gertrude had indeed preserved extensive organizational records. For other possessions, she meticulously prepared for her death with specific bequests. That she neither destroyed her papers nor donated them to an archive suggests that she recognized their value but did not want to be the agent of their preservation. It was the most significant unattended business that she left to her heirs.

In 1962 the honorary degree drama was reprised, this time with Hebrew Union College–Jewish Institute of Religion, the citadel of Reform Judaism. The provost proffering the Doctor of Humane Letters, Rabbi Samuel Sandmel, recalled Gertrude and Leslie warmly from twenty years earlier when he was Hillel director at Chapel Hill. After that, Sandmel had a distinguished academic career, publishing some twenty books. Gertrude responded that she enjoyed *A Jewish Interpretation of the New Testament*, but as for the honorary degree, she recited her familiar refrain: "Whatever made you think of an honorary degree for me! It seems too absurd. ... How would you ever explain such a proposal?" Sandmel answered that "it is our opinion your career is one of great distinction and serves as a model for other Jewish women to emulate in service both to Judaism and to the American community." She protested that her career was "so commonplace," her contribution "so infinitesimal." Why, she would feel like a "charlatan."[21] Her "no" stood.

Gertrude offered but perfunctory resistance in 1964 when Smith College announced that she was among the first class to be honored with Sophia Smith Medals for distinguished alumnae. Smith occupied a warm place in her heart, and its social justice ethos endeared it to her. She attended commencements, never missing an anniversary reunion of the class of '01. At one reunion, once again rooming with her classmate Lillian See, she heard of grape boycotts, an African American studies major, and the doubling of black enrollment. In 1966, at eight-six, she flew to Northampton for her sixty-fifth reunion, where she learned who was in a nursing home and who had broken her pelvis. The vibrant women of her college memories were now "old ladies in wheel chairs and walkers." She reluctantly agreed that "those Smith girls are so smart" to house her alumni class in the infirmary.[22]

Over the years her contributions to Smith scholarship funds totaled in the thousands, the latest of which was to support a student from Greensboro spending a year in Senegal for Operation Crossroads Africa. A letter from the development director began, "Since you have been so generous to Smith." When the college completed a chapel in 1955, Gertrude donated candelabras for Jewish Sabbath services, and fourteen years later she added a menorah. North Carolina had not yet had the critical mass to organize an alumni chapter—she returned from a gathering in Oxford in the 1930s all "aglow" though but four attended—but by 1964 numbers were sufficient for her to travel to Chapel Hill, where a Smith Alumnae Club formed.[23]

Gertrude felt grateful for her awards, but she could never take herself as seriously as those honoring her. In 1965 historian Guy Johnson announced that the North Carolina Human Relations Council was presenting Gertrude its first Howard Odum Award. At the ceremony, as the speaker sang her praises, Gertrude turned off her hearing aid, tuning back on when he finished. When asked to make remarks, she responded, "I'd enjoy this award just as much as if I actually deserved it." She found the occasion embarrassing. Later, she said of the framed certificate, "When I get tired of looking at it, I can put a picture in it." She tucked her Smith Medal in a drawer, feeling that it was not "seemly to keep it out on view." The medallion engraved by eminent artist Leonard Baskin did not impress. She thought the maiden depicted on the front holding an orb was "doing the twist," and the owl on the reverse "looks like a plucked chicken." When the family gathered in 1964 to celebrate Gertrude's eighty-fifth birthday, one youngster ran about with the medal draped from her neck.[24]

Nearing the End

Early in 1971 Gertrude's calendar book listed diminishing engagements. Having passed her ninety-first birthday the previous December, she was losing her customary energy, her heart weakening. Gertrude knew that she was dying. "She had come to peace with her way of living, and her way of thinking, and the things that mattered to her," David Weil observed. She joked to a visiting Anne Firor Scott and her husband that it was hard for her to read a book now that her memory lasted but five minutes. When she could not remember what to call a "jewelry box," she quipped to her niece Betty Weil, "It's the nouns that go first." She laughed. Stopping for a visit, Mina Kempton found Aunt Gertrude lying in bed in a white cotton nightgown, slippers neatly at her side. On her night table was William James's *The Varieties of Religious Experience* and a bone china demitasse cup of coffee. When her friend inquired, "How are you, Miss Gertrude," she responded, "There's nothing wrong with me except old age, and I'm afraid that's terminal!" She laughed again. On her deathbed, she was fascinated to hear her great-grand-niece Lesley describe the open classroom in her elementary school. "Did you like it?" she wanted to know. "Did it work? How did the students behave? How many teachers were there? How did they keep order?" Perhaps on a good day she would have Haywood Spearman take her there—could it be arranged?[25]

Gertrude would die as she had lived, on her own terms, in the very house—if not the very room—in which she was born. Over the years she had inventoried her household possessions, placing the recipient's name beside each vase, table, or bric-a-brac. Her lifestyle had been "modest beyond words," her great-nephew David observed, and she had been depleting her wealth with benefactions. "Toward the end of her life she had used up most of her inheritance," he noted. In her will she left her house and a lot, with a bequest of one hundred thousand dollars, to the family's Wayne Foundation to provide for a "modern, fire-proof library ... becoming to our City." She chose her plot in the Weil family section of Willow Dale Cemetery. She hired workers to tend it, keeping informed of the landscaping. Her desire was to be cremated, though that was not the traditional Jewish burial practice. She purchased the gown that she would wear. She wrote instructions for the funeral: no public ceremony but a simple home service led by the Goldsboro rabbi.[26]

In her final days, a nurse took station outside her downstairs bedroom. She tired easily, and visits were kept short. One nurse told a visitor, "I love her more every day."[27] Perhaps she held on through May when the North Carolina General Assembly, fifty years late, finally ratified the Nineteenth Amendment. Or perhaps she anticipated voting on the county referendum to build the new library. And then there was the Fiftieth Anniversary Convention of the NCAJW being held in mid-May at Oheb Sholom, the place of its birth. She liked to keep up.

On 30 May 1971, Gertrude Weil died in her sleep at four in the morning. Rabbi Tibor Fabian of Oheb Sholom led a home service. The family requested no flowers.

LEGACY

"Not Forgotten" is the title of the column in *Southern Cultures* in which Anne Firor Scott wrote her appreciation "Gertrude Weil and Her Times." Renown was not the ambition of a woman who described herself as of "retiring disposition." A North Carolina Highway Historical Marker stands before her restored home, but she wanted the house demolished to make space for the new public library. In 1984 the University of North Carolina at Chapel Hill hosted the conference "Women Working for Social Change: The Legacy of Gertrude Weil." Profiles continue to be written for encyclopedia and biographical dictionaries. Her achievements are examined in theses, dissertations, and scholarly tomes. The Jewish Women's Archive proclaimed her "A Woman of Valor" and created a website documenting her career.[1] She would dismiss the fuss. Gertrude Weil thought her ideals immortal, but not herself.

Gertrude Weil's public life began when women could not vote; children were exploited as industrial labor; African Americans were segregated and demeaned by racism; Jews were a homeless, pariah people; trade unionists were beaten and shot; alleged criminals were lynched; tuberculosis was rampant; and prisoners—including boys and girls—were brutalized. Twice she lived through a world at war. Over her near century Gertrude either led or facilitated social and political transformations. Spiritually, she wanted a change of hearts, and here her educational efforts have been felt. The parameters of the welfare state are debated today, but not government's responsibility to provide social security, hunger relief, or unemployment assistance. Health care is increasingly regarded as a right. Racial and gender equality have advanced if not yet found level ground. In 2008 North Carolinians voted for an African American as president and women as governor and U.S. senator. Materially, her legacy persists in Goldsboro with its modern public library, including a Gertrude Weil Auditorium, and the Mina Weil Park where children still gambol in the pool. At universities her endowments buy library books and provide scholarships. Thanks to her efforts and generosity, her German family survives into succeeding generations. Still others cite her as an inspiration for a meaningful life in public service. As for flowers: Loleta Powell of Princeton, North Carolina, has cultivated a hybrid iris "Gertrude Weil" and a daylily *Hemerocallis* "Gertrude Weil."

Yet Gertrude always insisted that she had not done much, nothing beyond the ordinary duty of any citizen. A self-proclaimed idealist, she held the torch. Gertrude's ambition was nothing less than systemic change—racial equality and social justice, labor rights and universal education, an end to war and poverty. Considering the categorical imperatives of her ambitions, her achievements could only be ameliorative. To paraphrase a Talmudic injunction, if it was not given to her to complete the task, neither did she desist from it. The family *Bildung*, expressed through her Judaism, imbued in her a perpetual desire to learn more, to expand her moral sympathies. The daughter who followed her mother as a benevolent volunteer, Federation Gertie found in the Women's Clubs a platform to expand her activism into public spheres. Like many progressive women, she believed that securing women's political rights would create social change. She utilized the League of Women Voters to advocate for children, women, and trade unionists, to lay the foundations of the welfare state. Raised in a white supremacist society, she grew increasingly aware that racial equality needed to become more than a topic of discussion and demanded disruptive action. In her inner life, no less than her public career, Gertrude mediated between her progressive ideals and the social conservatism of her native society.

In disparaging her efforts Gertrude implicitly acknowledged falling short. She often expressed frustration, sometimes exhaustion. Her social grace, ready laugh, and quick wit masked her moral anger. That she sympathized with radical youth in her later years reflected her recognition of unfulfilled ideals. Much today would disappoint her. Calling for the equitable distribution of wealth and expending her fortune for the commonweal, she would have despaired for a society befallen to rising income inequality and uneven concentrations of capital. An end to war was but a consummation devoutly to be wished. Her liberal Zionism, too, has been battered by cyclical wars and new migrations that transformed the democratic socialism that had founded Israel.

Gertrude was raised in a prospering Goldsboro, a boom city of a New South. Since her death, its population has fallen with the declining economic fortunes of agrarian eastern North Carolina. Almost 20 percent of its population now lives below the poverty line. Though opportunities are open today for African American students hardly conceivable in her time, Goldsboro High School has largely resegregated. Much of Goldsboro's once thriving downtown has devolved into second-hand stores, boarded windows, and storefront churches. The former high-end Weil Department Store has been rented to a low-end discounter. Gertrude, committed to the City Beautiful movement, would have been cheered by signs of renewal. Her home, whose architecture she deplored, has been returned to its pristine Victorian finery. When the Paramount Theater, built by the Weil brothers in

1882, burned in 2005, her great-nephew David oversaw its restoration into a community arts center.

On a more personal level, the values of family and community that were so dear to Gertrude have also struggled to survive. Typical of small-town Jews—as well as others of her class—family members moved elsewhere for education and careers. The intimate extended family bonds nurtured by Mina and Gertrude attenuated. The visiting and letter writing that kept Weils, Rosenthals, and Oettingers connected in mother's and daughter's day succumbed to mobility and individualism. Intramarriages with East European Jews and intermarriages with Christians ended the German-Jewish ethnic legacy of "our crowd." The Weil family saga gives evidence to the debate as to whether Reform Judaism can survive into a third generation. The North Carolina Association of Jewish Women faded away, excepting its college scholarship fund. Even her Jewish Home for the Aged closed as state Jewry grew too large and pluralistic for a single facility.

Gertrude had spent a lifetime reconsidering the "live issue" of Judaism. The prophetic, universalist Classical Reform Judaism that gave her life value has largely although not entirely yielded to a neotraditional Reform Judaism that renewed emphasis on ritual observance and Hebrew language. Gertrude had foreseen assimilation as inevitable once discriminatory barriers fell and cultural differences abated. To counterbalance these forces, she supported religious education and a commitment to Israel. Those remedies are still advocated today.[2]

In Goldsboro demography has played a larger role than theology in an evolving Judaism. Oheb Sholom congregation, which had centered her life, saw its membership dwindle by the late 1970s as the local economy declined. Soon after her death, its religious school ended, and by the 1980s the temple ceased to function as a house of worship. David and Emily Weil, grandchildren of her brother Leslie, have overseen preservation of its architectural integrity, but the building has now new uses. Its annex is a community kitchen that serves 125 daily, while its sanctuary houses the food pantry. Its reconstituted mission recalls Gertrude's frequent memory of the poor and hungry who came to her mother's door. She would have been saddened by the congregation's demise but uplifted by its community service. And that, indeed, too, was Gertrude Weil's legacy, her imagination in reinventing a Judaism that accommodated to her time and place, as in her rethinking of "What Judaism Means to Me."

Gertrude often said that her ambition was to live her ideals. Idealism has not fared well in the modern lexicon. To know one big thing is now seen as less human than to know many things. Gertrude was born in an era, and in a home, where values were certain and traditional. She was raised in the eternal verities of family, faith, and community, but she was educated in the new sciences of progress. Her argument in advancing social welfare beyond charity and benevolence was the necessity of research and the application of expertise. As an informed citizen who diligently studied the issues, she knew what was best. Indeed, many of her causes—women's suffrage, labor rights, and racial justice—were broadly unpopular in her community and state. White middle-class reformers had to overcome well-justified suspicions of elitism. Gertrude's advocacy of eugenics—a better child in a better environment—came from what is now regarded as utopian thinking that overlooked individual preferences or cultural differences. Eugenics did not endure as her achievement. Reason and science, legacies of the Enlightenment, are now also questioned not as tools of human betterment but for inspiring ideologies of inhumanity like racism or social engineering.

Spirituality balanced Gertrude's rationalism. Like her friend Frank Graham, she had a religious sensibility that affirmed the dignity and sanctity of each individual. Beyond public advocacy, her charity was quiet, personal, and neighborly. She expressed frustration with academic elitists who did not move beyond research and policy into direct action. She was the community organizer speaking in parlors, lobbying legislators, stuffing envelopes, making phone calls, or speaking in school auditoriums. Frequently she was thrust into leadership, but her preferred post was secretary, where she could do the busywork necessary to sustain her causes outside the spotlight. She focused on the personal dimension, which served as a corrective to the maternalism inherent in her elitist position as white, wealthy, and highly educated. Although a student of surveys and statistics, she was more likely to cite case studies and personal stories when making her arguments. Often, she recalled childhood memories of the poor knocking at her mother's door. Money was not just given—the recipient sat down for a talk.

Though certain of her opinions, Gertrude was not an ideologue. At a time when partisans of the left and right adhere to maximal positions, Gertrude's moderation serves as a reproach. Reason tempered her potential for radicalism. In her political work in the suffrage and labor movements she sought the middle ground and worked to reconcile opposing views and factions—although all knew where she stood. She was a "practical idealist."[3] Gertrude spoke most often as a humanist rather than as a feminist. As an affiliated Jew, she held to a universal rather than a parochial religion. A proud southerner who was northern educated and a world traveler, she saw her native region from inside and out. She acknowledge the reality of white supremacy when arguing for the women's vote, but she affirmed black enfranchisement. On child labor reform, she conceded state sovereignty rather than federal action. That self-deprecatory laugh, her ironic wit, would deflate any pretensions to a monolithic truth that would deprive the other of his or her humanity. Gertrude was keenly aware of the difference between her ideals and the ever-present reality, between what should be and what was. In addition to one big thing, she knew many things.

Gertrude lived comfortably with her contradictions as southern lady and New Woman, as a Jew in a Christian society. Those who knew her spoke of how centered, integrated, and seamless her character was. A home girl who lived ninety-two years in her dear Mama and Papa's house, she did not swath herself in the security of childhood but ventured into the world and struggled to change history. The guardian of inherited family values, she eschewed marriage and forged a public career. In defiance of her mother, she had insisted on a college education when such ambitions were thought unnecessary for a woman. She was the historic preservationist whose will provided for the demolition of her century-old home. Her African American servants answered to their first names even as black women sat in her parlor planning the city's desegregation. As a new *southern* woman, she wanted both social progress and social order.[4] She was an exemplary North Carolinian, embracing the competing values that still pull at the state today. In Gertrude they lived in happy harmony. One consolation of old age, she wrote, was that "one can be a conservative with impunity—and—more important—a progressive without embarrassment."[5]

Nearing death, Gertrude was looking forward. Lifelong she aspired to the new day. She committed to education, believing that it would instill feelings for social justice in succeeding generations. Much, she knew, remained to be done. Certainly, Weil descendants notable for philanthropy and public service have been conscious of that family legacy. Aunt Gertrude would have enjoyed the family gathering in Chapel Hill to attend the one hundredth anniversary of the Weil Lectures in American Citizenship.

Perhaps the lasting legacy of Gertrude Weil, then, is the example of her life. At a time when our political culture has turned cynical, her idealism serves as a corrective. At a time when celebrity has become an end in itself, and self-promotion the pathway to success, her modesty and unwillingness to take herself seriously return our attention to the content of her ideals, to economic justice, social equality, and global peace. She had presence. Her eyes sparkled. Everyone said that of her. And amidst all the complexities of the muddled history that she lived through, it was her holding aloft the torch of idealism, lighting the way to a better day, that remains her legacy to us all.

ACKNOWLEDGMENTS

I first express my gratitude to David and Emily Weil of Goldsboro. Beyond their insights and reminiscences, their hospitality, generosity, and community spirit brought to life the continuing presence of their beloved great-aunt. I thank them and Louis Weil of the Wayne Foundation and the Mid-Atlantic Foundation for helping to underwrite this project. Given the family's legacy, as one would expect, the extended Weil family was most gracious and forthcoming.

A Hadassah-Brandeis Institute Research Award provided me support to explore diverse and extensive sources, and I thank Debby Olins, program manager, for administering it. Beyond the generous support, I appreciate the confidence that the grant expressed for a biography of Gertrude Weil.

The State Archives of North Carolina holds 102 file boxes of Gertrude Weil Papers, and its search room became my home away from home. Its staff were not just expert and efficient but most welcoming. I thank them all: Kim Anderson, Gay Bradley, Bill Brown, Doug Brown, Dennis Daniels, Van Evans, Colleen Griffiths, Josh Hager, Larry Odzak, and Alison Thurman. Miss Gertrude would have been pleased that Marty Tschetter is the Local History and Reference Librarian at the Wayne County Public Library. The staffs of the Southern Historical Collection and North Carolina Collection at the University of North Carolina at Chapel Hill, Smith College Archives, and David M. Rubenstein Rare Book and Manuscript Library at Duke University made work a pleasure. The staff at the American Jewish Archives — Dr. Gary Zola, Kevin Proffitt, and Dana Herman — have been, as always, invaluable.

If this book has merit as scholarship, I owe much to the close and informed readings of Joyce Antler, Mark Bauman, and Deborah Dash Moore. When I asked Joyce Antler if she would expand her lecture on Gertrude Weil, "The Torch of Idealism," into a biography, she suggested that I do it. I always benefit from Mark Bauman's critiques even as he burdens me with overlooked sources and dismantles my cherished theses. I am especially grateful to the patient and professional staff of the University of North Carolina Press, particularly Mary Caviness, Gina Mahalek, Jessica Newman, Allison Shay, and Trish Watson. May every writer be so fortunate to have an editor as wise, agreeable, and forbearing as Elaine Maisner.

The Jewish Heritage Foundation of North Carolina has always been supportive, and I thank Henry Greene, Lynne Grossman, Eric Meyers, and Serena Elliott and remember gratefully the late Will Grossman. In the Southern Jewish Historical Society I have found both friends and colleagues, among them Jane Banov and Les Bergen, Janice Blumberg, Bonnie Eisenman, Marcie Cohen Ferris, Anton Hieke, Cathy Kahn, Scott Langston, Phyllis Leffler, Phyllis Levine, Adam Mendelsohn, Beth Orlansky, Dan Puckett, Dale Rosengarten, Stuart Rockoff, Barbara Tahsler, Ellen Umansky, Bernie Wax, Deb Weiner, Hollace and Bruce Weiner, Lee Shai Weissbach, and Stephen Whitfield.

Finally, there are friends and family who tolerated my sins of omission and commission: Barbara and Les Lang, Lynne Grossman, Ed Elkin, Linda Lipsky, Howard Weinberg, Maya and Ben Stang-Weinberg, Jessie Himmelstern, Henry Fuchs and Susan Rakeley, Cece Conway, Rachel Mills, John and Grace Curry, Marvin and Shirley Block, Rebecca Cerese, Lue Simopoulos, Sarah Kittner, Ed Levin, Elsa Liner, David Winer, Diane Wright, Tom Stern, Larry Green, Debbie and Jack Gross, Nancy Clapp and Steve Channing, Kathy Soule, Nancy Strauss, Vic and Sharon Fahrer, Pat and June Grimes, and Joe and Alison Kieber. John Rosenthal contributed to our long history with the jacket portrait. Beginning with my brother's family— Art, Carol, Jonny, Josh, and Lauren Rogoff—I am fortunate in having for relatives Jeffrey Drexler, Agi and Janos Nevai, Paulo and Tessa Drexler Ripper, Suzy Garfinkle, and my Pasternack cousins. I wrote this book consciously to pass along Miss Gertrude's legacy of a meaningful life to future generations. In that regard I think of my daughter, Lilah, and my son, Aaron. I thank them for keeping me humble and well fed with beer, pastry, and cheer.

Researching Miss Gertrude led me to reflect on the lives of women in my life. I recognized in them, too, a Jewish woman's good heart and devotion to family. My grandmother Jenny Cohen Rogoff and her daughter, my aunt Sylvia Pasternack, embraced selflessly those in need. My father, Nathan Rogoff, was very much a mother's son, generous and philanthropic. My grandmother Bertha Drexler was an immigrant who passed along her aspirations for education and high culture to my mother, Sally Drexler Rogoff, a school teacher who, too, was all about family. Writing this biography has made me more appreciative of my wife, Deborah, who embodies many of the virtues that drew me to Miss Gertrude. Her vocation has been the education and uplift from poverty of working-class girls. Thanks to her, my many hours spent before a pixilated screen were also days filled with kindness, laughter, and the beauty of flowers.

NOTES

ABBREVIATIONS

AJA   American Jewish Archives
AWMP   Alexander Worth McAlister Papers, Southern Historical Collection,
         University of North Carolina at Chapel Hill
ESAC   Equal Suffrage Amendment Collection, State Archives of North
         Carolina, Raleigh
ESANCP   Equal Suffrage Association of North Carolina Papers, State Archives
         of North Carolina, Raleigh
FPGP   Frank Porter Graham Papers, Southern Historical Collection,
         University of North Carolina at Chapel Hill
GWP   Gertrude Weil Papers, State Archives of North Carolina, Raleigh
MOCP   Mary O. Cowper Papers, Rubenstein Rare Book and Manuscript
         Library, Duke University, Durham, NC
NAWSA   National American Woman Suffrage Association
NCAJW   North Carolina Association of Jewish Women
NCC   North Carolina Collection, University of North Carolina at Chapel Hill
NCERAP   North Carolina Emergency Relief Administration Papers, State
         Archives of North Carolina, Raleigh
SJFP   Southgate Jones Family Papers, David M. Rubenstein Rare Book and
         Manuscript Library, Duke University, Durham, NC
WFP   Weil Family Papers, Southern Historical Collection, University of
         North Carolina at Chapel Hill

PREFACE

1. Anne Firor Scott, "Not Forgotten: Gertrude Weil and Her Times," *Southern Cultures*, 13, no. 1 (2007): 101.

2. Ibid., 89.

3. Ibid., 88.

4. Frank Graham, "We Come to Gertrude Weil in the Fullness of Our Hearts," B'nai B'rith dinner tribute, 1955, WFP; Marion Roydhouse, "The 'Universal Sisterhood of Women': Women and Labor Reform in North Carolina, 1900–1932" (Ph.D. diss., University of North Carolina at Chapel Hill, 1980), 263; Alexander Leidholdt, *Battling Nell: The Life of Southern Journalist Cornelia Battle Lewis, 1893–1956* (Baton Rouge: Louisiana State University Press, 2009), 60, 256.

5. Anne Firor Scott, *The Southern Lady: From Pedestal to Politics, 1830–1930* (Charlottesville: University Press of Virginia, 1995), x–xi; G. B. Morris to Gertrude Weil, 18 Sept. 1923, GWP.

6. Scott, *Southern Lady*, 210–11. I thank Joyce Antler for elucidating the doctrine of maternalism.

7. Louis D. Rubin Jr., *A Gallery of Southerners* (Baton Rouge: Louisiana State

University Press, 1982), xii. See Melissa Klapper, *Ballots, Babies, and Banners of Peace: American Jewish Women's Activism, 1890–1940* (New York: New York University Press, 2013), 10.

8. I thank Joyce Antler for highlighting "the torch of idealism," the subtitle of her popular lecture on Gertrude Weil. NCAJW, *Year Book*, 1926; Gertrude Weil, "Address of President, Fifth Annual Conference—Durham, 28 Feb. and 1 Mar. 1926," typescript, GWP; Gertrude Weil to A. W. McAlister, 29 Dec. 1944, AWMP.

9. Gertrude Weil to Mary O. Cowper, 9 Oct. 1927, GWP.

10. Eli Evans, *The Provincials: A Personal History of Jews in the South* (Chapel Hill: University of North Carolina Press, 2005).

11. See William Link, *North Carolina: Change and Tradition in a Southern State* (Wheeling, WV: Harlan Davidson, 2009), 314, 329; Anthony Badger, *North Carolina and the New Deal* (Raleigh, NC: Department of Cultural Resources, 1981), 91; Rob Christensen, *The Paradox of Tar Heel Politics: The Personalities, Elections, and Events That Shaped Modern North Carolina* (Chapel Hill: University of North Carolina Press, 2008); Paul Luebke, *Tar Heel Politics: Myths and Realities* (Chapel Hill: University of North Carolina Press, 1990). I thank Deborah Dash Moore for the insight of a "rooted cosmopolitan."

12. "Wayne's Weils," *State*, 21, no. 25 (21 Nov. 1953): 8.

13. Amy Meyers Krumbein, interview by the author, 5 June 2011.

CHAPTER 1

1. Emily Rose, *Portraits of Our Past: Jews of the German Countryside* (Philadelphia: Jewish Publication Society, 2001), 161.

2. Ibid., 211–12, 282; Stefan Rohrbacher, "From Württemberg to America: A Nineteenth-Century German-Jewish Village on Its Way to the New World," in Jonathan Sarna, ed., *The American Jewish Experience* (New York: Homes and Meier, 1997), 52. Quote from Amos Elon, *The Pity of It All: A Portrait of the German-Jewish Epoch, 1743–1933* (New York: Picador, 1993), 19, 273.

3. Quoted in Amos Elon, *The Pity of It All: A Portrait of the German-Jewish Epoch, 1743–1933* (New York: Picador, 1993), 19, 273; George Mosse, "Jewish Emancipation: Between *Bildung* and Respectability," in Jehuda Reinharz and Walter Schatzberg, eds., *The Jewish Response to German Culture: From the Enlightenment to the Second World War* (Hanover, NH: University Press of New England, 1985), 1–16. Weil notebook, GWP.

4. Yetta and Jacob's daughter Jeanette Weil arrived in Baltimore with items worth 111 florin. Bill of Lading for Jeanette Weil (later Oettinger), Jewish Museum of Maryland; Kala Rosenthal Herlands, interview by the author, 7 Apr. 2011. The border towns were Oberdorf, Oettingen, Nordlinger, Pfaumloch, and Katzenstein. The northern Bavarian communities were Furth, Ulm, and Uhfeld. Moses Rountree, *Strangers in the Land: The Story of Jacob Weil's Tribe* (Philadelphia: Dorrance, 1969), 103.

5. Rountree, *Strangers in the Land*, 103.

6. Ibid., 20; Henry Weil to Mimmi [Mina] Rosenthal, 3 Feb. and 17 June 1874.

7. See Hasia Diner, *Roads Taken: The Great Jewish Migrations to the New World and the Peddlers Who Forged the Way* (New Haven, CT: Yale University Press, 2015).

8. For one version of the Marcus quip, see "Where the Jews Came From: Background," www.americanjewisharchives.org/exhibits/gv/print/scholar-03.html (accessed 7 June 2016); *Goldsboro Messenger*, 3 Jan. 1887. Oettinger had a partner, Moses Frankfort of Norfolk, who lived in Baltimore while Jake Rosenthal, a relative who settled in Raleigh, managed his Goldsboro store.

9. Rose, *Portraits of Our Past*, 151. The Oettingers were from Nordlingen, on the Bavarian side of the Württemberg border.

10. Hugh Lefler, *History of North Carolina* (New York: Lewis Historical Publishing, 1956), 587, 388–89, 590–92.

11. Jewish peddlers include Aaron Lippman, Alex Strouse, and the Bloomingdale brothers, who achieved department store immortality in New York. The storekeeper and peddler Lippman is likely the Aaron Lippitz listed in the 1850 census.

12. Lefler, *History of North Carolina*, 388–89.

13. German Jewish storekeepers were H. M. Strouse, Falk Odenheimer, and Moses Einstein. Among family friends were members of Cobb, Daniels, Dortch, Hooper, Graves, Hollowell, Kirby, Borden, and Robinson families. Some community folklore claims the well was spiked with ice water.

14. North Carolina, vol. 14, p. 28; vol. 2, p. 41; vol. 3, p. 72F; vol. 4, p. 194, R. G. Dun & Co. Credit Report Volumes, Baker Library Historical Collections, Harvard Business School; J. M. Hollowell, *War-Time Reminiscences and Other Selections* (Goldsboro, NC: Goldsboro Herald, 1939), 9–10.

15. John Barrett, *The Civil War in North Carolina* (Chapel Hill: University of North Carolina Press, 1963), 346–48.

16. North Carolina, vol. 14, p. 14, R. G. Dun & Co. Credit Report Volumes. The sectarian test had been commonly ignored, and the state removed it in 1868.

17. Rountree, *Strangers in the Land*, 4, 7–10. Weil enterprises included the Building and Loan Association of Goldsboro, Goldsboro Ice Company, Carolina Rice Mills, Goldsboro Oil Company, Pioneer Tobacco Company, Wayne Agricultural Works, Goldsboro Savings Bank, and Goldsboro Storage and Warehouse Company.

18. Amy Crow, "'In Memory of the Confederate Dead': Masculinity and the Politics of Memorial Work in Goldsboro, North Carolina 1894–95," *North Carolina Historical Review* 83, no. 1 (2006): 31–32, 50.

19. Paul Gaston, *The New South Creed: A Study in Southern Myth-Making* (New York: Knopf, 1970), 4. Text of Grady's 1886 New South speech can be found at http://www.learnnc.org/lp/editions/nchist-newsouth/5489 (accessed 26 May 2016).

20. Quoted in Rountree, *Strangers in the Land*, 4.

21. Hugh Johnston Jr., *Oettinger's the Dependable Store*, typescript, 1976, Wilson County Public Library, Wilson, NC; Emil Rosenthal Papers, State Archives of North Carolina, Raleigh; Gertrude Weil to Mina Weil, 22 Sept. 1900, GWP.

22. Rountree, *Strangers in the Land*, 18–19.

23. Henry Weil to Mina Rosenthal, 14 Dec. 1873, GWP; Rountree, *Strangers in the Land*, 16.

24. Rountree, *Strangers in the Land*, 53–54; Eva Rosenthal to My dear, dear Children [Henry and Mina Weil], 9 Sept. 1875, GWP.

25. Josephus Daniels, *Tar Heel Editor* (Chapel Hill: University of North Carolina Press, 1939), 68, 106, 136. Kate Connor's son, R. D. W. Connor, founded the State Archives of North Carolina and was the first Archivist of the United States. Josephus Daniels later assisted Jewish refugees from Nazi Europe and spoke out as a Christian Zionist.

26. Jonathan Daniels to Gertrude Weil, 26 Dec. 1943; Collier Cobb to Mina Weil, 6 Feb. 1933, GWP.

27. Mina Rosenthal to Henry Weil, 24 Dec. 1887, GWP; Maurice Weinstein, ed., *Zebulon B. Vance and "The Scattered Nation"* (Charlotte, NC: Wildacres Press, 1995), 93.

28. The *Jewish South*, 19 Mar. 1878, reports that in nearby Tarboro D. Lichtenstein waited a year since his fiancé Hanna Zanders was but fifteen. See Leonard Rogoff, *Down Home: Jewish Life in North Carolina* (Chapel Hill: University of North Carolina Press, 2010), 90–91; Mina Weil to Henry Weil, 14 May 1874, GWP.
29. Henry Weil to Mina Rosenthal, 8 and 11 Dec. 1873 and 28 Jan. 1874; Mina Rosenthal to Henry Weil, 10 Dec. 1873 and 1 Feb. 1874, GWP.

30. Rountree, *Strangers in the Land*, 119; Henry Weil to Gertrude Weil, 10 Apr. 1899, GWP.

31. William Rosenau, *A Brief History of Congregation Oheb Shalom* (Baltimore: Guggenheimer, Weil and Co., 1903), 11.

32. *Goldsboro Argus*, undated newspaper clipping describing wedding of Edna Weil and Adolph Oettinger, GWP.

33. Rountree, *Strangers in the Land*, 115–25.

34. *Goldsboro Messenger*, 7 Dec. 1914. See Mary Hooper to Mina Weil, 27 Nov. 1885; Mattie Rosenthal to Mina Weil, 31 Jan. 1886, GWP. Gertrude was born in December and Herman in January, so they were closer in age than birth years suggest.

35. Hilda Einstein Weil, "The Lives of Leslie and Hilda Weil, Dedicated to My Five Children," 1950, typescript, 2, WFP.

36. Rountree, *Strangers in the Land*, 20; Leslie Weil to Mina Weil, 6 Dec. 1893; Eva Rosenthal to my dear Children, 2 Oct. 1881; Hattie Spier to Mina and Henry Weil, n.d.; Mary E. Hooper to Mina Weil, 27 Nov. 1885; Mattie Rosenthal to Mina Weil, New York, 31 Jan. 1886; Gertrude Weil to Mamma and Pappa, 3 June 1891, GWP. For neurasthenia as a specifically Jewish, feminine syndrome, see Ellen Umansky, *From Christian Science to Jewish Science: Spiritual Healing and American Jews* (Oxford: Oxford University Press, 2005), 8–9.

37. Henry Weil to Mina Rosenthal, 9 and 13 Feb. and 22 Apr. 1874, GWP; James Leloudis, *The New South: Pedagogy, Self, and Society in North Carolina, 1886–1920* (Chapel Hill: University of North Carolina Press, 1996), 99.

38. Henry Weil to Gertrude Weil, 9 Oct. 1898, GWP; Weil, "Lives of Leslie and Hilda Weil."

39. Zebulon B. Vance, *The Scattered Nation* (New York: Marcus Schnitzer, 1916), 54; Rountree, *Strangers in the Land*, 86–88.

40. Weil, "Lives of Leslie and Hilda Weil," 2.

41. Steven J. Whitfield, "The Braided Identity of Southern Jewry," *American Jewish History* 77, no. 3 (1988): 363. In Wilmington, NC, shellfish, tongue, and ice cream were served at Temple affairs. For Reform Judaism's refutation of the kosher laws, see "Reform Judaism: The Pittsburgh Platform (November 1885)," Jewish Virtual Library, http://www.jewishvirtuallibrary.org/jsource/Judaism/pittsburgh _program.html (accessed 4 Sept. 2012).

42. Leslie Weil to Gertrude Weil, 9 Dec. 1892; *The Book of Thoughts* (London: Marcus Ward, n.d.)—this autograph book, which asks writers to fill in responses to favorites in music, art, and literature, as well as life's big questions, dates to circa 1876–92, Gertrude's childhood years; Sol Weil to Henry and Mina Weil, 24 Mar. 1875, GWP. See Anton Hieke, *Jewish Identity in the Reconstruction South: Ambivalence and Adaptation* (Berlin: DeGruyter, 2013), 306–9. Hieke downplays the persistence of German culture among immigrants. He finds that the characterization of the second wave as "German" overstates its national origins. That is not to say that German nationality did not persist among the Weils, although the family's German culture faded over generations.

43. Mina Weil to Henry Weil, 14 and 27 Feb. 1874; Mina Weil to Leslie Weil, 13 and 17 May 1893; Gertrude Weil to My Dear Ones, 12 Apr. 1898, GWP.

44. Melissa Klapper, *Jewish Girls Coming of Age in America, 1860–1920* (New York: New York University Press, 2005), 70.

45. Rountree, *Strangers in the Land*, 95–96.

46. Gertrude Weil to my dear ones, 11 Sept. 1892; Henry Weil to Mina Weil, 27 July 1893, GWP.

47. Young Folk's Literary Society, *Literary Times*, 1890–91, GWP.

48. See Klapper, *Jewish Girls*, 188; Etta Spier to Helen and Gertrude Weil, 27 Nov. 1898, GWP.

49. Frank Porter Graham, "We Come to Gertrude Weil," WFP.

50. Klapper, *Jewish Girls*, 32; Henry Weil to Gertrude Weil, 7 Dec. 1898 and 15 Jan. 1899; Gertrude Weil to Henry Weil, 12 June 1900, GWP.

51. Henry Weil to Mina Weil, 27 Mar. 1876, GWP; Rountree, *Strangers in the Land*, 88; Paula Hyman, *Gender and Assimilation in Modern Jewish History: The Roles and Representation of Women* (Seattle: University of Washington Press, 1995), 111. For Herman Park, see Rountree, *Strangers in the Land*, 48–52.

52. Anne Firor Scott, *The Southern Lady: From Pedestal to Politics, 1830–1930* (Charlottesville: University Press of Virginia, 1995), 141; Faith Rogow, *Gone to Another Meeting: The National Council of Jewish Women* (Tuscaloosa: University of Alabama Press, 1993), 61.

53. Hilda Weil, "Recollection of Youthful Days Spent in Goldsboro" *Goldsboro News-Argus*, 13 Aug. 1954; Charity Organization Society of Goldsboro, NC, annual report, 1916, GWP.

54. "For Woman's College, University of North Carolina," remarks delivered at the dedication of the Mina Weil Dormitory at the Woman's College, typescript, 14 Sept. 1941, Wayne County Public Library, Goldsboro, NC; Rountree, *Strangers in the Land*, 96, 116, 135.

55. Mina Weil to Leslie Weil, 19 Nov. 1893, GWP.

56. Mina Weil to Gertrude Weil, 22 Apr. 1900; Mina Weil to Janet Weil, 3 Oct. 1911, GWP.

57. Chatauqua Circle [Goldsboro] Minutes and notebooks, ca. 1892–95, 25, 2 May, n.y.; 5 Oct., 8 Nov. 1893, GWP. The Ladies Benevolent Society formed in 1884 and a year later called itself the Hebrew Ladies Aid Society.

58. Henry Weil to Mina Rosenthal, 17 Feb. 1874, GWP.

59. Fr. Lawrence Newman to H. Weil and Brothers, Goldsboro, NC, n.d., WFP.

60. Mina Weil to Gertrude Weil, 21 Sept. 1900; Henry Weil to Mina Rosenthal, 12 Jan. 1874, GWP.

61. Henry Weil to Mimmi [Mina] Weil, 12 Jan. 1874 and 25 Nov. 1875; Mina Weil to Gertrude Weil, 21 Sept. 1900; Gertrude Weil to Leslie Weil, 17 Mar. 1893; Leslie Weil to Henry and Mina Weil, 2 Sept. 1881; Solomon Weil to Henry and Mina Weil, 7 May 1875; Leslie Weil to dear ones, 12 Mar. 1892; Gertrude Weil to Leslie Weil, 17 Mar. 1893, GWP; Mina Weil to Hilda and Leslie Weil, 9 Apr. 1930, WFP.

62. Mina Rosenthal to Henry Weil, 15, 22, and 24 Feb. 1874, GWP.

63. *Goldsboro Messenger*, 7 Jan. 1884.

64. "The Programme for the Dedication of Temple Oheb Sholom of Goldsboro, North Carolina, Friday, December 31, 1886," WFP; *Goldsboro Daily Argus*, 1 Jan. 1887.

65. See Emily Weil, *Temple Oheb Sholom, Goldsboro, North Carolina* (Goldsboro, NC: Temple Oheb Sholom, 2000), 7, 8; *Goldsboro Daily Argus*, 1 Jan. 1887.

66. Amy Meyers Krumbein, interview by the author, 5 June 2011.

67. "Digest of the Minutes of the Oheb Sholom Congregation, 1883–1958," typescript, 3, 5, AJA.

68. Ibid., 6, 7; Rountree, *Strangers in the Land*, 71–74.

69. Karla Goldman, *Beyond the Synagogue Gallery: Finding a Place for Women in American Judaism* (Cambridge, MA: Harvard University Press, 2000), 2, 9. See Hyman, *Gender and Assimilation*.

70. Henry Weil to Mina Weil, 28 Sept. 1895; Henry Weil to Mina Rosenthal, 6, 17 Feb. 1874; Mina Weil to Janet Weil, n.d. Feb. 1910, GWP.

71. Gertrude Weil Diary, 13 Jan. and 5 Feb. 1891; Gertrude Weil to Leslie Weil, 17 Mar. 1879, GWP; Klapper, *Jewish Girls*, 179.

72. Gertrude's statement on prejudices quoted in Rountree, *Strangers in the Land*, 129; H. Weil & Bros. ledger, WFP. See Hieke, *Jewish Identity*; Henry Weil to Mimmi [Mina] Rosenthal, 13 May 1874; Henry Weil to Mimmi [Mina] Weil, 29 Apr. 1873; Rountree, *Strangers in the Land*, 24–25, 29–30; Henry Weil to Mimmi [Mina] Rosenthal, 6 Aug. 1874; Henry Weil to Gertrude Weil, 3 Nov. 1896, GWP.

73. Mina Weil to Gertrude Weil, 2, 9 Nov. 1898, GWP; Jim Leloudis, *Schooling the New South: Pedagogy, Self, and Society in North Carolina, 1880–1920* (Chapel Hill: University of North Carolina Press, 1999), 137; *Jewish South*, 24 Nov. 1898.

74. Susie Fulghum to Gertrude Weil, 4 Mar., 1896; Hilda Weil to Gertrude Weil, 12 Dec. 1900; Gertrude Weil to My Dear Ones, 23 Oct. 1896, GWP; Patrick Valentine, *The Rise of a Southern Town: Wilson, North Carolina, 1849–1920* (Baltimore: Gateway Press, 2002), 73.

75. Leslie Weil to Hilda Einstein, Sept 24, 1893, WFP; Henry Weil to Mina Rosenthal, 17 Feb. 1874; Rosa Kaufman to Mina Weil, 30 Nov. 1894, GWP; Scott, *Southern Lady*, 170, 176–77.

CHAPTER 2

1. Hugh Lefler, *History of North Carolina* (New York: Lewis Historical Publishing, 1956), 651, 642; Melissa Klapper, *Jewish Girls Coming of Age in America, 1860–1920* (New York: New York University Press, 2005), 74; Charles Orr Jr., *Charles Brantley Aycock* (Chapel Hill: University of North Carolina Press, 1961), 73; *Goldsboro Messenger*, 5 Sept. 1881; James Leloudis, *The New South: Pedagogy, Self, and Society in North Carolina, 1886–1920* (Chapel Hill: University of North Carolina Press, 1996), 107, xiii.

2. In 1894 Henry Weil had given the University of North Carolina at Chapel Hill a copy of Heinrich Graetz's *History of the Jews*. Five years later a $1,000 donation heated and decorated the library and created the Henry Weil Collection in Political and Social Science.

3. Mina Weil to Leslie Weil, 19 Nov. 1893; Gertrude Weil to Leslie Weil, 17 Mar. 1893; Leslie Weil to Gertrude Weil, 6 Mar. 1892; "Smith College (Gertrude), Examinations, Themes, Etc., 1900–1901," GWP; Leloudis, *New South*, 58.

4. Hilda Weil, "Recollection of Youthful Days Spent in Goldsboro," *Goldsboro News-Argus*, 13 Aug. 1954.

5. This report dates to 1909, after Gertrude graduated, but the issue of prayer and Bible reading persisted for decades as did Jewish protests. See B'nai B'rith Leopold Zunz Lodge No. 364 minutes, 1886–1970, AJA.

6. *Round Table*, 8 Dec. 1893; *Goldsboro Weekly Argus*, 30 May 1895.

7. Joan Johnson, *Southern Women at the Seven Sister Colleges: Feminist Values and Social Activism, 1875–1915* (Athens: University of Georgia Press, 2008), 3; Klapper, *Jewish Girls*, 34; Hilda Einstein Weil, "The Lives of Leslie and Hilda Weil, Dedicated to My Five Children," 1950, typescript, 2, WFP.

8. Sarah Wilkerson-Freeman, "The Emerging Political Consciousness of Gertrude Weil: Education and Women's Clubs, 1879–1914" (M.A. thesis, University of North Carolina at Chapel Hill, 1986), 7–8; *Round Table*, 22 Dec. 1893.

9. Klapper, *Jewish Girls*, 98–99, 103–04; survey quoted in Lisa Aronson, "After College, at Home: One Hundred Round Robin Letters from Smith College Women, 1908–1912," undated typescript, 3, Smith College Archives, Northampton, MA. See Joyce Antler, *The Journey Home: How Jewish Women Shaped Modern America* (New York: Schocken, 1997), 56.

10. Handbook, Columbia University in the City of New York, Teacher's College, 1898–99, 11; Henry Weil to Mina Weil, 5 Oct. 1895, GWP.

11. Katie (Kala) Strauss to My Beloved Sister Mina, 31 Oct. 1895; Horace Mann School Announcement, 1896–97; Susie Fulghum to Gertrude Weil, 4 Mar. 1896, GWP; Caroll Smith-Rosenberg, "The Female World of Love and Ritual: Relations between Women in Nineteenth-Century America," in Linda Kerr and Jane Sherron De Hart, eds., *Women's America: Refocusing the Past* (New York: Oxford University Press, 2004), 168–69, 171.

12. Gertrude Weil to My Dear Ones All, 31 Oct. 1895 and 8 Feb. and 16 Apr. 1896, GWP. "Mr. Untermeyer" was likely Samuel Untermyer, a prominent Jewish lawyer and political leader.

13. Gertrude Weil to My Dear Ones, 5 Oct. and 23 Nov. 1895 and 23 Mar. 1896, GWP. Temple Emanuel, largest synagogue in America, was a bastion of Classical Reform Judaism located at 5th Avenue and 43rd Street. Rabbi Kaufmann Kohler's Temple Beth-El was located at 5th Avenue and 76th Street.

14. Gertrude Weil to My Dear Ones, 10 Nov. 1895 and 1 Feb. 1896, GWP.

15. Gertrude Weil to My Dear Ones, 16 Nov. and 1 Dec. 1896 and 20 Apr. and 19 May 1897, GWP.

16. Gertrude Weil to My Dear Ones, 13 Dec. 1895, 28 Feb. and 17 May 1896, 18 and 21 Mar. and 26 June 1897, GWP.

17. Gertrude Weil to My Dear Ones, 5, 18, and n.d. Mar. 1897, GWP.

18. See Wilkerson-Freeman, "Emerging Political Consciousness of Gertrude Weil," 22–23; Gertrude Weil to Dear Ones, 7 June 1897; Mina Weil to Gertrude Weil, 9 and 19 May 1897, GWP.

19. Wilkerson-Freeman, "Emerging Political Consciousness of Gertrude Weil," 24.

20. See "Smith College (Gertrude)."

21. Gertrude Weil to Mina Weil, 8 Nov. 1897, 31 Jan., 6 Mar., and 30 Oct. 1898, and 16 Jan. 1899; Mina Weil to Gertrude Weil, 2 Nov. 1898, GWP; Helen Horowitz, "Smith College and Changing Conceptions of Educated Women," in Ronald Story, ed., *Five Colleges: Five Histories* (Amherst: University of Massachusetts Press, 1992), 86, 91.

22. Mina Weil to Gertrude Weil, n.d. Oct. 1897, 22 Sept. 1898, and n.d. 1900; Gertrude Weil to Mina Weil, 12 Jan. 1900, GWP; Smith-Rosenberg, "The Female World of Love and Ritual," 175.

23. Mina Weil to Gertrude Weil, n.d. Oct. 1897, 22 Sept. 1898, and n.d. 1900; Gertrude Weil to Mina Weil, 12 Jan. 1900, GWP.

24. Gertrude Weil to My Dear Ones, 7 Oct. 1898, n.d. and 30 Jan. 1900; Mina Weil to Gertrude Weil, 20 Sept. 1899; Gertrude Weil to addressee unknown, circa 1898, GWP.

25. Mina Weil to Gertrude Weil, 13 Oct. 1897; Gertrude Weil to My Dear Ones, 7 Oct. 1897 and 17 Oct. 1898, GWP.

26. Wilkerson-Freeman, "Emerging Political Consciousness of Gertrude Weil," 30–31. See "Smith College (Gertrude)"; Gertrude Weil to My Dear Ones, 21 Jan. 1900, GWP.

27. Wilkerson-Freeman, "Emerging Political Consciousness of Gertrude Weil," 30–31. See "Smith College (Gertrude)."

28. "Smith College (Gertrude)."

29. Gertrude Weil to Mina Weil, 27 Apr. 1898 and 4 Nov. 1900; Gertrude Weil to Henry Weil, 4 May 1898; Gertrude Weil to My Dear Ones, 9 May 1898, GWP.

30. Gertrude Weil to My Dear Ones, 21 Jan. 1900 and 15 Jan. 1901; Anna Moffatt to Gertrude Weil, 17 Feb. 1901; "Music Programme, Class of Ninety-Nine," 19 June 1899; Program for *White Aprons*, Smith College, 21 Mar. 1901, GWP.

31. "Home Culture Clubs," privately printed pamphlet, n.d., GWP.

32. Gertrude Weil to Dear Ones, 11 Feb. 1900; Mina Weil to Gertrude Weil, n.d. and 28 Oct. 1900, GWP.

33. Gertrude Weil to Mina Weil, 2 Dec. 1900; Mina Weil to Gertrude Weil, 9 and 10 Oct. 1898; Gertrude Weil to My Dear Ones, 25 Oct. 1898 and 12 Mar. 1900, GWP.

34. The poem appeared on a dinner card for the senior class. See Gertrude Weil to Dear Ones, 30 Nov. 1900, GWP. Her roommates were Anna Collins, Louise Kilton, and Jessica Gray. Historian George Tindall and sociologist John Shelton Reed define white Southerners as an ethnic group with their distinct cuisine, music, dialect, religiosity, attitude, flag, and anthem. See George Tindall, *The Ethnic Southerners* (Baton Rouge: Louisiana State University Press, 1976) or John Shelton Reed, *One South: An Ethnic Approach to Regional Culture* (Baton Rouge: Louisiana State University Press, 1982).

35. Martha Cosley[?] to Gertrude Weil, 28 Aug. 1901; Gertrude Weil to My Dear Ones, 30 Oct. 1898 and 29 Aug. 1899, GWP.

36. Gertrude Weil to My Dear Ones, 21 Mar. 1901; Leslie Weil to Gertrude Weil, 2 July 1900, 31 Jan. 1899, GWP.

37. Gertrude Weil to Mina Weil, 31 Jan. 1899 and 1 Feb. 1900, GWP.

38. Gertrude Weil to Mina Weil, 31 Jan. and 4 Oct. 1899 and 1 Feb 1900; Gertrude Weil to no addressee, 11 June 1900, GWP.

39. Mina Weil to Gertrude Weil, 8 Dec. 1897; "The Nineteen-Wonder or Ten Years After," Smith Alumnae Class of 1901 10th Reunion, Northampton, MA, brochure, 17 June 1911, GWP; Wilkerson-Freeman, "Emerging Political Consciousness of Gertrude Weil," 33: Johnson, *Southern Women*, 4–5.

40. *Goldsboro Argus*, 10 May 1898. Mina shared with Gilman a disposition toward nervous disease. Although Gilman wrote sympathetically of "the hideous injustice of the Christian to the Jew," after living in New York she became anti-Semitic. Charlotte Perkins Gilman, *Women and Economics* (Berkeley: University of California Press, 1998), 78.

41. Gertrude Weil to Dear Ones, 12 and 20 Nov. 1898, GWP.

42. Mina Weil to Gertrude Weil, 16 and 20 Nov. 1898, GWP. Clara Jones Royall, married to politician and manufacturer George Royall, left her husband for New York. Their son Kenneth Royall served as Truman's secretary of war.

43. Goldsboro Women's Club, "Fortieth Anniversary Dinner Program," 23 Mar. 1939, NCC; Henry Weil to Gertrude Weil, 10 Apr. 1899; Gertrude Weil to Mina Weil, 18 Apr. 1899, GWP.

44. Mina Weil to Gertrude Weil, 17 Apr. 1899 and 20 Apr. 1900, GWP.

45. Mina Weil to Gertrude Weil, 21 Sept. 1900, GWP.

46. Gertrude Weil to Mina and Henry Weil, 22 Sept. 1900, GWP. Herman received a similar letter from Mina but responded perfunctorily.

47. Gertrude Weil, "On my way to Boston," typescript, 8 Apr. 1901, GWP.

48. Manual quoted in Joyce Antler, "'After College, What?': New Graduates and the Family Claim," *American Quarterly* 32, no. 4 (1980): 418–19—this discussion borrows from Antler's themes; Gertrude Weil to Mrs. Henry Weil, 18 Apr. 1901, GWP.

49. Mina Weil to Gertrude Weil, 23 Apr. 1901; Gertrude Weil to Mrs. Henry Weil, 28 Apr. 1901, GWP.

50. Mina Weil to Gertrude Weil, 7 May 1901, GWP.

51. Klapper, *Jewish Girls*, 85.

52. Gertrude Weil to [no salutation], 13 May 1901, GWP.

53. Sarah Weil to Gertrude Weil, 17 June 1901; Joe Rosenthal to Mina Weil, 23 June 1901, GWP.

54. See Antler, "'After College, What?,'" 409–13; Jane Addams, *Democracy and Social Ethics* (Cambridge, MA: Belknap Press of Harvard University Press, 1964), 82–86; Jane Addams, *Twenty Years at Hull-House* (New York: Macmillan, 1942), 118–20. For letters of women's self-effacement, see Beulah [Evans] to you, dear, dear girl, 20 Feb. 1901; and Louise to Gertrude, 12 May 1901, GWP.

55. Gertrude Weil to My Dear Ones, 28 Apr. 1901, GWP; Barbara M. Solomon, *In the Company of Educated Women: A History of Women and Higher Education in America* (New Haven, CT: Yale University Press, 1985), 119, 126–27, 132, 134.

56. Sarah Weil to Gertrude Weil, 17 July 1901, GWP.

57. Mina Weil to Gertrude Weil, 7 May 1901, GWP.

58. *New York Times*, 7 May 1901; *Goldsboro Weekly Argus*, 2 May 1901.

CHAPTER 3

1. Anna [Collins] to Gertrude Weil, 17 Aug. and 2 Sept. 1901 and 1 Jan. 1905; Martha Cosley[?] to Gertrude Weil, 28 Aug. 1901, GWP.

2. See Joan Johnson, *Southern Women at the Seven Sister Colleges: Feminist Values and Social Activism, 1875–1915* (Athens: University of Georgia Press, 2008), 92; Joyce Antler, "'After College, What?': New Graduates and the Family Claim," *American Quarterly* 32, no. 4 (1980): 410–11; Jane Addams, *Democracy and Social Ethics* (New York: Macmillan, 1920), 93.

3. Sarah Weil to Gertrude Weil, 17 June 1901; Mina to Gertrude Weil, 13 Mar. 1902; Gertrude Weil to My Dear Ones, 16 Mar. 1902, GWP. Given Mina's frequent travels to spas and resorts, Gertrude continued to correspond with her mother even after returning home.

4. Adams, *Democracy and Social Ethics*, 87; [Gertrude Weil] to Mary [Brinson], ca. 1903, GWP. This letter is unsigned but in Gertrude's hand; it is likely a draft of a mailed letter.

5. Isaac Oettinger to Gertrude Weil, 11 Aug. 1901; Beulah Evans to Gertrude Weil, 7 Oct. 1901; Betty B to Gertrude Weil, 29 Jan. 1902; Henry Weil to Mina Weil, ca. Jan. or Feb. 1902; Gertrude Weil to Janet Weil, 19 and n.d. Feb. 1909 and 18 Oct. 1910, GWP.

6. Antler, "'After College, What?,'" 409–10; [Gertrude Weil] to Mary [Brinson], ca. 1903, GWP.

7. Mina Weil to Gertrude Weil, 23 Aug. 1907; Gertrude Weil to Janet Weil, 18 Mar. 1909, GWP.

8. William Toll, *The Making of an Ethnic Middle Class: Portland Jewry over Four Generations* (Albany: SUNY Press, 1982), 52–55; Karen Manners Smith,

"New Paths to Power: 1890–1920," in Nancy F. Cott, ed., *No Small Courage: A History of Women in the United States* (Oxford: Oxford University Press, 2000), 390; Nancy M. Cowan, "Gertrude Weil and Her Fight for the Nineteenth Amendment," history paper, University of North Carolina at Charlotte—the story of Henry's "fit" over Gertrude's suitors is credited to Mrs. Emil Rosenthal, Gertrude's cousin; Hattie [Spier or Joseph?] to Mina Weil, 5 Mar. 1906; Joe Rosenthal to Mina Weil, 8 Mar. 1906; Jess to Gertrude Weil, 4 Dec. 1904 and 1 Jan. 1909; Leslie Weil to Gertrude Weil, 25 Mar. 1902, GWP.

9. Gertrude Weil to Dear Ones, 21 Mar. and 7 Apr. 1902, GWP.

10. Gertrude Weil to Dear Ones, 21 Mar. 1902; Mr. Frank to Gertrude Weil, 4 May 1902; Henry [?] to Gertrude Weil, 20 Feb. 1904; Alexander Blumberg to Gertrude Weil, 5 Feb. 1905; Gertrude Weil to Isaac Heller, 26 June 1908; Isaac Heller to Gertrude Weil, 25 July 1908; George Thompson to Gertrude Weil, 19 Jan., 22 Mar., and 21 Apr. 1909, 23 Mar. 1910, and 8 Jan. 1911, GWP; *Goldsboro News-Argus*, 3 June 1971.

11. Victor Jelenko to Gertrude Weil, 7 Apr. 1907 and 6 and 28 Feb. 1911. Jelenko was perhaps a Weil cousin: L. Carl Jelenko addressed Gertrude's mother as "Aunt Mina." L. Carl Jelenko to Mina Weil, 16 Nov. 1938, GWP.

12. Victor Jelenko to Gertrude Weil, 5 Sept. 1909 and 28 Feb. 1911, GWP.

13. Victor Jelenko to Gertrude Weil, 29 Apr. 1909, GWP.

14. Victor Jelenko to Gertrude Weil, 29 May 1908 and 26 Apr. 1910, GWP.

15. Victor Jelenko to Gertrude Weil, 2 Mar. 1908 and 6 Nov. and 19 Dec. 1910; Mina Weil to Janet Weil, 1 Mar. 1912; Bessie B[lum] to Gertrude Weil, 19 Feb. 1912, GWP. Minna Rosenheim was Gertrude's companion at Cornell.

16. Amy Meyers Krumbein, interview by the author, 5 June 2011—Graham did not wed until 1932, when he was forty-six; Bessie B[lum] to Gertrude Weil, 19 Feb. 1912; Gertrude Weil to My Dear Ones, 6 Dec. 1912; Janet Weil to Gertrude Weil, 24 June 1914, GWP.

17. [Frances Towers] to Gertrude Weil, 7 July and 6 Nov. 1909; Rosa Kaufman to Mina Weil, 15 Sept. 1904; Sallie Kirby to Gertrude Weil, 29 June 1909 and 24 Dec. 1913; Gertrude Weil to Janet Weil, 18 Feb. 1911, GWP.

18. Gertrude Weil to Mina Weil, 26 and 27 July and 4, 7, 18 Aug. 1912; Harriet Payne to Gertrude Weil, 26 July 1912, GWP.

19. Quoted in Cowan, "Gertrude Weil, n.p. Cowan quotes her undated interview with Gertrude's cousin Mrs. Emil [Miriam] Rosenthal." Louis Weil, telephone interview by the author, 29 Aug. 2014; Harriet Payne to Gertrude Weil, 21 Oct. 1915, 18 Dec. 1916, 15 Mar. and 17 July 1917, 25 Jan. 1918, and 22 Mar. 1921, GWP.

20. William Chafe, *The Paradox of Change: American Women in the Twentieth Century* (New York: Oxford University Press, 1991), 9; Faith Rogow, *Gone to Another Meeting: The National Council of Jewish Women* (Tuscaloosa: University of Alabama Press, 1993), 55; Lynn Gordon, *Gender and Higher Education in the Progressive Era* (New Haven, CT: Yale University Press, 1990), 32. The quote is from Caroll Smith-Rosenberg, "The Female World of Love and Ritual: Relations between Women in Nineteenth-Century America," in Linda Kerr and Jane Sherron De Hart,

eds., *Women's America: Refocusing the Past* (New York: Oxford University Press, 2004), 172, 173, 178, 180. Cissy Weil, interview by the author, 17 March 2011.

21. Gertrude Weil to Janet Weil, 10 Dec. 1910, GWP; Anne Firor Scott, *Women's Associations in American History* (Chicago: University of Illinois Press, 1991), 80; Moses Rountree, *Strangers in the Land: The Story of Jacob Weil's Tribe* (Philadelphia: Dorrance, 1969), 99.

22. Kahn and Co. to Mrs. Henry Weil, 7 Jan. 1903; Kala Rosenthal to Gertrude Weil, 10 Dec. 1902, GWP.

23. Mina Weil to Janet Weil, 25 Nov. 1908; Ruth Heyn Weil to Gertrude Weil, 15 Sept. 1910, GWP.

24. Mina Weil to Gertrude Weil, 22 Feb. 1908; Mina Weil to Janet Weil, 3 Oct. 1911, GWP; *North Carolina Federation of Women's Clubs Year Book*, 1915–16, and "Program of the Fourth Annual Session of the North Carolina Conference for Social Service," Charlotte, 23–26 Jan. 1916, NCC; minutes, Goldsboro B'nai B'rith, 29 Sept. 1913, AJA; Rountree, *Strangers in the Land*, 117. Marcus Jacobi and David Stern joined the lobbying effort against the constitutional amendment. Collected Weil papers do not mention the lynching of Leo Frank in 1915, which traumatized Atlanta Jewry. That North Carolina Jewry was not overly reactive to the Frank trial and lynching suggests perhaps that the case did not resonate broadly or deeply across the Upper South.

25. See Chafe, *Paradox of Change*, 16; and Scott, *Women's Associations*, 24. Gertrude's uncle Elias Ries, a celebrated inventor, repaid her father's investment with some 150 patents on electronic devices, including light switches, rheostats, and train signals.

26. George Kirby to Mrs. Weil, 28 Apr. 1909; Mina Weil to Gertrude Weil, 20 Sept. 1910, GWP; *Goldsboro Weekly Argus*, 5 Nov. 1903.

27. Teaching friends included Frances Towers, Sallie Kirby, Susie Fulghum, Etta Spier, and Florence Mayerberg. Ethel Gowler to Gertrude Weil, 6 Jan. 1915, GWP.

28. Book order, handwritten list, 1912, GWP; Sallie Borden Hatton to Gertrude Weil, 24 Dec. 1906; Liz Kohn to Gertrude Weil, 6 May 1912; Gertrude Weil to Rosa Kaufman, 5 Nov. 1913, GWP.

29. *Goldsboro Weekly Argus*, 25 Feb. 1914; Travel Journal, 1915, GWP.

30. Gertrude Weil to Henry Weil, 26 June 1906; Gertrude Weil to My Dear Ones, 10 and 22 July 1906, GWP.

31. Mina Weil to My Dear Ones, 4 June 1903, GWP. Correspondence does not mention Etta and Claribel Cone of Gertrude's Baltimore crowd, who in their Paris sojourns became intimates of Gertrude Stein and collectors of Matisse and Picasso. The Cones also visited their brother Moses's Blowing Rock estate.

32. Gertrude Weil to My Dear Ones, 29 July and 3 Aug. 1906, GWP.

33. Mina Weil to Gertrude Weil, 11 June 1904; Gertrude Weil to Mina and Janet Weil, 31 July 1905; Gertrude Weil to My Dear Ones, 15 June 1904, GWP.

34. Mina Weil to Gertrude Weil, 19 June 1910; Rosa Kaufman to Mina Weil, 31 Aug. 1903; Gertrude Weil to My Dear Ones, 26 May 1904; Hotel Commodore, Put-in-Bay Island, Lake Erie, Dinner Grub Schedule, 22 June 1910; Gertrude Weil to Mina and Henry Weil, 26 Mar. 1908, GWP.

35. Gertrude Weil to the President Women's Club of Goldsborough [Mina Weil], 7 Apr. 1902, GWP.

36. Gertrude Weil to Henry and Mina Weil, 15 Apr. and 4 May 1902; Gertrude Weil to Mina Weil, 27 May 1910; Gertrude Weil to Janet Weil, 18 Mar. 1911; Victor Jelenko to Gertrude Weil, 28 Apr. 1909, GWP.

37. *Goldsboro Argus*, 2 Aug. 1909; Erica Simmons, *Hadassah and the Zionist Project* (Lanham, MD: Rowman and Littlefield, 2006), 1–3; Rountree, *Strangers in the Land*, 103–9. See Laura Schor, *The Best School in Jerusalem: Annie Landau's School for Girls, 1900–1960* (Waltham, MA: Brandeis University Press, 2013).

38. Central Conference of American Rabbis, "Declaration of Principles, Oct. 27, 2004: 'The Pittsburgh Platform'—1885," https://ccarnet.org/rabbis-speak/platforms /declaration-principles (accessed 6 Mar. 2016); "Jewish People (Israel)," undated notes, GWP.

39. Annie Landau to Mina Weil, 11 Sept. 1910; Henry Weil to My Dear Ones, 22 Mar. 1909, GWP.

40. Eva [Rosenthal] to My Dear Ones, Mar. 1905; Herman Weil to Janet Weil, Mar. 1905; Mina Weil to Janet Weil, 10 and 17 Jan. 1912, GWP; Chafe, *Paradox of Change*, 10, 13; Scott, *Women's Associations*, 141; Hugh Lefler, *History of North Carolina* (New York: Lewis Historical Publishing, 1956), 651; Rob Christensen, *The Paradox of Tar Heel Politics: The Personalities, Elections, and Events That Shaped Modern North Carolina* (Chapel Hill: University of North Carolina Press, 2008), 42–45.

41. For women's labor see Glenda Gilmore, "Gender and Jim Crow: Sarah Dudley Pettey's Vision of the New South," *North Carolina Historical Review* 68, no. 3 (1991): 276; Gertrude Weil to My Dear Ones, 1 May 1902; Lillian See to Gertrude Weil, 10 Dec. 1902; Mina Weil to Gertrude Weil, 26 July 1906; Gertrude Weil to Janet Weil, 8, 25 Nov. 1908, GWP. Gertrude's sister Janet wrote philanthropist Therese Loeb Schiff requesting work in a New York settlement. Janet Weil to Mina Weil, 13 Apr. 1913; Mina Weil to Janet Weil, 29 June 1913, GWP.

42. *Goldsboro News-Argus News*, 6 Dec. 1964; Rountree, *Strangers in the Land*, 136; "The Need of a State-wide Survey of Social and Economic Condition of Women and Girls in North Carolina," undated typescript, GWP.

43. Scott, *Women's Associations*, 1, 89, 96, 102–03. The Woman's Christian Temperance Union was founded nationally in 1874 and in North Carolina in 1883. Marni Davis, *Jews and Booze: Becoming American in the Age of Prohibition* (New York: New York University Press, 2012), 41–42; Milton Ready, *The Tar Heel State: A History of North Carolina* (Columbia: University of South Carolina Press, 2005), 315–16. Union leader Francis Willard later urged alliances with Jewish and Catholic women. Solomon Bear, founder of Wilmington's Temple of Israel, was president of the North Carolina Liquor Dealers, Distillers, and Grape Growers' Association. "Negroes, Jews and Beerkegs," handwritten untitled manuscript, n.d., GWP.

44. The Jewish women met under the rubric of the religious parliament rather than the woman's congress. See Mary McCune, *"The Whole Wide World, without Limits": International Relief, Gender Politics, and American Jewish Women, 1893–1930* (Detroit, MI: Wayne State University Press, 2005), 206n26; Anne Firor Scott

suggests that both NCAJW and the state Federation were inspired by the fair, but Cotten did not organize the state Federation until nine years later.

45. Rosa Kaufman to Mina Weil, 28 May 1906, GWP; Rogow, *Gone to Another Meeting*, 239; Linda Kuzmack, *Women's Cause: The Jewish Woman's Movement in England and the United States, 1881–1933* (Columbus: Ohio State University, 1990), 2–3, 155.

46. Chafe, *Paradox of Change*, 17.

47. Rogow, *Gone to Another Meeting*, 1, 4, 11, 120–21. The General Federation of Women's Clubs closed membership to sectarian organizations but invited the NCAJW to join as a literary rather than as a religious society, a condition that the NCAJW debated but could not accept. Scott, *Women's Associations*, 188; Mina Weil to Janet Weil, 2 Jan. 1912, GWP.

48. Mina Weil to Janet Weil, 25 Mar. 1911, GWP.

49. Mina to My Dear Little Girl, 29 Mar. 1902; *North Carolina Federation of Women's Clubs Year Book*, 1915–16; *Goldsboro Daily Argus*, 4 Apr. 1902.

50. Sallie Southall Cotten, *History of the North Carolina Federation of Women's Clubs, 1901–1925* (Raleigh, NC: Edwards and Broughton, 1925), 1, 2, 3, 57, 67, http://docsouth.unc.edu/nc/cottenss/cottenss.html; *Goldsboro Daily Argus*, 4 Apr. 1902.

51. Like most historians, Cotten described Sorosis of New York, a literary society founded in 1868, as the first woman's club, followed by a General Federation in 1889. Sallie Southall Cotton to Gertrude Weil, 12 May 1912; Gertrude Weil to Mina Weil, 7 Apr. 1902; North Carolina Federation Women's Club Reports, 1907–57, GWP; Cotten, *History*, 9.

52. Sarah Wilkerson-Freeman, "The Emerging Political Consciousness of Gertrude Weil: Education and Women's Clubs, 1879–1914" (M.A. thesis, University of North Carolina at Chapel Hill, 1986), 56, 57; Margaret Lovell Gibson to Gertrude Weil, 8 Mar. 1908, GWP.

53. *North Carolina Federation of Women's Clubs Year Book*, 1903, 1908–9, NCC; *Goldsboro Weekly Argus*, 11 July 1901; Lefler, *History of North Carolina*, 737, 741.

54. *Goldsboro Weekly Argus*, 26 Feb. 1903.

55. Quoted in Cotten, *History*, 92.

56. Untitled newspaper clipping, 20 Feb. 1908, GWP; Eva to My Dear Ones, n.d. Mar. 1905; Mina Weil to Janet Weil, 10 and 17 Jan. 1912; Gertrude Weil to Francis Squire Potter, n.d. [ca. Sept. 1912]; Francis Squire Potter to Gertrude Weil, 25 Oct. 1912, GWP; *Goldsboro Daily Argus*, 18 Mar. 1913.

57. Wilkerson-Freeman, "Emerging Political Consciousness of Gertrude Weil," 62–63; newspaper clipping, 2 Feb. 1908; Margaret Lovell Gibson to Gertrude Weil, 8 Mar. 1908, GWP; *North Carolina Federation of Women's Clubs Year Book*, 1917–18; *Goldsboro Weekly Argus*, 19 Mar. 1903.

58. Gertrude Weil to Mina Weil, 27 May 1910, GWP.

59. See *Goldsboro Weekly Argus*, 26 March, 10 April, 14 August 1902. Robinson's support of the club is recalled in *Goldsboro News*, 14 Feb. 1928.

60. William Powell, "McKelway, Alexander Jeffrey," in William Powell, ed., *Dictionary of North Carolina Biography* (Chapel Hill: University of North Carolina Press, 1991), 4:157–58; *Goldsboro Daily Argus*, 4 May 1905.

61. Julius Cone to Gertrude Weil, 3 Mar. 1909; David Stern to Gertrude Weil, 30 Mar. 1910, GWP; Scott, *Women's Associations*, 165.

62. Scott, *Women's Associations*, 155; Mina Weil to Gertrude Weil, 30 Jan. 1913; outline of work for 1902–3 Child Study Department of the Goldsboro Woman's Club, GWP.

63. *Goldsboro Daily Argus*, 6 May 1915; Susan Graham to Gertrude Weil, 31 Aug. 1916, GWP; Jane Jerome Camhi, *Women against Women: American Anti-Suffragism, 1880–1920* (Brooklyn, NY: Carlson, 1994), 112.

64. Sallie Borden Hatton to Gertrude Weil, 24 Dec. 1906; Kate Burr Johnson to Gertrude Weil, 29 Jan. 1919, GWP.

65. *Goldsboro Weekly Argus*, 26 Mar., 10 Apr., and 14 Aug. 1902. North Carolina governor Charles B. Aycock, architect of black disfranchisement, defended black civil rights and called up the militia to confront lynch mobs.

66. Gertrude Weil to David Stern, n.d. [ca. Nov. 1910], GWP.

67. Sallie Southall Cotten, *A Line a Day Book, 1908–1912*, 3 July 1912, NCC; Sallie Southall Cotten to Gertrude Weil, 29 June 1913; Gertrude Weil to Mina Weil, 27 May 1910, GWP; *Wilson Daily Times*, 21 May 1915.

68. Gertrude Weil to Francis Squire Potter, n.d. [ca. Sept. 1912]; Francis Squire Potter to Gertrude Weil, 25 Oct. 1912, GWP.

69. Kate Burr Johnson to Gertrude Weil, 19 July 1919, GWP.

70. Scott, *Women's Associations*, 152; *North Carolina Federation of Women's Clubs Year Book*, 1908–9.

71. *Goldsboro News*, 15 Aug. 1914.

72. Scott, *Women's Associations*, 140.

73. Sallie Kirby to Gertrude Weil, 20 Mar. 1907, GWP. See Rogow, *Gone to Another Meeting*, 78–83.

74. Harriette Hammer Walker, *Busy North Carolina Women* (Asheboro, NC: privately printed, 1930), 77; Cotten, *History*, 44.

75. *Raleigh News and Observer*, 5 May 1909; *Everything*, 28 Nov. 1913, GWP.

76. Quoted in Rogow, *Gone to Another Meeting*, 6. An educational pioneer, Meyer was antisuffragist, believing in separate gender spheres, although her social-activist sister Maud Nathan was strongly pro. Scott, *Women's Associations*, 82.

77. Gertrude Weil to Janet Weil, 10 Dec. 1910, GWP.

78. *Everything*, 28 Nov. 1913, GWP.

CHAPTER 4

1. Quoted in Nancy Cowan, "Gertrude Weil and Her Fight for the Nineteenth Amendment," undated typescript, Special Collections, University of North Carolina at Charlotte Library.

2. *Raleigh News and Observer*, 27 Apr. 1919; Cotten quoted in Sarah Wilkerson-Freeman, "The Emerging Political Consciousness of Gertrude Weil: Education and Women's Clubs, 1879–1914" (M.A. thesis, University of North Carolina at Chapel Hill, 1986), 64; Sarah Weil to Walter Clark, 28 May 1913, Walter Clark Papers, State Archives of North Carolina, Raleigh.

3. E. C. Brooks to Gertrude Weil, 19 May 1908, GWP.

4. Moses Rountree, *Strangers in the Land: The Story of Jacob Weil's Tribe* (Philadelphia: Dorrance, 1969), 103; "General Federation of Women's Clubs Official Ballot," 17 May 1910; "The Nineteen-Wonder or Ten Years After," Smith Alumnae Class of 1901 10th reunion program, Northampton, MA, 17 June 1911; Louise [Kilton] to Gertrude Weil, 22 Jan. 1909, GWP.

5. Sallie Southall Cotten to Walter Clark, n.d., Walter Clark Papers; Walter McKenzie Clark, "Address by Chief Justice Walter Clark before the Federation of Women's Clubs, New Bern, N. C., 8 May, 1913," 18, 24, http://docsouth.unc.edu/nc/clark13/menu.html; Sarah Weil to Walter Clark, 28 May 1913, WFP.

6. *Raleigh News and Observer*, 27 Jan. 1915.

7. *Goldsboro Daily Argus*, 18 Mar. 1913 and 17 Apr. 1915.

8. *Raleigh News and Observer*, 29 Jan. 1912; Mina to Gertrude Weil, 25 Feb. 1912, GWP.

9. *Raleigh News and Observer*, 29 Jan. 1912; Mina to Gertrude Weil, 25 Feb. 1912; "The Cry of the Children" undated typescript; "The Need of a State-wide Survey of Social and Economic Condition of Women and Girls in North Carolina," undated typescript, GWP.

10. *Goldsboro Daily Argus*, 18 Mar. 1913 and 17 Apr. 1915.

11. Moses Rountree, "Red Cross Chapter," 27 Apr. 1964, GWP.

12. Gertrude quote in William Breen, "Southern Women in the War: The North Carolina Woman's Committees, 1917–1919," *North Carolina Historical Review* 60, no. 3 (1978): 268–69; Glenda Gilmore, *Gender and Jim Crow: Women and the Politics of White Supremacy in North Carolina, 1896–1920* (Chapel Hill: University of North Carolina Press, 1996), 195.

13. Harriet Payne to Gertrude Weil, Thanksgiving 1917; Gertrude Weil to Dear Friend and Patriot, 3 Dec. 1918, GWP.

14. Anne Firor Scott, "Gertrude Weil and Her Times," Weil Symposium, University of North Carolina at Chapel Hill, 17 Mar. 1984, WFP; Liberty Loan Committee in Wayne County, "A Bond in Every Home," undated flyer; Mamie Latham to Gertrude Weil, 19 Oct. 1918, GWP.

15. Gertrude Weil to Mina Weil, 24 Mar. 1918; Harriet Payne to Gertrude Weil, 23 Mar., 2 Apr., n.d. May, and 24 June 1918 and 25 Jan. 1919; GWP.

16. Arthur Bluethenthal to Mina Weil, 25 May 1918; Mina Weil to Gertrude Weil, 21 June 1918, GWP; Edward Blum, undated newspaper article, n.d. [ca. 1918], GWP.

17. Gertrude Weil, open letter, 31 Jan. 1919; George Franklin to Gertrude Weil, n.d.; Thoughts on Armistice Day, undated typescript, GWP.

18. See Leonard Rogoff, *Down Home: Jewish Life in North Carolina* (Chapel Hill: University of North Carolina Press, 2010), 187–88. The North Carolina Plan consisted of a Jewish Relief Day by gubernatorial proclamation and a statewide Union Prayer Service to pledge funds.

19. Lillian See to Gertrude Weil, 19 Jan. 1919; Helen Chamberlain to Gertrude Weil, 1 Feb. 1919, GWP; Rountree, *Strangers in the Land*, 116–17.

20. Julia Dameron to Gertrude Weil, 23 Dec. 1918, GWP. When the Legislative Council formed in 1921, the coalition included the North Carolina Federation of

Women's Clubs, the Equal Suffrage League of North Carolina, the North Carolina Teachers' Assembly, and the North Carolina Educational Association.

21. A Citizen of Goldsboro to Dear Sir, 18 July 1919, GWP.

CHAPTER 5

1. NCAJW, *Year Book*, 1926; Gertrude Weil, "Address of President, Fifth Annual Conference—Durham, 28 Feb. and 1 Mar. 1926," typescript, GWP.

2. Anne Firor Scott, "Not Forgotten: Gertrude Weil and Her Times," *Southern Cultures* 13, no. 1 (2007): 101.

3. Paula Hyman, *Gender and Assimilation in Modern Jewish History: The Roles and Representation of Women* (Seattle: University of Washington Press, 1995), 165–66; Victor Jelenko to Gertrude Weil, 28 and 29 Apr. 1909; Gertrude Weil to Henry and Mina Weil, 15 Apr. 1902; Gertrude Weil to Mina Weil, 27 May 1910; Gertrude Weil to Janet Weil, 18 Mar. 1911, GWP.

4. Linda Gordon Kuzmack, *Woman's Cause: The Jewish Woman's Movement in England and the United States, 1881–1933* (Columbus: Ohio State University Press, 1990), 99, 105; Janice Rothschild Blumberg, "Sophie Weil Browne: From Rabbi's Wife to Clubwoman," *Southern Jewish History* 9 (2006): 1–33; *American Jewish Times*, Sept. 1937, 74. Progressive Jewish women were typically Reform Jews of German origin, but Schneiderman was Russian, and Nathan was Sephardic. Wald, a German Jew, was not religious but maintained Jewish associations. Jewish women activists in North Carolina include Edna Lichtenfels of Asheville, Minna Weill and Rhea White of Charlotte, and Flora Stern, Etta Spier, and Laura Weill Cone of Greensboro.

5. Gertrude Weil to My Dear Ones, 6 Dec. 1912, GWP; Jonathan Sarna, "'To Quicken the Religious Consciousness of Israel': The NFTS National Committee on Religion, 1913–1933," in Carole Balin, Dana Herman, Jonathan Sarna, and Gary Zola, eds., *Sisterhood: A Centennial History of Women in Reform Judaism* (Cincinnati, OH: Hebrew Union College Press, 2013), 663–65.

6. Eli Evans, *The Provincials: A Personal History of Jews in the South* (Chapel Hill: University of North Carolina Press, 2005), 92. Amy Meyers Krumbein, interview by the author, 5 June 2011. German Jewish women like Lily Kronheimer of Durham, Emma Schiff Simmonds of Charlotte, and Helen Elias of Raleigh played congregational roles similar to Gertrude's. The Heiligs and Meyers, immigrant families, started with a second-hand store in Goldsboro in 1911 and built the nation's largest retail furniture chain.

7. Amy Meyers Krumbein, interview by the author, 5 June 2011.

8. Henrietta Szold to Mina Weil, 2 Feb. 1921, GWP.

9. Digest of the minutes of the Oheb Sholom congregation, 1883–1958, 6, AJA.

10. [Oheb Sholom] Religious School Report—1919–20; Religious School Report, 1922–23, 3 June 1923, GWP; Emma Edwards, "History of the NCAJW," undated mimeographed typescript, 9, GWP; Hyman, *Gender and Assimilation*, 154–55, 160–61; Melissa Klapper, "Peace Is Truly Our Mission: NFTS and the Peace Movement," in Balin et al., *Sisterhood*, 275.

11. Undated, handwritten notes for talk; [Oheb Sholom], Religious School Report, 1922–23 (3 June 1923), GWP.

12. School commencement, 7 June 1925; Purim entertainment, 17 Mar. 1935, GWP.

13. Amy Meyers Krumbein, interview by the author, 5 June 2011; Muriel Kramer Offerman, interview by the author, 6 June 2014.

14. [Oheb Sholom], Religious School Report, 1922–23.

15. Lecture notes, undated manuscript, GWP; Hyman, *Gender and Assimilation*, 9, 156.

16. NCAJW, *Year Book*, 1923, 5, GWP.

17. Edwards, "History of the NCAJW," 5. The first fieldworker, Sadie Lee Bear, soon left, and Hattie Spier Weinberg, Gertrude's Goldsboro cousin, succeeded her. Mizrachi, the women's Orthodox Zionist society, also had a presence in North Carolina.

18. Gertrude Weil, Chair NCAJW Advisory Committee, report, 21 Mar. 1936, GWP.

19. Kittner quoted in Leonard Rogoff, *A History of Temple Emanu-El: An Extended Family, Weldon, North Carolina* (Durham, NC: Jewish Heritage Foundation of North Carolina, 2007), 55–56; Sylvia Levy to Gertrude Weil, 25 Oct. 1930; Edwards, "History of the NCAJW," 5, GWP. NCAJW friends included Sylvia Margolis in Williamston, Min Klein in High Point, and Hinda Honigman in Gastonia.

20. Karla Goldman, *Beyond the Synagogue Gallery: Finding a Place for Women in American Judaism* (Cambridge, MA: Harvard University Press, 2000), 202; Kuzmack, *Woman's Cause*, 147. Edna Lichtenfels of Asheville and Etta Spier and Laura Weill Cone of Greensboro served both the North Carolina League of Women Voters and NCAJW; Digest of the minutes of the Oheb Sholom congregation. In 1922 Spier asked the Greensboro temple board to grant women equal membership, but the men needed a year to reflect.

21. NCAJW program, Sixth Conference, 6–8 Mar. 1927, GWP.

22. NCAJW, *Year Book*, 1923, 6; "Report on North Carolina Presented by Rabbi Gustave Falk, Regional Director, Southeast," 13 Sept. 1929, GWP, quoted in Edwards, "History of the NCAJW," 5.

23. See Jonathan Sarna, "The Cult of Synthesis in American Jewish Culture," *Jewish Social Studies*, n.s., 5, no. 1/2 (1999): 52–79.

CHAPTER 6

1. Gertrude Weil to Mrs. T. D. Jones, 26 July 1920, SJFP.

2. *Goldsboro News*, 23 Mar. 1928; Elna Green, *Southern Strategies: Southern Women and the Woman Suffrage Question* (Chapel Hill: University of North Carolina Press, 1997), xv, 17.

3. Green, *Southern Strategies*, xv, 19.

4. Linda Gordon Kuzmack, *Woman's Cause: The Jewish Woman's Movement in England and the United States, 1881–1933* (Columbus: Ohio State University Press, 1990), 134, 144, 147; *Washington Jewish Week*, 24 Aug. 2015. Another figure was

Carolyn Katzenstein of Philadelphia, who also had North Carolina family ties, perhaps to the Weil family.

5. *Goldsboro News-Argus*, 3 May 1971. In the 1912 North Carolina Democratic primary for U.S. Senate, prosuffrage Walter Clark lost to conservative, antisuffrage Furnifold Simmons.

6. *Raleigh News and Observer*, 16 Jan. 1914.

7. Karen Manners Smith, "New Paths to Power: 1890–1920," in Nancy Cott, ed., *No Small Courage: A History of Women in the United States* (Oxford: Oxford University Press, 2000), 397.

8. Frances Towers to Gertrude Weil, 21 Apr. 1913; Harriet Payne to Gertrude Weil, 11 June 1915, GWP.

9. The 1913 incorporation papers in the North Carolina secretary of state's office record the "Equal Suffrage League of North Carolina." Organizational stationery and other documents list the "Equal Suffrage Association of North Carolina." A 1915 resolution names the "North Carolina Equal Suffrage Association." In correspondence both "League" and "Association" are mentioned. Some secondary sources regard the league and association as separate, but all have identical leadership. Perhaps "Association" was adopted to stress affiliation with NAWSA. The League of Women Voters was founded under NAWSA. For clarity, here the organization will be designated by the most commonly used title, Equal Suffrage Association of North Carolina. See "Finding Guide," 3, ESAC.

10. Mina Weil to Janet Weil, 13 Jan. 1914, GWP.

11. See A. Elizabeth Taylor, "The Woman Suffrage Movement in North Carolina, Part I," *North Carolina Historical Review* 38, no. 1 (1961): 48–49, 53–54.

12. Rosa Kaufman to Mina Weil, 13 Nov. 1904; Louise to Gertrude Weil, 22 Jan. 1909; Liz Kohn to Gertrude Weil, 16 May 1912; Frances Towers to Gertrude Weil, 21 Apr. 1913; F. T. Towers to Gertrude Weil, 21 Apr. 1913; Harriet Payne to Gertrude Weil, 21 Oct. 1915, GWP; A. Elizabeth Taylor, "The Woman Suffrage Movement in North Carolina, Part II," *North Carolina Historical Review* 38, no. 2 (1961): 176.

13. Mina Weil to Janet Weil, 20 June 1912, GWP.

14. Harriet Payne to Gertrude Weil, 21 Oct. 1915, GWP; *Raleigh News and Observer*, 16 Jan. 1914 and 12 Nov. 1914; *Proceedings of the Second Annual Convention of the Equal Suffrage Association of North Carolina, October 29, 1915* (Asheville: Equal Suffrage League of North Carolina, 1915), 11.

15. *Proceedings of the Second Annual Convention*, 4, 29.

16. Taylor, "Woman Suffrage Movement, Part I," 55.

17. *Raleigh News and Observer*, 30 Jan. and 19 Feb. 1915; undated clipping, GWP.

18. *Proceedings of the Second Annual Convention*, 9.

19. Anonymous letter from "a prominent Goldsboro suffragist," newspaper clipping, 27 Oct. 1916, GWP.

20. Green, *Southern Strategies*, 5.

21. Ibid., 175.

22. Taylor, "Woman Suffrage Movement, Part I," 61; Green, *Southern Strategies*, 27–28.

23. Catt used the Committee on Organization as her base to rebuild NAWSA, a step to presidency. Gertrude took the same route at the state level; Gertrude Weil to Laura Stern [Cone], 27 July 1917, SJFP.

24. Sallie Southall Cotten, *History of the North Carolina Federation of Women's Clubs, 1901–1925* (Raleigh, NC: Edwards and Broughton, 1925), 118–20, http://docsouth.unc.edu/nc/cottenss/cottenss.html; Gertrude Weil to Laura Stern [Cone], 27 July 1917, GWP; "North Carolina Suffrage Story," clipping, 8 Feb. 1919, MOCP.

25. Quoted in Taylor, "Woman Suffrage Movement, Part II," 177.

26. Cotten, *History*, 127, 137, 138; Equal Suffrage Association of North Carolina leaders active in Federation included Clara Lingle, Barbara Henderson, and Laura Holms Reilley.

27. Equal Suffrage Association of North Carolina, Goldsboro, NC, typescript, 11 Feb. 1918, GWP.

28. Carrie Chapman Catt to Gertrude Weil, 1 Apr. 1918, GWP.

29. Walter Clark to Gertrude Weil, 4 Apr. 1918, GWP. Clark named state legislator Gallatin Roberts and U.S. congressman Zebulon Weaver, both Democrats from mountain Buncombe County, as woman suffrage stalwarts.

30. President [Catt] to Mrs. John S. Cunningham, 18 July 1918, GWP; *Greensboro Daily Record*, 19 Apr. 1918.

31. Rob Christensen, *The Paradox of Tar Heel Politics: The Personalities, Elections, and Events That Shaped Modern North Carolina* (Chapel Hill: University of North Carolina Press, 2008), 49–50.

32. Carrie Chapman Catt to Gertrude Weil, 26 Apr. 1919; Mrs. W. A. Graham to Helen Gardener, 29 Apr. 1918, GWP; Taylor, "Woman Suffrage Movement, Part II," 178.

33. Justina Leavitt Wilson, ed., *Handbook of the National American Woman Suffrage Association and Proceedings of the Jubilee Convention (1869–1919)* (New York: National Woman Suffrage Publishing, 1919), 288–89.

34. Carrie Chapman Catt to Gertrude Weil, 16 May 1918; Carrie Chapman Catt to Gertrude Weil, 18 July 1918; *Raleigh News and Observer*, undated clipping, GWP; Nettie Rogers Shuler, *Report of the Corresponding Secretary: Jubilee Convention of the National American Woman Suffrage Association* (New York: National Woman's Suffrage Publishing, 1919), 4–5.

35. Harriett Elliott to Gertrude Weil, 5 Jan. 1919; Julia Alexander to Walter Clark, 17 Apr. 1919, GWP; *Greensboro Daily Record*, 8 Feb. 1919.

36. Taylor, "Woman Suffrage Movement, Part II," 179.

37. Undated typescript, ca. Aug. 1920, GWP; endorsements reprinted in *Raleigh News and Observer*, 8, 9, 11 Aug. 1920, GWP. Suffragist industrialists included Julius Cone, Julian S. Carr, and John Motley Morehead.

38. Gertrude Weil to Walter Clark, 12 Apr. 1919, GWP; quoted in Moses Rountree, *Strangers in the Land: The Story of Jacob Weil's Tribe* (Philadelphia: Dorrance, 1969), 133.

39. *Raleigh News and Observer*, 28 Feb. 1919.

40. Gertrude Weil to My Dear Suffragist, 12 Mar. 1919, ESANCP.

41. *League of Women Voters* [newsletter], vol. 1, no. 1 (Apr. 1919): 1, 2, GWP.

42. Gertrude Weil to Suffragists All Over State, 22 Apr. 1919, ESANCP.43. "Resolution," Equal Suffrage Association of North Carolina," 23 July 1919; Gertrude Weil to Dear Sir, 11 Apr. 1919, ESANCP.

44. Gertrude Weil to Sam Brinson, 18 May 1919; Gertrude Weil to Walter Clark, 22 May 1919, GWP; Aubrey L. Brooks and Hugh T. Lefler, eds., *The Papers of Walter Clark*, Vol. 2, *1902-1924* (Chapel Hill: University of North Carolina Press, 1950), 403.

45. Undated clipping, *Raleigh News and Observer*, GWP. This article is found among clippings dated March–May 1920.

46. Mrs. T. D. Jones to Gertrude Weil, 15 Feb. 1918; Gertrude Weil to Mrs. Jones, 26 Feb. 1918; Furnifold Simmons to Mrs. T. D. Jones, 25 May 1918; Lee Overman to Mrs. T. D. Jones, 5 June 1918, SJFP.

47. Walter Clark to Gertrude Weil, 4 June 1919, ESANCP.

48. "Gertrude Weil Address to North Carolina Division of the United Daughters of the Confederacy, High Point," 7 Oct. 1919, ESANCP; "Mary O. T. Cowper Topical Series," 6 Sept. 1919, MOCP.

49. Gertrude Weil to Mrs. Jones, 2 May, 1919, SJFP; Green, *Southern Strategies*, 15.

50. Gertrude Weil to James Sprunt, 11 Aug. 1919, with undated clipping, John Sprunt Hill Papers, Rubenstein Rare Book and Manuscript Library, Duke University, Durham, NC; Gertrude Weil to Mrs. Jones, 17 Feb. 1919; Gertrude Weil to Mrs. E. L. Travis, Halifax, 27 Oct. 1919, ESANCP. Borrowing a National Woman's Party tactic, Cowper organized "propaganda" plays.

51. Carrie Chapman Catt telegram to Gertrude Weil, 5 Jan. 1920, ESANCP; "Announcement of Dinners and Luncheons to Be Held in Connection with the Victory Convention of the National American Woman Suffrage Association and the First Congress of the League of Women Voters, Chicago, IL, 12–18 Feb., 1920"; A School for Education for Citizenship; *Handbook of the National American Woman Suffrage Association Proceedings of the Victory Convention National American Woman Suffrage Association (1869-1920) and First National Congress League of Women Voters (Chicago Ill., 12-18 Feb. 1920)*, 176–77, GWP.

52. Mrs. H. W. Chase and Gertrude Weil to the Clubwomen of North Carolina, 6 Aug. 1919, ESANCP. The school's sponsors, the Federation's Civics Department and Committee on Citizenship, were chaired, respectively, by Lucetta Chase, wife of the president of the University of North Carolina at Chapel Hill, and Gertrude; Gertrude Weil to Dear President, 26 Mar. 1920, ESANCP.

53. Carrie Chapman Catt to Gertrude Weil, 29 Mar. 1920, ESANCP.

54. Gertrude Weil to Carrie Chapman Catt, 3 Apr. 1920, ESANCP.

55. President [Carrie Chapman Catt] to Mrs. John Cunningham, 18 July 1918; Gertrude Weil to Carrie Chapman Catt, 3 Apr. 1920; Gertrude Weil to W. L. Long, 4 Apr. 1920, ESANCP.

56. Gertrude Weil to Carrie Chapman Catt, 3 Apr. 1920, ESANCP.

57. "The Coup d'Etat of the Tar Heel State," *Women's Citizen*, 17 Apr. 1920. The coup was led by Mary Graham, Cornelia Jerman, and Delia Dixon-Carroll.

58. *Raleigh News and Observer*, 16 May 1920. F. P Hobgood led the pro-federal

amendment floor fight, while T. J. Warren headed the anti-amendment platform committee.

59. Jason Gray to Gertrude Weil, 25 May 1920; NAWSA to Miss Weil, 21 June 1920, ESANCP; *Raleigh News and Observer*, July 1920; Elna C. Green, "Those Opposed: The Antisuffragists in North Carolina, 1900–1920," *North Carolina Historical Review* 67, no. 3 (1990): 323–35.

60. *Greensboro Daily News*, 30 July 1920; *Raleigh News and Observer*, 29 July 1920, ESANCP.

61. Green, *Southern Strategies*, 46, 112, 113; *Raleigh News and Observer*, 24 July 1920. The Richmond organizer was Carrie Preston Davis.

62. Green, *Southern Strategies*, 102.

63. *Raleigh News and Observer*, 24 July 1920. Episcopal Bishop Joseph Blount Cheshire joined the antisuffrage league's advisory board where his wife was an activist. Green, *Southern Strategies*, 17, 185; Jane Jerome Camhi, *Women against Women: American Anti-Suffragism, 1880–1920* (Brooklyn: Carlson, 1994), 224. See also Gerda Lerner, *The Woman in American History* (Menlo Park, CA: Addison-Wesley 1971), 110, 140.

64. Green, *Southern Strategies*, 58, 62, 66–67.

65. Camhi, *Women against Women*, 216; "Madam President, Members of the Convention and Friends," typescript, 27 Apr. 1920, GWP; *Raleigh News and Observer*, 10 May 1925.

66. Green, *Southern Strategies*, 66–67; Private Secretary to Mr. James Sprunt to Gertrude Weil, 29 July 1920, GWP.

67. Green, *Southern Strategies*, 31, 38; Weil referred to Goldsboro as "un-suffrage minded." Quoted in *Goldsboro News-Argus*, 3 May 1971.

68. Gertrude Weil to Carrie Chapman Catt, 9 July 1920, ESANCP.

69. Green, *Southern Strategies*, 52; Camhi, *Women against Women*, 224, citing Eleanor Flexner, *Century of Struggle* (New York: Atheneum, 1968), 294.

70. Green, *Southern Strategies*, 113, 122, 124; Rose Young to James Evans, 18 June 1920, ESANCP.

71. Mary Garret Hayt and Nettie Rogers Shuler to Dear President, 25 June 1920; Gertrude Weil to Dear Friend, 21 June 1920, ESANCP; Gertrude Weil, "A Good Thing for Women," *Everywoman's Magazine*, July–Aug. 1920, 7, 8, 9; Taylor, "Woman Suffrage Movement, Part II," 186–87; *Raleigh News and Observer*, 4 Aug. 1920.

72. "North Carolina Branch of the Southern League for the Rejection of the Susan B. Anthony Amendment," typescript, July 1920, ESAC; Glenda Gilmore, *Gender and Jim Crow: Women and the Politics of White Supremacy in North Carolina, 1896–1920* (Chapel Hill: University of North Carolina Press, 1996), 204.

73. "NAWSA Position on the Race Question: Letter to the New Orleans Times-Democrat, March 1903," in Mary Jo Buhle and Paul Buhle, eds., *The Concise History of Woman Suffrage Selections from the Classic Work of Stanton, Anthony, Gage, and Harper* (Urbana: University of Illinois Press, 1978), 350. This letter was prepared by the NAWSA board of officers. Green, *Southern Strategies*, 10; Shuler, *Report of the Corresponding Secretary*, 9.

74. Margaret Clark Neal, "North Carolina Conference for Social Service Records

of Its Twenty-Five Years," typescript, 7 Apr. 1938, NCC, 45, 47; Gilmore, *Gender and Jim Crow*, 200.

75. These broadsides are available at both MOCP and GWP.

76. Gertrude Weil to George Wilcox, 4 Aug. 1920; Floyd Triplett to Rosie Young, 21 June 1920; Gertrude Weil and Mrs. Palmer Jerman to George Wilcocks [*sic*], 24 July 1920, ESANCP; Gilmore, *Gender and Jim Crow*, 210; "Makes for White Supremacy," *Woman Citizen*, n.d., GWP.

77. Gertrude Weil to Sam Brinson, 18 May 1919; Gertrude Weil to J. O. Carr, 8 July 1919, ESANCP.

78. *League of Women Voters* [newsletter] 1, no. 1 (Apr. 1919): 2, GWP; quoted in Aileen Kraditor, *The Ideas of the Woman Suffrage Movement, 1890–1900* (New York: Norton, 1981), 197. See Gertrude Weil, "A Good Thing for Women," 8; Green, *Southern Strategies*, xii.

79. Gertrude Weil to Dear Suffragist, 10 July 1920, SJFP; Gertrude Weil to Mrs. K. A. Pittman, 22 July 1920, ESANCP. Endorsers included the North Carolina Federation of Women's Clubs, the North Carolina Business and Professional Women's Clubs, and the Society of Friends; F. P. Hobgood to Gertrude Weil, 22 July 1920, ESANCP.

80. Carrie Chapman Catt to Gertrude Weil, 1 July 1920; Carrie Chapman Catt to Mrs. John Cunningham, 18 July 1918, GWP.

81. Marion Roydhouse, "The 'Universal Sisterhood of Women': Women and Labor Reform in North Carolina, 1900–1932" (Ph.D. diss., University of North Carolina at Chapel Hill, 1980), 132; Carrie Chapman Catt to Gertrude Weil, 1 July 1920; Equal Suffrage Association of North Carolina, annual report, Nov. 1914, GWP.

82. Gertrude Weil to Carrie Chapman Catt, 9 July 1920, ESANCP; Carrie Chapman Catt to Gertrude Weil, 1 July 1920, GWP.

83. J. W. Bailey to Miss Weil, 25 July 1920, ESANCP; *Raleigh News and Observer*, 8 Aug. 1920.

84. *Raleigh News and Observer*, 26 July 1920. ESANCP.

85. Gertrude Weil to Mrs. Jones, 21 July 1920; Gertrude Weil to Mrs. T. D. Jones, 3 Aug. 1920; "Gene" Clark to Mrs [Mattie Logan] Jones, 5 Feb. 1918, SJFP.

86. Gertrude Weil to Mrs. Jones, 29 July 1920, SJFP; Office of the North Carolina Equal Suffrage League, photograph, ca. 1920, call no. N.60.4.38, State Archives of North Carolina, Raleigh; Alexander Leidholdt, *Battling Nell: The Life of Southern Journalist Cornelia Battle Lewis, 1893–1956* (Baton Rouge: Louisiana State University Press, 2009), 60–61.

87. "North Carolina Legislature Should Ratify the Suffrage Amendment," broadside, ESANCP.

88. *Greensboro Daily News*, 22 June 1920, GWP; Gertrude Weil, untitled, undated typescript, ESANCP.

89. Annie Bock to B. G. Crisp, 19 July 1920, ESANCP; Weil, "Good Thing for Women," 8.

90. Gertrude Weil to George Wilcox, 24 July and 4 Aug. 1920, ESANCP.

91. "Lest We Forget: While Suffragists Plead, the Poison Works!," *State's Defense*, 16 Aug. 1920, ESANCP.

92. Carrie Chapman Catt to Gertrude Weil, 6 and 7 Aug. 1920, ESANCP.

93. Elizabeth Jones to Gertrude Weil, 9 Aug. 1920; untitled clipping, *Charlotte Observer*, 11 Aug. 1920, ESANCP.

94. "Telegram to the General Assembly of Tennessee," Raleigh, N.C., 11 Aug. 1920. ESANCP; Gertrude's typescript of the telegram includes her handwritten comment, GWP; *Charlotte Observer*, 12 Aug. 1920.

95. *Raleigh News and Observer*, 14 Aug. 1920.

96. Ibid.

97. Quoted in Taylor, "Woman Suffrage Movement, Part II," 187.

98. *Raleigh News and Observer*, 5 Oct. 1925; Carrie Chapman Catt to Gertrude Weil, 19 Aug. 1920, ESANCP.

99. Carrie Chapman Catt to Gertrude Weil, 19 and 23 Aug. 1920, ESANCP; *State of North Carolina Public Laws ad Resolutions Passed by the General Assembly at Its Extra Session of 1920* (Raleigh: Commercial Printing Co., 1920), 181.

100. Undated, untitled newspaper clipping, ca. Aug. 1920, ESANCP.

101. Gertrude Weil to My dear Friend Suffragist, 13 Aug. 1920, ESANCP.

102. Mina Weil to Gertrude Weil, n.d., 1920; Margaret Tyler to Gertrude Weil, 21 Aug. 1920; Lila Ripley Barnwell to Gertrude Weil, 30 Aug. 1920; Carrie Chapman Catt to Gertrude Weil, 23 Aug. 1920, ESANCP; *Raleigh News and Observer*, 14 Mar. 1965.

103. *Raleigh News and Observer*, 10 May 1925; L. J. H. Mewborn to Gertrude Weil, 26 Aug. 1920, ESANCP.

104. Quoted in Taylor, "Woman Suffrage Movement, Part II," 189.

CHAPTER 7

1. Gertrude Weil to [no salutation], 24 Sept. 1920, ESAC.

2. *Goldsboro News-Argus*, 6 Jan. 1932. Employing an innovative business model, the Goldsboro Woman's Club financed its building with income from a service station, cafeteria, and rental apartments.

3. Frank Graham to Gertrude Weil, 7 Sept. 1928; Nathan O'Berry to Mrs. Mina Weil, 20 Apr. 1928; Hope Chamberlain to Gertrude Weil, 28 Feb. 1927; Nell Battle Lewis to Gertrude Weil, 29 May 1925, GWP.

4. Quoted in Moses Rountree, *Strangers in the Land: The Story of Jacob Weil's Tribe* (Philadelphia: Dorrance, 1969), 142; W. J. Jones to Gertrude Weil, 10 Apr. 1930; Dan [Powell] to Gertrude Weil, 7, 8 Feb. 1930; Margaret Maye to Mrs. Weil, 12 Feb. 1931; Martha [Boswell] to Gertrude Weil, 29 Nov. 1929, GWP. One Weil fellow, Clara Guiguard, went to the University of Chicago, married distinguished sociologist Robert Faris, and became a lifelong family friend. Leslie Weil lent tuition to a farmer's son, Albert Coates, to attend Harvard Law School. Coates later founded the UNC Institute of Government.

5. Canceled checks, 1923–39; Gertrude Weil to Mr. Peterson, n.d., ca. Dec. 1920; Frances Towers Doggett to Gertrude Weil, 24 Jan. 1921, GWP.

6. Gertrude Weil to Mary O. Cowper, 20 June 1924, MOCP.

7. Charles Abernethy to Gertrude Weil, 11 Dec. 1926, GWP.

8. Alice Boyden to Gertrude Weil, 24 Feb. 1917, GWP; Mina Bluethenthal Kemp-

ton, "Gertrude was my aunt ...," undated typescript, WFP; Mrs. A. E. [Florie] Alt-meyer to Mina Weil, 5 June 1927; Mary Berenson to Mrs. Altmeyer, 13 June 1927; Rachel Berenson Perry to Gertrude Weil, 31 Dec. 1932, GWP. Bernard Berenson was at least a nominal convert to Christianity, and biographers debate his Jewishness.

9. Harriet Payne to Gertrude Weil, 7 Dec. 1923, 28 Feb. 1927, and 28 July 1928, GWP.

10. W. T. Couch to Gertrude Weil, 22 Apr. 1927, GWP.

11. *New York Times*, 4 Sept. 1921 and 8 July 1927; Rob Christensen, *The Paradox of Tar Heel Politics: The Personalities, Elections, and Events That Shaped Modern North Carolina* (Chapel Hill: University of North Carolina Press, 2008), 38.

12. Harriet Payne to Gertrude Weil, 24 Sept. 1924; G. B. Morris to Gertrude Weil, 18 Sept. 1923, GWP. Morris praised "Christ-like" Nathaniel Jacobi, who underwrote dormitories at Goldsboro's Odd Fellows orphanage.

13. See Van Vann Newkirk, *Lynching in North Carolina: A History, 1865–1941* (Jefferson, NC: McFarland, 2009), 86, 93.

14. Christensen, *Paradox of Tar Heel Politics*, 38; *Monthly News*, Jan. 1928, MOCP.

15. "The Memorial Idea," undated typescript; Sallie Southall Cotten to Laura Cone, 28 July 1927, GWP.

16. Gertrude Weil, "North Carolina League of Women Voters," typescript, 11 Oct. 1920, GWP.

17. Marion Roydhouse, "The 'Universal Sisterhood of Women': Women and Labor Reform in North Carolina, 1900–1932" (Ph.D. diss., University of North Carolina at Chapel Hill, 1980), 140–41; "Members of the North Carolina League of Voters, and Friends," undated typescript, GWP.

18. Gertrude Weil, "The Social Program of the National League of Women Voters," *Journal of Social Forces* 1 (Nov. 1922): 55.

19. I. G. Greer to Gertrude Weil, 15 June 1922, GWP; Roydhouse, "'Universal Sisterhood of Women,'" 138; *Raleigh News and Observer*, 18 July, 5 Sept., and 27 Nov. 1920.

20. Weil, "Social Program"; E. C. Branson to Gertrude Weil, 22 Sept. 1922, GWP. Sociologists at the University of North Carolina at Chapel Hill included Branson, Howard Odum, Harold Meyer, Guy Johnson, and Guion Johnson. See Paul Gaston, *The New South Creed* (New York: Knopf, 1970), 5. Many "New Souths" have been proclaimed: after Reconstruction, after World War I, and after the civil rights move-ment. All were efforts to move beyond the racist myth that enshrined white racial superiority.

21. Roydhouse, "'Universal Sisterhood of Women,'" 4, 142. Its first incarnation was as the Legislative Council of North Carolina Women with Ida Hook as presi-dent. Founders were the North Carolina Federation of Women's Clubs, the North Carolina Federation of Business and Professional Women's Clubs, and the state Woman's Christian Temperance Union.

22. William Link, *The Paradox of Southern Progressivism, 1880–1930* (Chapel Hill: University of North Carolina Press, 1992), xi; Johanna Schoen, *Choice and Coercion: Birth Control, Sterilization, and Abortion in Public Health and Welfare*

(Chapel Hill: University of North Carolina Press, 2005), 9; Gertrude Weil to Belle Sherwin, 31 Mar. 1928; Charles Laughinghouse to Gertrude Weil, 2 June and 1 July 1930, GWP.

23. Gertrude Weil, "North Carolina League of Women Voters," typescript, 14 Dec. 1920; "Minutes of the Second Annual Convention of the North Carolina League of Women Voters, Greensboro," 16 Feb. 1922, GWP.

24. "Minutes of the Second Annual Convention"; Civics Department, "Goldsboro Woman's Club Annual Report," 12 Apr. 1922, GWP.

25. Louise Young, *In the Public Interest: The League of Women Voters, 1920–1970* (New York: Greenwood Press, 1989), 2, 49; *Monthly News*, Oct. 1925, MOCP.

26. Young, *In the Public Interest*, 61; Gertrude Weil to Mrs. Douglas, 9 Apr. 1928, GWP; Kathryn Nasstrom, "'More Was Expected of Us': The North Carolina League of Women Voters and the Feminist Movement in the 1920s" (history thesis, University of North Carolina at Chapel Hill, 1998), 84; "too much being done for mothers today" quoted in Hazel M[oore] to Gertrude Weil, 13 Feb. 1931, GWP.

27. Belle Sherwin to Gertrude Weil, 20 Jan. 1928; George Collins to Gertrude Weil, 27 Sept. 1927; "Minutes of the Second Annual Convention"; "Maternal and Infant Hygiene," undated typescript, GWP.

28. Roydhouse, "'Universal Sisterhood of Women,'" 239; "Minutes of the Second Annual Convention."

29. Quoted in Nasstrom, "'More Was Expected of Us,'" 309.

30. "To the League of Women Voters from A. W. McLean," *Monthly News*, May 1924, MOCP.

31. Quoted in Roydhouse, "'Universal Sisterhood of Women,'" 231, 258.

32. Young, *In the Public Interest*, 67.

33. *Monthly News*, Oct. 1925, MOCP.

34. "She Has 'Em Guessing," undated newspaper clipping; Sallie Southall Cotten to Gertrude Weil, 6 June 1922, GWP; "Editorial: Gertrude Weil's Legacy," WFP; *Charlotte Herald*, 23 June 1922; *Raleigh Times*, 29 June 1922; *Goldsboro News*, 1 July 1922.

35. Young, *In the Public Interest*, 73; I. G. Greer to Gertrude Weil, 15 June 1922; Walter Clark to Gertrude Weil, 1 Aug. 1922, GWP; *Goldsboro News*, 1 July 1922; *Raleigh Times*, 29 and 31 July 1922; *Asheville Times*, 27 July 1922.

36. Young, *In the Public Interest*, 91; *Goldsboro News*, 1 July 1922; Gertrude Weil to Club President, 29 May 1924, MOCP.

37. "Martin Cottage, Blowing Rock, N. C.," undated typescript; Gertrude Weil to Mrs. Mosher, 12 Feb. 1928, GWP.

38. Quoted in Roydhouse, "'Universal Sisterhood of Women,'" 265.

39. Gertrude Weil to Miss Williams, 16 June 1922, GWP; Frank Graham, "We Come to Gertrude Weil in the Fullness of Our Hearts," B'nai B'rith dinner tribute, 1955, undated typescript, FPGP; Gertrude Weil to Mary O. Cowper, 29 June and 25 Aug. 1924, MOCP.

40. "Minutes of the Second Annual Convention"; Gertrude Weil to Mrs. Moore, 12 Apr. 1928, GWP; Gertrude Weil to Mary O. Cowper, 6 June 1924, MOCP.

41. Gertrude Weil to Mary O. Cowper, 4 Apr. 1924, MOCP; Mrs. S. McMahon

to Gertrude Weil, 23 Mar. 1923, GWP; Carrie Chapman Catt to Maud Wood Park, Easter Sunday 1922, League of Women Voters, Library of Congress, Washington, DC; "drifting" comment quoted in Barbara Stuhler, *For the Public Record: A Documentary History of the League of Women Voters* (Westport: Greenwood, 2000), 68.

42. Young, *In the Public Interest*, 83; Belle Sherwin to Gertrude Weil, 3 Oct. 1928; Gertrude Weil to Belle Sherwin, 10. Oct. 1928, GWP,

43. Gertrude Weil to Mrs. Miller, 11 Sept. 1928, GWP; Gertrude Weil to Mary O. Cowper, 8 Mar. 1924, MOCP.

44. *Goldsboro Daily Argus*, 16 Feb. 1924.

45. Quoted in Roydhouse, "'Universal Sisterhood of Women,'" 240.

46. Ibid., 381; Guion Griffis Johnson, interview by Mary Frederickson, 17 May 1974 (G-00290-2), Southern Oral History Program Collection (4007), http://docsouth .unc.edu/sohp/html_use/G-0029-2.html.

47. Gertrude Weil to Penrhyn Stanlaws, 16 Aug. 1922; "The Immorality of Our Fashions," undated handwritten note, GWP.

48. Gertrude Weil to Mrs. Walter Crowell, 21 Mar. 1927, GWP; Linda Gordon Kuzmack, *Woman's Cause: The Jewish Woman's Movement in England and the United States, 1881–1933* (Columbus: Ohio State University Press, 1990), 159.

49. For DuBois on the Talented Tenth, see http://teachingamericanhistory.org /library/document/the-talented-tenth/ (accessed 6 June 2016).

50. Belle Sherwin to Gertrude Weil, 21 and 31 May 1928; "Minutes of the Second Annual Convention." The North Carolina League of Women Voters dropped "censorship" and instead called for "wholesome" movies.

51. L. B. McBrayer to Gertrude Weil, 4 Aug. 1923; Gertrude Weil to Mr. Peterson, n.d.; untitled, undated typescript of antituberculosis report, GWP.

52. Decisions Committee, 7 Mar. and n.d. May 1928; Decisions Committee, Bureau for Social Service, report, 28 Jan. 1931; Decisions Committee, annual report, Jan. 1930 and Jan. 1932, GWP.

53. "The Cry of the Children," undated typescript, GWP.

54. Ibid.; president's report, Goldsboro Bureau for Social Service, 12 Jan. 1927, GWP.

55. See Mary Hoffschwelle, *The Rosenwald Schools of the American South* (Gainesville: University of Florida Press, 2006).

56. *Winston Salem Journal*, 2 May 1928.

57. Maud Turman to Gertrude Weil, 28 Nov. 1928; "A Review of the History and Work of the Special Committee on Interracial Problems, National League of Women Voters," undated typescript, GWP.

58. Gertrude Weil to Clara Cox, 19 Apr. 1928; Gertrude Weil to Adele Clark, 19 Apr. 1928, GWP.

59. See Newkirk, *Lynching in North Carolina*, 6; Christensen, *Paradox of Tar Heel Politics*, 86; Oheb Sholom Sisterhood program honoring Mrs. Henry Weil, 2 Feb. 1933; C. Dillard to Kind Friend, 8 Feb. 1929, GWP. In a prescient letter, Nathan O'Berry lamented the white man's inability to recognize the African-American's humanity and anticipated "ten years from now" when he hoped feelings would be different; Nathan O'Berry to Mina Weil, 20 Apr. 1928, GWP.

60. Jeffrey Crow, Paul Escott, and Flora Hatley, *A History of African Americans in North Carolina* (Raleigh, NC: Office of Archives and History). 136; Charity Organization Society, Goldsboro, NC, annual report, 1926, GWP.

61. Crow et al., *History of African Americans*, 137; canceled checks, 1923–39.

62. Link, *Paradox of Southern Progressivism*, 251, 252, 256–57, 260. Among the Commission on Interracial Cooperation members were W. C. Jackson, Clara Cox, Howard Odum, and Laura Cone.

63. Quoted in Virginia Wooten Gulledge, *The North Carolina Conference for Social Service: A Study of Its Development and Methods* (Chapel Hill: North Carolina Conference for Social Service, 1942), 51.

64. W. C. Jackson to The New Member of the North Carolina Commission on Interracial Cooperation, 5 July 1932; Laurence Oxley to Miss Weil, 9 Jan. 1932, GWP.

65. Bertha Newell to Miss Weil, 31 Jan. 1931, GWP; "Excerpt from Program of the Conference of the State Committee of Women for the Prevention of Lynching, November 1, 1930," Jewish Women's Archive, http://jwa.org/media/excerpt-from -program-of-conference-of-state-committee-of-women-for-prevention-of-lynching (accessed 22 Dec. 2013); John Shelton Reed, "An Evaluation of an Anti-Lynching Organization," *Southern Problems* 16 (Fall 1968): 175. See Jacquelyn Dowd Hall, *Revolt against Chivalry: Jessie Daniel Ames and the Women's Campaign against Lynching* (New York: Columbia University Press, 1979), x. Ames was a Texan who moved to North Carolina.

66. Link, *Paradox of Southern Progressivism*, 239, 260–61, 267; John Egerton, *Speak Now against the Day: The Generation before the Civil Rights Movement in the South* (Chapel Hill: University of North Carolina Press, 1994), 166.

67. *Monthly News*, May 1925, MOCP; "Today Anniversary of Founding of Women's Club," *Goldsboro News*, 23 Mar. 1928.

68. Department of International Co-operation to Prevent War, annual report, Charlotte, NC, 9 Mar. 1926; International Co-operation to Prevent War, annual report of state chairman, Chapel Hill, NC, 10 Mar. 1927, GWP; *Monthly News*, Mar. 1927, MOCP; Young, *In the Public Interest*, 63, 124; Melissa Klapper, *Ballots, Babies, and Banners of Peace: American Jewish Women's Activism, 1890–1940* (New York: New York University Press, 2013), 140.

69. Kuzmack, *Woman's Cause*, 3; Committee on International Relations, annual report, High Point, NC, May 1928; Gertrude Weil to Mrs. Miller, 11 Sept. 1928, GWP; *Monthly News*, Feb. 1929, MOCP.

70. Mary Anderson to Mary O. Cowper, 8 Dec. 1927; National Women's Trade Union League, "Women Voters Stand by Women Trade Unionists," typescript, 18 Apr. 1921, GWP.

71. Quoted in Roydhouse, "'Universal Sisterhood of Women,'" 281, 307–8; *Monthly News*, Apr. 1926, MOCP.

72. Roydhouse, "'Universal Sisterhood of Women,'" 308, 309, 311, 315; *Southern Textile Bulletin*, 26 Nov. 1931. Clark's father was Justice Walter Clark, Gertrude's suffrage ally.

73. E. C. Carter to Mary O. Cowper, 26 Feb. 1926; Angus McLean to Gertrude Weil, 24 July 1926, GWP.

74. *Monthly News*, Mar. 1927, MOCP.

75. Roydhouse, "'Universal Sisterhood of Women,'" 160, 312, 313, 314–15, 316–18; Gertrude Weil to Gov. W. A. McLean, n.d.; "His Excellency, W. A. McLean, Governor," undated typescript, GWP. The state attorney general ruled that the Child Welfare Commission was not authorized to conduct the survey.

76. *Monthly News*, Mar. 1926, MOCP; *Raleigh News and Observer*, 20 July 1926; *Goldsboro News-Argus*, 21 July 1926; Gertrude Weil to H. F. Seawell, Harriet Elliott, Annie O'Berry, Mary Henderson, Clara Cox, 18 July 1926, GWP.

77. Gertrude Weil to Mrs. Henry Harris, 14 Jan. 1928, GWP.

78. Roydhouse, "'Universal Sisterhood of Women,'" 292.

79. Young, *In the Public Interest*, 96–97.

80. "Report of Acting Chairman," Mar. 1923–24, *Monthly News*, Mar. 1923, MOCP.

81. Quoted in Roydhouse, "'Universal Sisterhood of Women,'" 296–97; Sarah Matthews to Minnie Fisher Cunningham, 26 Aug. 1924, League of Women Voters, Library of Congress, Washington, DC.

82. Roydhouse, "'Universal Sisterhood of Women,'" 297; Link, *Paradox of Southern Progressivism*, 170.

83. Roydhouse, "'Universal Sisterhood of Women,'" 297. Wiley Swift of the "aggressive" nonprofit National Child Labor Committee complained that its North Carolina affiliate's "quiet ways" were ineffective. Quoted in Link, *Paradox of Southern Progressivism*, 176.

84. Roydhouse, "'Universal Sisterhood of Women,'" 300, 312–13, 321.

85. Ibid., 295, 296.

86. Ibid., 301, 298; Stuhler, *For the Public Record*, 139–40; Nasstrom, "'More Was Expected of Us,'" 42.

87. "Passing an 8 Hour Law for Children," undated typescript, GWP.

88. "The American Child: Again North Carolina," typescript, June 1927; Wiley Swift to Gertrude Weil, 6 Mar. 1928, GWP. The legislature previously defeated bills requiring compulsory school attendance until sixteen or to prevent children from working in dangerous environments.

89. Roydhouse, "'Universal Sisterhood of Women,'" 299, 300, 302–3.

90. Gertrude Weil to Mary O. Cowper, 30 July 1926, MOCP; Cowper quoted in Nasstrom, "'More Was Expected of Us,'" 44; Young, *In the Public Interest*, 93.

91. Young, *In the Public Interest*, 93; Linda Kuzmack, *Women's Cause: The Jewish Woman's Movement in England and the United States, 1881–1933* (Columbus: Ohio State University, 1990), 171; annual report of president, seventh annual convention, Chapel Hill, typescript, 10 Mar. 1927, GWP.

92. Belle Sherwin to Gertrude Weil, 5 and 6 Oct. 1927, GWP.

93. *New York Times*, 1 July 1927; Roydhouse, "'Universal Sisterhood of Women,'" 254n67; "Greetings to the D.A.R. Convention," Raleigh, 27 Mar. 1928, GWP.

94. Nasstrom, "'More Was Expected of Us,'" 59; Gertrude Weil to Julia Margaret

Hicks, 9 Oct. 1927; Paul Blanshard, *Labor in Southern Cotton Mills* (New York: New Republic, 1927); Paul Blanshard to Mary O. Cowper, 7 May and 16 Nov. 1927, GWP. Other invitees were Josephus Daniels, Frank Graham, and Kate Burr Johnson.

95. Graham, "We Come to Gertrude Weil"; Roydhouse, "'Universal Sisterhood of Women,'" 304; Gertrude Weil to Mary O. Cowper, 9 Oct. 1927; Mary O. Cowper to Gertrude Weil, 10 Oct. 1927, GWP.

96. *Monthly News*, Sept. 1927, MOCP; Huldah Moorhead to Gertrude Weil, 28 Oct. 1928: Moorhead stated Cowper was "really appreciated" in Asheville; Mary Cowper to Gertrude Weil, 7 Nov. 1928; Myrtle Miller to Miss Weil, 28 May 1928; Elizabeth Cotten to Gertrude Weil, 10 Dec. 1928; Mary O. Cowper to Gertrude Weil, 21 Nov. 1928; Eleanor Mosher to Mrs. Arthur Ringland, 22 Feb. 1928; Gertrude Weil to Huldah Moorhead, 18 Apr. 1928; Belle Sherwin to Gertrude Weil, 3 Oct. 1928; Gertrude Weil to Belle Sherwin, 10. Oct. 1928, GWP.

97. Belle Sherwin to Gertrude Weil, 16 Feb. 1928, GWP.

98. "Gertrude Weil," Jewish Women's Archive, Women of Valor web exhibit, http://jwa.org/womenofvalor/weil/social-service (accessed 24 Jan. 2014); "Adult Education in Citizenship," typescript, Mar. 1928; Mary Grace Canfield to Gertrude Weil, 14 Apr. 1932; Harold Glasgow to Gertrude Weil, 21 May 1934, GWP.

99. Young, *In the Public Interest*, 94–95; Roydhouse, "'Universal Sisterhood of Women,'" 258–59; Mary O. Cowper to Laura Cone, 25 Feb. 1928; Gertrude Weil to Belle Sherwin, 21 June 1928, GWP. Gertrude wrote Sherwin that the one supportive legislator was W. O. Saunders, who, she noted, was "(considered) radical."

100. Gertrude Weil to Dear Member of the Board, 2 Oct. 1928; Gertrude Weil to Gertrude Ely, 30 Sept. 1928, GWP. Gertrude's remark is curious since she well knew that Cornelia Jerman and Gladys Tillett endorsed Smith.

101. "Why I Would Not Vote for Hoover," undated handwritten notes; "Some Moral Issues of the Present Campaign," typescript, 1928, GWP; Jonathan D. Sarna, "The Jewish Vote in Presidential Elections," *Sh'ma* (blog), 1 Jan. 2012, http://shma .com/2012/01/the-jewish-vote-in-presidential-elections.

102. "Readers Write of Problems," undated newspaper clipping; Gladys Tillett to Gertrude Weil, 13 Dec. 1928; Mary O. Cowper to President [Gertrude Weil], 7 Nov. 1928, GWP. Gertrude did not think Prohibition was "realistic" with bootleg flowing freely and advocated Alcohol Beverage Control stores so that the state could earn revenue. "Readers Write of Problems."

103. Warren Ashby, *Frank Porter Graham: A Southern Liberal* (Winston-Salem, NC: Blair, 1980), 68–70; Gulledge, *North Carolina Conference for Social Service*, 36–37. Other members of the Central Committee on Code included W. C. Jackson, A. W. McAlister, and Clarence Poe.

104. Graham, "We Come to Gertrude Weil"; Frank Graham to Mrs. Weil, 25 Feb. 1930, GWP.

105. Christensen, *Paradox of Tar Heel Politics*, 71; Gertrude Weil to R. W. Hogue, 13 July 1930, GWP.

106. Canceled checks, 1923–39. For Fred Beal, see http://ncpedia.org/biography /beal-fred-erwin (accessed 2 June 2016).

107. Roydhouse, "'Universal Sisterhood of Women,'" 338, 342, 343.

108. Gertrude Weil to Mary O. Cowper, 7, 15 Sept. 1924; *Monthly News*, May, July–Aug., and Oct. 1929, MOCP; Harriet Payne to Gertrude Weil, 24 Dec. 1928, GWP.

109. *Monthly News*, July–Aug. and Oct. 1929, MOCP; Frank Porter Graham to Kemp Battle, 5 Oct. 1929, FPGP; *Monthly Bulletin*, June 1928 and Mar. 1930, MOCP.

110. *Monthly News*, Oct. 1929, MOCP.

111. Quoted in Roydhouse, "'Universal Sisterhood of Women,'" 324, 358; Nell Battle Lewis, "Whose Fault Is It" and "Incidentally," Feb. 1929, Nell Battle Lewis Papers, State Archives of North Carolina, Raleigh; Milton Ready, *The Tar Heel State: A History of North Carolina* (Columbia: University of South Carolina Press, 2005), 328.

112. *Monthly News*, May and June 1929, MOCP.

113. Roydhouse, "'Universal Sisterhood of Women,'" 350; *Southern Textile Bulletin*, 26 Sept. 1929.

114. Roydhouse, "'Universal Sisterhood of Women,'" 323, 347–48, 349, 354; *Monthly Bulletin*, Dec. 1929, MOCP; Bertha Newell attended and Bulus Bagby Swift testified before the house committee.

115. Frank [Porter Graham] to Gertrude [Weil], 13 Dec. 1929, GWP; Harriet Herring to Gertrude Weil, 5 Feb. 1930, FPGP. Graham also asked Clara Cox and A. W. McAlister to lead.

116. Roydhouse, "'Universal Sisterhood of Women,'" 358. The short-lived Blue Ridge Conference of 1930 led to a coalition, the Southern Council on Women and Children in Industry, but it died for lack of finances and committed workers. Its mission and legislative program overlapped with those of the North Carolina League of Women Voters, but conservative women of the state's Federation of Women's Clubs constrained it. Hugh MacRae to Gertrude Weil, 13 May 1930, GWP. MacRae, a leader of the Wilmington race riot of 1898, was a real estate entrepreneur in coastal Carolina, where he promoted scientific agriculture and immigrant farm colonies, including in 1939 Van Eeden for European Jewish refugees. Frank Porter Graham to Hugh McRae, 1 May, 21 June, and 9 July 1930; Gertrude Weil to Frank [Graham], 25 June 1931, FPGP; Ready, *Tar Heel State*, 336; Harriet Herring to Gertrude Weil, 29 May 1930, GWP.

117. Roydhouse, "'Universal Sisterhood of Women,'" 363, 366–68; *Monthly Bulletin*, Dec. 1929, MOCP. The Legislative Council called upon Gertrude, as well as Mary Cowper, Elsie Riddick, and Bulus Swift, to testify before the House Judiciary Committee. 118. Roydhouse, "'Universal Sisterhood of Women,'" 372; canceled checks, 1936, GWP.

119. Roydhouse, "'Universal Sisterhood of Women,'" 372.

120. *Monthly News*, Mar. 1930, MOCP.

121. Young, *In the Public Interest*, 98–99; *Monthly News*, May 1930, MOCP. The National Woman's Party also dwindled from 35,000 in 1920 to 1,000 in 1930.

122. Roydhouse, "'Universal Sisterhood of Women,'" 370.

123. Ibid., 202; "Southern Summer School for Women Workers in Industry," undated brochure, GWP. The camp moved from Arden to Burnsville to Hendersonville.

124. Avery Baker to Gertrude Weil, 2 Mar. 1932; Louise Leonard McLaren to Gertrude Weil, 6 June 1932, GWP. Southern Summer School for Women Workers in Industry's advisory board included Frank Porter Graham, Dean Alice Baldwin of Duke, and William Birthright of the American Federation of Labor. Roydhouse, "'Universal Sisterhood of Women,'" 93, 177, 198.

125. Nasstrom, "'More Was Expected of Us,'" 315–16; Roydhouse, "'Universal Sisterhood of Women,'" 193, 215–19.

126. Quoted in Christensen, *Paradox of Tar Heel Politics*, 75.

127. Quoted in Nasstrom, "'More Was Expected of Us,'" 307; *Monthly News*, Feb. 1928, MOCP. See *Greensboro Daily Record*, 12 Jan. 1928.

128. Roydhouse, "'Universal Sisterhood of Women,'" 373.

129. Graham, "We Come to Gertrude Weil"; *Monthly News*, Feb. 1930, MOCP; Beverly Gage, "Left Turn," *New York Times Magazine*, 17 Jan. 2016, 15.

CHAPTER 8

1. Dr. J. M. T. Finney Jr. to Leslie Weil, 25 Nov. 1932, WFP.

2. Gertrude Weil to Leslie and Hilda Weil, n.d., WFP.

3. Martha Boswell to Gertrude Weil, 2 Jan. 1933; Rachel Berenson Perry to Gertrude Weil, 21 Mar. 1933, GWP.

4. "Harriet L. Payne," handwritten eulogy, 27 Dec. 1950, GWP.

5. Kala Rosenthal Herlands, interview by the author, 7 Apr. 2011; A. Helen Martikainen, interview by the author, 16 June 2011; Roy Brown to Gertrude Weil, 10 June 1943; Marjorie [no last name] to Gertrude, 12 June 1943, GWP.

6. Frank Graham to Mina Weil, 4 Jan. 1932; Jake Oettinger to Coz Mina, 5 Jan. 1932; Eli Oettinger to Cousin Mina, 5 Jan. 1932, GWP.

7. See "Goldsboro, North Carolina," *Encyclopedia of Southern Jewish Communities*, Goldring/Woldenberg Institute of Southern Jewish Life, http://www.isjl.org /north-carolina-goldsboro-encyclopedia.html (accessed 3 June 2016); Augusta [?] to Mrs. Weil, 11 July 1935, GWP.

8. H. C. Valentine & Co. Antiques to Miss Weil, 9 Feb. 1933; canceled checks, 1932, 1933, GWP.

9. Gertrude Weil to Ella Waddill, 21 Apr. 1936, GWP.

10. Gertrude Weil, "Knowing, Coordinating, and Developing Our Social Resources in Goldsboro," speech typescript, Jan. 10, 1938, Local History Room, Wayne County Public Library.

11. Ready, *Tar Heel State*, 324; Rob Christensen, *The Paradox of Tar Heel Politics: The Personalities, Elections, and Events That Shaped Modern North Carolina* (Chapel Hill: University of North Carolina Press, 2008), 66.

12. Martha Boswell to dear friends, 23 Dec. 1930, GWP; Christensen, *Paradox of Tar Heel Politics*, 62.

13. Decisions Committee, [Goldsboro] Bureau for Social Services, annual report, 28 Jan. 1931 and Jan. 1932, GWP.

14. Christensen, *Paradox of Tar Heel Politics*, 65; Kemp Battle to Gertrude Weil, 22 Aug. 1934; Annie Bost to Gertrude Weil, 28 July 1934, GWP. The consolidated university system at first consisted of the flagship campuses in Raleigh, Greensboro, and Chapel Hill.

15. Marion Roydhouse, "The 'Universal Sisterhood of Women': Women and Labor Reform in North Carolina, 1900–1932" (Ph.D. diss., University of North Carolina at Chapel Hill, 1980), 382; Gertrude Weil to Lucy Randolph Mason, 3 May 1932, GWP.

16. Lucy Mason to Frank Graham, 28 and 29 Dec. 1932; Lucy Morgan to Gertrude Weil, 28 Dec. 1932; Lucy Randolph Mason to Frank Graham, 29 Dec. 1932, FPGP. This new council included Gertrude and League cohorts Mary Cowper, Cornelia Jerman, Bertha Newell, Clara Cox, and Harriet Elliott. Also joining were attorney Kemp Battle, editor Hiden Ramsey, and publisher Clarence Poe. A. W. McAlister to Gertrude Weil, 11 and 18 Oct., 8 and 30 Nov., and 4 and 9 Dec. 1932; Gertrude Weil to A. W. McAlister, 4 Nov. and 4 Dec. 1932 and 19 Feb. 1933; Frank Graham to Ella Waddill, 14 May 1932; A. W. McAlister to Ella Waddill, 30 June 1932; NCAJW, *Year Book*, 1934–35, 6–7, GWP.

17. NCAJW, *Year Book*, 1934–35, 6–7. Emma Edwards and her cousins Etta Spier and Miriam Rosenthal also represented NCAJW to the council.

18. Annie Bost to Gertrude Weil, 9 May 1934; A. W. McAlister to Mrs. W. B. Waddill, 30 June 1932, GWP.

19. See Sarah Wilkerson-Freeman, "From Clubs to Parties: North Carolina Women in the Advancement of the New Deal," *North Carolina Historical Review* 68, no. 3 (1991): 320–39; Gardner quoted in Christensen, *Paradox of Tar Heel Politics*, 77.

20. Anthony Badger, *North Carolina and the New Deal* (Raleigh, NC: Department of Cultural Resources, 1981), 38; Johanna Schoen, *Choice and Coercion: Birth Control, Sterilization, and Abortion in Public Health and Welfare* (Chapel Hill: University of North Carolina Press, 2005), 10.

21. Ready, *Tar Heel State*, 237. After the 1931 bank failure, O'Berry and her father-in-law, Nathan, an old friend of Mina Weil, raised $5,000 for local relief; Mrs. Thomas O'Berry, "Wayne County, Nov. 1932," NCERAP; Wayne County Superintendent of Public Welfare, Board of Public Welfare, to Mrs. Henry Weil, 4 Dec. 1934; Mrs. Mina Weil to Mr. Cutter, 26 Mar. 1932, GWP.

22. Badger, *North Carolina and the New Deal*, 40; J. S. Kirk, Walter A. Cutter, and Thomas W. Morse, eds., *Emergency Relief in North Carolina* (Raleigh: North Carolina Emergency Relief Commission, 1936), 14, 70, http://docsouth.unc.edu/nc/emergencyrelief/emergencyrelief.html; Z. G. Hollowell to Gertrude Weil, 15 Aug. 1933; Mrs. Thomas O'Berry to R. H. Edwards, 31 Aug. 1933, GWP; Annie O'Berry to Local Advisory Boards, North Carolina Emergency Relief Agency, 30 Aug. 1933, GWP.

23. Ready, *Tar Heel State*, 333; Badger, *North Carolina and the New Deal*, 47.

24. Gertrude Weil to Annie O'Berry, 29 Aug. 1933; Annie O'Berry to Gertrude Weil, 31 Aug. 1933, GWP.

25. Mrs. Thomas O'Berry, Wayne County, reports for Mar.-Apr. 1933; Goldsboro Bureau for Social Service, Wayne County, Reports for Mar.-Apr. 1933, NCERAP.

26. Kirk et al., *Emergency Relief in North Carolina*, 70.

27. Badger, *North Carolina and the New Deal*, 43 (see also Wilkerson-Freeman, "From Clubs to Parties," 339); Martha Boswell to Gertrude Weil, 4 Feb. 1934 and 25 Dec. 1935; Gertrude Weil, untitled typescript, North Carolina State Board of Charities and Public Welfare file, GWP.

28. Ready, *Tar Heel State*, 53, 330, 333.

29. Badger, *North Carolina and the New Deal*, 29–30; Mina Weil to Gertrude Weil, 12 Sept. 1934, GWP; Ready, *Tar Heel State*, 329–30.

30. Ready, *Tar Heel State*, 30, 78, 333, 339; Badger, *North Carolina and the New Deal*, 71, 13.

31. "On Knowing, Coordinating, and Developing our Social Resources in Goldsboro," speech to the Goldsboro Kiwanis Club, 10 Jan. 1938, GWP.

32. Badger, *North Carolina and the New Deal*, 39.

33. Ready, *Tar Heel State*, 335.

34. Mrs. Thomas [Annie] O'Berry, Supervisor Wayne County, Nov. 1932, typescript report, NCERAP; Gertrude Weil to Lawrence Oxley, 19. Jan. 1933, GWP; Margaret Clark Neal, "North Carolina Conference for Social Service Records of Its Twenty-Five Years," typescript, 7 Apr. 1938, NCC, 180, 183, 185, 187. Committee members from the University of North Carolina at Chapel Hill and North Carolina College for Negroes (later North Carolina Central University) in Durham included Fannie Bickett, Clara Cox, Guy Johnson, W. C. Jackson, and Howard Odum.

35. John Egerton, *Speak Now against the Day: The Generation before the Civil Rights Movement in the South* (Chapel Hill: University of North Carolina Press, 1994), 191. Among those staying home were Jessie Daniel Ames, Howard Odum, and Lillian Smith. Odum, more interested in research than in activism, differed with Graham on organizational approaches to regional problems and was less tolerant of leftists; Clark Foreman, interview by Jacquelyn Hall and William Finger, 16 Nov. 1974 (B-0003), Southern Oral History Program Collection (4007), http://docsouth.unc.edu/sohp/B-0003/excerpts/excerpt_2617.html.

36. North Carolina Conference for Social Service board of directors meeting, Minutes, 29 Oct. 1942 and 27 July 1943, AWMP; Lucy Randolph Mason to Gertrude Weil, 29 Apr. and 4 May 1932; Gertrude Weil to Lucy Randolph Mason, 3 May 1932; "Personality in News: Miss Gertrude Weil," undated newspaper clipping, GWP; Virginia Wooten Gulledge, *The North Carolina Conference for Social Service: A Study of Its Development and Methods* (Chapel Hill: North Carolina Conference for Social Service, 1942), 44.

37. Badger, *North Carolina and the New Deal*, 92; Martha Boswell to Gertrude Weil, 25 Dec. 1935, GWP.

38. Gertrude Weil to A. W. McAlister, 5 Mar. 1940 and 19 Jan. and 7 Dec. 1941, AWMP; Gulledge, *North Carolina Conference for Social Service*, 65, 71.

39. Melissa Klapper, *Ballots, Babies, and Banners of Peace: American Jewish Women's Activism, 1890–1940* (New York: New York University Press, 2013), 147; Eleanor Dwight Jones to Gertrude Weil, 19 Nov. 1930, GWP. Ella Waddill, a women's club activist and public health officer in Vance County, also led the move for birth control.

40. Hazel Moore to Gertrude Weil, 12 Feb. 1931 and 23 Mar. 1932, GWP.

41. Klapper, *Ballots, Babies, and Banners of Peace*, 72, 81, 85; Gertrude Weil to Margaret Sanger, 25 Feb. 1932; Margaret Sanger to Gertrude Weil, 3 Mar. 1932, GWP. References in Gertrude's engagement books to "Margaret Sanger" are to Margaret Heyn Sanger, Gertrude's cousin—and Ruth Heyn Weil's sister—from Ohio.

42. *Birth Control News Letter*, June 1925; Hazel Moore to Gertrude Weil, 13 Feb. 1931, GWP.

43. Hazel Moore to Gertrude Weil, 12 and 13 Feb. 1931, GWP.

44. Hazel Moore to Gertrude Weil, 12 Feb. 1931, GWP.

45. A. W. McAlister, "North Carolina Conference for Social Welfare," 26 Apr. 1932; "Statement Concerning the Present Situation of the Birth Control Program in North Carolina," 1 Nov. 1938; Woodbridge Morris to Gertrude Weil, 22 June 1939; Hazel Moore to Gertrude Weil, 27 June n.d. [likely dates to 1939 since it mentions merger of national birth control groups], GWP.

46. George Lawrence to Mina Weil, 30 Apr. 1935; George Lawrence, "Something Ought to Be Done about It," undated typescript, 26 Apr. 1935; North Carolina Mental Hygiene Society brochure, [1936]. Its mission was to prevent "nervous and mental disorders," promote legislation, and raise standards of care. Other members included Annie O'Berry, Kemp Battle, and Janet Weil Bluethenthal. Harry Crane to Gertrude Weil, 9 July 1936, GWP; Klapper, *Ballots, Babies, and Banners of Peace*, 147. In 1936 the North Carolina Mental Hygiene Society invited Gertrude to become a "tentative" executive committee member.

47. Schoen, *Choice and Coercion*, 71; quoted in Gulledge, *North Carolina Conference for Social Service*, 43; North Carolina Maternal Health League, "A Population Program for North Carolina," 1941, GWP.

48. Gertrude Weil to Margaret Sanger, 25 Feb. 1932; E. S. Gosney to Mina Weil, 3 July 1931, GWP; *Raleigh News and Observer*, 10 May 1925.

49. Decisions Committee, "Bureau for Social Service Report," 29 June 1933, GWP; Tom Belton, "Eugenics Board," in William Powell, ed., *Encyclopedia of North Carolina* (Chapel Hill: University of North Carolina Press, 2006), 402.

50. Schoen, *Choice and Coercion*, 7; quoted in Gulledge, *The North Carolina Conference for Social Service*, 43; Neal, "North Carolina Conference for Social Service," 137, 168; "Minutes, Annual Meeting of Conference—Raleigh—1934," North Carolina Conference for Social Service, GWP.

51. Schoen, *Choice and Coercion*, 121, 125, 138, 212.

52. Ibid., 138. The critique against eugenics is part of the larger reassessment of Enlightenment thinking for social engineering and scientific disparagement of minorities. Sanger deplored linkage between birth control and race or religion and urged African Americans to create a program.

53. Gertrude Weil to David Rankin Barbee, 10 Jan. 1928; "President's Report, Goldsboro Bureau for Social Service," 12 Jan. 1927, GWP; Klapper, *Ballots, Babies, and Banners of Peace*, 170; Schoen, *Choice and Coercion*, 22, 24.

54. Clarence Gamble to Gertrude Weil, 10 Nov. 1947; Gertrude Weil to Clarence Gamble, 23 Nov. 1947, GWP; Schoen, *Choice and Coercion*, 108. Schoen claims that blacks constituted 75 per cent of those sterilized. For an updated assessment, see

Lutz Kaelber, "Eugenics/Sexual Sterilizations in North Carolina," https://www.uvm.edu/~lkaelber/eugenics/NC/NC.html (accessed 7 June 2016).

55. Schoen, *Choice and Coercion*, 105.

56. Eduard Lindeman to Gertrude Weil, 30 Apr. 1936; "Summer Playground, 1939," handwritten notes, GWP; Mina Bluethenthal Kempton, "Gertrude was my aunt ...," undated typescript, WFP.

57. Elsa Ernst to Gertrude Weil, 19 Feb. 1939, GWP; Gertrude Weil to A. W. McAlister, 27 Nov. 1942 and 14 Jan. 1943, AWMP. Gertrude's passion for the farm colony for white girls became entangled in racial and partisan politics when Annie Bost, commissioner of the Board of Charities and Public Welfare, wanted to fund a "new institution for Colored girls." In her 1943 letter to McAlister, Gertrude endorsed the school, but not at the expense of the white program. She suspected a "political plot" by the "State Prison ring" more interested in patronage than the welfare of blacks.

58. Martikainen interview.

59. Ibid. Martikainen also cited University of North Carolina at Chapel Hill public health educators Milton Rosenau and Lucy Morgan as inspirations.

60. W. C. Jackson to Gertrude Weil, 4 Apr. 1946, GWP.

61. William MacNider to Gertrude Weil, 8 Sept. 1933, GWP; Gertrude Weil to A. W. McAlister, 27 Oct. 1940, AWMP.

62. Hilda Einstein Weil, "The Lives of Leslie and Hilda Weil, Dedicated to My Five Children," typescript, 1950, WFP; Herman Weil's self-written eulogy, undated typescript, WFP; Frank Porter Graham to Gertrude Weil, 24 June 1946; W. C. Jackson to Gertrude Weil, 12 and 23 Dec. 1946; Gertrude Weil to W. C. Jackson, 18 Dec. 1946, GWP.

63. "Opening of Fall Term, Woman's College—U.N.C.," 14 Sept. 1941, GWP.

64. Moses Rountree, *Strangers in the Land: The Story of Jacob Weil's Tribe* (Philadelphia: Dorrance, 1969), 129; Beverly Gage, "Left Turn," *New York Times Magazine*, 17 Jan. 2016, 63; Foreman interview; Mary Price Adamson, interview by Mary Frederickson, 19 Apr. 1976 (G-0001), Southern Oral History Program Collection (4007), http://docsouth.unc.edu/sohp/G-0001/G-0001.html.

65. Thomas Krueger, *Promises to Keep: The Southern Conference for Human Welfare, 1938–1948* (Nashville, TN: Vanderbilt University Press, 1967), 133–34, 164–65.

66. Warren Ashby, *Frank Porter Graham: A Southern Liberal* (Winston-Salem, NC: Blair, 1980), 233.

67. Ibid., 233, 237; Kempton, "Gertrude was my aunt"; Virginia Foster Durr, interview by Sue Thrasher, 16 Oct. 1977 (G-0023-3), Southern Oral History Program Collection (4007), http://docsouth.unc.edu/sohp/G-0023-3/excerpts/excerpt_3053.html; Egerton, *Speak Now against the Day*, 178–192.

68. Foreman interview; Christensen, *Paradox of Tar Heel Politics*, 131–32; Krueger, *Promises to Keep*, 185–86.

69. Institute for the Arts and Humanities, "Weil Lecture on American Citizenship," http://iah.unc.edu/events/lectures/weil (accessed 13 Apr. 2014); Gertrude Weil to A. W. McAlister, 19 Jan. 1941 and 25 July 1944, AWMP.

70. "Lines Written Attending My First Pen Club Meeting," Poems (Pen Club), n.d., GWP. The poems are undated, but the names and topical references suggest 1930s.

CHAPTER 9

1. Gertrude Weil to Mary Grace Canfield, 24 Aug. 1934, GWP.

2. Gertrude Weil to A. W. McAlister, 18 May 1940, AWMP.

3. Kemp Battle to Frank Graham, 17 Nov. 1936, FPGP; Jonathan Sarna, "The 'Mythical Jew' and the "Jew Next Door,'" in David Gerber, ed., *Anti-Semitism in American History* (Urbana: University of Illinois Press, 1986), 57–78.

4. See Edward Halperin, "Frank Porter Graham, Isaac Hall Manning, and the Jewish Quota at the University of North Carolina Medical School," *North Carolina Historical Review* 67, no. 4 (1990): 393–95; William MacNider to Mina Weil, 8 Sept. 1933 and 27 Mar. 1937, GWP.

5. Hadley Cantril, *Public Opinion, 1935-1946* (Princeton, NJ: Princeton University Press, 1951), 384; Mrs. Allen V. DeFord to Leslie Weil, 21 June 1938, WFP.

6. NCAJW, *Year Book*, 1934–35, 25, GWP.

7. Nell Battle Lewis, "Incidentally," undated newspaper clipping; NCAJW, *Year Book*, 1937–38, 23, GWP. The Alien Registration Act passed in 1940. An NCAJW statewide survey found only 3 percent of foreign-born Jews lacked citizenship.

8. David Wyman, *The Abandonment of the Jews: America and the Holocaust, 1941-1945* (New York: Pantheon Books, 1984), 211.

9. NCAJW, *Year Book*, 1935–36, 27, GWP.

10. President's address, temple sisterhood, 6 Jan. 1932; "Temple Sisterhood of Goldsboro, Annual Report of President—6 Jan 1932," GWP.

11. "Purim Entertainment," 17 Mar. 1935; Jewish Sunday School materials, 15 Dec. 1935 and 26 Jan. 1936, GWP.

12. "Temple Sisterhood of Goldsboro, Annual Report of President"; E. Eustler to F. W. Simmons, 9 Nov. 1925, GWP.

13. NCAJW, *Year Book*, 1937–38, 33–34; NCAJW, *Year Book*, 1928–39, 81, GWP.

14. Emma Edwards, "The History of the North Carolina Association of Jewish Women," 30, https://archive.org/details/historyofnorthca00oedwa (accessed 6 June 2016); NCAJW, *Year Book*, 1936–36, 51–53, GWP. Hillel leaders were Goldsboro rabbi Iser Freund and Greensboro's Sidney Stern Sr., a Weil cousin by marriage.

15. Mark Bauman, "Role Theory and History," in Mark Bauman, ed., *Dixie Diaspora* (Tuscaloosa: University of Alabama Press, 2006), 242.

16. A. W. McAlister to Gertrude Weil, 15 Dec. 1933; Gertrude Weil to A. W. McAlister, 14 and 18 Dec. 1933 and 9 Sept. 1934, AWMP; A. W. McAlister to no salutation, 31 Dec. 1944, GWP.

17. A. W. McAlister to W. T. Bost, 21 Nov. 1938, AWMP.

18. Gertrude Weil, "In Times of Crises," speech typescript, Danville, VA, 20 May 1941, GWP.

19. Gertrude Weil to Belle Sherwin, 31 Mar. 1934; Golda Watson to Gertrude Weil, 21 July 1934; Gladys Tillett to Gertrude Weil, 25 July 1934; Courtney Sharpe

to Gertrude Weil, 15 July 1935, GWP. Gertrude and her sister, Janet, were also involved with the North Carolina Council for Prevention of War, associated with a national council.

20. Melissa Klapper, *Ballots, Babies, and Banners of Peace: American Jewish Women's Activism, 1890–1940* (New York: New York University Press, 2013), 119; Kala Rosenthal Herlands, interview by the author, 7 Apr. 2011; "In Times of Crises," GWP. Rabbi Stephen Wise of New York's Free Synagogue, whom Gertrude greatly admired, had spoken as a pacifist in 1932 but now urged America's entry into the war.

21. Martha Boswell to Gertrude Weil, 19 July 1943, GWP; Martha Gash Boswell Papers, 1940–1941, 1968–1969, State Archives of North Carolina, Raleigh, http://digital.ncdcr.gov/cdm/ref/collection/p16062coll15/id/112; Klapper, *Ballots, Babies, and Banners of Peace*, 190–91.

22. Emil and Marie Oettinger to Mina Weil, 28 Dec. 1930; Fritz Herzberg to dear Cousin, 8 Oct. 1931, GWP.

23. Grete Oettinger to Mina Weil, 9 Sept. 1938, GWP.

24. Ibid.; Quoted in Julian Pleasants, "The Senatorial Career of Robert Rice Reynolds, 1933–1945" (Ph.D. diss., University of North Carolina at Chapel Hill, 1971), 465–66, 494, 496–97, 545; "Breckinridge Long," *Wikipedia*, http://en.wikipedia.org/wiki/Breckinridge_Long (accessed 12 May 2014); "War Refugee Board," *Wikipedia*, http://en.wikipedia.org/wiki/War_Refugee_Board (accessed 12 May 2014); Wyman, *Abandonment of the Jews*, 5–6, 124–26.

25. General Information Regarding Visas for Immigrants, Department of State, Washington, July, 1937; "United States of America, County of Wayne, State of North Carolina, "I, Gertrude Weil … " [affidavit typescript], GWP.

26. Sworn statement, Department of State, Visa Division, 9 Sept. 1941; R. H. Edwards to Whom It May Concern, 12 Feb. 1940; Paul Garrison to Whom It May Concern, 13 Feb. 1940; R. M. to Davis no addressee, 14 Feb. 1940; Jas. Crawford to no addressee, 13 Feb. 1940; Mina Weil to Whom It May Concern, 12 Feb. 1940, GWP.

27. Bankers Trust to Mrs. Weil, 8 Feb. 1939; Emil Oettinger to Mina and Gertrude Weil, 9 Aug. 1936; Anna Rosenbaum to Mina and Gertrude Weil, 21 and 29 Sept. 1936, GWP.

28. Emil Oettinger to Mina Weil, 12 Sept. 1937, GWP.

29. Emil Oettinger to Mina Weil, 7 Mar. 1940; Max Oettinger to Dear Cousin, 11 Sept. 1939, GWP.

30. Alice Fischer to Mina Weil, 2 Feb. and 7 Apr. 1939; Bankers Trust remittance to Mr. Fritz Herzberg and Alice Fischer, May 16 and June 11, 1940; Alice Fischer to Dear Cousin, 1 Apr. and 12 Sept. 1939, GWP.

31. Olga Fortgang to Mrs. Weil, 16 May 1939; Alice Fischer to Dear Cousin, 26 Jan. 1940; Otto Birnbaum to Gertrude Weil, 8 Sept. 1939; Walter Oppenheim to Mina Weil, 20 June 1939, GWP.

32. Gertrude Weil to American Export Lines, 2 July 1941; Lise Witten to Gertrude Weil, 31 Aug 1941; [?] Schmidt to Miss Gertrude, 20 Oct. 1941, GWP.

33. Mina Weil to Gertrude Weil, 10 Dec. 1938, GWP.

34. Margaret Lovell Gibson to Gertrude Weil, 9 Nov. 1940; Amy S. J[acobs] to Gertrude Weil, n.d.; Margaret Norwood to Gertrude Weil, 26 Nov. 1940, GWP.

35. Marie Birnbaum to Department of State, Immigration Section, 16 July 1941; Hans Lederer to Gertrude Weil, 17 July 1941; Gertrude Weil to Visa Division, Department of State, 29 July 1941, GWP.

36. Fritz Herzberg to Liebe Cousine, 19 Oct. and 16 Nov. 1941; Gertrude Weil to Consul Frankfort, 22 Feb. 1940; A. M. Warren to Graham Barden, 16 Sept. 1941, GWP.

37. Emil Oettinger to Gertrude Weil, 7 Dec. 1941, GWP.

38. Alice Fischer to Gertrude Weil, 2 Aug. 1941 and 14 Mar. 1942, GWP.

39. Graham Barden telegram to Gertrude Weil, n.d., GWP.

40. Mr. Schmidt to Gertrude Weil, 20 Oct. 1941; Gertrude Weil to Hebrew Sheltering and Immigrant Aid Society, 1 Dec. 1941; Gertrude Weil to American Joint Distribution Committee, 1 Jan. 1942; Isaac Asofksy to Gertrude Weil, 15 Dec. 1941, GWP.

41. A. M. Warren, Chief Visa Division, to Gertrude Weil, 22 Jan. 1942; Emil Oettinger to Dear Cousins, 18 Apr. 1942; Raymond Gittleman to Anne Lise Witten, 30 Apr. 1942; Gertrude Weil to Eliot Coulter, n.d.; Gertrude Weil to Graham Barden, 8 June 1942; Gertrude Weil to Raymond Gittleman, 8 June 1942; Notice of Hearing to Gertrude Weil, Department of State, 20 June 1942, GWP.

42. Henrietta Szold to Mrs. Weil, 24 Feb. 1939, GWP. Among the families were the Sterns in Greensboro, Meyers in Enfield, Katzensteins in Warren Plains, and Lichtenfels in Asheville. Mrs. Raphael Tourover of Hadassah visited Goldsboro seeking support "in rescuing 1200 children for whom we have certificates who were stranded in Germany"; William Haber to Emil Rosenthal, 8 Jan. 1940, GWP.

43. "Jewish War Record, Goldsboro North Carolina, 1941–1945," 6, 9, 10, 11, WFP.

44. "The Adolescent Girl in the War Camp Area," North Carolina Conference for Social Service, GWP.

45. Elsie Fiason to Gertrude, 27 June 1943, GWP; "Jewish War Record, Goldsboro North Carolina, 1941–1945," 6, 9, 10, 11, WFP.

46. Russel Engle to Gertrude Weil, 23 Jan. 1943; Paul Kessler to Gertrude Weil, 13 July 1943; Stephen S. Wise to Gertrude Weil, 17 Sept. 1943; Gabe Jackson to Gertrude Weil, 6 Oct. 1943; Anna Shapiro to Gertrude Weil, n.d.; Sheldon Datz to Gertrude Weil, n.d.; Gertrude Weil to Chaplain Goode, 17 Sept. 1942; Bryon Ginsburg to Gertrude Weil, n.d., GWP.

47. Marjorie to Gertrude, 12 June 1943, GWP.

48. Mrs. George Butler to Gertrude Weil, 9 June 1943; Sadie [?] to Gertrude Weil, 9 June 1943; Roy Brown to Gertrude Weil, 10 June 1943; Marjorie [?] to Gertrude Weil, 12 June 1943; Harriet Elliott to Gertrude Weil, 16 June 1943; Hope Summerall Chamberlain to Gertrude Weil, 31 June 1943; Martha Boswell to Gertrude Weil, 28 June and 19 July 1943; Harriet Elliot to Gertrude Weil, 16 June 1943; M. G. Canfield to Gertrude Weil, 30 June 1943, GWP.

49. Gertrude Weil to A. W. McAlister, 27 Jan. 1943, AWMP.

50. Martha Boswell to Gertrude Weil, 19 July 1943; Hope Summerall Chamberlain to Gertrude Weil, 31 June 1943, GWP.

51. Emil Oettinger to Gertrude Weil, 14 Aug. 1946; Elizabeth Rosenthal to Gertrude Weil, 11 Aug. and 8 Sept. 1945, GWP.

CHAPTER 10

1. Speech transcript, Raleigh, 20 May 1941; "Talk at Beth Or Temple, Sisterhood Sabbath," speech transcript, Raleigh, 12 May 1944; "In Times of Crises," speech transcript, Danville, VA, 20 May 1941, GWP. See Martin P. Beifield Jr., "'Let Her Works Praise Her in the Gates," paper presented at the symposium "Women Working for Social Changes: The Legacy of Gertrude Weil," 7 Mar. 1984, Women's Studies Program, University of North Carolina at Chapel Hill, 15, AJA.

2. Azriel Eisenberg to Gertrude Weil, 18 Nov. 1952, 12 June 1953, 12 Sept. 1957, and 4 Sept. 1968; Gertrude Weil to Azriel Eisenberg, 3 Jan. 1953, GWP.

3. David Weil, interview by the author, 13 Dec. 2012; Goldsboro Temple Sisterhood minutes, 10 Oct. 1957, GWP.

4. Muriel Kramer Offerman, interview by the author, 6 June 2014; Amy Meyers Krumbein, interview by the author, 5 June 2011.

5. Solomon Herbst to Gertrude Weil, 14 Sept. 1955 and 23 Sept. 1957, GWP; Rabbi Solomon Herbst to Dear Colleague, 1 Mar. 1953, AJA.

6. Engagement books, 1953; Goldsboro Temple Sisterhood minutes, 1931, Gertrude Weil to my dear sisters of the Sisterhood, 5 Jan. 1955, GWP.

7. "Introduction of Frank P. Graham at a Meeting of the NCAJW," Greensboro, NC, 18 Apr. 1950, GWP.

8. NCAJW, *Year Book*, 1948–49; Mrs. Max Miller to Hilda Goldstone, 24 Apr. 1950; Hilda Goldstone to Irene Miller, 25 Apr. 1950; Gertrude Weil to Irene Miller, 30 Oct. 1950, GWP.

9. "In Times of Crises."

10. "Sin in the World," undated handwritten notes, GWP.

11. "Survival for What?," undated handwritten notes, GWP. To her niece Betty Weil, a college student in the 1940s, Gertrude confessed that "I'm really a secular humanist" but that she felt culturally Jewish. More typically she expressed spirituality. Elizabeth Weil Fisher, telephone interview by the author, 18 Aug. 2014; "In Times of Crises."

12. "Talk at Beth Or Temple"; "Survival for What?," GWP.

13. Untitled notes, 19 Feb. 1952; "My Concept of God Is Creative Essence, Ultimate Reality, Infinite Truth, Universal Being," typescript, Summer 1955, GWP.

14. Michael Meyer, *Response to Modernity: A History of the Reform Movement in Judaism* (Detroit, MI: Wayne State University Press, 1995), 64–67; "Why Study So Much Jewish History," handwritten notes, 15 May 1958, GWP.

15. "Survival for What?"

16. "In Times of Crises."

17. Ibid.; "Talk at Beth Or Temple."

18. "In Times of Crises."

19. "Talk at Beth Or Temple"; "Sin in the World."

20. Untitled notes, 19 Feb. 1952, GWP.

21. "What I Expect of a Sermon: A Symposium for Laymen," *American Judaism* 3, no. 3 (1954): 5–6; "What I Should Like of a Sermon," undated handwritten manuscript, GWP.

22. Rabbi Solomon Herbst to Dear Colleague, 1 Mar. 1953, AJA; Joanne Blueth-enthal and Arthur Bluethenthal, interview by the author, 17 May 2011; Elizabeth Weil Fisher, telephone interview by the author, 18 Aug. 2014.

23. Jonathan Sarna, *American Judaism: A History* (New Haven, CT: Yale University Press, 2004), 222; Kala Rosenthal Herlans, interview by the author, 17 Apr. 2011; Ida Cohn Dortch, "In Memoriam," handwritten proclamation, undated, Jewish Heritage Foundation of North Carolina Collection, Rubenstein Rare Book and Manuscript Library, Duke University, Durham, NC.

24. Rabbi Solomon Herbst to Dear Colleague, 1 Mar. 1953, AJA; [no author] to Miss Gertrude, 16 Jan. 1970, GWP.

25. "In Times of Crises"; "Talk at Beth Or Temple."

26. "What Judaism Means to Me," Jewish Women's Archive, Women of Valor web exhibit, http://jwa.org/womenofvalor/weil/what-judaism-means-to-me/study -of-judaism (accessed 7 June 2016. 1, 2).

27. Ibid.

28. Ibid., 3–5.

29. Undated, untitled notes, 19 Feb. 1952; untitled poem (first line "The waves of light stream from the far-off sun"), "Poems (Pen Club)," n.d., GWP.

30. "What Judaism Means to Me," 5.

31. Ibid., 5.

32. Ibid., 5. Gertrude never cited Rabbi Mordecai Kaplan, who inspired the Reconstructionist movement, but her rationalism, naturalism, commitment to Jewish peoplehood, and belief in Judaism as a civilization parallels his thought. Gertrude, an avid reader of Jewish literature, would have been acquainted with his extensive writings.

33. Bernard Berger to Gertrude Weil, 4 Dec. 1938, GWP.

34. "What Is the Status of Zionism," *New Palestine* 10, no. 18 (1926): 426–28; Women's Zionist Organization of America, "Zionist Public Relations," Integrated Kit no. 2, 1951–52, GWP.

35. Henrietta Szold to Mrs. Weil, 24 Feb. 1939, GWP.

36. "Impressions of Israel—May 1962," Jews Israel subject file, GWP; Avi Shavit, *My Promised Land: The Triumph and Tragedy of Israel* (New York: Spiegel and Grau, 2013), 149–51. Shavit is Joseph and Sarah Bentwich's grandson; travel diary, 2 May 1962, GWP.

37. Engagement book, 1962; "Impressions of Israel," GWP. Joseph Bentwich's father, Herbert, a British barrister, founded the British Zionist Federation in 1899.

38. Engagement book, 16 Mar. 1952, GWP; Jewish Women's Archive, "Gertrude Weil, Morris Leder, and Eleanor Roosevelt, April 4, 1955" (photograph), http://jwa .org/media/gertrude-weil-right-with-eleanor-roosevelt-and-morris-leder (accessed 31 July 2014); Beifield, "'Let Her Works Praise Her'"; quoted in Eli Evans, *The Provincials: A Personal History of Jews in the South* (Chapel Hill: University of North Carolina Press, 2005), 93.

39. Joe Berk to Gertrude Weil, 9 Jan. 1968; "The Prime Minister's Message," in Women's Zionist Organization of America, "Zionist Public Relations," 8, GWP.

40. John Cunningham, "A Significant Move," in *Talks on Timely Topics* (reprint; Commission on Interracial Cooperation, n.d.), GWP.

CHAPTER 11

1. "A very enthusiastic audience . . . ," undated newspaper clipping, engagement books, 1949, 1951, GWP.

2. Nannie Frederick to Gertrude Weil, 28 Nov. 1944, GWP.

3. "In Times of Crises," speech transcript, Danville, VA, 20 May 1941, GWP; Jacquelyn Dowd Hall, *Revolt against Chivalry: Jessie Daniel Ames and the Women's Campaign against Lynching* (New York: Columbia University Press, 1979), 259.

4. John Egerton, *Speak Now against the Day: The Generation before the Civil Rights Movement in the South* (Chapel Hill: University of North Carolina Press, 1995), 314–15; Anthony Badger, *North Carolina and the New Deal* (Raleigh, NC: Department of Cultural Resources, 1981), 92.

5. Executive committee meeting, North Carolina Commission on Interracial Cooperation, typescript, 14 Oct. 1946; C. C. Spaulding, Edgar Thompson, and Guy Johnson, "Report of Special Committee on Principles and Aims," Commission on Interracial Cooperation, 27 Sept. 1947, GWP. In 1942 the eleven Goldsboro members also included Rabbi Iser Freund, several cousins, and C. Dillard, principal of the African-American high school.

6. Spaulding et al., "Report of Special Committee on Principles and Aims"; North Carolina Commission on Interracial Cooperation, typescript, 17 Feb. 1948; executive committee meeting report, Commission on Interracial Cooperation, 7 June 1949, GWP.

7. "To Secure These Rights: The Report of the President's Committee on Civil Rights," Harry S. Truman Library and Museum, http://www.trumanlibrary.org/civilrights/srights1.htm (accessed 20 Mar. 2016).

8. Gertrude Weil to Lillian Smith, 7 July 1953, GWP.

9. *Goldsboro News-Argus*, 31 May 1971.

10. Nelle Morton to Gertrude Weil, 23 Apr. 1948, GWP; Egerton, *Speak Now against the Day*, 422–23. Gertrude advised Jones that "a visit to Governor Cherry would be wasted effort," but Cherry expressed concern only with Graham's obedience to state, not divine, law. Jones became pastor of the interracial Community Church in Chapel Hill.

11. Howard Covington and Marion Ellis, *Terry Sanford: Politics, Progress, and Outrageous Ambitions* (Durham, NC: Duke University Press, 1999), 176–77.

12. Gertrude Weil to Dear Editor, 31 Aug. 1956, GWP.

13. See Leonard Rogoff, *Down Home: Jewish Life in North Carolina* (Chapel Hill: University of North Carolina Press, 2010), 288. The North Carolina Council on Human Relations also opposed; Covington and Ellis, *Terry Sanford*, 176; Gertrude Weil to Dear Editor, 31 Aug. 1956, GWP; Clive Webb, *Fight against Fear: Southern Jews and Black Civil Rights* (Athens: University of Georgia, 2001), 147–48.

14. Rogoff, *Down Home*, 287–88.

15. Webb, *Fight against Fear*, 148–68.

16. Harry Golden to Gertrude Weil, 21 Jan. 1957, GWP. See Kimberly M. Hart-

nett, *Carolina Israelite: How Harry Golden Made Us Care about Jews, the South, and Civil Rights* (Chapel Hill: University of North Carolina Press, 2015).

17. *Goldsboro News-Argus*, 3 May 1971; Joanne Bluethenthal and Arthur Bluethenthal, interview by the author, 17 May 2011.

18. Gertrude Weil to Charles Graves, 19 Nov. 1952; "Some Suggested Ways to Make Goldsboro a Better Place," typescript of editorial for *Goldsboro Argus*, Mar. 1955, GWP.

19. Herman Weil to Page Benton, 15 Jan. 1958, GWP; Eugene Price, interview by the author, 20 Aug. 2014.

20. *Raleigh News and Observer*, 14 Mar. 1965; William Chafe, *Never Stop Running: Allard Lowenstein and the Struggle to Save American Liberalism* (New York: Basic Books, 1993), 39, 41.

21. Gertrude Weil to Dear Sirs, F. W. Woolworth Company, 14 Apr. 1960, GWP; Emily Weil, interview by the author, 13 Dec. 2012.

22. Robert Mayer, Charles King, Anne Borders-Patterson, and James McCullough, *The Impact of School Desegregation in a Southern City: A Case Study in the Analysis of Educational Policy* (Lexington, KY: Lexington Books, 1974), 16; Shelley Leder and Arnold Leder, interview by the author, 20 Aug. 2014.

23. *Raleigh News and Observer*, 14 Mar. 1965.

24. Quoted in Covington and Ellis, *Terry Sanford*, 296.

25. Robert Korstad and James Leloudis, *To Right These Wrongs: The North Carolina Fund and the Battle to End Poverty and Inequality in 1960s America* (Chapel Hill: University of North Carolina Press, 2010), 72.

26. Ibid., 73–74.

27. *Goldsboro News-Argus*, 30 May and 10 and 20 June 1963.

28. *Goldsboro News-Argus*, 12 and 14 June 1963.

29. *Goldsboro News-Argus*, 17 and 18 June 1963; Mary Ann Lachat, "Desegregation in Goldsboro, North Carolina: A Case Study," (June 1973), 17. http://files.eric.ed.gov/fulltext/ED117278.pdf (accessed 10 June 2016).

30. *Goldsboro News-Argus*, 19 July 1963; Barbara Berkeley to Dear Member, 13 and 29 Apr. 1964, GWP.

31. *Goldsboro News-Argus*, 14 Nov. 1963 and 13 Feb. 1964.

32. Rev. Elbert Williams to Gertrude Weil, 9 Dec. 1967, GWP.

33. Arabia Bunn to Mrs. Weils [*sic*], 8 Nov. 1961; Walter Foster to Gertrude Weil, 27 Apr. 1962, GWP; *Goldsboro News-Argus*, 31 May 1971; Moses Rountree, *Strangers in the Land: The Story of Jacob Weil's Tribe* (Philadelphia: Dorrance, 1969), 130.

34. *Goldsboro New-Argus*, 13 Feb. 1964.

35. Mina Bluethenthal Kempton, "Gertrude was my aunt . . . ," undated typescript, WFP.

36. Ibid.; Abram Weil to Linda, Alan, and Carol, 27 Nov. 1967, WFP; Bluethenthal and Bluethenthal interview.

37. Emily Weil interview; Elizabeth Weil, telephone interview by the author, 18 Aug. 2014.

38. Mayer et al., *Impact of School Desegregation*, 16, 21. In the sociological study the Weils are named "Farrow," but it is unmistakably them, as penciled into a copy at

the Wayne County Public Library. Rabbi Solomon Herbst to Dear Colleague, 1 Mar. 1952, GWP.

39. Mayer et al., *Impact of School Desegregation*, 26, 107.

CHAPTER 12

1. Mina Bluethenthal Kempton, "Gertrude was my aunt …," undated typescript, WFP; Ellen-Fairbanks Diggs Bodman, "Weil, Gertrude," *NCPedia*, 1996, http://ncpedia.org/biography/weil-gertrude-0 (accessed 21 July 2014); *Raleigh News and Observer*, 14 Mar. 1965; Moses Rountree, *Strangers in the Land: The Story of Jacob Weil's Tribe* (Philadelphia: Dorrance, 1969), 136.

2. Engagement book, 8 Apr. 1957 and 19 Mar. 1959, GWP.

3. Pocket travel diaries, 1950, 1951, GWP; see 2–20 Aug. 1950 for North Carolina travel; Elizabeth Weil, telephone interview by the author, 18 Aug. 2014.

4. Estelle Ries to Gertrude Weil, 7 Nov. 1964, GWP.

5. Elizabeth Weil interview.

6. Kempton, "Gertrude was my aunt …"; Kala Rosenthal Herlans, interview by the author, 17 Apr. 2011; Cissy Weil, interview by the author, 17 Mar. 2011; Elizabeth Weil interview.

7. Joanne Bluethenthal and Arthur Bluethenthal, interview by the author, 17 May 2011; Janet Bluethenthal to Gertrude Weil, 1 Feb. 1961, GWP.

8. "Opening of Fall Term, Woman's College–U.N.C.," 14 Sept. 1941; Lavinia Engle to Gertrude Weil, 9 Feb. 1962; Frances Doggett to Gertrude Weil, 22 Oct. 1969, GWP.

9. Leslie Weil Paley, telephone interview by the author, 28 Aug. 2014; Frank Graham, "We Come to Gertrude Weil in the Fullness of Our Hearts," undated typescript, WFP; "At length I seem to have come out with a degree of mental calm …," handwritten manuscript, 4 Dec.[?] 1957, GWP.

10. Louise Alexander telegram to Gertrude Weil, 6. Aug. 1947; "Harriet Payne," typescript eulogy, 27 Dec. 1950, GWP.

11. "At length I seem to have come out with a degree of mental calm."

12. Travel diary, Mar. and Apr. 1956, GWP.

13. Eugene Price, interview by the author, 20 Aug. 2014; The Great Books Foundation Readers Aids, "Sophocles: Antigone," "Plutarch," "Tolstoy," 1957, brochures, GWP.

14. Eugene Price, interview by the author; Solomon Herbst to Dear Colleague, 1 Mar. 1952, GWP.

15. The North Carolina Legislative Council, note from Hattie Parrott to Gertrude Weil, 24 Oct. 1956; Ingis Fletcher to Gertrude Weil, 6 Dec. 1954; William Friday to Gertrude Weil, 1 Mar. 1957, GWP; Bluethenthal and Bluethenthal interview.

16. *Winston Salem Journal*, 4 May 1964.

17. Frank Graham, *Charles Brantley Aycock of North Carolina: The South's Greatest Education Governor* (n.p., 1951?), 14, NCC; Howard Covington and Marion Ellis, *Terry Sanford: Politics, Progress and Outrageous Ambitions* (Durham, NC: Duke University Press, 1999), 244.

18. I. F. Stone to Gertrude Weil, 20 Dec. 1952, GWP.

19. Charles Jonas to Gertrude Weil, 16 Nov. 1954; Gertrude Weil to Harold Stassen, 24 Mar. 1955; Gertrude Weil to Basil Whitener, 29 Apr. 1957, GWP.

20. "Scott, Kerr" subject file, May 1954, GWP; Harry Golden, "Gertrude Weil," undated typescript, Harry Golden Papers, Special Collections, University of North Carolina at Charlotte.

21. Rob Christensen, *The Paradox of Tar Heel Politics: The Personalities, Elections, and Events That Shaped Modern North Carolina* (Chapel Hill: University of North Carolina Press, 2008), 141–42.

22. Engagement book, 21 and 22 June 1950, GWP, quoted in Rountree, *Strangers in the Land*, 132.

23. Gertrude Weil to Nell Battle Lewis, 13 Apr. 1950, GWP; *Raleigh News and Observer*, 2 and 9 Apr. 1950.

24. Emil Oettinger to Gertrude Weil, 29 July 1950; Gertrude Weil to Frank Graham, 26 June 1950; Gertrude Weil to Gladys Tillett, 26 June 1950, GWP; Robert Korstad and James Leloudis, *To Right These Wrongs: The North Carolina Fund and the Battle to End Poverty and Inequality in 1960s America* (Chapel Hill: University of North Carolina Press, 2010), 149.

25. "Scott, Kerr" subject file.

26. Rountree, *Strangers in the Land*, 132; Gertrude Weil, "At Chi Omega 'Tapping,'" 6 Apr. 1951, GWP.

27. Gertrude Weil to Edward K. Graham, 21 Jan. 1952; Edward K. Graham to Gertrude Weil, 24. Jan. 1952, GWP; citation of Gertrude Weil for the honorary degree of doctor of humane letters, conferred by the Woman's College of the University of North Carolina, 2 June 1952, AJA.

28. Simcha Kling to Gertrude Weil, 15 Mar. 1955; Gertrude Weil to Harry Golden, 29 Dec. 1955, GWP; Graham, "We Come to Gertrude Weil."

CHAPTER 13

1. Louis Weil, telephone interview by the author, 29 Aug. 2014.

2. Anne Firor Scott, *The Southern Lady: From Pedestal to Politics, 1830–1930* (Charlottesville: University Press of Virginia, 1995), 261; Nell Hirschberg to Gertrude Weil, Feb. 1968, GWP; Louis Weil interview.

3. Leslie Weil Paley, telephone interview by the author, 28 Aug. 2014; Lesley Weil, interview by the author, 13 Dec. 2012; Louis Weil, telephone interview by the author, 29 Aug. 2014.

4. Joanne Bluethenthal and Arthur Bluethenthal, interview by the author, 17 May 2011; David Weil, interview by the author, 13 Dec. 2012.

5. Edward K. Graham Jr. to Gertrude Weil, 8 Feb. 1956, University Archives, University of North Carolina at Greensboro; Emily Weil, interview by the author, 13 Dec. 2012.

6. Engagement books, 1952–57, GWP.

7. "G. W. C. Nominates Miss Gertrude Weil as Woman of the Year," typescript, 2 Feb. 1953, WFP; Mildred Oliver to Gertrude Weil, 15 Jan. 1958, GWP; Shelley Leder and Arnold Leder, interview by the author, 20 Aug. 2014.

8. Report of J. A. Branch, business manager, University of North Carolina, typescript, 1965, GWP; Leder and Leder interview.

9. Guion Griffis Johnson, interview by Mary Frederickson, 17 May 1974 (G-00290-2), Southern Oral History Program Collection (4007), http://docsouth .unc.edu/sohp/html_use/G-0029-2.html; Robert Korstad and James Leloudis, *To Right These Wrongs: The North Carolina Fund and the Battle to End Poverty and Inequality in 1960s America* (Chapel Hill: University of North Carolina Press, 2010), 149.

10. Leder and Leder interview.

11. Johanna Schoen, *Choice and Coercion: Birth Control, Sterilization, and Abortion in Public Health and Welfare* (Chapel Hill: University of North Carolina Press, 2005), 11. See also Korstad and Leloudis, *To Right These Wrongs*.

12. Mina Bluethenthal Kempton, "Gertrude was my aunt …," undated typescript, WFP.

13. Bluethenthal and Bluethenthal interview; Sally Kempton, "Cutting Loose," *Esquire* (July 1970), 53; Kempton, "Gertrude was my aunt"; Emily Weil interview.

14. Lesley Weil, interview by the author, 13 Dec. 2012; Leslie Weil Paley interview; Emily Weil interview; Anne Firor Scott, "Gertrude Weil and Her Times," *Southern Cultures* 13, no. 1 (2007): 88.

15. David Weil interview; Lesley Weil interview.

16. Leslie Weil Paley interview; Emily Weil interview; Louis Weil interview.

17. Moses Rountree, *Strangers in the Land: The Story of Jacob Weil's Tribe* (Philadelphia: Dorrance, 1969), 136–37; Elizabeth Weil, telephone interview by the author, 18 Aug. 2014.

18. *Raleigh News and Observer*, 14 Mar. 1965; Scott, *Southern Lady*, 261; Eli Evans, *The Provincials: A Personal History of Jews in the South* (Chapel Hill: University of North Carolina Press, 2005), 92–93.

19. Rountree, *Strangers in the Land*; Moses Rountree, "Miss Gertrude," *Goldsboro News-Argus*, 3 Jun 1971; Betsy Marsh, "A Legend in Her Lifetime," *Raleigh News and Observer*, 14 Mar. 1965; Gertrude Weil to Grace [Tillett?], 17 Mar. 1965, WFP.

20. Margaret Grierson to Gertrude Weil, 13 Nov. 1964, GWP; Elizabeth Weil interview; Scott, *Southern Lady*, 261. Great-nephews Louis and Allen Weil later donated another 6,000 items, 22.5 linear feet, of family and business material to the Southern Historical Collection at the University of North Carolina at Chapel Hill.

21. Samuel Sandmel to Gertrude Weil, 10 and 19 Jan. 1962; Gertrude Weil to Samuel Sandmel, undated letter drafts, GWP.

22. Bluethenthal and Bluethenthal interview; Elizabeth Weil interview.

23. Herbert Heston to Gertrude Weil, 1 Mar. 1966; Richard Unsworth to Gertrude Weil, 16 Apr. 1958; Rabbi Yechiael Lander to Gertrude Weil, 3 June 1969; Mina Weil to My Dear Children., n.d. [ca. 1930s], GWP.

24. Frank Warren, "Miss Gertrude Weil," *Goldsboro News-Argus*, 6 Dec. 1964; Bluethenthal and Bluethenthal interview; *Raleigh News and Observer*, 14 Mar. 1965.

25. Scott, "Gertrude Weil"; David Weil interview; Lesley Weil interview; Elizabeth Weil interview.

26. Henry Weil to Arnold Edgerton, 28 Jan. 1961, GWP.

27. *Goldsboro News-Argus*, 3 June 1971.

LEGACY

1. Anne Firor Scott, "Not Forgotten: Gertrude Weil and Her Times," *Southern Cultures*, 13, no. 1 (2007); "Gertrude Weil," Jewish Women's Archive, Women of Valor web exhibit, http://jwa.org/womenofvalor/weil (accessed 6 June 2016).

2. Eli Evans, *The Provincials: A Personal History of Jews in the South* (Chapel Hill: University of North Carolina Press, 2005), 93. Gertrude suggested that Jewish men, not women, intermarried with Christians, although that was not wholly the case in her own family.

3. "Practical idealist" appears in the obituary for Mina Bluethenthal Kempton, but it applies equally to the aunt who inspired her. "Mina Bluethenthal Kempton," *Trenton (NJ) Times*, 1 Aug. 2010, http://obits.nj.com/obituaries/trenton/obituary .aspx?pid=144387169 (accessed 17 Aug. 2014).

4. Dewey Grantham, *The Reconciliation of Progress and Tradition* (Knoxville: University of Tennessee Press, 1983), xviii; Joan Johnson, *Southern Women at the Seven Sister Colleges: Feminist Values and Social Activism, 1875–1915* (Athens: University of Georgia Press, 2008), 4.

5. "At length I seem to have come out with a degree of mental calm . . . ," manuscript, 4 Dec.[?] 1957, GWP.

INDEX

Page numbers in italics refer to photographs.

Belk, Henry, 275
Ben-Gurion, David, 247
Bentonville, NC, 7, 8
Bentwich family, 245
Berenson, Bernard, 44, 143
Berenson, Rachel (Perry), 44, 185
Berenson, Senda, x, 44, 45, 268
Berenson family, 44–45, 144, 268
Berger, Bernard, 243
Bickett, Fanny, 137, 146–47, 180
Bickett, Thomas, 88, 93, 117, 122–24, 128, 131–32, 136–37, 139
Bicycling, 19, 40
Bildung, ix, 2–4, 10, 31, 34, 101, 157, 235, 286
Birnbaum, Mizzi (Burnham), 220, 222–23, 227, 265
Birnbaum, Otto, 220, 222
Birth control, 81–82, 157–59, 197–200
Blanshard, Paul, 172
Blowing Rock, NC, 63, 113, 143
Bluethenthal, Arthur (1891–1918), 92–93
Bluethenthal, Arthur (1923–2013), 266
Bluethenthal, Herbert, 92, 143, 224
Bluethenthal, Joanne, 262, 266, 276
Bluethenthal, Mina (Kempton), 143, 181, 207, 261–62, 264, 266, 279, 284
B'nai B'rith, 28, 33, 213, 273
Booth, Maud, 38
Borden, Ethel, 66
Bost, Annie, 190, 193–94
Bost, W. T., 215
Boswell, Martha, 184, 189, 193, 197, 217, 227
Boy Scouts, 203, 277
Brandeis, Louis, 201, 236, 244
Branson, E. C., 148
Breckenridge, Madeline, 110
Brinson, Mary, 56
Brinson, Sam, 119
Brown, Charlotte Hawkins, 129, 161
Browne, Sophie W., 97
Brown v. Board of Education, 253
Bryan, William Jennings, 90, 111, 117

Burns, Lucy, 108
Butler, Marion, 115

Cable, George Washington, 43
Cable, Mary, 41, 43, *44*
Cabot, Caroline, 39, 47
Calisch, Edward, 72
Camp Osceola, 104
Canfield, M. G., 226
Cardozo, Benjamin, 236
Carr, Julian S., 117–18, 133
Carter, E. C., 165–66
Catt, Carrie Chapman: and League of Women Voters, 140, 146, 151–52, 155, 173; nativism of, 75, 217; as organizer, 112–16; peace advocacy of, 120, 138, 162–63, 183, 216–17; and North Carolina ratification, 110, 115, 122–23, 127–28, 130–32, 13–36, 138; and Winning Plan, 112–13. *See also* Weil, Gertrude
Chamberlain, Hope, 36, 141, 227
Chapel Hill, NC, 68, 154, 172, 173, 252
Charity Organization Society, 85, 94, 141–42, 157, 160
Charles B. Aycock Memorial, 269–70
Charlotte, NC, 107, 111, 255, 259, 263
Chatauqua, 23
Cheshire, J. B., 125
Chesnutt, Charles, 35
Children's Home Society, 158
Chi Omega, 272–73
Christian Science, 61, 70, 233, 236
Cincinnati, 24, 80, 97, 104
Citizenship School, 148, 163, 179
City Beautiful, 78, 79, 203, 287
Civil War, viii, 7, 8
Civil Works Administration, 91
Clark, David, 165, 181
Clark, Walter, 88–89, 110, 112, 115–21, 126, 128–33, 153
Class conflict, 107, 157, 168, 289
Clement, Lilian Exum, 110, 147, 152
Cliffs of Neuse State Park, 264
Cobb, Collier, 11

McCarthyism, 270–71
McKelway, Dr. A. J., 80
McMahon, Maria, 121, 132, 136, 155
McPheeters, Samuel, 187, 204, 266, 274
McPheeters, Virginia, 187, 266, 269, 281
Meir, Golda, 245
Melba, Nellie, x, 54
Meredith College, 120
Methodists, 6, 10, 15, 23, 24, 77, 111
Mewborn, L. J. H., 139
Meyer, Annie Nathan, 86
Miller, Irene, 233
Mindel, Alan, 102
Mitchell, S. Weir, 45
Moffatt, Adeline, 47, 83
Mooney, Tom, 180
Moore, A. M., 129, 135
Moore, Hazel, 197–99
Moorhead, Huldah, 172
Morgenstern, Julian, 104
Morgenthau, Henry, Jr., 212
Morris, G. B., viii, 145
Morrison, Cameron, 116, 140, 152
Moses, Max, 26
Mosher, Eleanor, 172
Mount Holyoke College, 34, 39
Multiculturalism, 1, 18, 45
Municipal housekeeping, 73–74
Muscle Shoals, Ala., 173

Nathan, Maud, 98, 108
National American Woman Suffrage Association, 88, 108–10, 116, 118, 121–24, 127, 129–30, 132, 133, 146
National Association for the Advancement of Colored People, 159, 253, 258–59
National Association Opposed to Woman Suffrage, 125
National Child Labor Committee, 81, 170, 179, 190
National Conference of Christians and Jews, 212
National Consumers League, 52, 76, 142, 189

National Council of Jewish Federations and Welfare Funds, 212
National Council of Jewish Women, 75–76, 80, 82, 85, 86, 98, 102–4, 163, 198, 216, 254
National Federation of Temple Sisterhoods, 98, 216
National Refugee Service, 218, 224
National Textile Workers Union, 176–78
National Woman's Party, 108, 110–13, 116, 121–22, 147, 171
Nazism, 201–2, 211–12, 215, 216, 235–36, 243, 265
Neal, W. W., 136
Needleman, Joseph, 146
Newbold, N. C., 196
New Deal, 182, 187, 191–97, 206
Newell, Bertha, 162
New Orleans, 255
New South, viii, 8, 9, 15, 23, 32, 52, 55, 118, 125, 317n20
New Woman, vii–x, 32, 39, 40, 44, 46, 47, 54, 55, 79, 86, 126, 168, 229, 290
New York, 5, 15, 18, 25, 35, 36, 38, 50–51, 54, 68, 71, 76, 102, 143, 265
Nickolic-Podrinsky, Vera, 274
Niebuhr, Reinhold, 163
Northampton, MA, 39–40, 68, 283
North Carolina A&T, 257
North Carolina Association of Jewish Men, 213
North Carolina Association of Jewish Women, 96, 102–5, 190, 212, 214, 232–33, 237, 247, 264–65, 269, 285, 288
North Carolina Birth Control Committee, 199
North Carolina Board of Rabbis, 254
North Carolina College for Negroes, 238, 257
North Carolina Conference for Social Service, 89–90, 129, 135, 161, 175, 183, 188, 190–91, 195–97, 199, 201, 210, 215, 225, 277
North Carolina Council on Human Relations, 251, 256, 259, 284

Shuler, Nettie, 115

Simkhovitch, Mary Kingsbury, 50

Simmons, Furnifold, 114–17, 120, 123, 128, 130, 131, 136–37, 163, 175–76

Sisterhood, Oheb Sholom, 98, 100, 163–64, 211, 213, 225, 232, 280

Sisterhoods, National Federation of, 102–3, 105, 163, 213, 237, 240

Smith, A. J., 191

Smith, Al, 146, 174, 177

Smith, Lillian, 162, 250–52

Smith, Willis, 271

Smith College, vii, 34, 39–47, *44*, 142, 231; alumni, 55–56, 80, 133, 238, 266; Jews at, 40–42, 44–45, 233; and careerism, 50–53; curriculum at, 42–43; feminism at, 40, 42, 45–46, 50–51; and race, 43, 67, 249; and social justice, 42–44, 50–51, 86; and suffrage, 43, 88; Smith Medal, 282–84

Social Gospel, 22, 53, 74, 75, 97

Socialism, 47, 60–61, 135, 156, 173, 183, 194, 206–8, 270

Socialist Party of America, 173

Social Security, 194

Solomon, Hannah, 85

Southeastern Economic Conference, 179

Southern Conference for Human Welfare, 196, 206–7

Southern identity, 45, 301n34. *See also* Southern Lady

Southern Lady, vii–x, 10, 40, 49, 51, 55, 79, 85–86, 107, 109–10, 119, 126, 137, 138, 168, 229, 277, 290

Southern Region Council, 250

Southern Summer School for Women Workers in Industry, 181

Southern Textile Bulletin, 165, 181

Southern Women's Rejection League, 125, 127–28

Spaulding, C. C., 251

Spearman, Haywood, 187, 238, 261–62, 275–76, 281, 285

Spier, Amelia, 16

Spier, Etta, 16, 19, 30, 34, 104, 201

Spier, Hattie, 30

Spier family, 13, 16, 19, 29

Sports, 21, 45, 65

Sprunt, James, 126

Stacy, Horace, 138

Stanlaws, Penrhyn, 156

Stanton, Elizabeth Cady, 38, 75, 134

Stassen, Harold, 270

State Normal and Industrial School. *See* Woman's College

Steinem, Paula, 70

Sterilization, 200–203

Stern, David, 60, 81, 83

Stetson, Charlotte Perkins. *See* Charlotte Perkins Gilman

Stevenson, Adlai, 272

Stone, I. F., 270

Stonewall Jack School, 82, 149

Straus, Esther, 80

Strauss family, 265

Stringfield, Lamar, 215

Student Nonviolent Coordinating Committee, 257

Suffrage, 43, 46, 64, 85, 88–89, 91, 103, 106–39, 168; in Britain, 86; and Susan B. Anthony Amendment, 113–14, 120, 129–30, 135. *See also* Antisuffragists; Catt, Carrie Chapman; Equal Suffrage Association of North Carolina; Weil, Gertrude

Swalin, Benjamin, 277

Swift, Bulus Bagby, 179–80

Swift, Wiley, 170, 179

Syrians, 57

Szold, Benjamin, 12

Szold, Henrietta, x, 12, 71–73, 75, 99–100, 224, 243–44. *See also* Hadassah; Zionism

Taft, William Howard, 91

Temple Beth Or, 236

Temple Emanuel (Greensboro), 104

Temple Emanuel (New York), 36, 71

Tennessee, 106, 107, 120, 123–24, 131, 133, 135, 136, 138, 139

Legal aspects of midwifery

4th Edition

QUAY
BOOKS

A division of MA Healthcare Ltd

Other titles in the series include

Legal Aspects of Health and Safety 2nd Edition
Legal Aspects of Medicines 2nd Edition
Legal Aspects of Patient Confidentiality 2nd Edition
Legal Aspects of Pain Management 2nd Edition
Legal Aspects of Consent 2nd Edition
Legal Aspects of Death

Note

Healthcare practice and knowledge are constantly changing and developing as new research and treatments, changes in procedures, drugs and equipment become available.

The author and publishers have, as far as is possible, taken care to confirm that the information complies with the latest standards of practice and legislation.